FRANK MILLER'S

SIN CITY ®

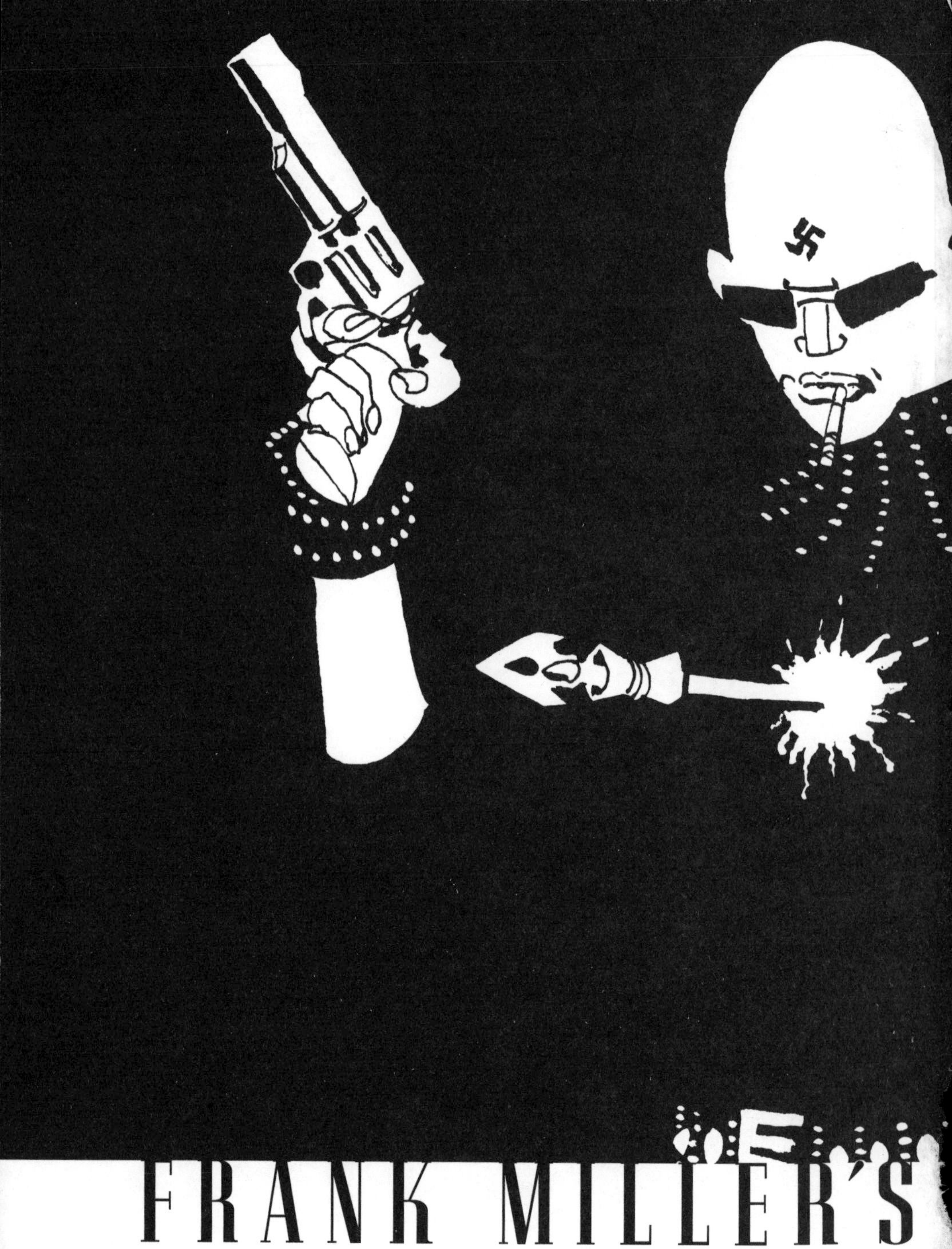

FRANK MILLER'S

THE BIG FAT KILL

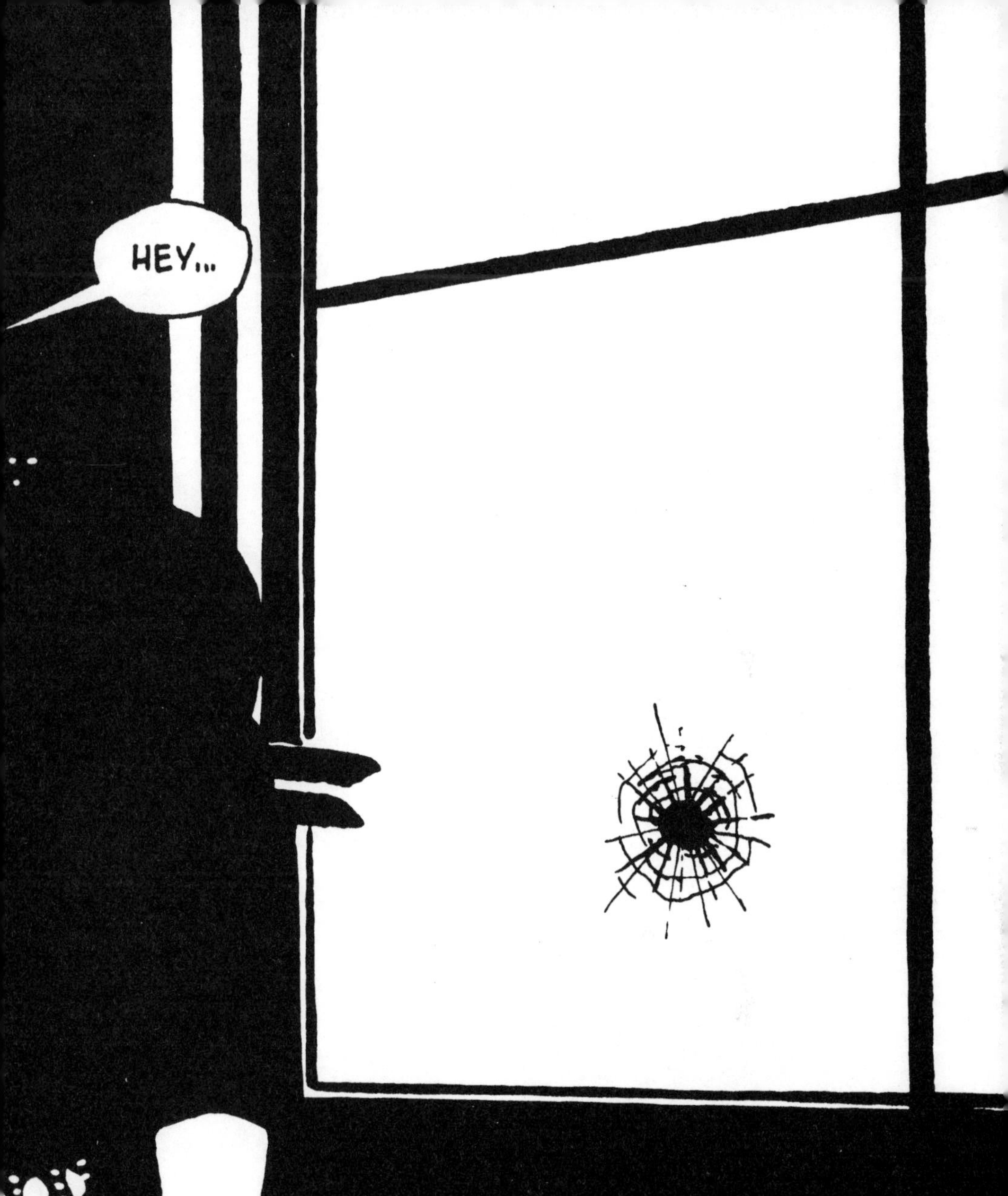
HEY...

SIN CITY®

DARK HORSE BOOKS™

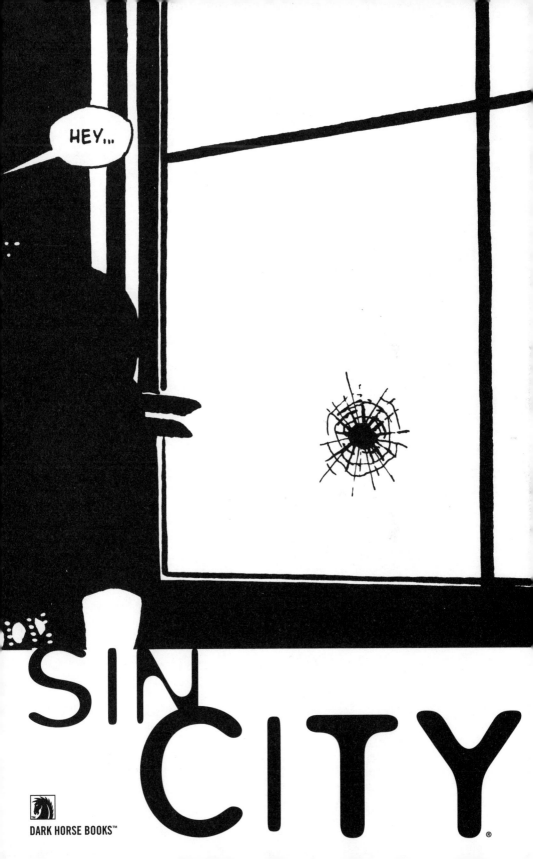

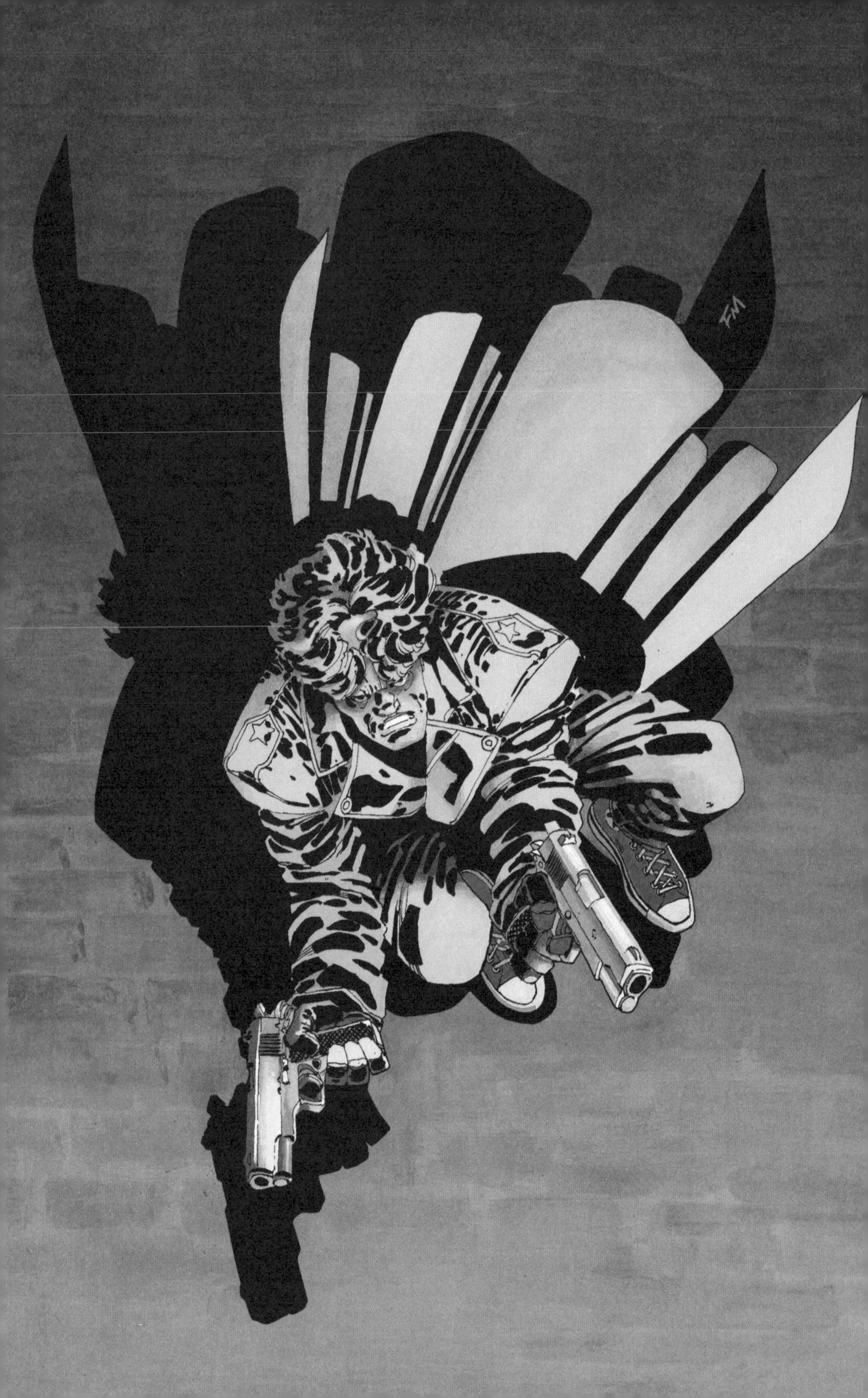

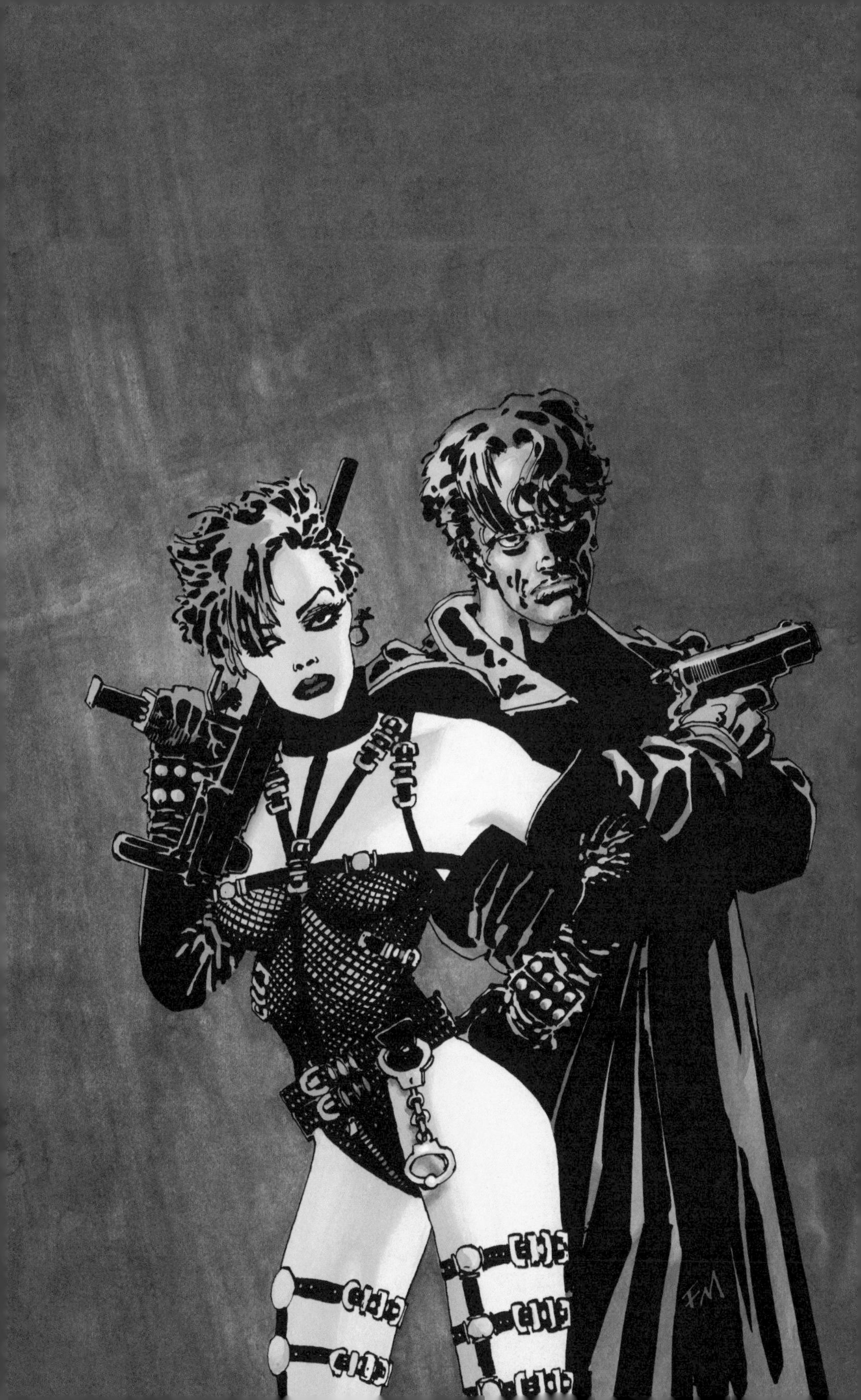

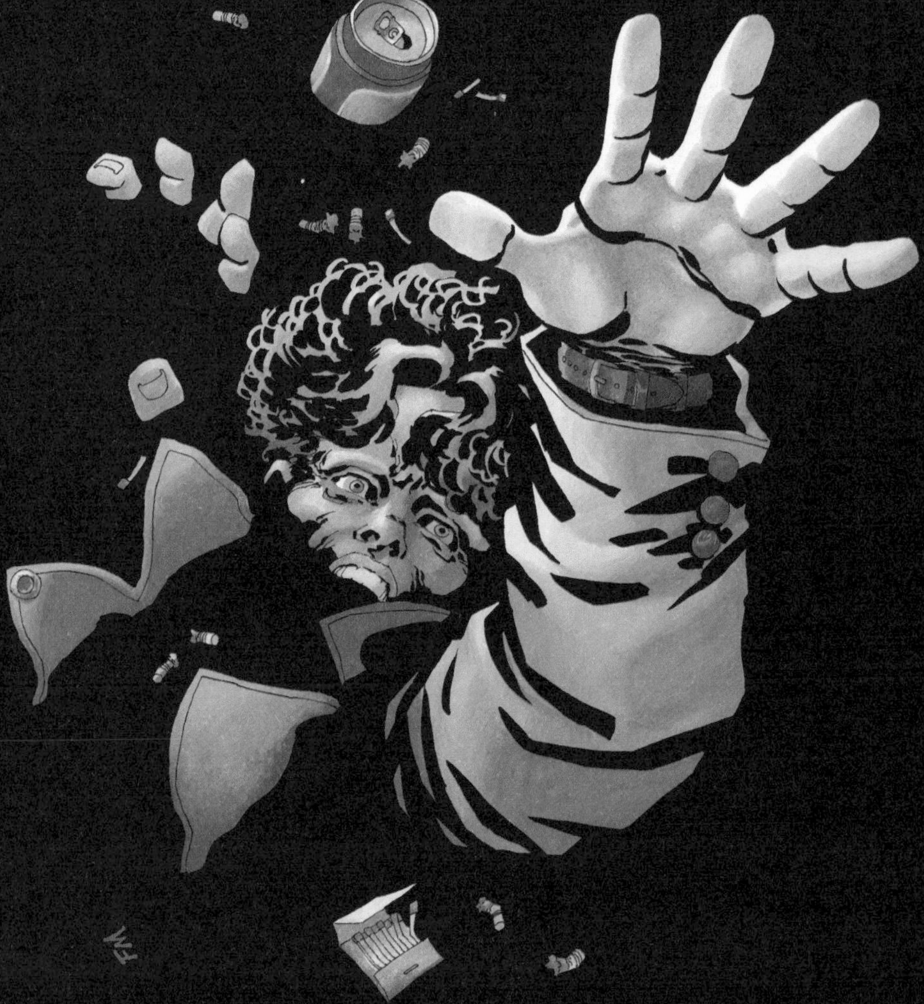

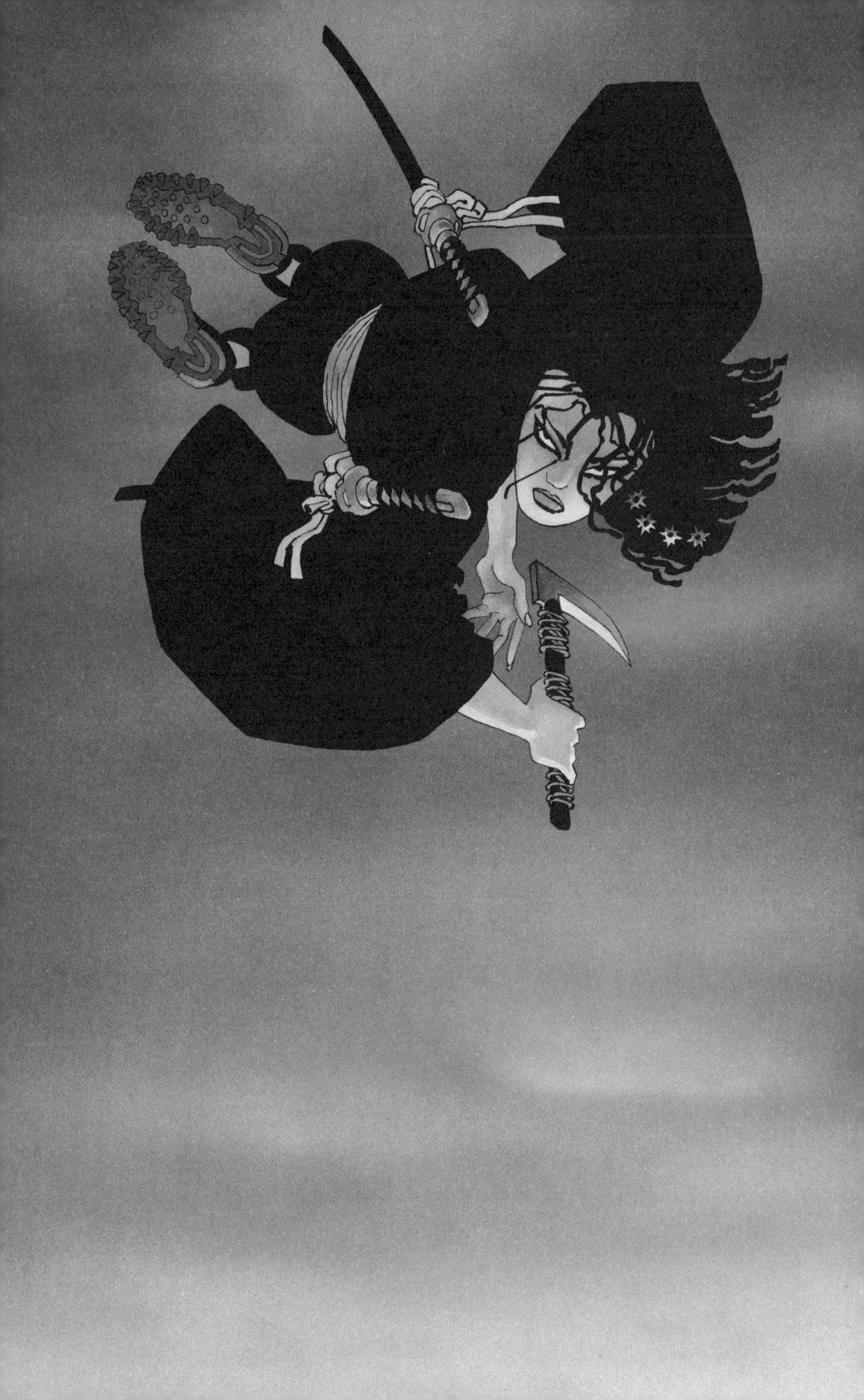

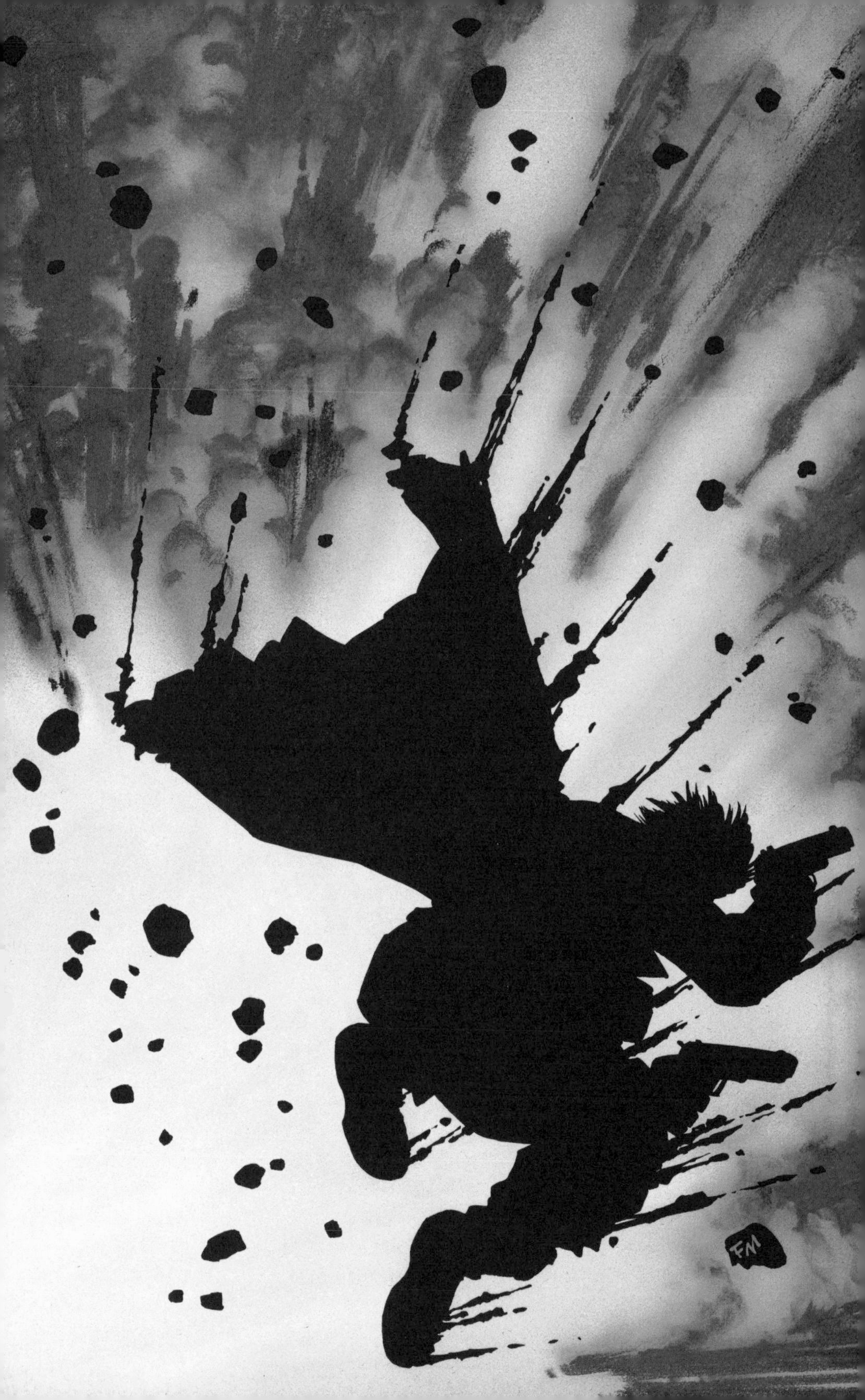
FM

CHAPTER 0

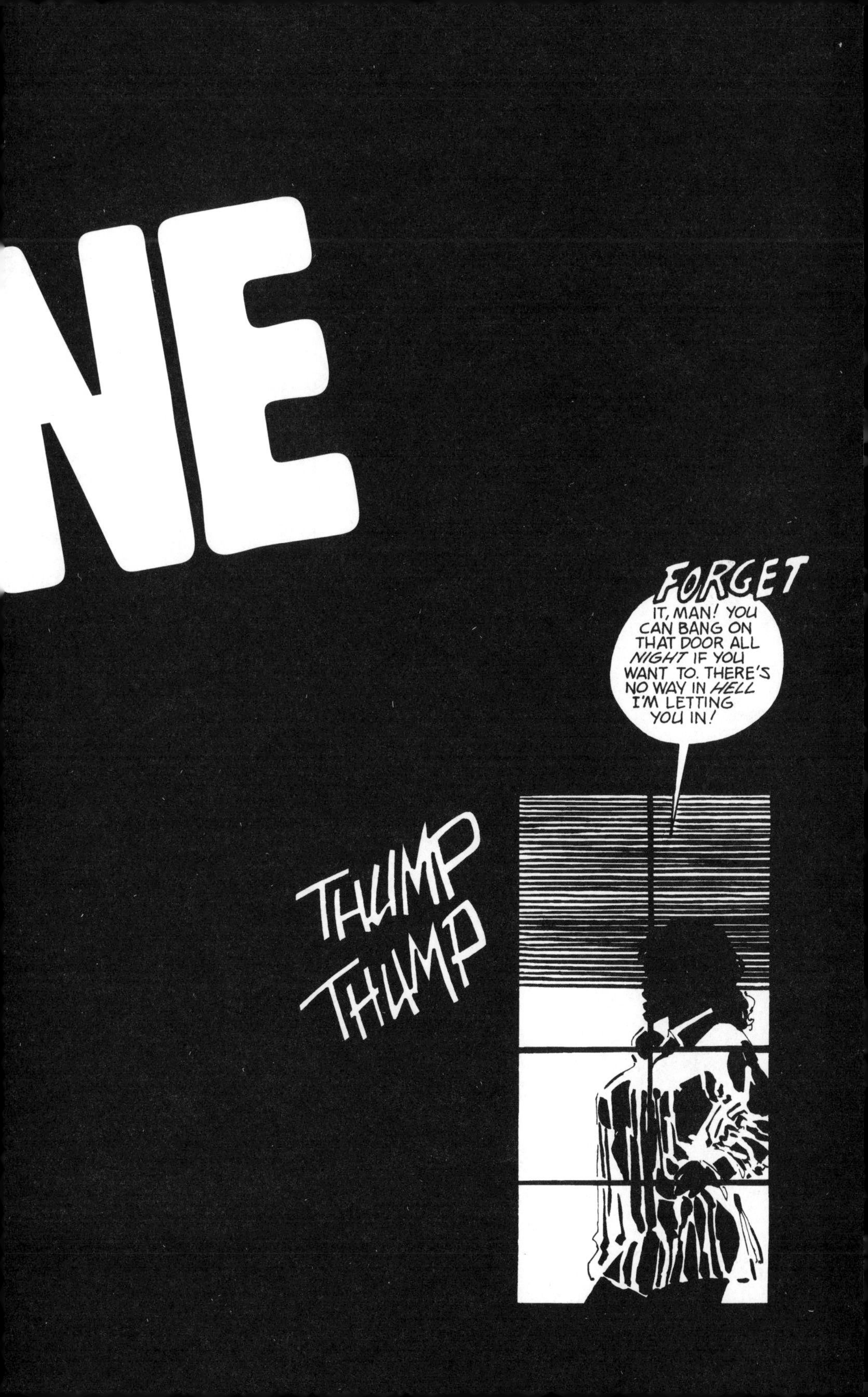
NE
FORGET IT, MAN! YOU CAN BANG ON THAT DOOR ALL NIGHT IF YOU WANT TO. THERE'S NO WAY IN HELL I'M LETTING YOU IN!
THUMP THUMP

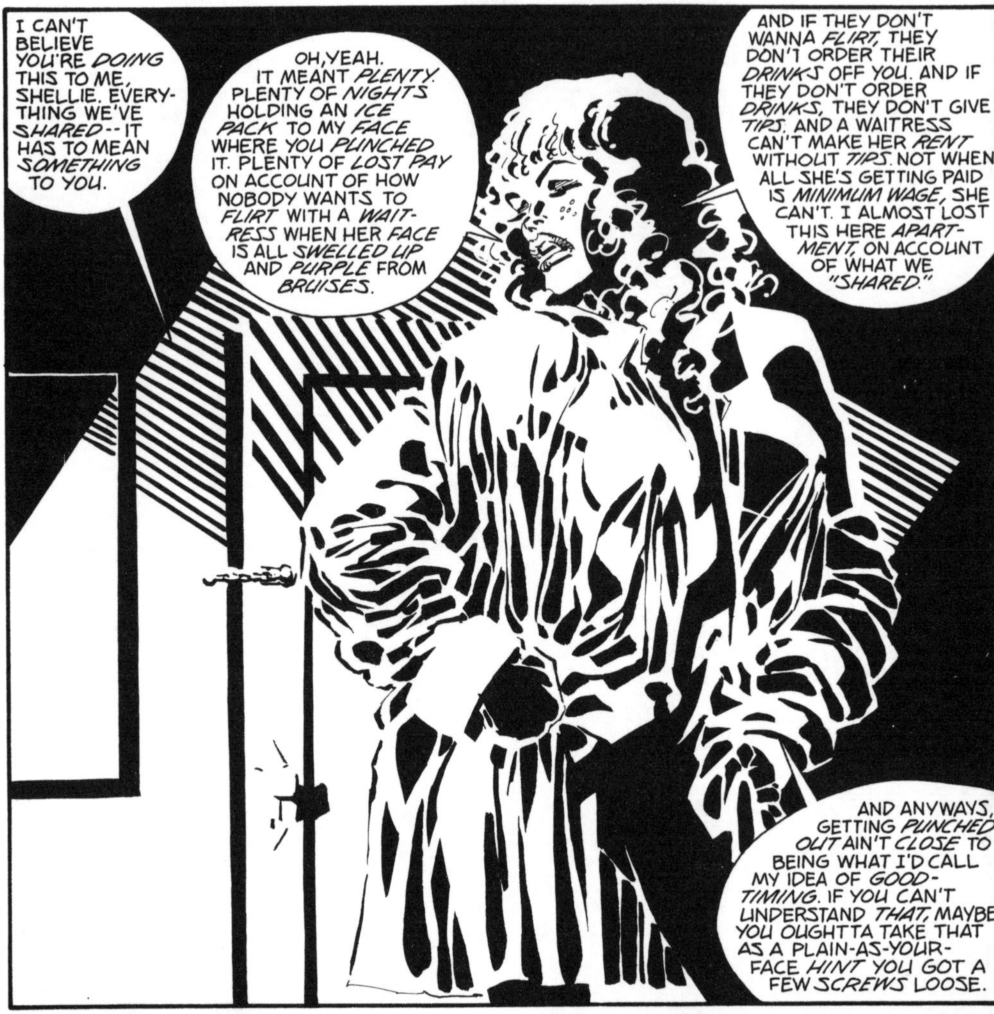
I CAN'T BELIEVE YOU'RE DOING THIS TO ME, SHELLIE. EVERYTHING WE'VE SHARED--IT HAS TO MEAN SOMETHING TO YOU.
OH, YEAH. IT MEANT PLENTY. PLENTY OF NIGHTS HOLDING AN ICE PACK TO MY FACE WHERE YOU PUNCHED IT. PLENTY OF LOST PAY ON ACCOUNT OF HOW NOBODY WANTS TO FLIRT WITH A WAITRESS WHEN HER FACE IS ALL SWELLED UP AND PURPLE FROM BRUISES.
AND IF THEY DON'T WANNA FLIRT, THEY DON'T ORDER THEIR DRINKS OFF YOU. AND IF THEY DON'T ORDER DRINKS, THEY DON'T GIVE TIPS. AND A WAITRESS CAN'T MAKE HER RENT WITHOUT TIPS. NOT WHEN ALL SHE'S GETTING PAID IS MINIMUM WAGE, SHE CAN'T. I ALMOST LOST THIS HERE APARTMENT, ON ACCOUNT OF WHAT WE "SHARED."
AND ANYWAYS, GETTING PUNCHED OUT AIN'T CLOSE TO BEING WHAT I'D CALL MY IDEA OF GOOD-TIMING. IF YOU CAN'T UNDERSTAND THAT, MAYBE YOU OUGHTTA TAKE THAT AS A PLAIN-AS-YOUR-FACE HINT YOU GOT A FEW SCREWS LOOSE.

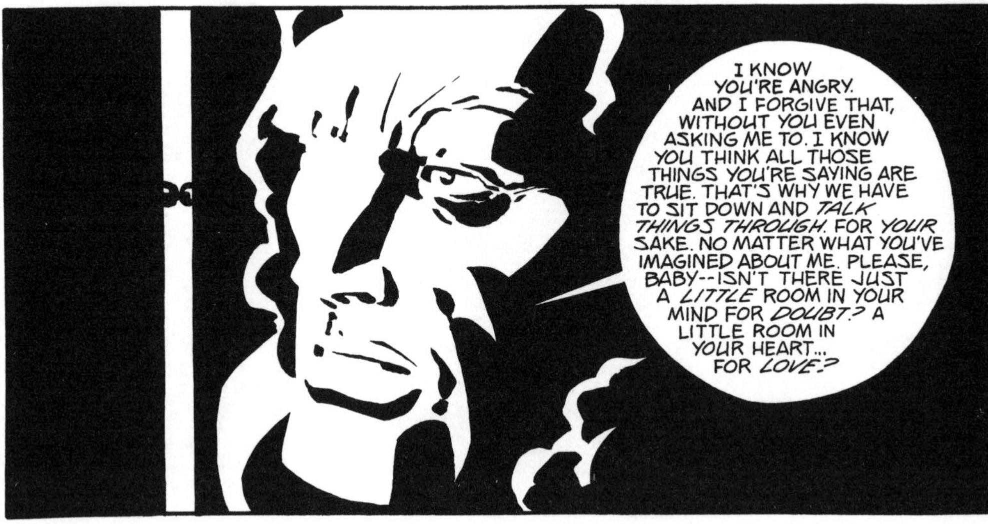
I KNOW YOU'RE ANGRY. AND I FORGIVE THAT, WITHOUT YOU EVEN ASKING ME TO. I KNOW YOU THINK ALL THOSE THINGS YOU'RE SAYING ARE TRUE. THAT'S WHY WE HAVE TO SIT DOWN AND TALK THINGS THROUGH. FOR YOUR SAKE. NO MATTER WHAT YOU'VE IMAGINED ABOUT ME. PLEASE, BABY--ISN'T THERE JUST A LITTLE ROOM IN YOUR MIND FOR DOUBT? A LITTLE ROOM IN YOUR HEART... FOR LOVE?

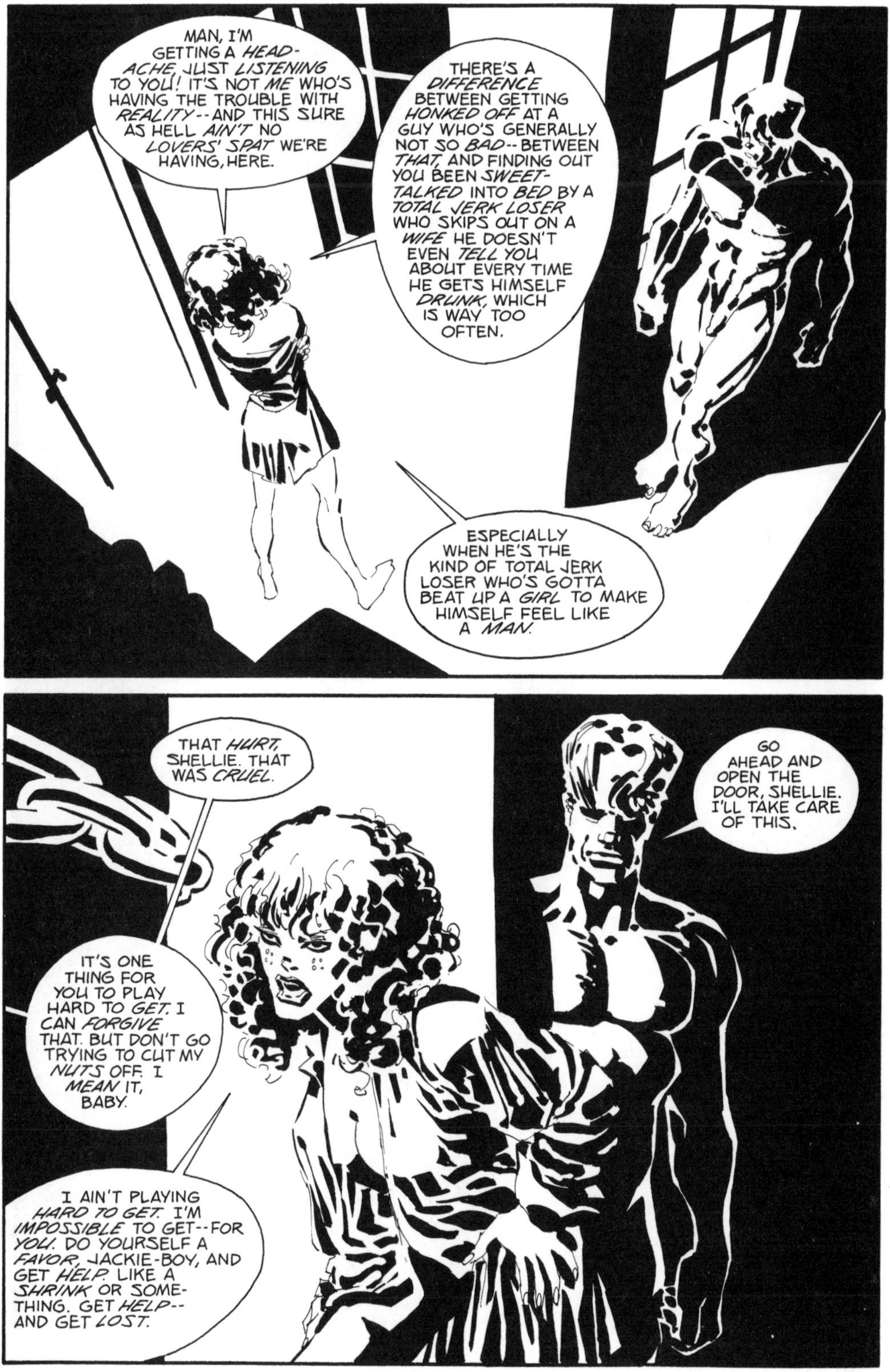
MAN, I'M GETTING A HEAD-ACHE, JUST LISTENING TO YOU! IT'S NOT ME WHO'S HAVING THE TROUBLE WITH REALITY--AND THIS SURE AS HELL AIN'T NO LOVERS' SPAT WE'RE HAVING, HERE.
THERE'S A DIFFERENCE BETWEEN GETTING HONKED OFF AT A GUY WHO'S GENERALLY NOT SO BAD--BETWEEN THAT, AND FINDING OUT YOU BEEN SWEET-TALKED INTO BED BY A TOTAL JERK LOSER WHO SKIPS OUT ON A WIFE HE DOESN'T EVEN TELL YOU ABOUT EVERY TIME HE GETS HIMSELF DRUNK, WHICH IS WAY TOO OFTEN.
ESPECIALLY WHEN HE'S THE KIND OF TOTAL JERK LOSER WHO'S GOTTA BEAT UP A GIRL TO MAKE HIMSELF FEEL LIKE A MAN.
THAT HURT, SHELLIE. THAT WAS CRUEL.
IT'S ONE THING FOR YOU TO PLAY HARD TO GET. I CAN FORGIVE THAT. BUT DON'T GO TRYING TO CUT MY NUTS OFF. I MEAN IT, BABY.
GO AHEAD AND OPEN THE DOOR, SHELLIE. I'LL TAKE CARE OF THIS.
I AIN'T PLAYING HARD TO GET. I'M IMPOSSIBLE TO GET--FOR YOU. DO YOURSELF A FAVOR, JACKIE-BOY, AND GET HELP. LIKE A SHRINK OR SOME-THING. GET HELP--AND GET LOST.

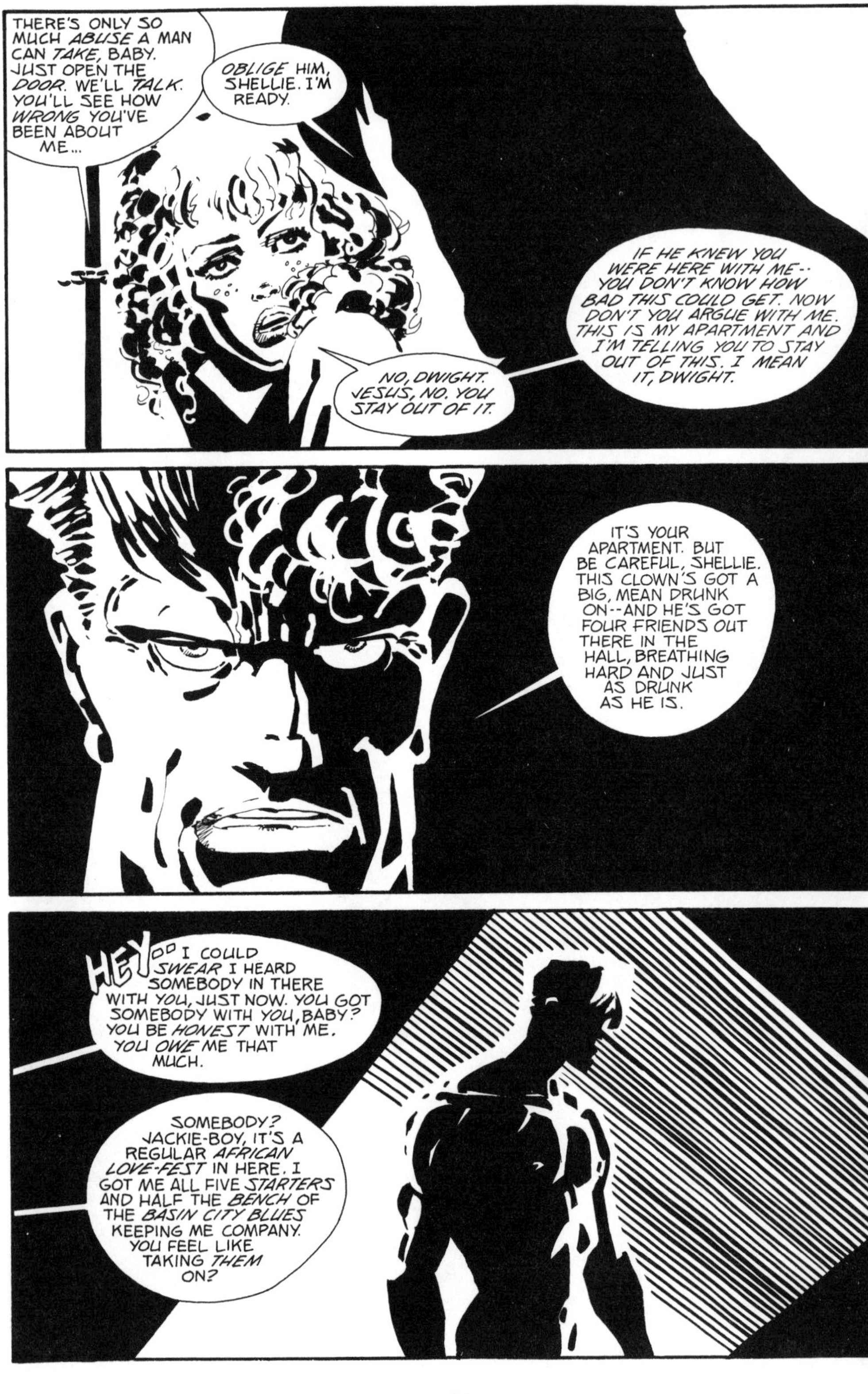
THERE'S ONLY SO MUCH ABUSE A MAN CAN TAKE, BABY. JUST OPEN THE DOOR. WE'LL TALK. YOU'LL SEE HOW WRONG YOU'VE BEEN ABOUT ME...
OBLIGE HIM, SHELLIE. I'M READY.
NO, DWIGHT. JESUS, NO. YOU STAY OUT OF IT.
IF HE KNEW YOU WERE HERE WITH ME-- YOU DON'T KNOW HOW BAD THIS COULD GET. NOW DON'T YOU ARGUE WITH ME. THIS IS MY APARTMENT AND I'M TELLING YOU TO STAY OUT OF THIS. I MEAN IT, DWIGHT.
IT'S YOUR APARTMENT. BUT BE CAREFUL, SHELLIE. THIS CLOWN'S GOT A BIG, MEAN DRUNK ON--AND HE'S GOT FOUR FRIENDS OUT THERE IN THE HALL, BREATHING HARD AND JUST AS DRUNK AS HE IS.
HEY.. I COULD SWEAR I HEARD SOMEBODY IN THERE WITH YOU, JUST NOW. YOU GOT SOMEBODY WITH YOU, BABY? YOU BE HONEST WITH ME. YOU OWE ME THAT MUCH.
SOMEBODY? JACKIE-BOY, IT'S A REGULAR AFRICAN LOVE-FEST IN HERE. I GOT ME ALL FIVE STARTERS AND HALF THE BENCH OF THE BASIN CITY BLUES KEEPING ME COMPANY. YOU FEEL LIKE TAKING THEM ON?

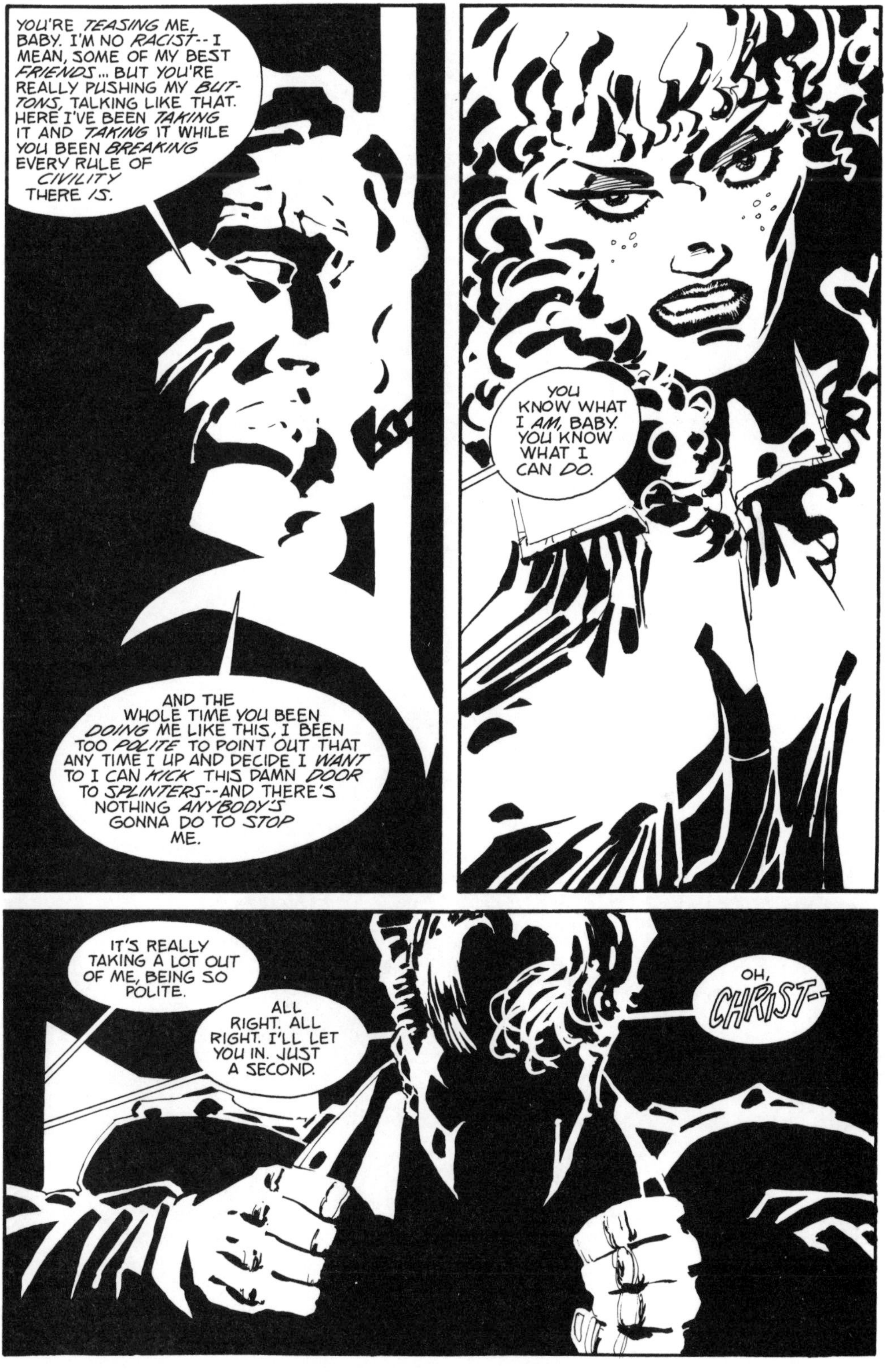
YOU'RE TEASING ME, BABY. I'M NO RACIST-- I MEAN, SOME OF MY BEST FRIENDS... BUT YOU'RE REALLY PUSHING MY BUTTONS, TALKING LIKE THAT. HERE I'VE BEEN TAKING IT AND TAKING IT WHILE YOU BEEN BREAKING EVERY RULE OF CIVILITY THERE IS.
AND THE WHOLE TIME YOU BEEN DOING ME LIKE THIS, I BEEN TOO POLITE TO POINT OUT THAT ANY TIME I UP AND DECIDE I WANT TO I CAN KICK THIS DAMN DOOR TO SPLINTERS--AND THERE'S NOTHING ANYBODY'S GONNA DO TO STOP ME.
YOU KNOW WHAT I AM, BABY. YOU KNOW WHAT I CAN DO.
IT'S REALLY TAKING A LOT OUT OF ME, BEING SO POLITE.
ALL RIGHT. ALL RIGHT. I'LL LET YOU IN. JUST A SECOND.
OH, CHRIST--

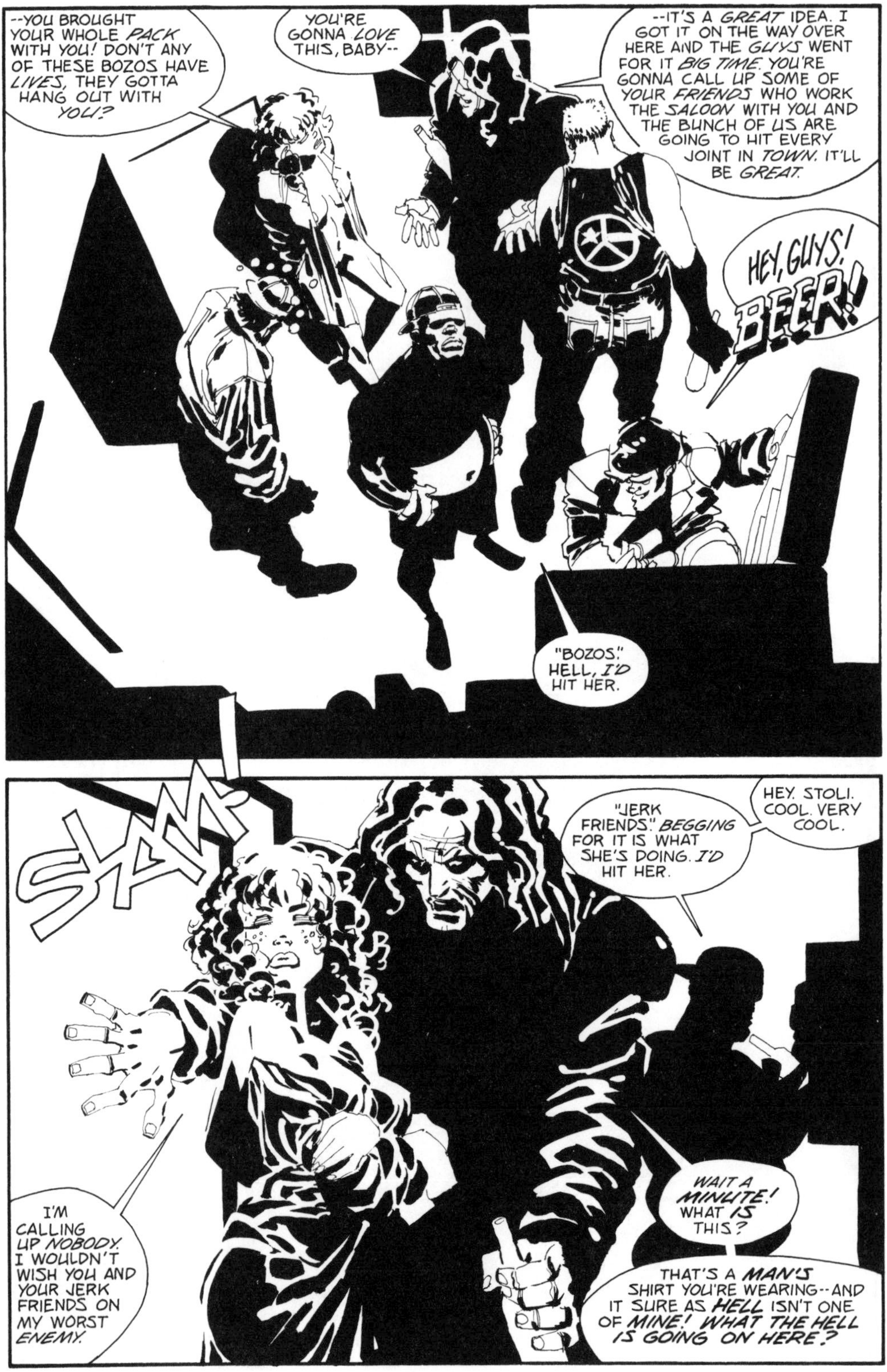
--YOU BROUGHT YOUR WHOLE PACK WITH YOU! DON'T ANY OF THESE BOZOS HAVE LIVES, THEY GOTTA HANG OUT WITH YOU?
YOU'RE GONNA LOVE THIS, BABY--
--IT'S A GREAT IDEA. I GOT IT ON THE WAY OVER HERE AND THE GUYS WENT FOR IT BIG TIME. YOU'RE GONNA CALL UP SOME OF YOUR FRIENDS WHO WORK THE SALOON WITH YOU AND THE BUNCH OF US ARE GOING TO HIT EVERY JOINT IN TOWN. IT'LL BE GREAT.
HEY, GUYS! BEER!
"BOZOS." HELL, I'D HIT HER.
SLAM!
"JERK FRIENDS." BEGGING FOR IT IS WHAT SHE'S DOING. I'D HIT HER.
HEY. STOLI. COOL. VERY COOL.
I'M CALLING UP NOBODY. I WOULDN'T WISH YOU AND YOUR JERK FRIENDS ON MY WORST ENEMY.
WAIT A MINUTE! WHAT IS THIS?
THAT'S A MAN'S SHIRT YOU'RE WEARING--AND IT SURE AS HELL ISN'T ONE OF MINE! WHAT THE HELL IS GOING ON HERE?

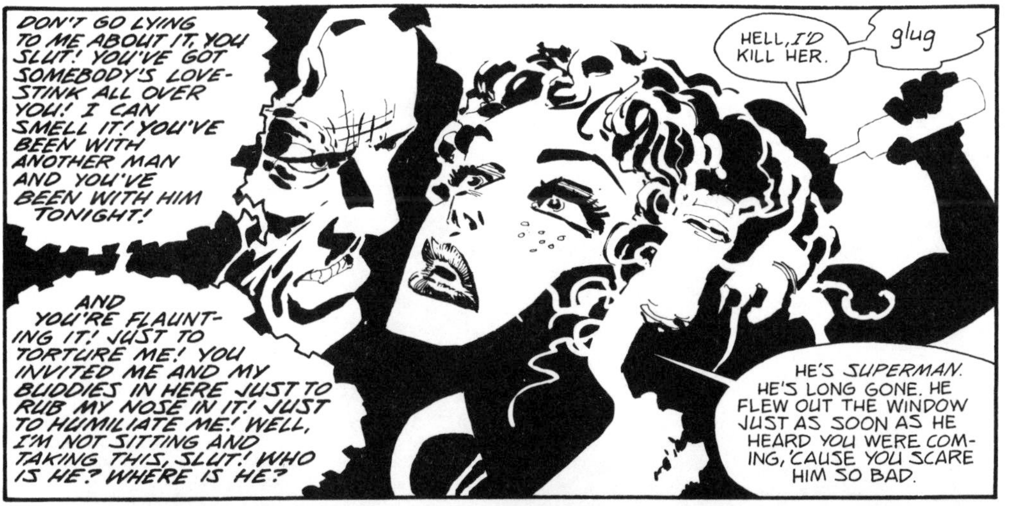
DON'T GO LYING TO ME ABOUT IT, YOU SLUT! YOU'VE GOT SOMEBODY'S LOVE-STINK ALL OVER YOU! I CAN SMELL IT! YOU'VE BEEN WITH ANOTHER MAN AND YOU'VE BEEN WITH HIM TONIGHT!
HELL, I'D KILL HER.
glug
AND YOU'RE FLAUNTING IT! JUST TO TORTURE ME! YOU INVITED ME AND MY BUDDIES IN HERE JUST TO RUB MY NOSE IN IT! JUST TO HUMILIATE ME! WELL, I'M NOT SITTING AND TAKING THIS, SLUT! WHO IS HE? WHERE IS HE?
HE'S SUPERMAN. HE'S LONG GONE. HE FLEW OUT THE WINDOW JUST AS SOON AS HE HEARD YOU WERE COMING, 'CAUSE YOU SCARE HIM SO BAD.

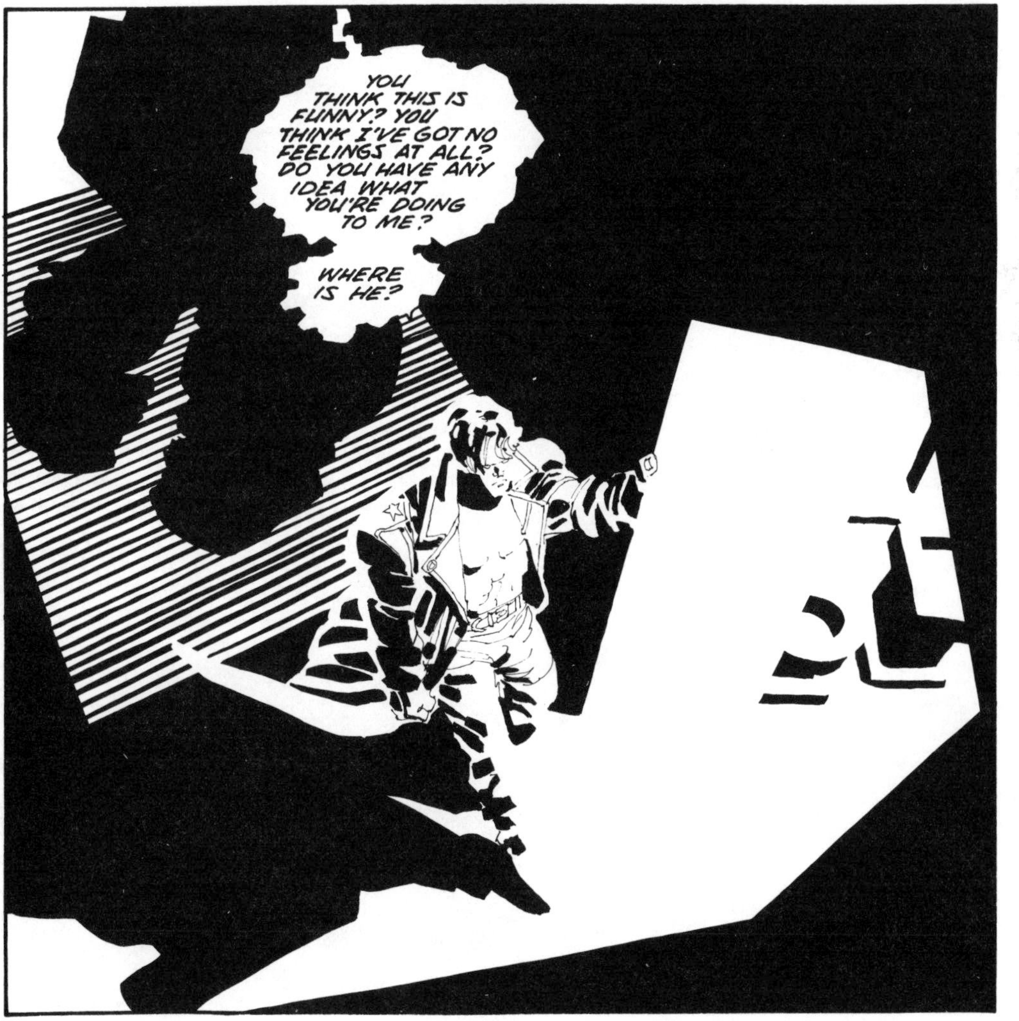
YOU THINK THIS IS FUNNY? YOU THINK I'VE GOT NO FEELINGS AT ALL? DO YOU HAVE ANY IDEA WHAT YOU'RE DOING TO ME?
WHERE IS HE?

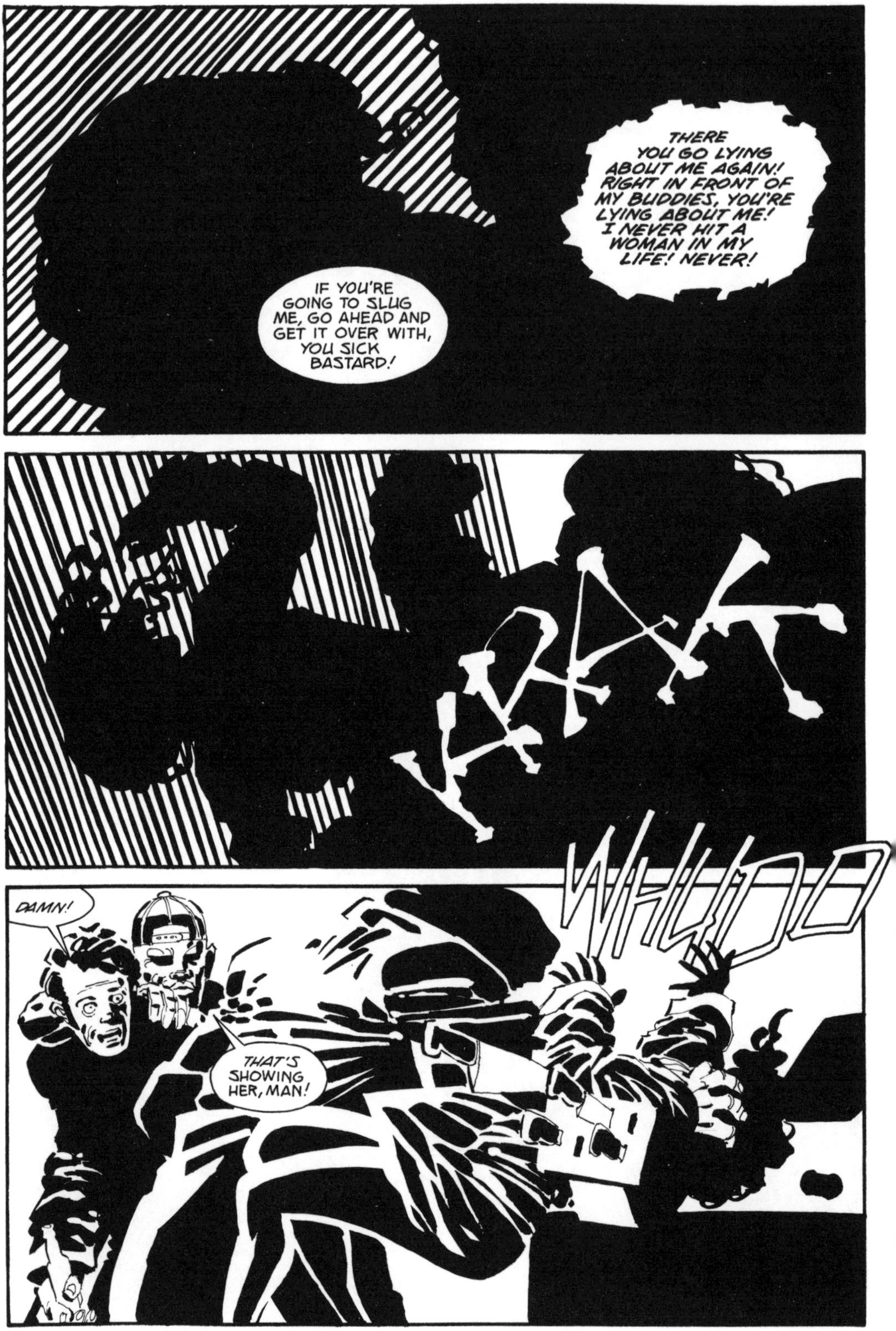
THERE YOU GO LYING ABOUT ME AGAIN! RIGHT IN FRONT OF MY BUDDIES, YOU'RE LYING ABOUT ME! I NEVER HIT A WOMAN IN MY LIFE! NEVER!
IF YOU'RE GOING TO SLUG ME, GO AHEAD AND GET IT OVER WITH, YOU SICK BASTARD!
KRAK
WHUDD
DAMN!
THAT'S SHOWING HER, MAN!

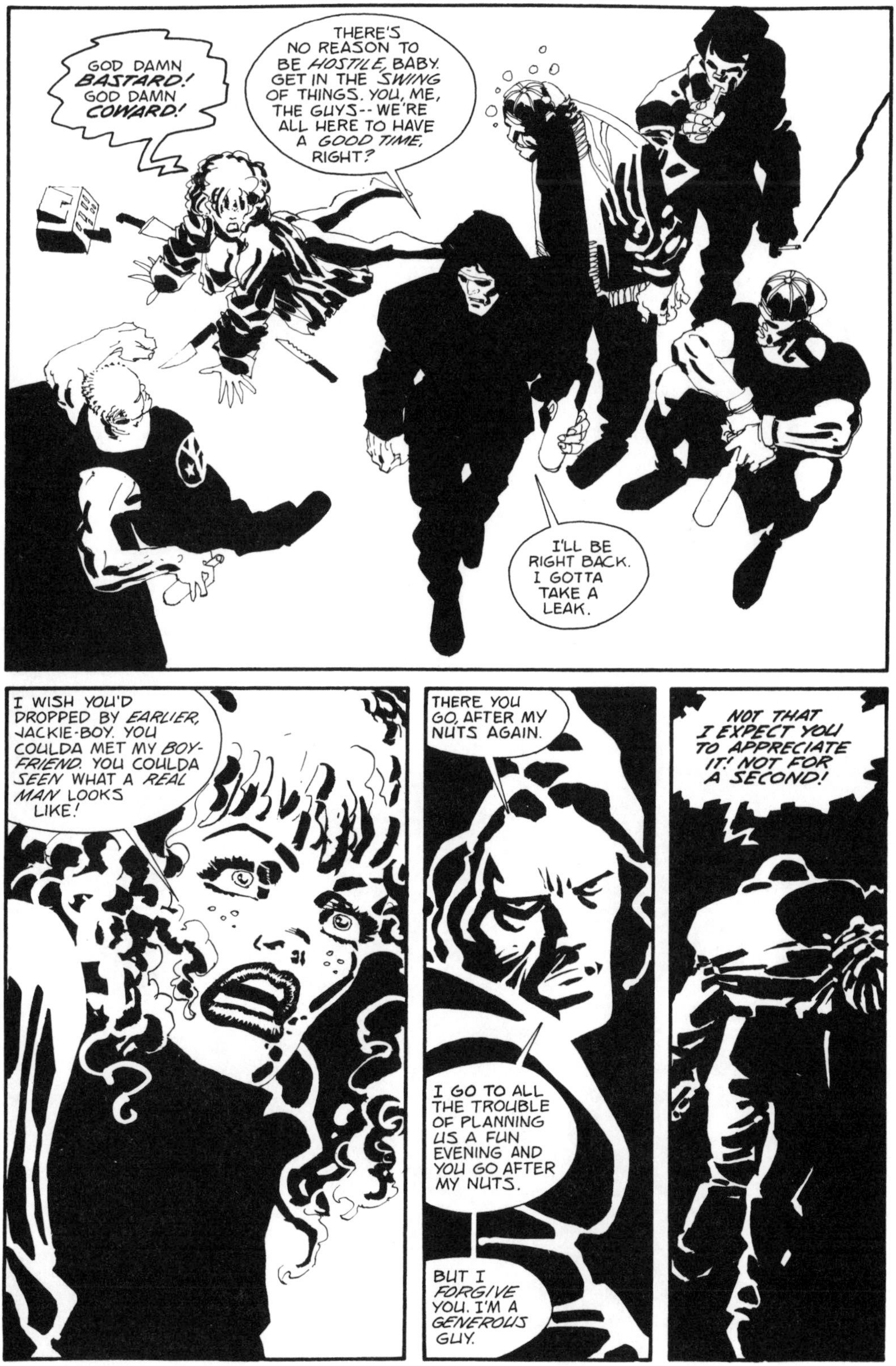
GOD DAMN BASTARD! GOD DAMN COWARD!
THERE'S NO REASON TO BE HOSTILE, BABY. GET IN THE SWING OF THINGS. YOU, ME, THE GUYS-- WE'RE ALL HERE TO HAVE A GOOD TIME, RIGHT?
I'LL BE RIGHT BACK. I GOTTA TAKE A LEAK.
I WISH YOU'D DROPPED BY EARLIER, JACKIE-BOY. YOU COULDA MET MY BOY-FRIEND. YOU COULDA SEEN WHAT A REAL MAN LOOKS LIKE!
THERE YOU GO, AFTER MY NUTS AGAIN.
I GO TO ALL THE TROUBLE OF PLANNING US A FUN EVENING AND YOU GO AFTER MY NUTS.
BUT I FORGIVE YOU. I'M A GENEROUS GUY.
NOT THAT I EXPECT YOU TO APPRECIATE IT! NOT FOR A SECOND!

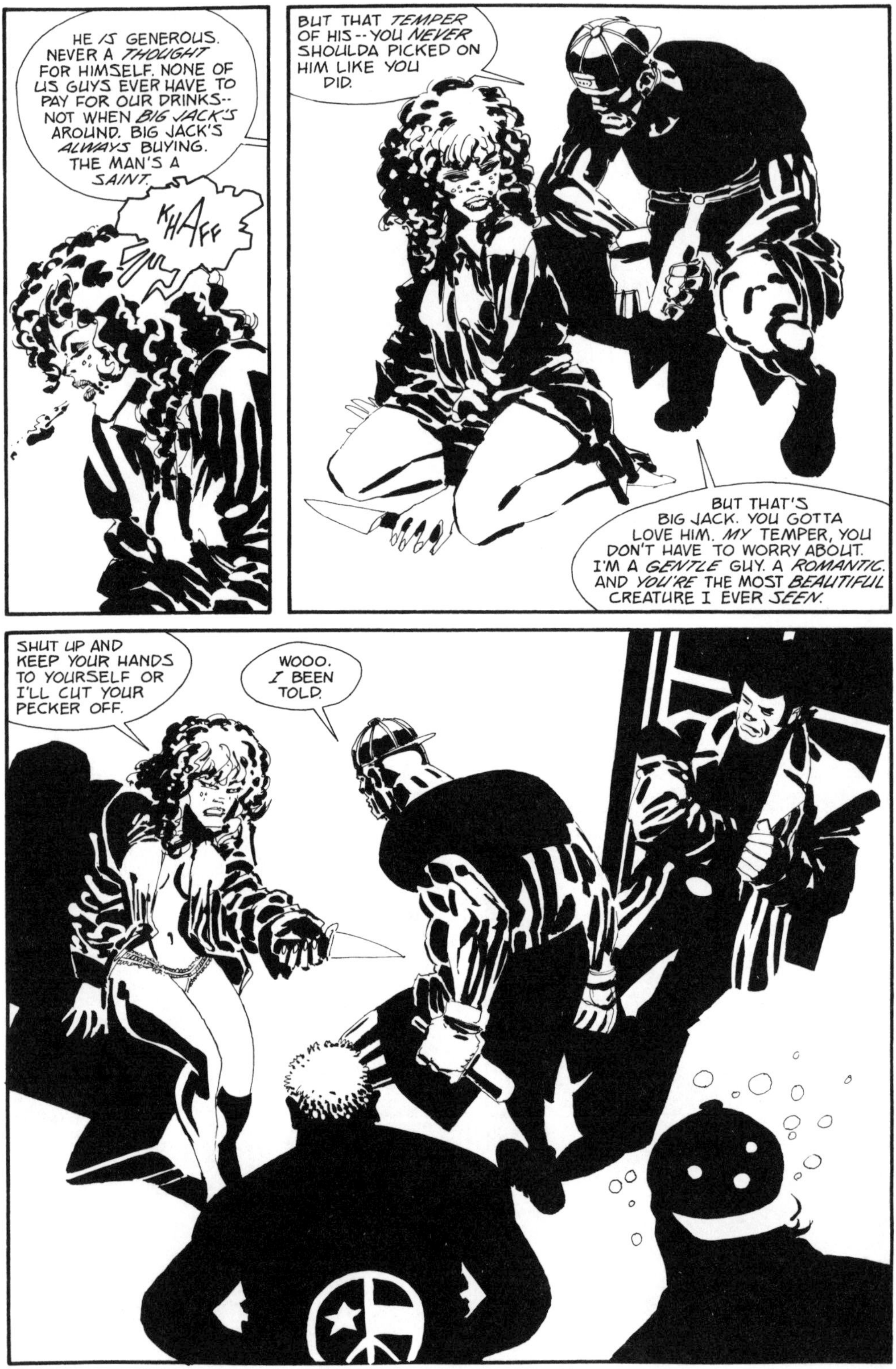
HE IS GENEROUS. NEVER A THOUGHT FOR HIMSELF. NONE OF US GUYS EVER HAVE TO PAY FOR OUR DRINKS-- NOT WHEN BIG JACK'S AROUND. BIG JACK'S ALWAYS BUYING. THE MAN'S A SAINT.
KHAFF
BUT THAT TEMPER OF HIS--YOU NEVER SHOULDA PICKED ON HIM LIKE YOU DID.
BUT THAT'S BIG JACK. YOU GOTTA LOVE HIM. MY TEMPER, YOU DON'T HAVE TO WORRY ABOUT. I'M A GENTLE GUY. A ROMANTIC. AND YOU'RE THE MOST BEAUTIFUL CREATURE I EVER SEEN.
SHUT UP AND KEEP YOUR HANDS TO YOURSELF OR I'LL CUT YOUR PECKER OFF.
WOOO. I BEEN TOLD.

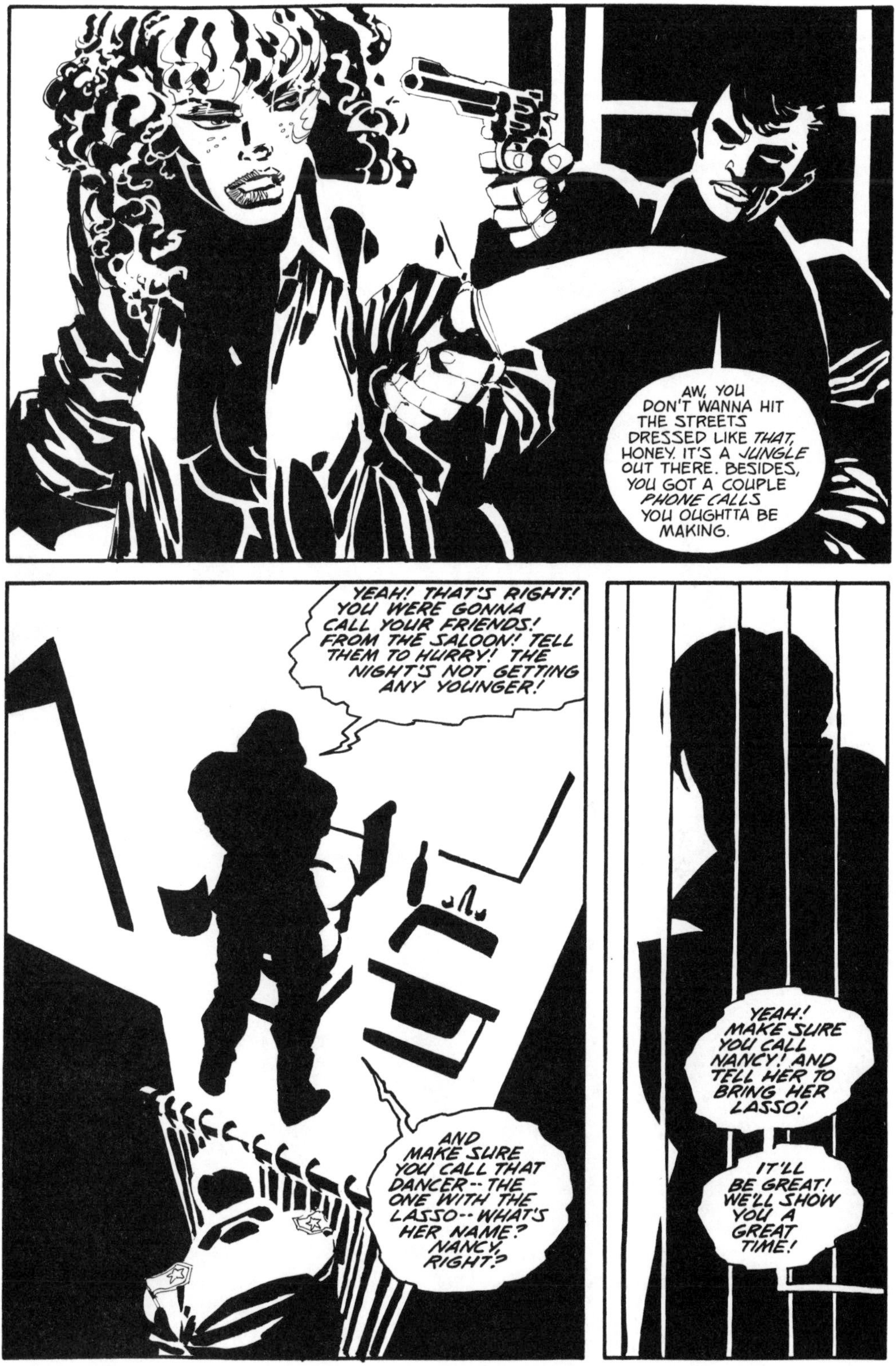
AW, YOU DON'T WANNA HIT THE STREETS DRESSED LIKE THAT, HONEY. IT'S A JUNGLE OUT THERE. BESIDES, YOU GOT A COUPLE PHONE CALLS YOU OUGHTTA BE MAKING.
YEAH! THAT'S RIGHT! YOU WERE GONNA CALL YOUR FRIENDS! FROM THE SALOON! TELL THEM TO HURRY! THE NIGHT'S NOT GETTING ANY YOUNGER!
AND MAKE SURE YOU CALL THAT DANCER-- THE ONE WITH THE LASSO-- WHAT'S HER NAME? NANCY, RIGHT?
YEAH! MAKE SURE YOU CALL NANCY! AND TELL HER TO BRING HER LASSO!
IT'LL BE GREAT! WE'LL SHOW YOU A GREAT TIME!

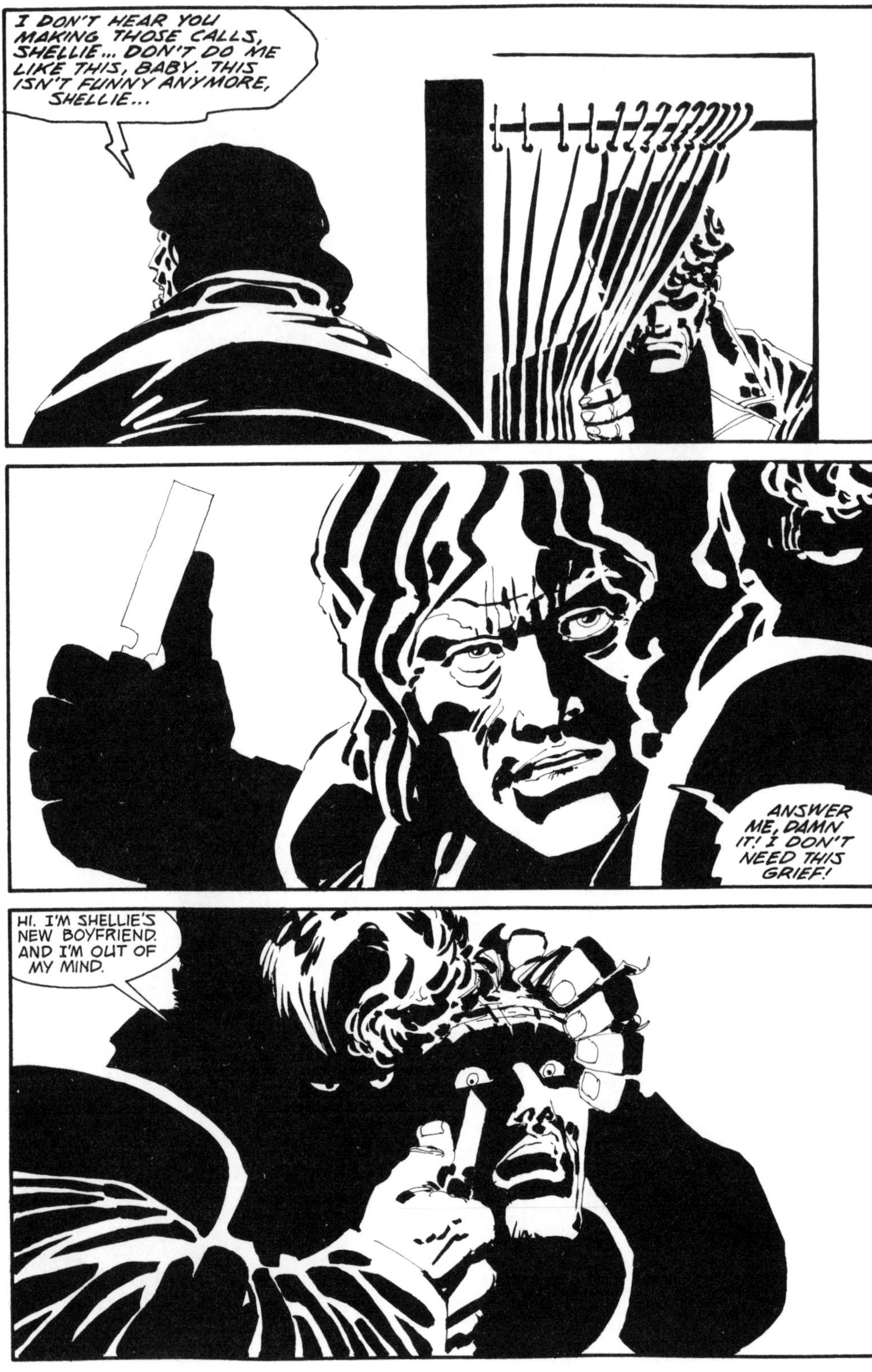
I DON'T HEAR YOU MAKING THOSE CALLS, SHELLIE... DON'T DO ME LIKE THIS, BABY. THIS ISN'T FUNNY ANYMORE, SHELLIE...
ANSWER ME, DAMN IT! I DON'T NEED THIS GRIEF!
HI. I'M SHELLIE'S NEW BOYFRIEND. AND I'M OUT OF MY MIND.

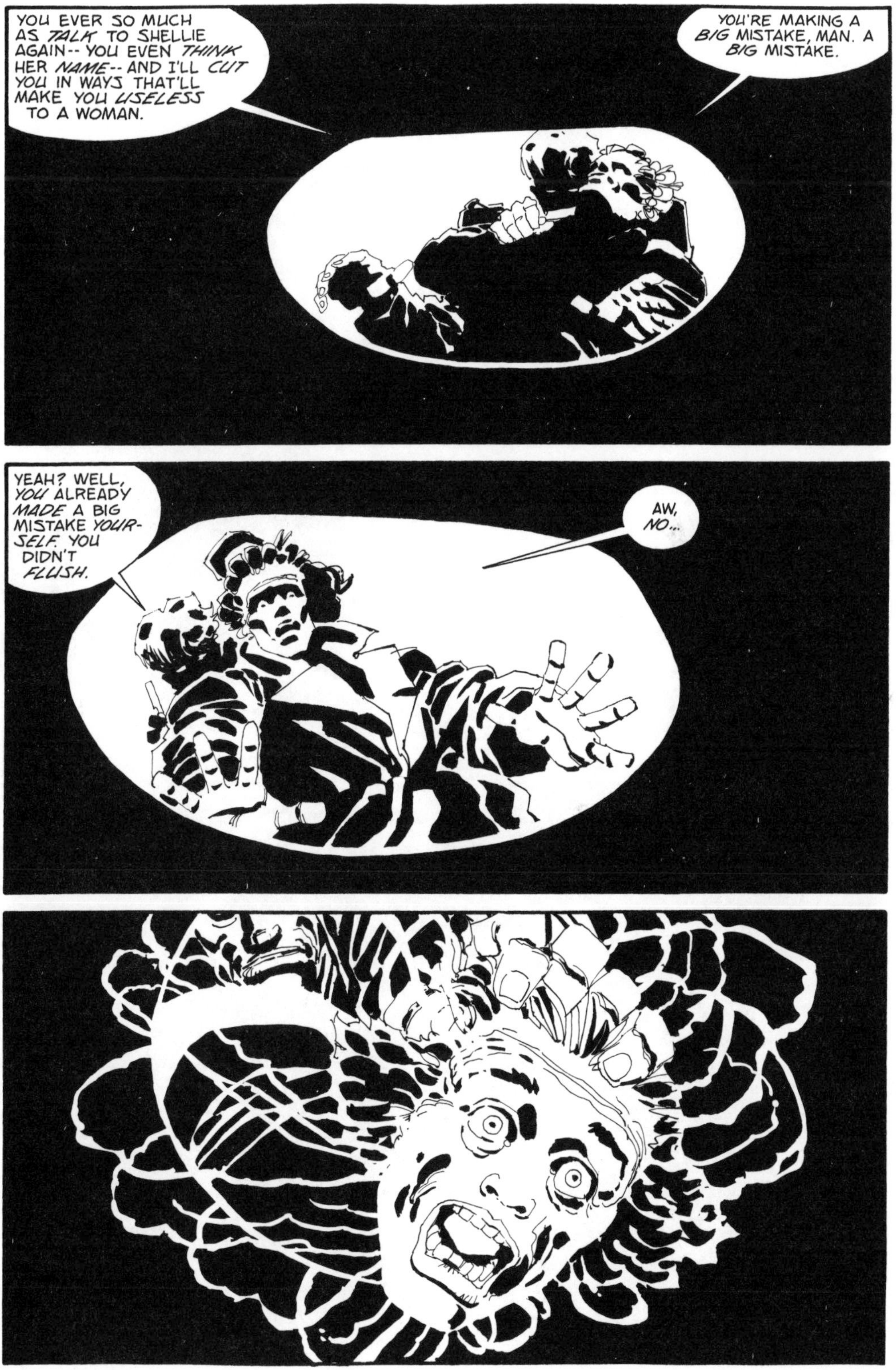
YOU EVER SO MUCH AS TALK TO SHELLIE AGAIN-- YOU EVEN THINK HER NAME-- AND I'LL CUT YOU IN WAYS THAT'LL MAKE YOU USELESS TO A WOMAN.
YOU'RE MAKING A BIG MISTAKE, MAN. A BIG MISTAKE.
YEAH? WELL, YOU ALREADY MADE A BIG MISTAKE YOURSELF. YOU DIDN'T FLUSH.
AW, NO...

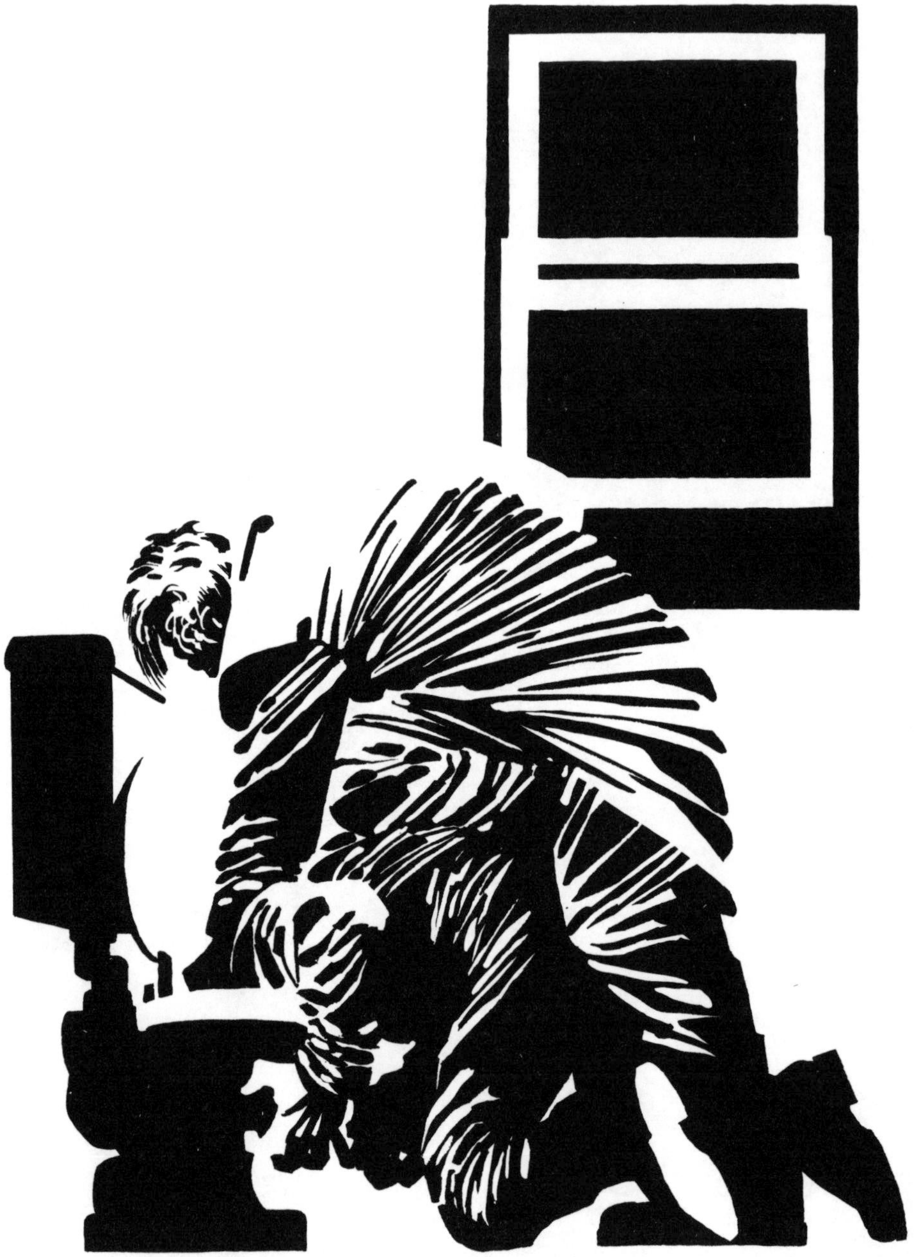

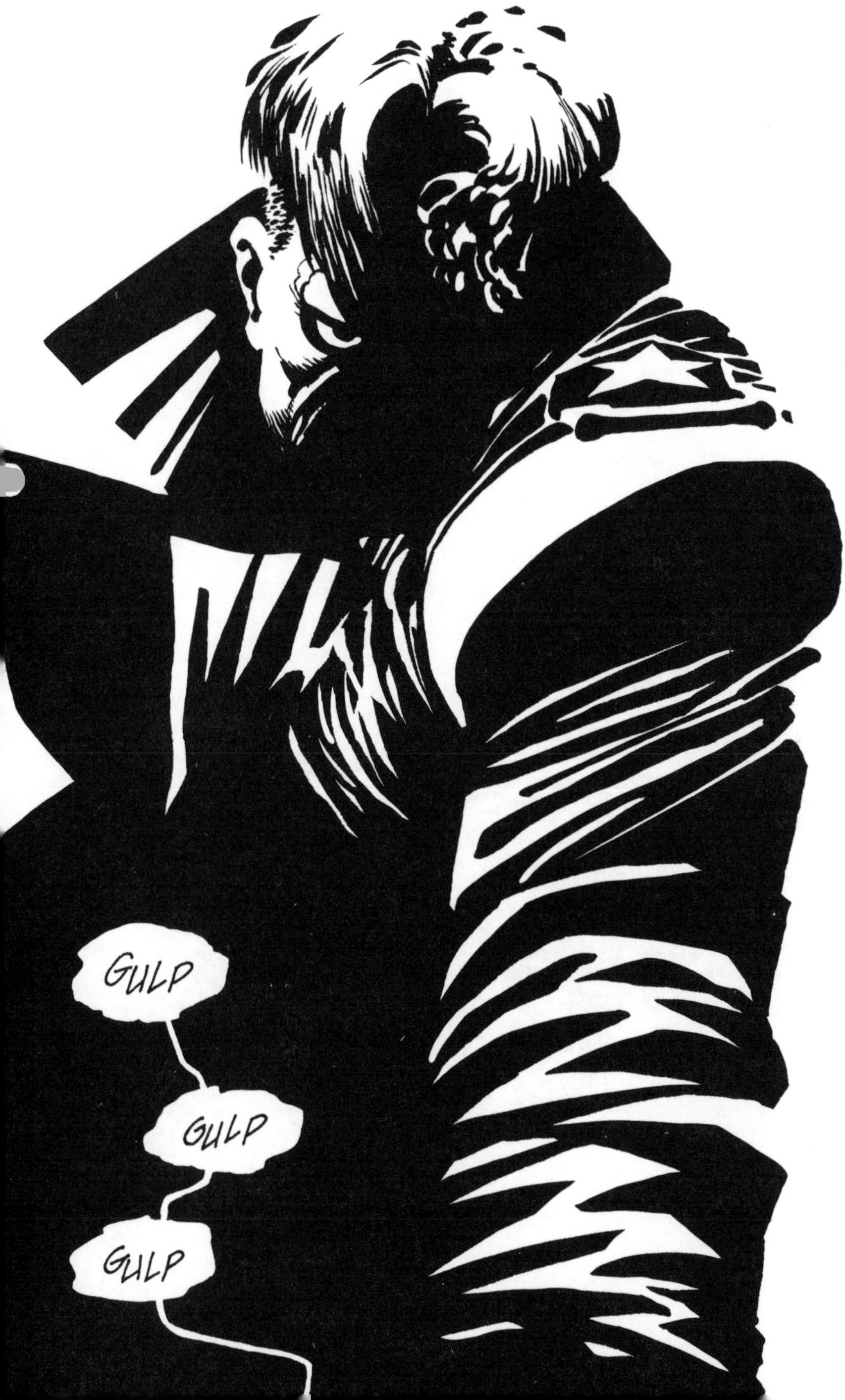
GULP
GULP
GULP

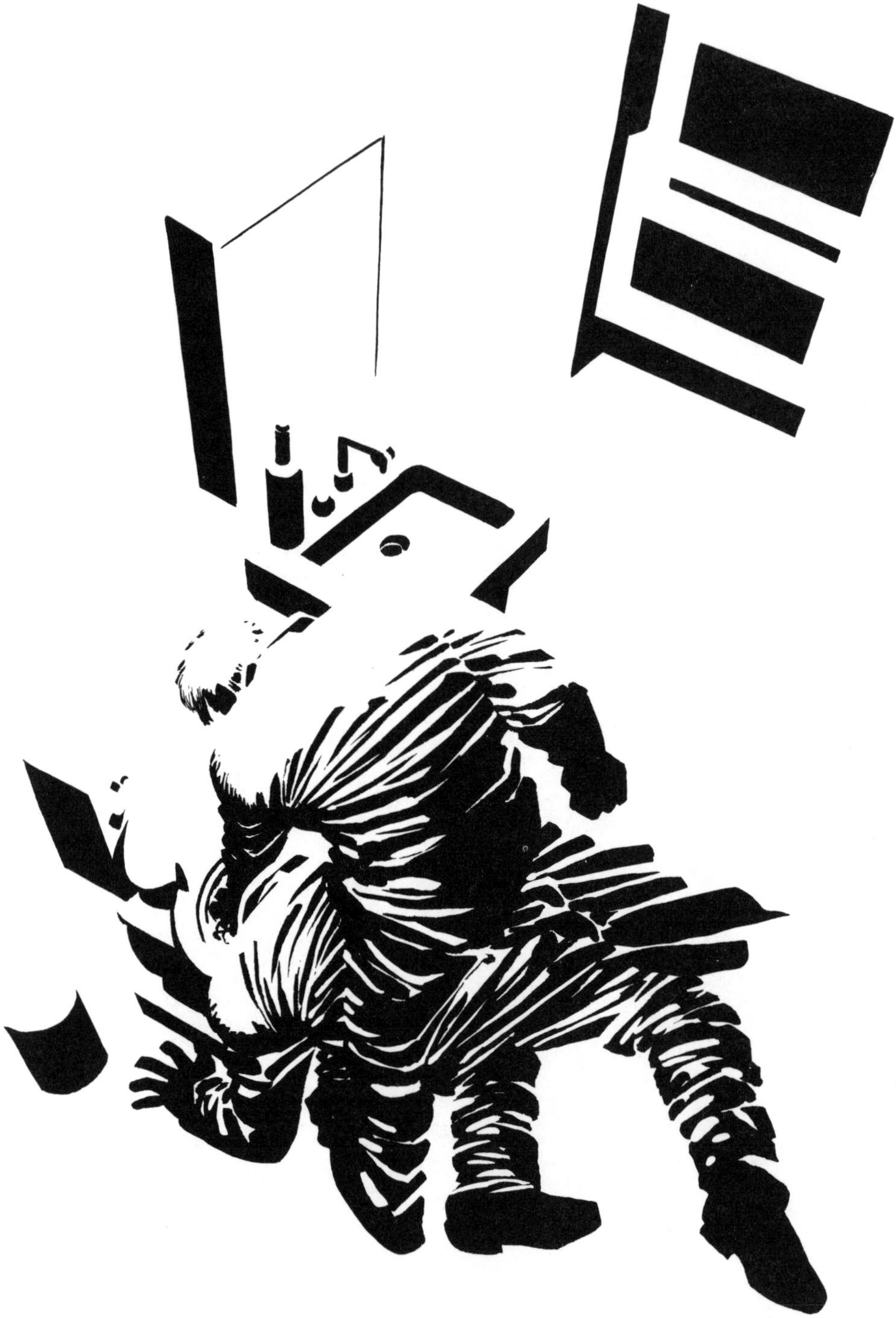

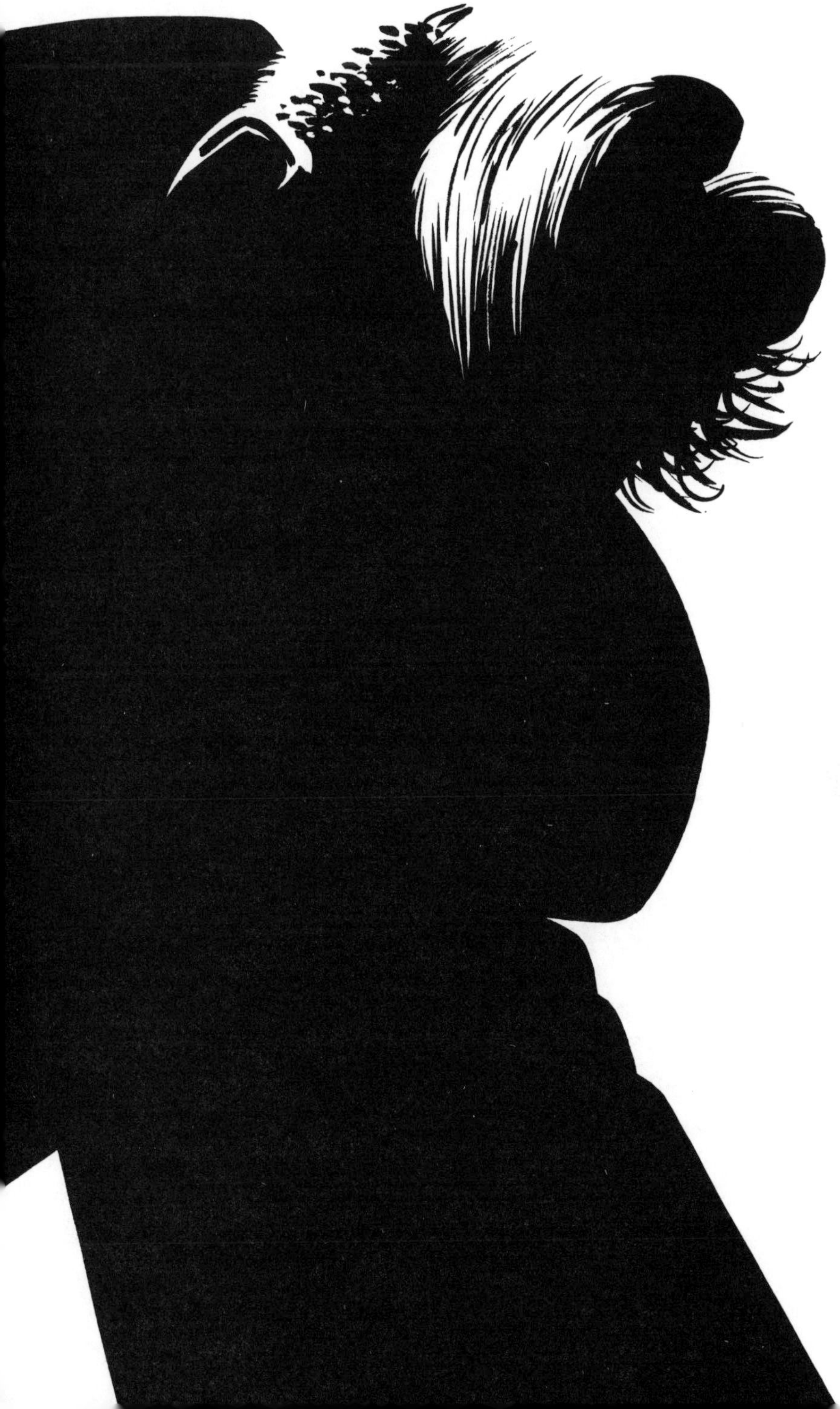

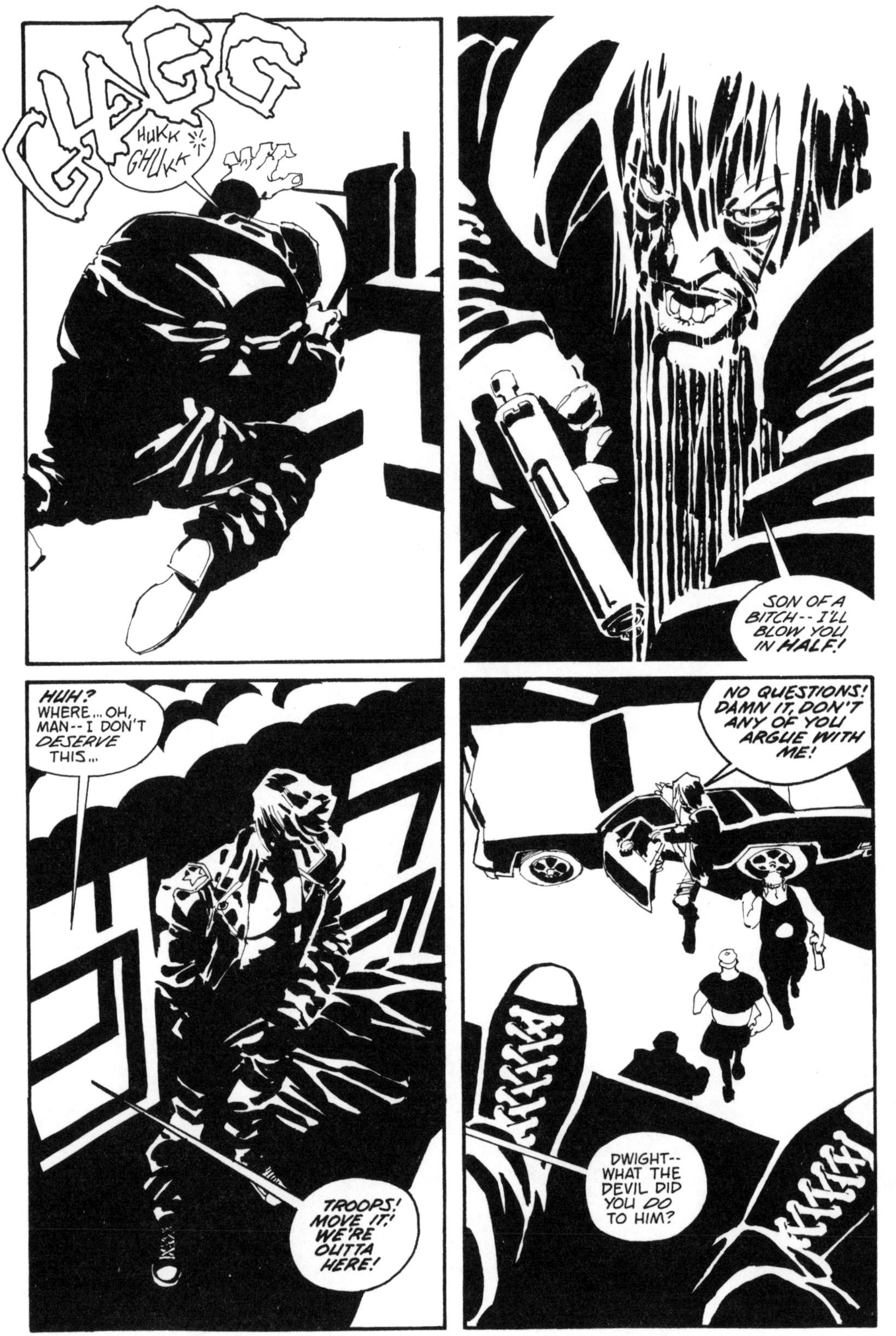
GAGG
HUKK GHUKK
SON OF A BITCH-- I'LL BLOW YOU IN HALF!
HUH? WHERE... OH, MAN-- I DON'T DESERVE THIS...
TROOPS! MOVE IT! WE'RE OUTTA HERE!
NO QUESTIONS! DAMN IT, DON'T ANY OF YOU ARGUE WITH ME!
DWIGHT-- WHAT THE DEVIL DID YOU DO TO HIM?

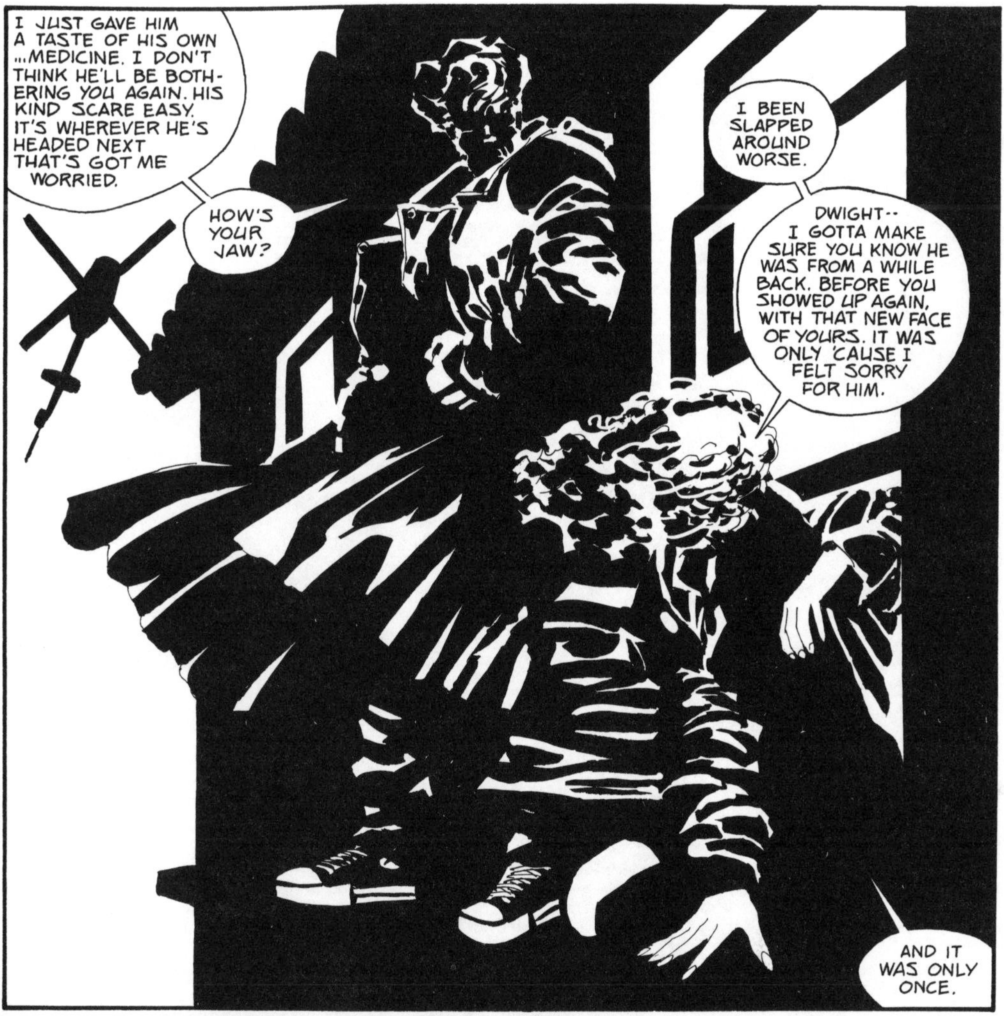
I JUST GAVE HIM A TASTE OF HIS OWN ...MEDICINE. I DON'T THINK HE'LL BE BOTHERING YOU AGAIN. HIS KIND SCARE EASY. IT'S WHEREVER HE'S HEADED NEXT THAT'S GOT ME WORRIED.
HOW'S YOUR JAW?
I BEEN SLAPPED AROUND WORSE.
DWIGHT-- I GOTTA MAKE SURE YOU KNOW HE WAS FROM A WHILE BACK. BEFORE YOU SHOWED UP AGAIN, WITH THAT NEW FACE OF YOURS. IT WAS ONLY 'CAUSE I FELT SORRY FOR HIM.
AND IT WAS ONLY ONCE.

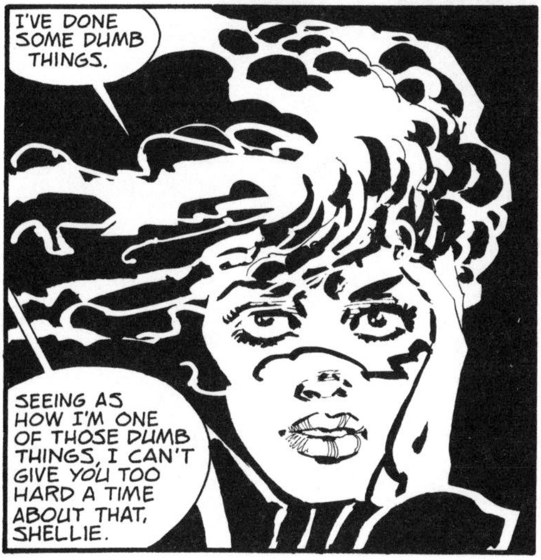
I'VE DONE SOME DUMB THINGS.
SEEING AS HOW I'M ONE OF THOSE DUMB THINGS, I CAN'T GIVE YOU TOO HARD A TIME ABOUT THAT, SHELLIE.

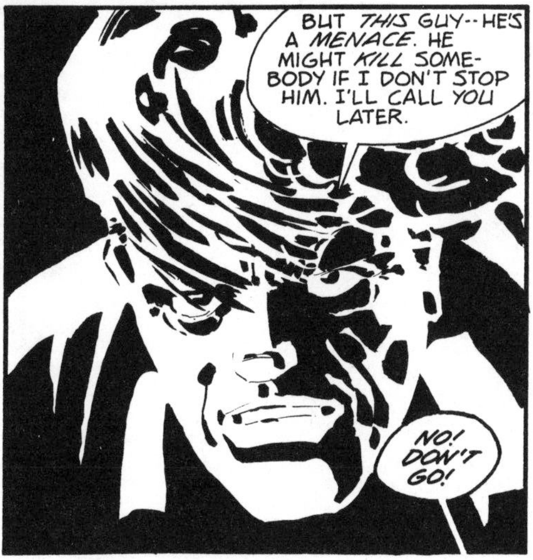
BUT THIS GUY--HE'S A MENACE. HE MIGHT KILL SOMEBODY IF I DON'T STOP HIM. I'LL CALL YOU LATER.
NO! DON'T GO!

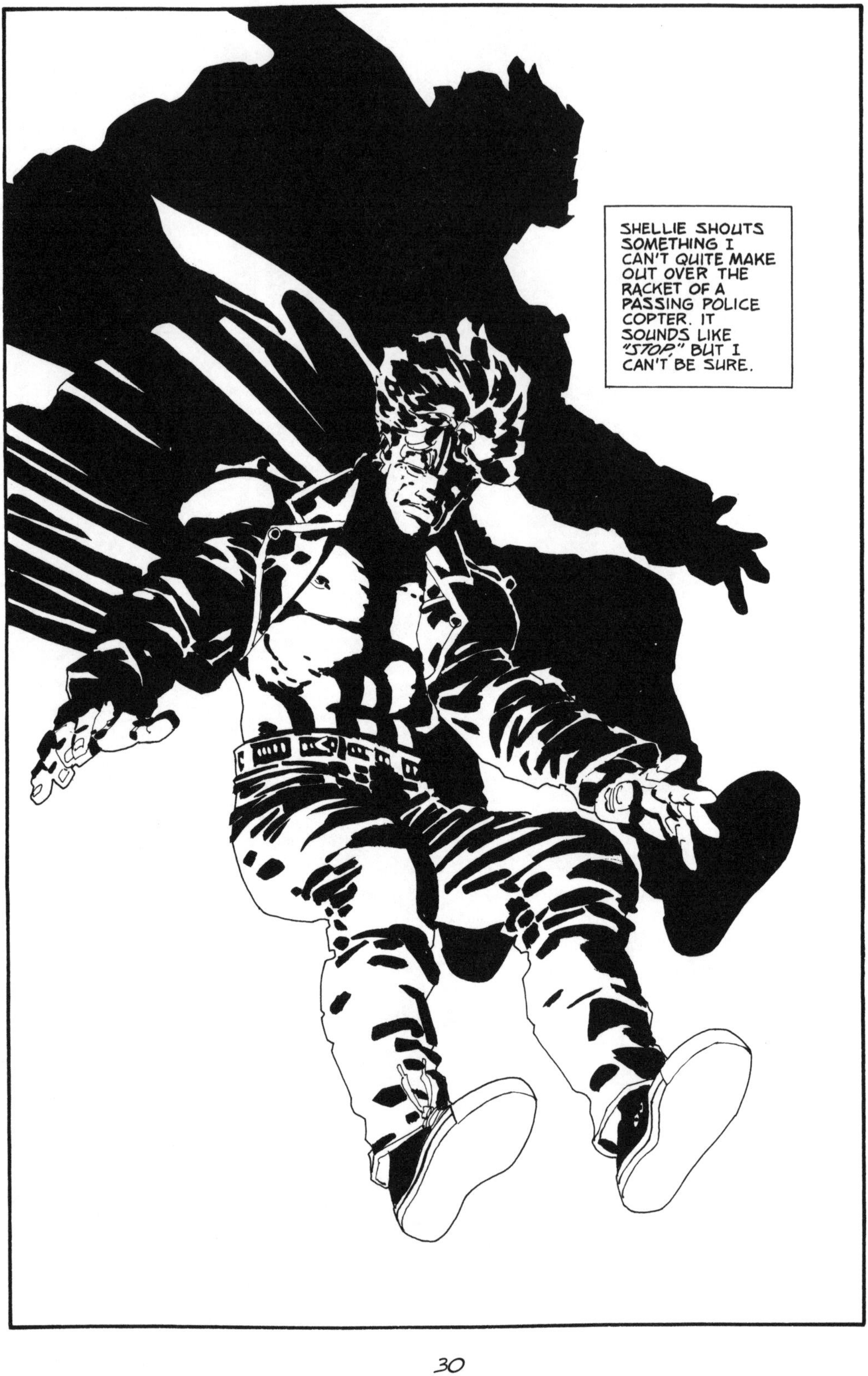
SHELLIE SHOUTS SOMETHING I CAN'T QUITE MAKE OUT OVER THE RACKET OF A PASSING POLICE COPTER. IT SOUNDS LIKE "STOP," BUT I CAN'T BE SURE.

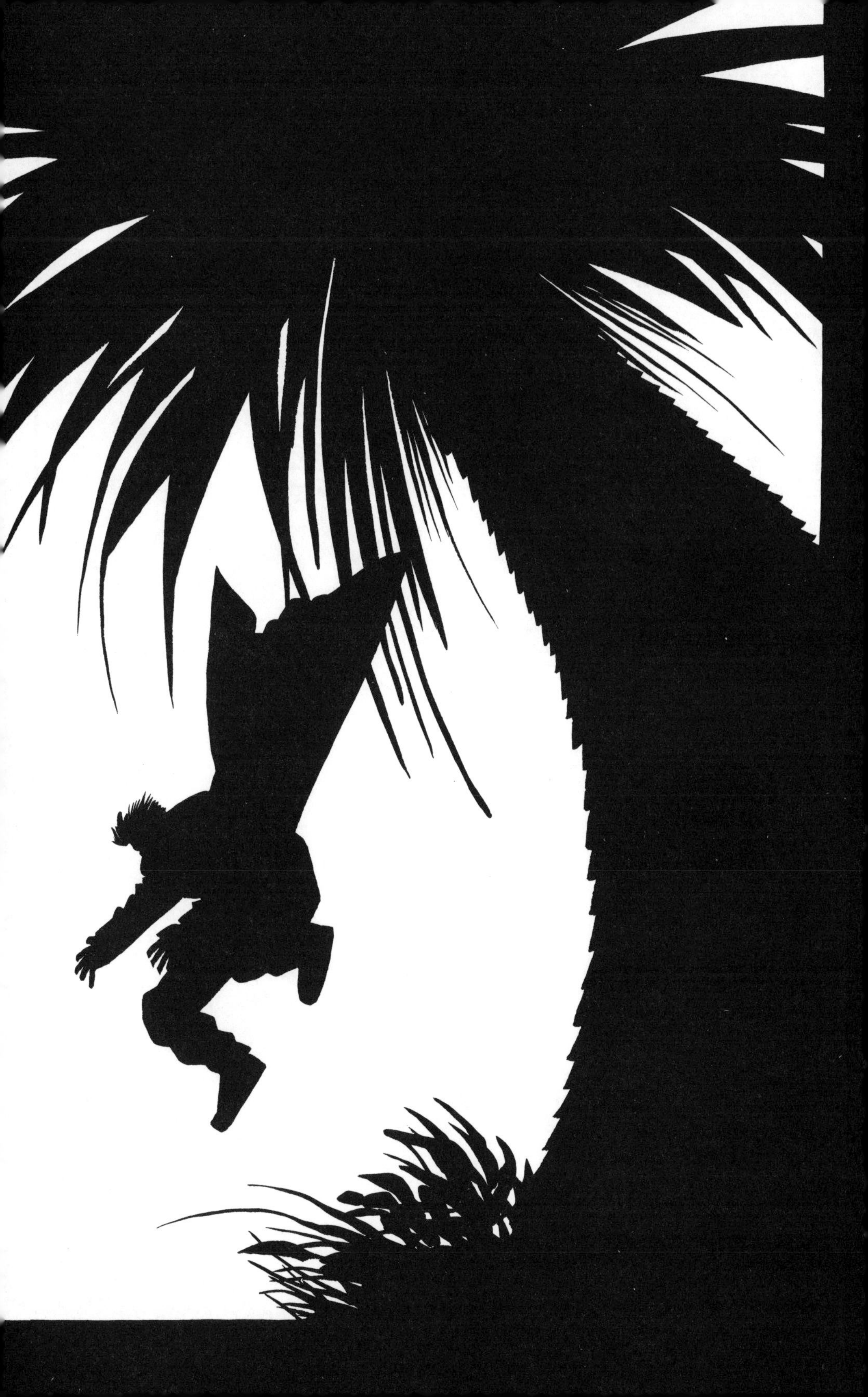

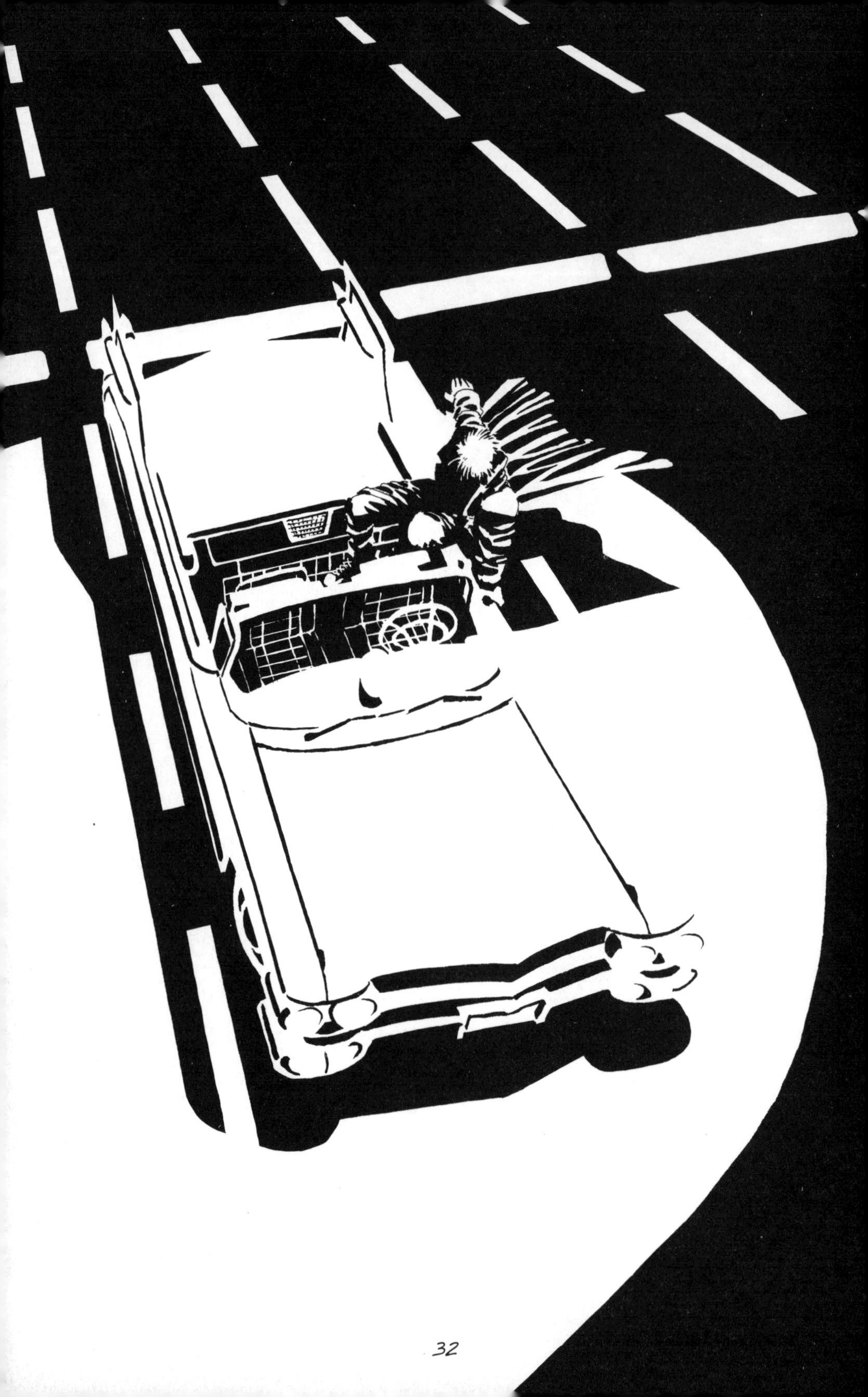

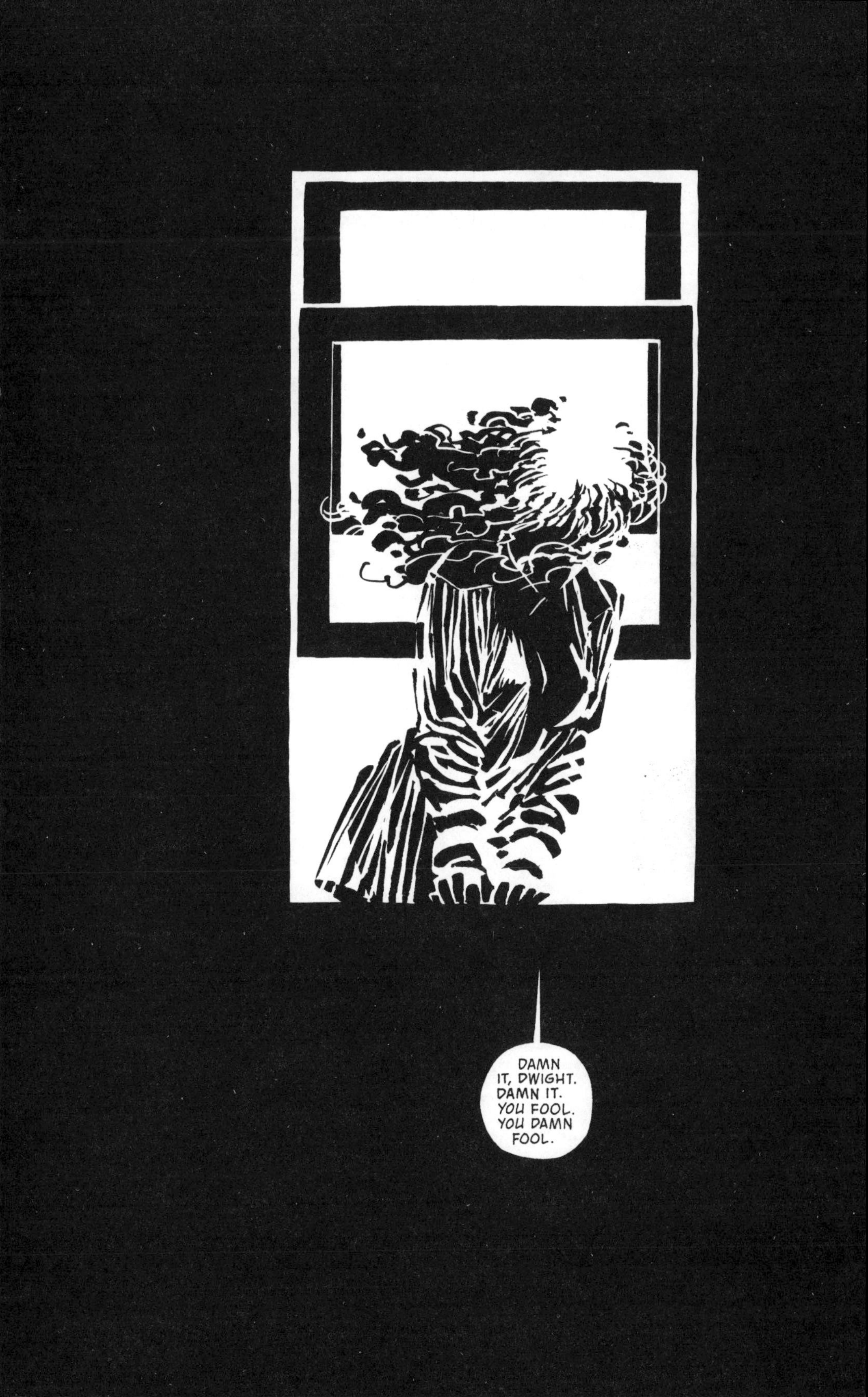
DAMN IT, DWIGHT. DAMN IT. YOU FOOL. YOU DAMN FOOL.

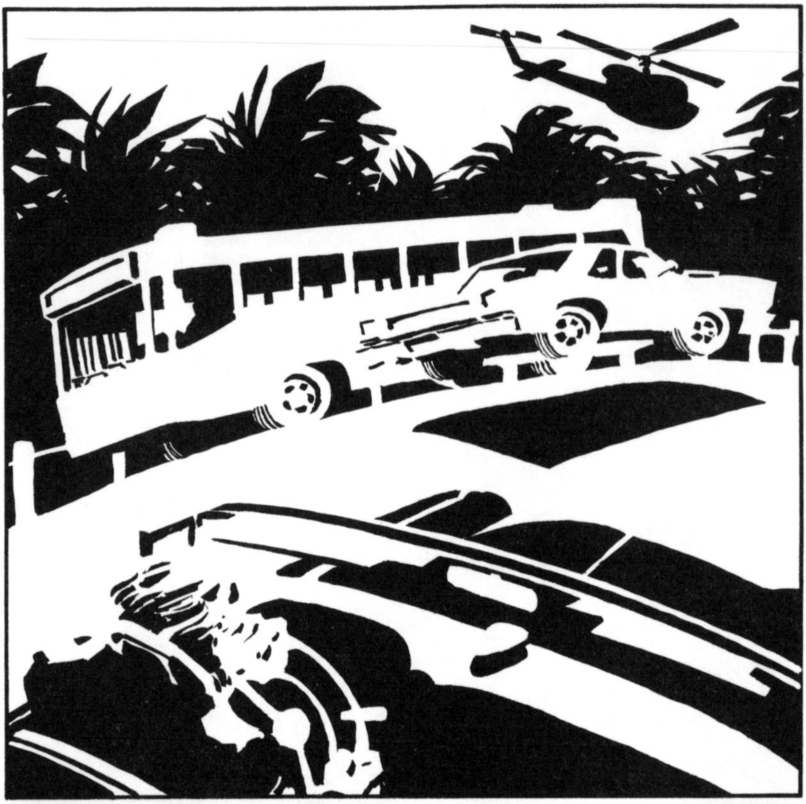

I MAKE MY WAY TO MY CADDY AND KICK IT INTO GEAR AND CUT ACROSS THE PARK TO PICK UP JACKIE-BOY HEADING LIKE A BAT OUT OF HELL UP THE HILL. THE CONDITION HE'S IN, HE WOULDN'T NOTICE IT IF I WAS SITTING RIGHT THERE IN HIS BACK SEAT WITH HIS BUDDIES, SO THERE'S NO NEED TO PLAY IT CUTE. I SNUGGLE UP RIGHT BEHIND HIM, KEEPING PACE AT A WAY-TOO-FAST EIGHTY-FIVE AND LEAVING MYSELF OPEN FOR ALL THE TROUBLE IN THE WORLD.

SPEEDING. IT'S A GOOD WAY TO GET YOURSELF NOTICED. AND IF YOU'RE A MURDERER WITH A NEW FACE WHO'S ONE FINGERPRINT CHECK AWAY FROM THE FAST TRACK TO THE GAS CHAMBER LIKE I AM, THE LAST THING YOU WANT IS TO GET NOTICED.

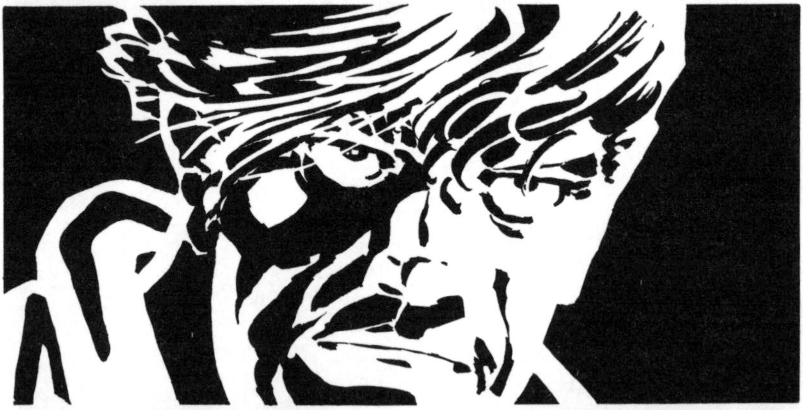

IT'S A CHANCE I SHOULDN'T BE TAKING, BUT I CAN'T JUST GO HOME AND FORGET ABOUT IT AND LET JACKIE-BOY AND HIS PALS FIND THEIR FUN. THEY'RE A PACK OF PREDATORS AND THEY'RE OUT FOR BLOOD TONIGHT. A WOMAN'S BLOOD.

THEY WON'T GET IT. I'M IN NO HURRY TO KILL ANYBODY EVER AGAIN, BUT I'LL KILL THEM IF I HAVE TO.

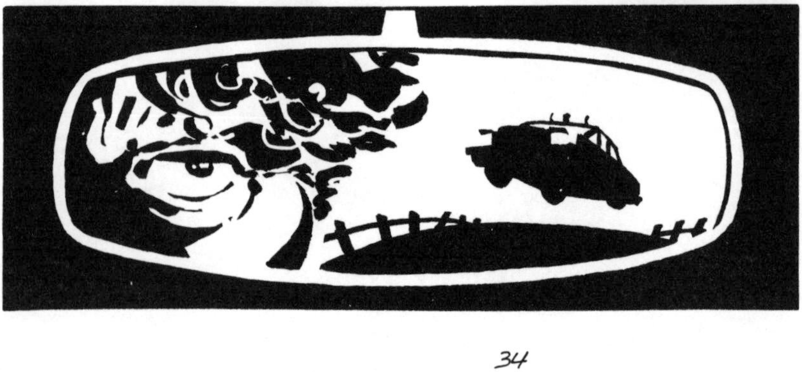

THEN I HEAR A BANSHEE CRY, COMING UP FAST.

I'VE BEEN *NOTICED.*

I DON'T HAVE *NEARLY* ENOUGH CASH ON ME TO *BRIBE* THIS COP...

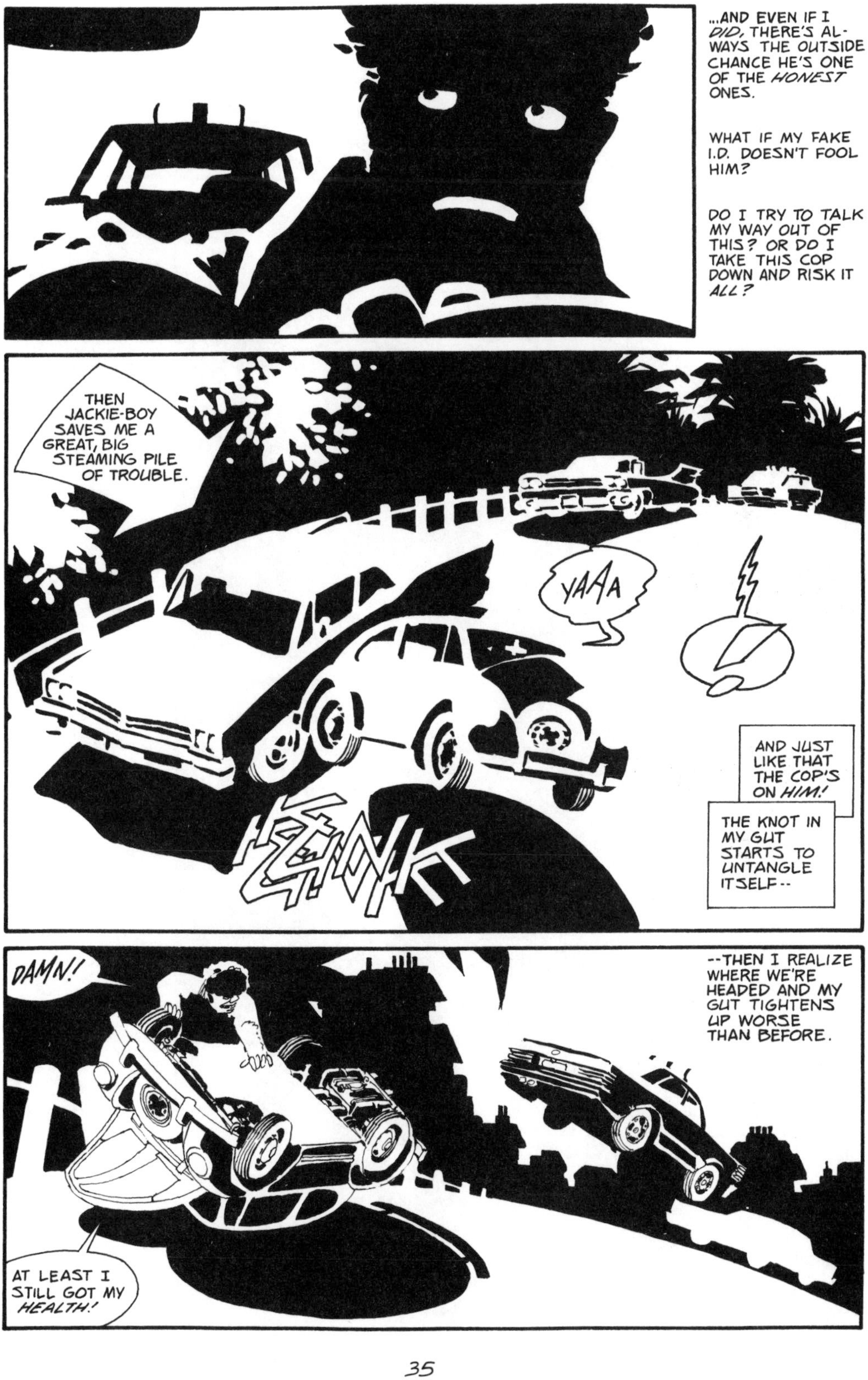
...AND EVEN IF I *DID,* THERE'S ALWAYS THE OUTSIDE CHANCE HE'S ONE OF THE *HONEST* ONES.
WHAT IF MY FAKE I.D. DOESN'T FOOL HIM?
DO I TRY TO TALK MY WAY OUT OF THIS? OR DO I TAKE THIS COP DOWN AND RISK IT *ALL?*
THEN JACKIE-BOY SAVES ME A GREAT, BIG STEAMING PILE OF TROUBLE.
YAAA
AND JUST LIKE THAT THE COP'S ON *HIM!*
THE KNOT IN MY GUT STARTS TO UNTANGLE ITSELF--
DAMN!!
--THEN I REALIZE WHERE WE'RE HEADED AND MY GUT TIGHTENS UP WORSE THAN BEFORE.
AT LEAST I STILL GOT MY *HEALTH!*

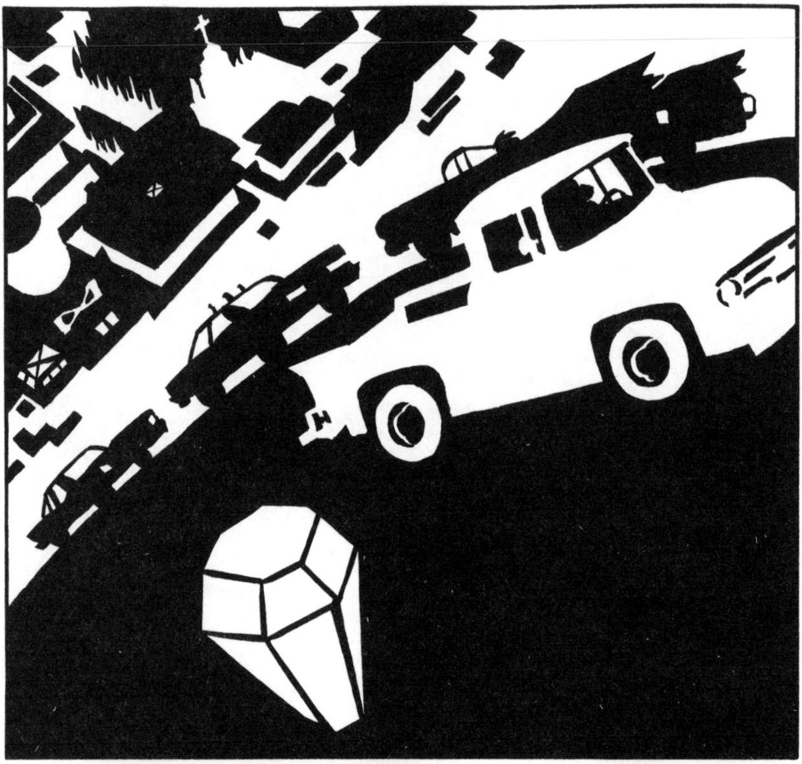

JACKIE-BOY'S LEADING US STRAIGHT TO OLD TOWN.

DAMN IT!

JUST SECONDS AGO EVERYTHING WAS PERFECT. THE COP WAS GOING TO PULL THEM OVER AND NAIL THEM FOR DRUNK DRIVING. HE WAS GOING TO FIND AT LEAST TWO PISTOLS ON THEM, FOR WHICH IT'S A SAFE BET THEY DON'T HAVE PERMITS. MAYBE THEY'D EVEN RESIST ARREST, JUST TO MAKE MY JOY COMPLETE. THEY'D BE SITTING IN THE SLAMMER FOR MONTHS, OFF THE STREETS AND NO DANGER TO ANYBODY.

BUT NO, THE BUM HAS TO MAKE A RUN INTO OLD TOWN AND MAKE A MESS OUT OF EVERYTHING.

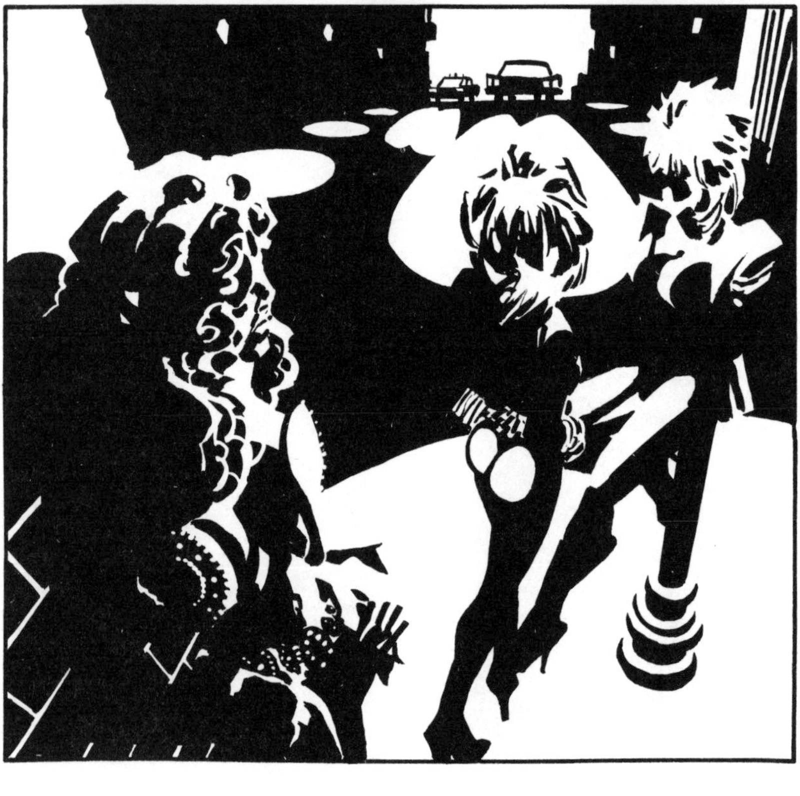

THE COP SHUTS UP HIS SIREN, NOT SURE HOW TO PLAY IT. HE KNOWS HE'S NOT THE LAW. NOT IN OLD TOWN.

THE LADIES ARE THE LAW HERE, BEAUTIFUL AND MERCILESS. IF YOU'VE GOT THE CASH AND YOU PLAY BY THE RULES, THEY'LL MAKE ALL YOUR DREAMS COME TRUE. BUT IF YOU CROSS THEM, YOU'RE A CORPSE.

OFFICER, MAKE BOTH OUR LIVES BETTER AND TURN THE HELL AROUND AND GET THE HELL OUT OF HERE. LEAVE JACKIE-BOY TO ME.

YOU KNOW HOW THE GIRLS ARE.

THE LAST THING OLD TOWN NEEDS IS A DEAD COP.

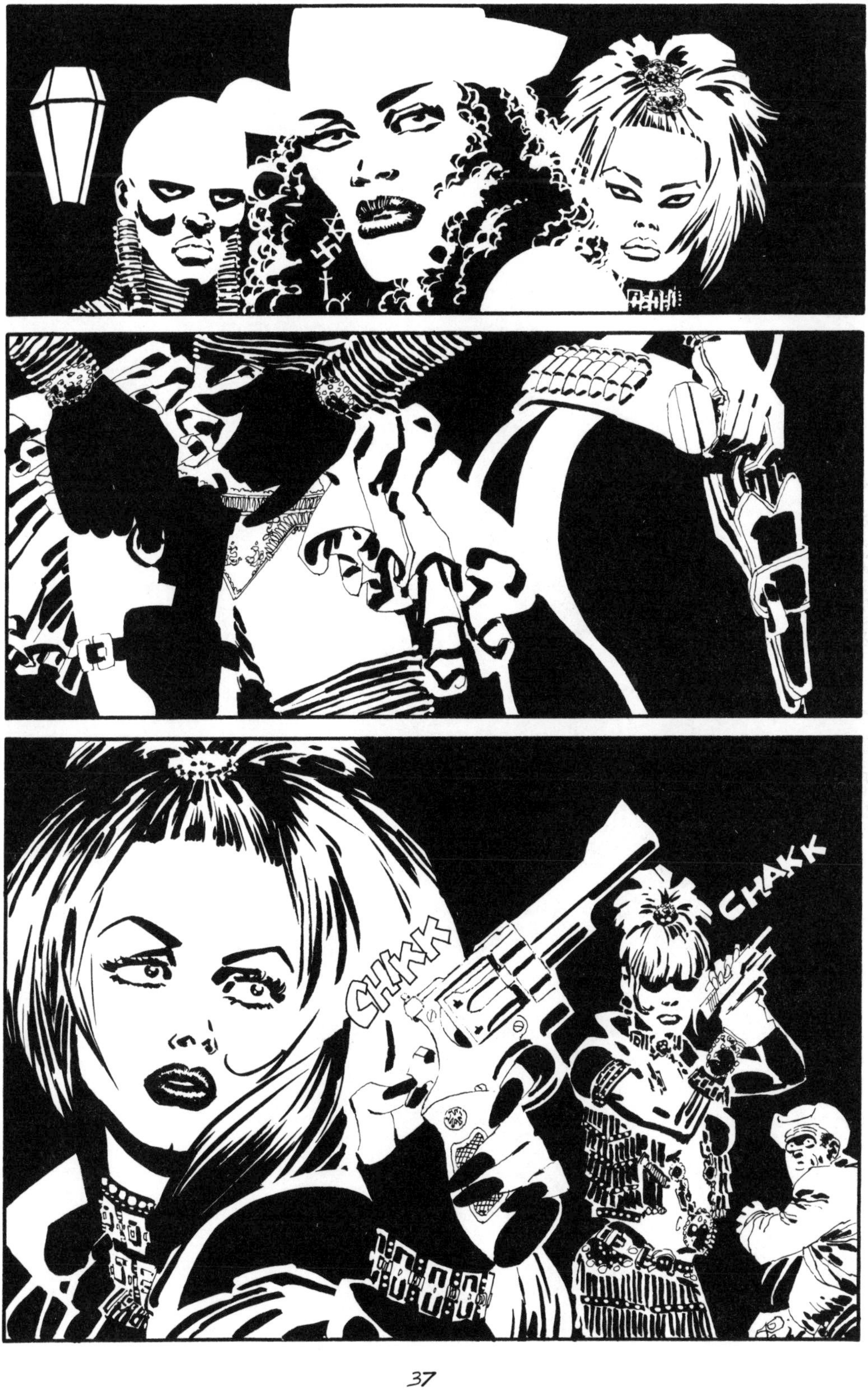
CHAKK
CHAKK

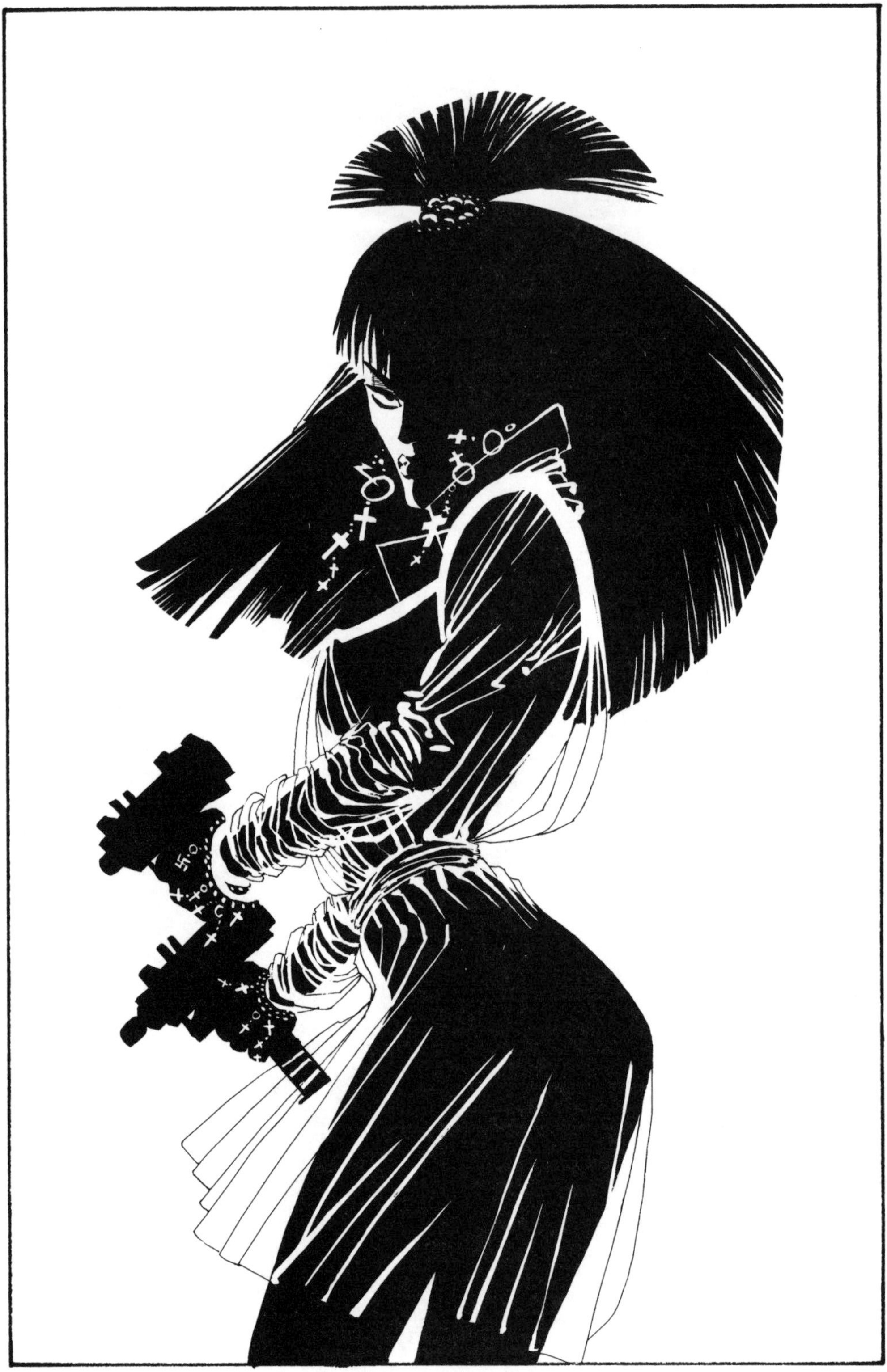

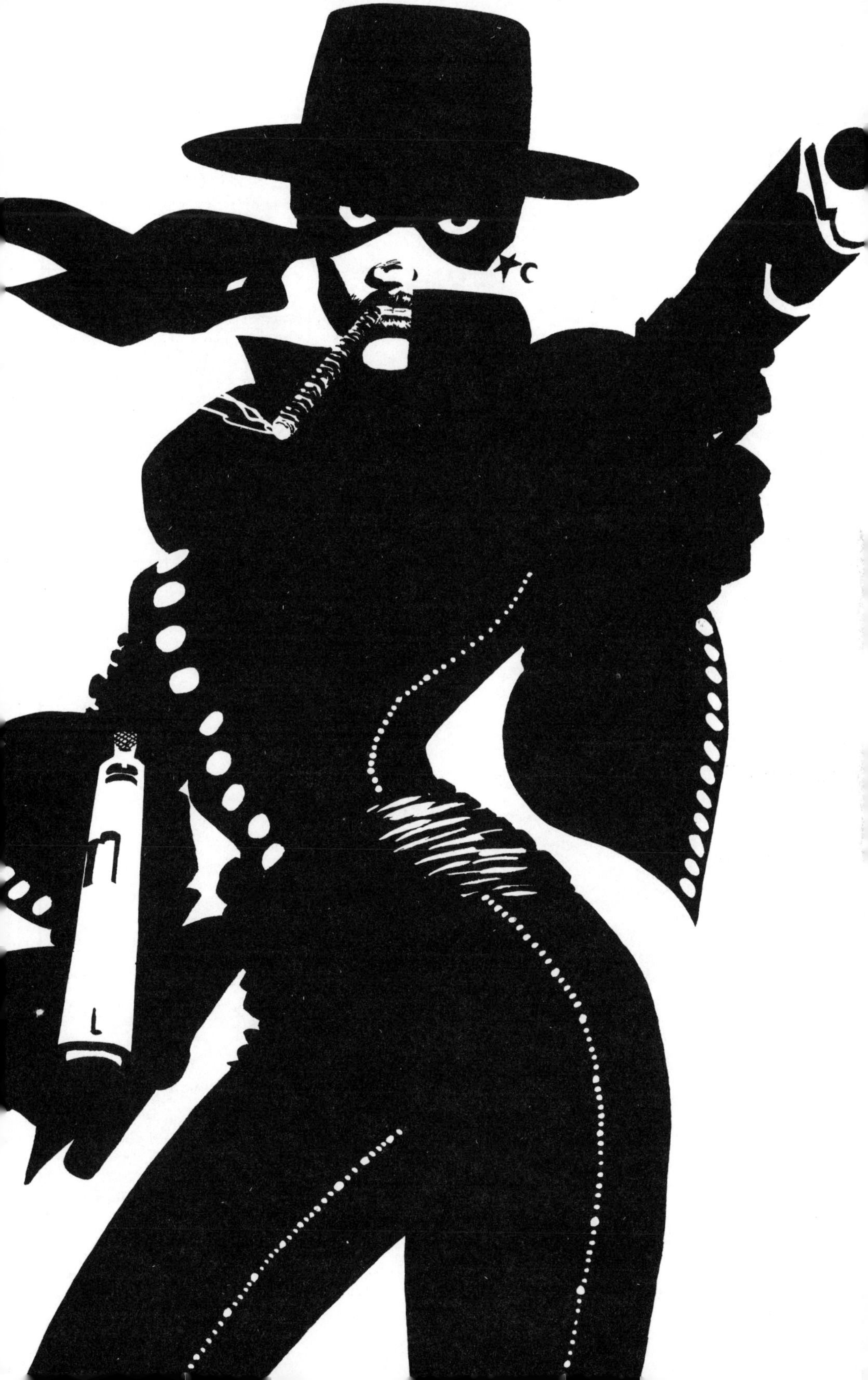

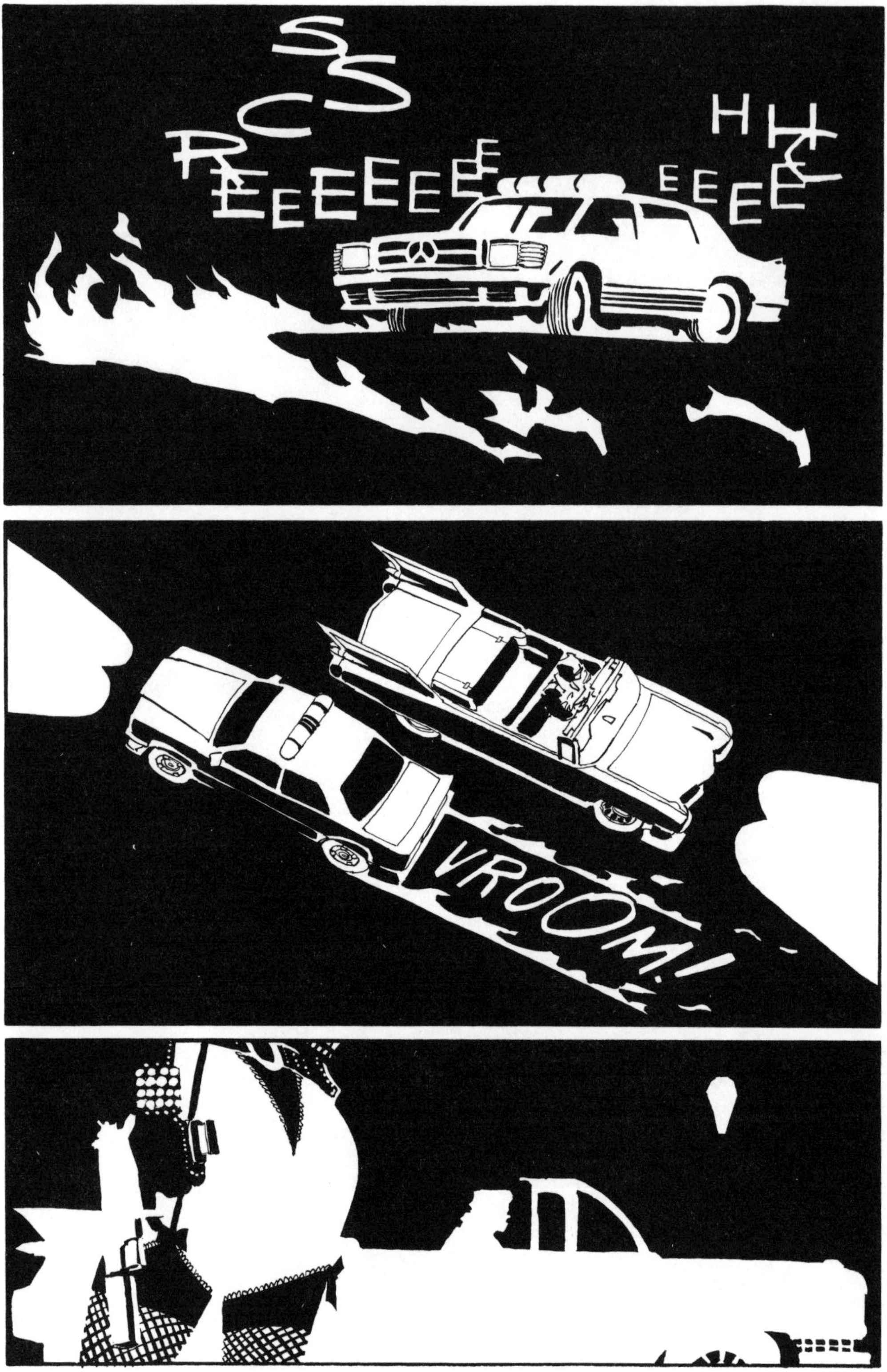
SSCREEEEEEEEE
VROOM!

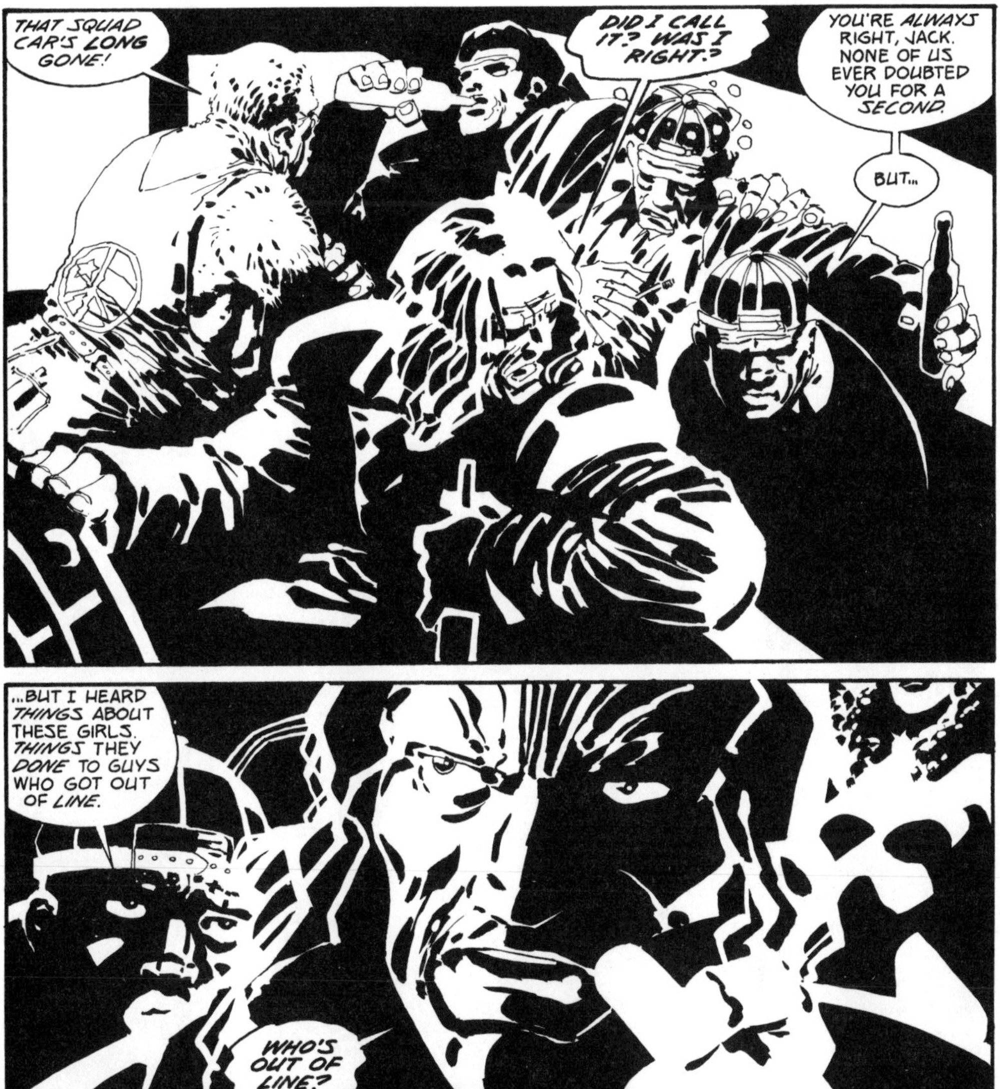
THAT SQUAD CAR'S LONG GONE!
DID I CALL IT? WAS I RIGHT?
YOU'RE ALWAYS RIGHT, JACK. NONE OF US EVER DOUBTED YOU FOR A SECOND.
BUT...
...BUT I HEARD THINGS ABOUT THESE GIRLS. THINGS THEY DONE TO GUYS WHO GOT OUT OF LINE.
WHO'S OUT OF LINE?

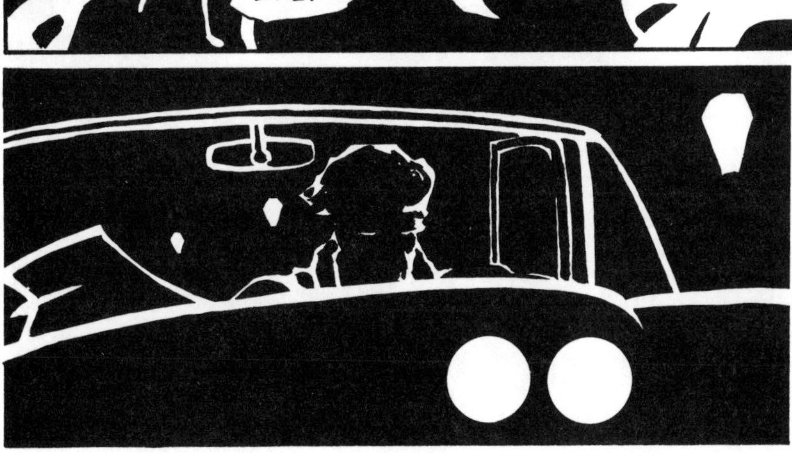

THEY WEAVE THEIR WAY DOWN SIDE STREETS, KEEPING AWAY FROM THE LIGHTS AND THE CROWDS, LOOKING FOR A WOMAN WHO'S ALONE AND DEFENSELESS.

LOOKING FOR PREY.

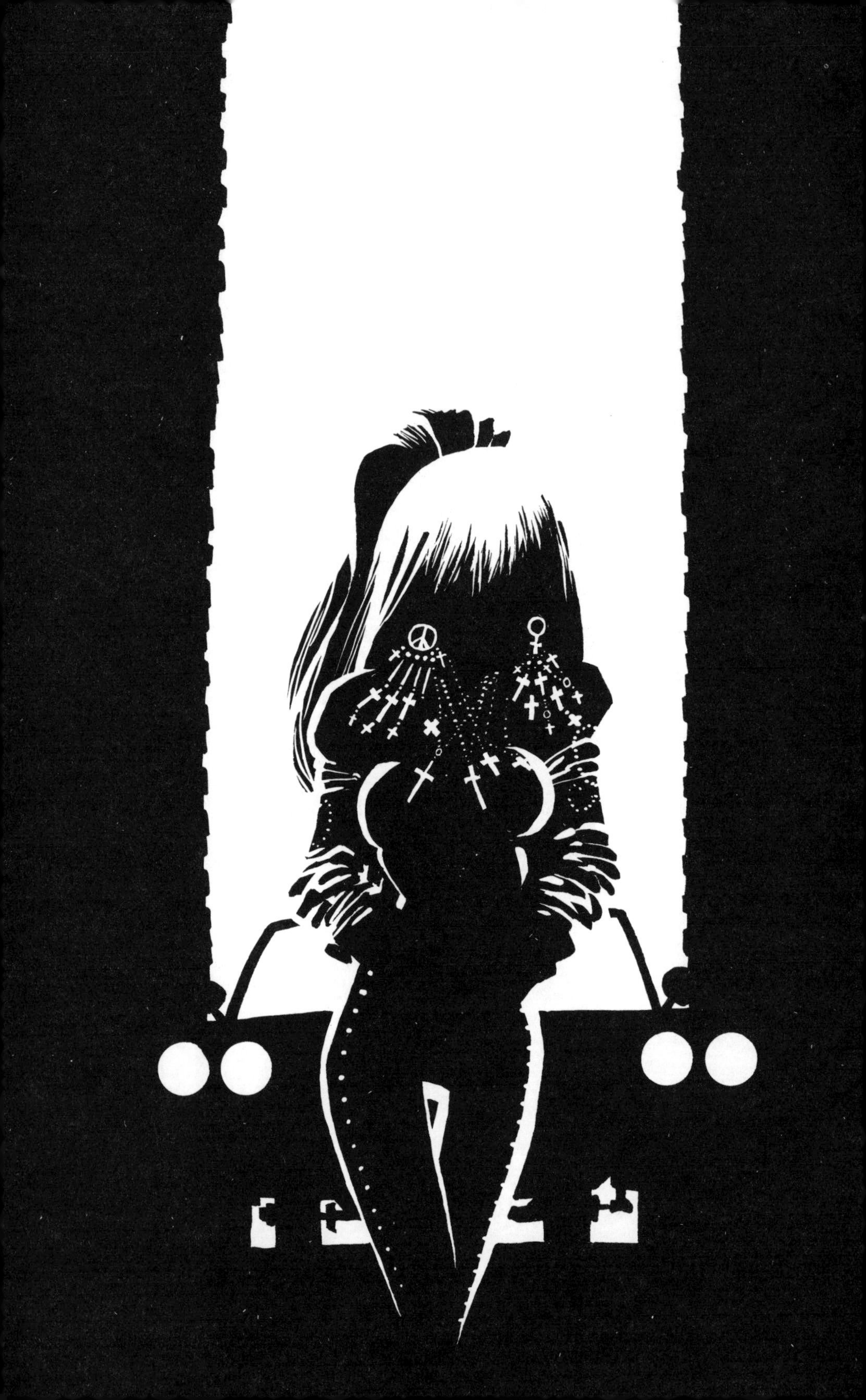

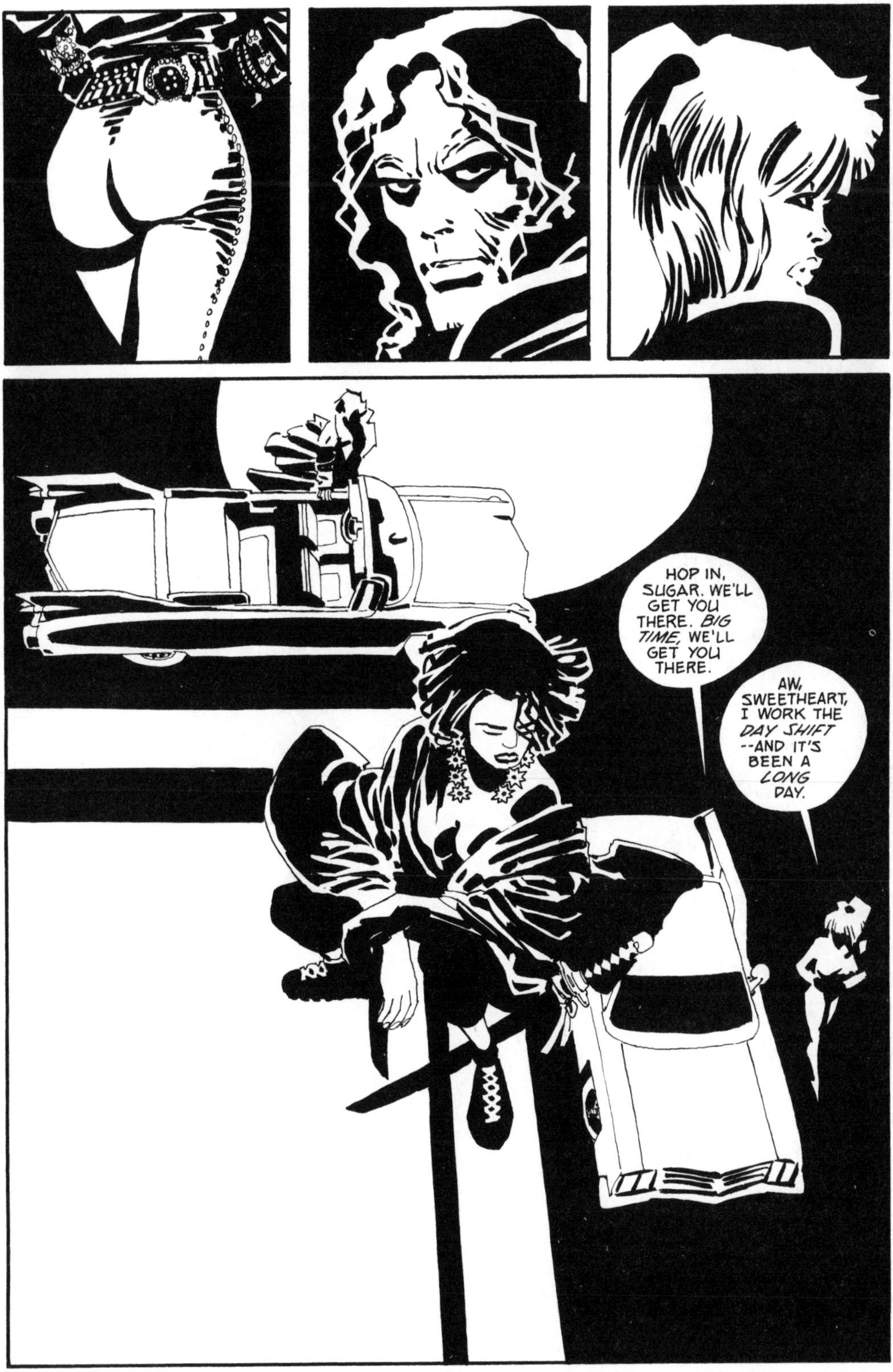
HOP IN, SUGAR. WE'LL GET YOU THERE. *BIG TIME,* WE'LL GET YOU THERE.
AW, SWEETHEART, I WORK THE *DAY SHIFT* --AND IT'S BEEN A *LONG* DAY.

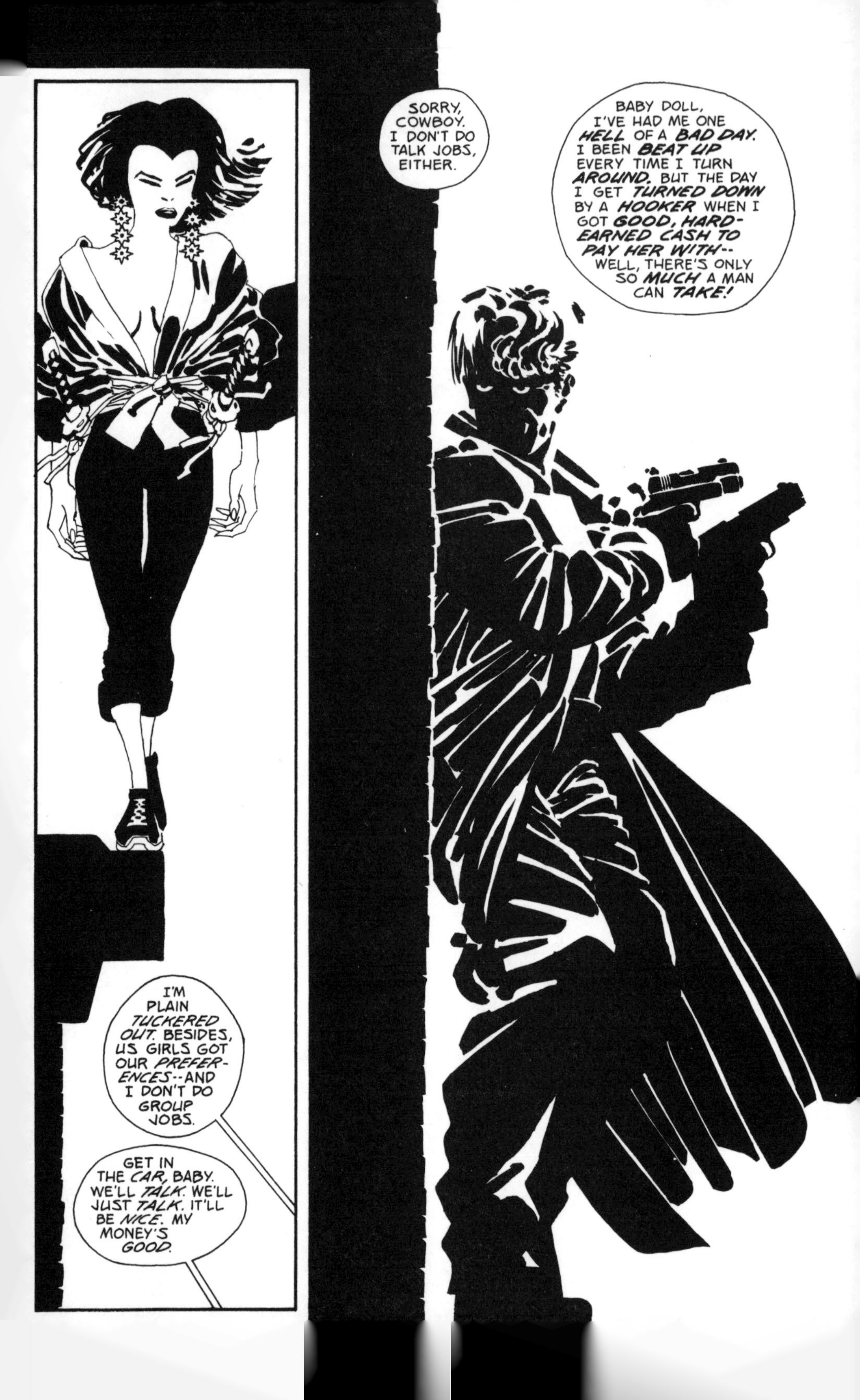
I'M PLAIN TUCKERED OUT. BESIDES, US GIRLS GOT OUR PREFER-ENCES--AND I DON'T DO GROUP JOBS.
GET IN THE CAR, BABY. WE'LL TALK. WE'LL JUST TALK. IT'LL BE NICE. MY MONEY'S GOOD.
SORRY, COWBOY. I DON'T DO TALK JOBS, EITHER.
BABY DOLL, I'VE HAD ME ONE HELL OF A BAD DAY. I BEEN BEAT UP EVERY TIME I TURN AROUND. BUT THE DAY I GET TURNED DOWN BY A HOOKER WHEN I GOT GOOD, HARD-EARNED CASH TO PAY HER WITH-- WELL, THERE'S ONLY SO MUCH A MAN CAN TAKE!

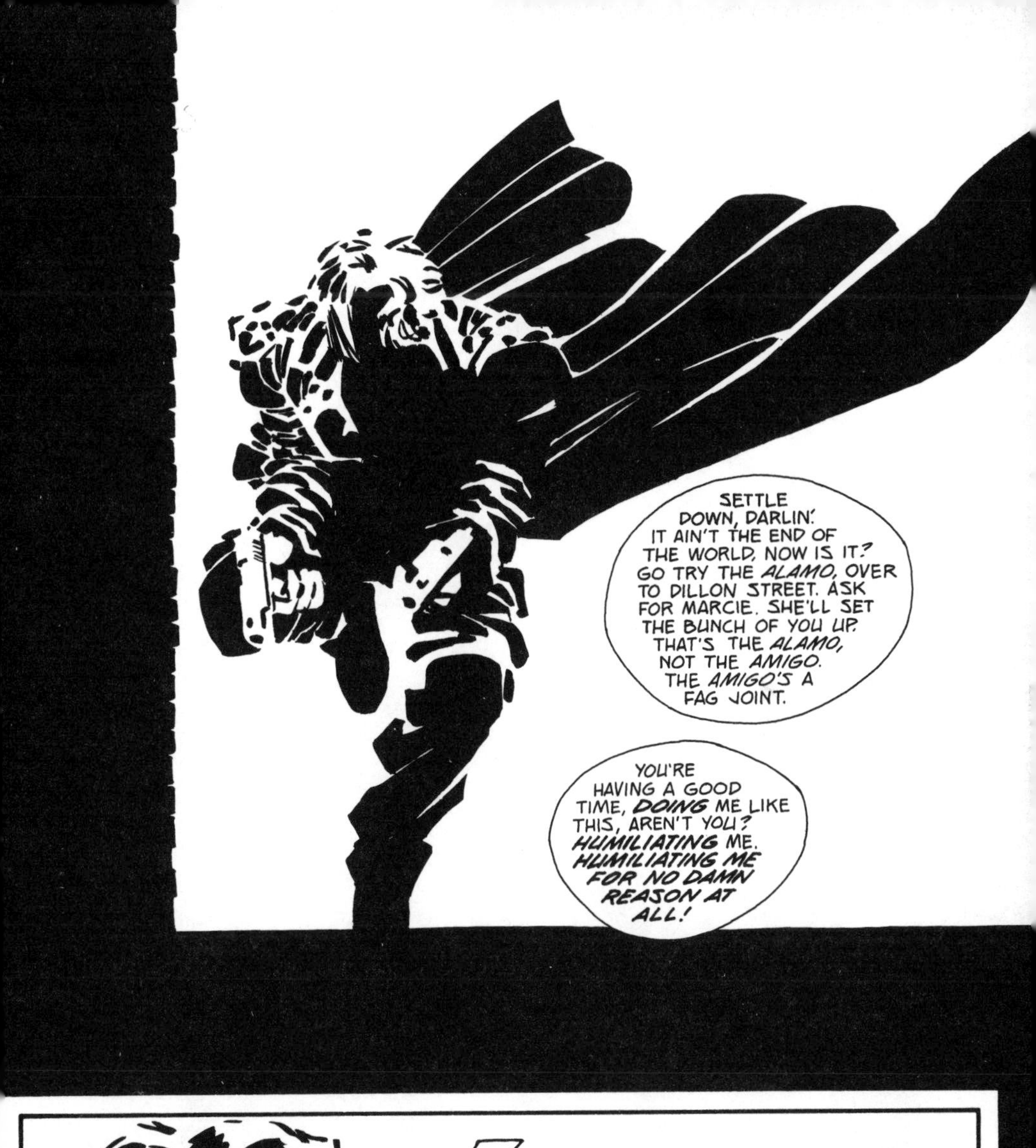
SETTLE DOWN, DARLIN'. IT AIN'T THE END OF THE WORLD, NOW IS IT? GO TRY THE *ALAMO*, OVER TO DILLON STREET. ASK FOR MARCIE. SHE'LL SET THE BUNCH OF YOU UP. THAT'S THE *ALAMO*, NOT THE *AMIGO*. THE *AMIGO'S* A FAG JOINT.
YOU'RE HAVING A GOOD TIME, ***DOING*** ME LIKE THIS, AREN'T YOU? ***HUMILIATING*** ME. ***HUMILIATING ME FOR NO DAMN REASON AT ALL!***

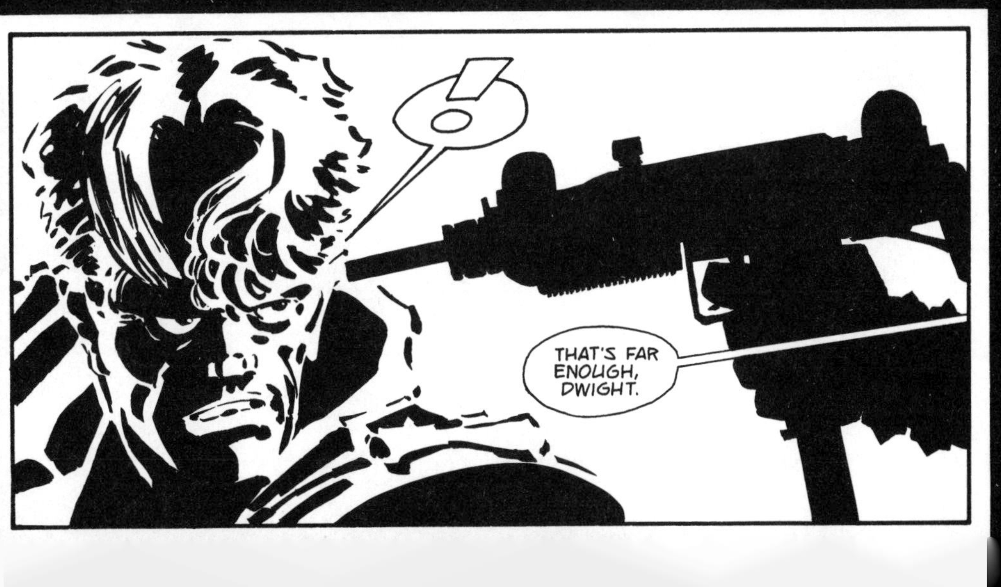
!
THAT'S FAR ENOUGH, DWIGHT.

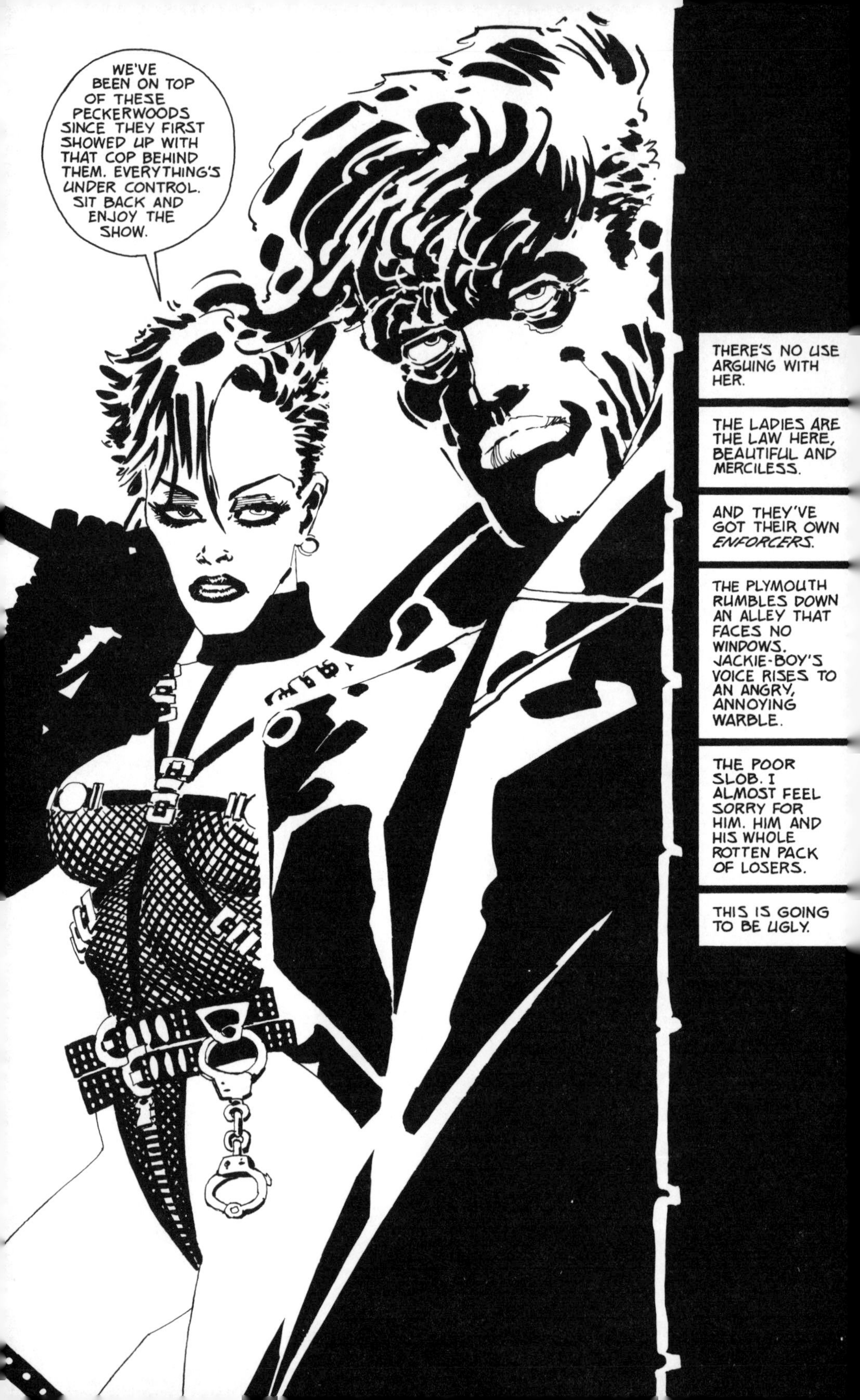
WE'VE BEEN ON TOP OF THESE PECKERWOODS SINCE THEY FIRST SHOWED UP WITH THAT COP BEHIND THEM. EVERYTHING'S UNDER CONTROL. SIT BACK AND ENJOY THE SHOW.
THERE'S NO USE ARGUING WITH HER.
THE LADIES ARE THE LAW HERE, BEAUTIFUL AND MERCILESS.
AND THEY'VE GOT THEIR OWN *ENFORCERS*.
THE PLYMOUTH RUMBLES DOWN AN ALLEY THAT FACES NO WINDOWS. JACKIE-BOY'S VOICE RISES TO AN ANGRY, ANNOYING WARBLE.
THE POOR SLOB. I ALMOST FEEL SORRY FOR HIM. HIM AND HIS WHOLE ROTTEN PACK OF LOSERS.
THIS IS GOING TO BE UGLY.

CHAPTER TWO

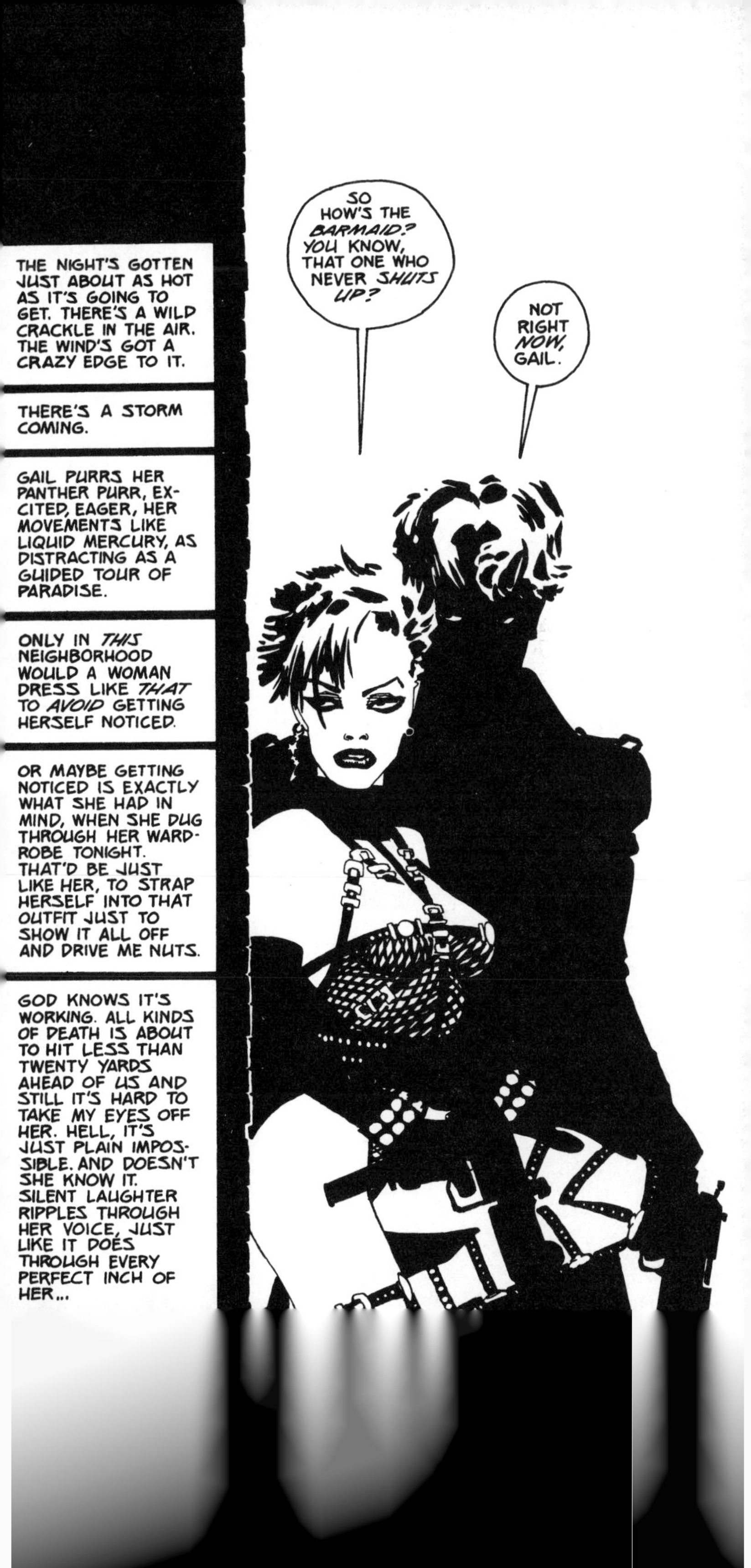
THE NIGHT'S GOTTEN JUST ABOUT AS HOT AS IT'S GOING TO GET. THERE'S A WILD CRACKLE IN THE AIR. THE WIND'S GOT A CRAZY EDGE TO IT.
THERE'S A STORM COMING.
GAIL PURRS HER PANTHER PURR, EXCITED, EAGER, HER MOVEMENTS LIKE LIQUID MERCURY, AS DISTRACTING AS A GUIDED TOUR OF PARADISE.
ONLY IN THIS NEIGHBORHOOD WOULD A WOMAN DRESS LIKE THAT TO AVOID GETTING HERSELF NOTICED.
OR MAYBE GETTING NOTICED IS EXACTLY WHAT SHE HAD IN MIND, WHEN SHE DUG THROUGH HER WARDROBE TONIGHT. THAT'D BE JUST LIKE HER, TO STRAP HERSELF INTO THAT OUTFIT JUST TO SHOW IT ALL OFF AND DRIVE ME NUTS.
GOD KNOWS IT'S WORKING. ALL KINDS OF DEATH IS ABOUT TO HIT LESS THAN TWENTY YARDS AHEAD OF US AND STILL IT'S HARD TO TAKE MY EYES OFF HER. HELL, IT'S JUST PLAIN IMPOSSIBLE. AND DOESN'T SHE KNOW IT. SILENT LAUGHTER RIPPLES THROUGH HER VOICE, JUST LIKE IT DOES THROUGH EVERY PERFECT INCH OF HER...
SO HOW'S THE BARMAID? YOU KNOW, THAT ONE WHO NEVER SHUTS UP?
NOT RIGHT NOW, GAIL.

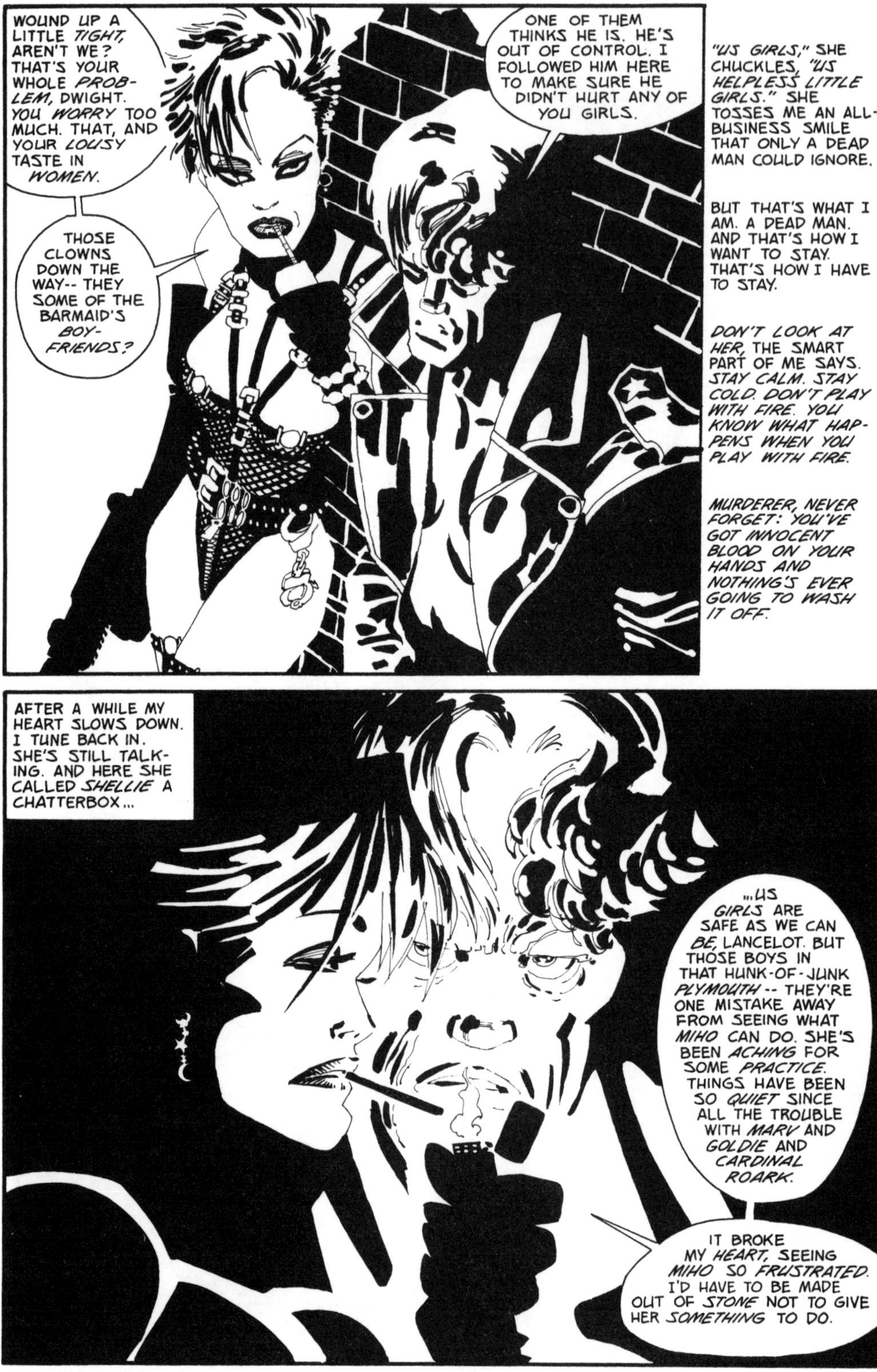
WOUND UP A LITTLE *TIGHT,* AREN'T WE? THAT'S YOUR WHOLE *PROBLEM,* DWIGHT. *YOU WORRY* TOO MUCH. THAT, AND YOUR *LOUSY* TASTE IN *WOMEN.*
ONE OF THEM THINKS HE IS. HE'S OUT OF CONTROL. I FOLLOWED HIM HERE TO MAKE SURE HE DIDN'T HURT ANY OF YOU GIRLS.
"US GIRLS," SHE CHUCKLES, *"US HELPLESS LITTLE GIRLS."* SHE TOSSES ME AN ALL-BUSINESS SMILE THAT ONLY A DEAD MAN COULD IGNORE.
BUT THAT'S WHAT I AM. A DEAD MAN. AND THAT'S HOW I WANT TO STAY. THAT'S HOW I HAVE TO STAY.
THOSE CLOWNS DOWN THE WAY-- THEY SOME OF THE BARMAID'S *BOY-FRIENDS?*
DON'T LOOK AT HER, THE SMART PART OF ME SAYS. *STAY CALM. STAY COLD. DON'T PLAY WITH FIRE. YOU KNOW WHAT HAPPENS WHEN YOU PLAY WITH FIRE.*
MURDERER, NEVER FORGET: YOU'VE GOT INNOCENT BLOOD ON YOUR HANDS AND NOTHING'S EVER GOING TO WASH IT OFF.
AFTER A WHILE MY HEART SLOWS DOWN. I TUNE BACK IN. SHE'S STILL TALKING. AND HERE SHE CALLED *SHELLIE* A CHATTERBOX...
...US *GIRLS* ARE SAFE AS WE CAN *BE,* LANCELOT. BUT THOSE BOYS IN THAT HUNK-OF-JUNK *PLYMOUTH* -- THEY'RE ONE MISTAKE AWAY FROM SEEING WHAT *MIHO* CAN DO. SHE'S BEEN *ACHING* FOR SOME *PRACTICE.* THINGS HAVE BEEN SO *QUIET* SINCE ALL THE TROUBLE WITH *MARV* AND *GOLDIE* AND *CARDINAL ROARK.*
IT BROKE MY *HEART,* SEEING *MIHO* SO *FRUSTRATED.* I'D HAVE TO BE MADE OUT OF *STONE* NOT TO GIVE HER *SOMETHING* TO DO.

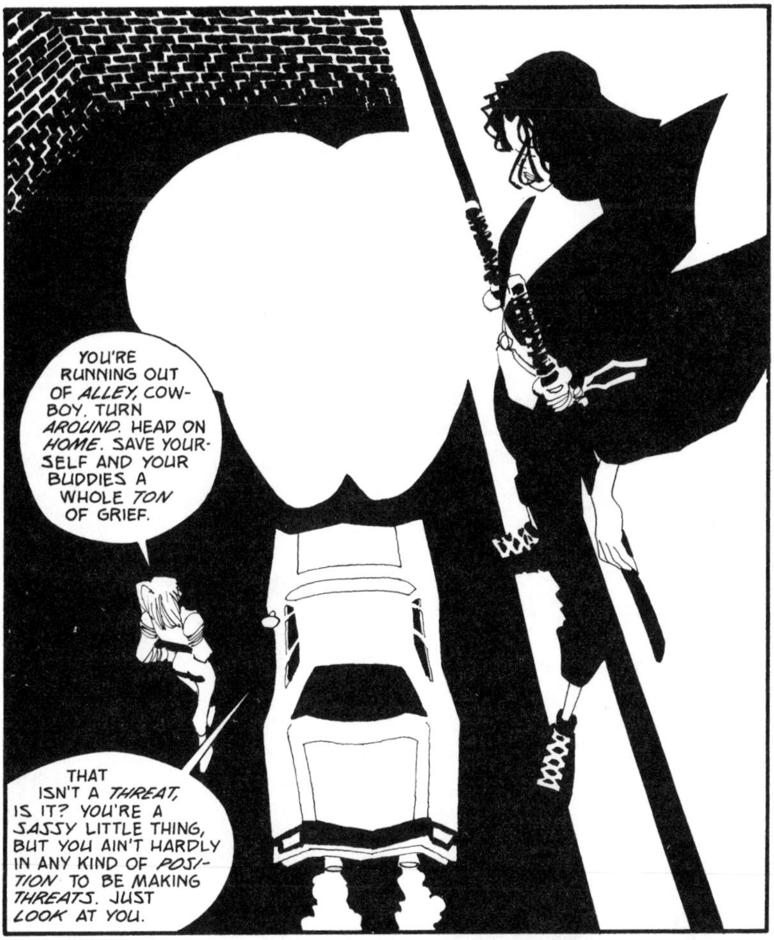
YOU'RE RUNNING OUT OF *ALLEY*, COWBOY. TURN *AROUND*. HEAD ON *HOME*. SAVE YOURSELF AND YOUR BUDDIES A WHOLE *TON* OF GRIEF.
THAT ISN'T A *THREAT*, IS IT? YOU'RE A *SASSY* LITTLE THING, BUT YOU AIN'T HARDLY IN ANY KIND OF *POSITION* TO BE MAKING *THREATS*. JUST *LOOK* AT YOU.

DISTANT DESERT THUNDER. IT ROLLS ON FOREVER.

GAIL GIVES ME A QUICK ELBOW TO THE RIBS AND GIGGLES AT HOW I PRACTICALLY JUMP OUT OF MY SKIN. SHE GUIDES MY GLANCE UPWARD TO THE PIXIE PERCHED AT THE ROOF'S EDGE.

DEADLY LITTLE MIHO.

THOSE POOR SLOBS. THOSE STUPID, DRUNKEN SLOBS. LESS THAN TEN MINUTES AGO I WAS READY TO KILL THEM MYSELF. NOW I ALMOST WANT TO RUN AFTER THEM AND TELL THEM TO GET THEIR SORRY BUTTS THE HELL OUT OF HERE BEFORE IT'S TOO LATE.

BUT I WOULDN'T GET TEN STEPS. THE LADIES ARE THE LAW, HERE. IT'S SUICIDE TO CROSS THEM.

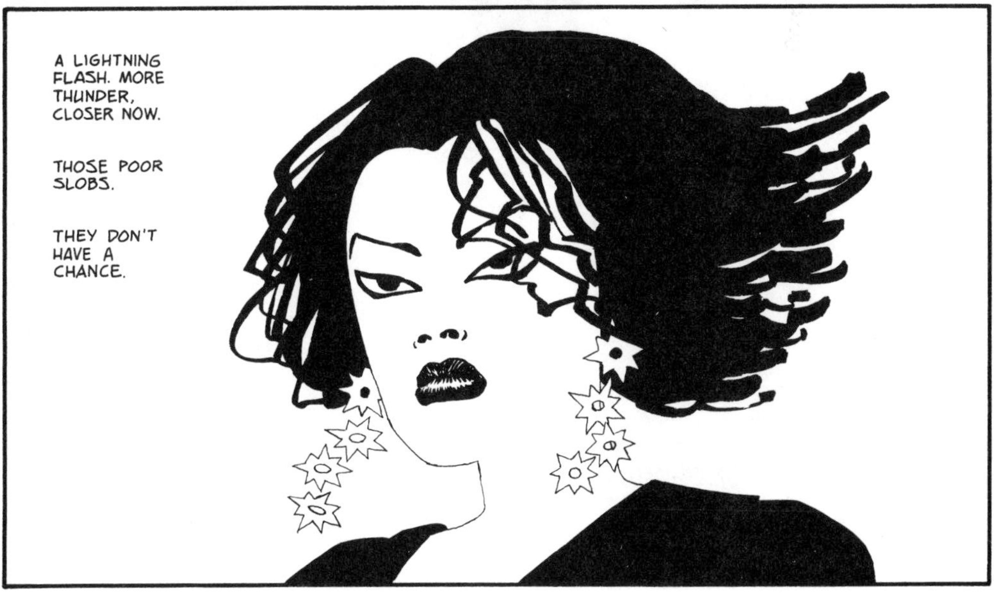
A LIGHTNING FLASH. MORE THUNDER, CLOSER NOW.
THOSE POOR SLOBS.
THEY DON'T HAVE A CHANCE.

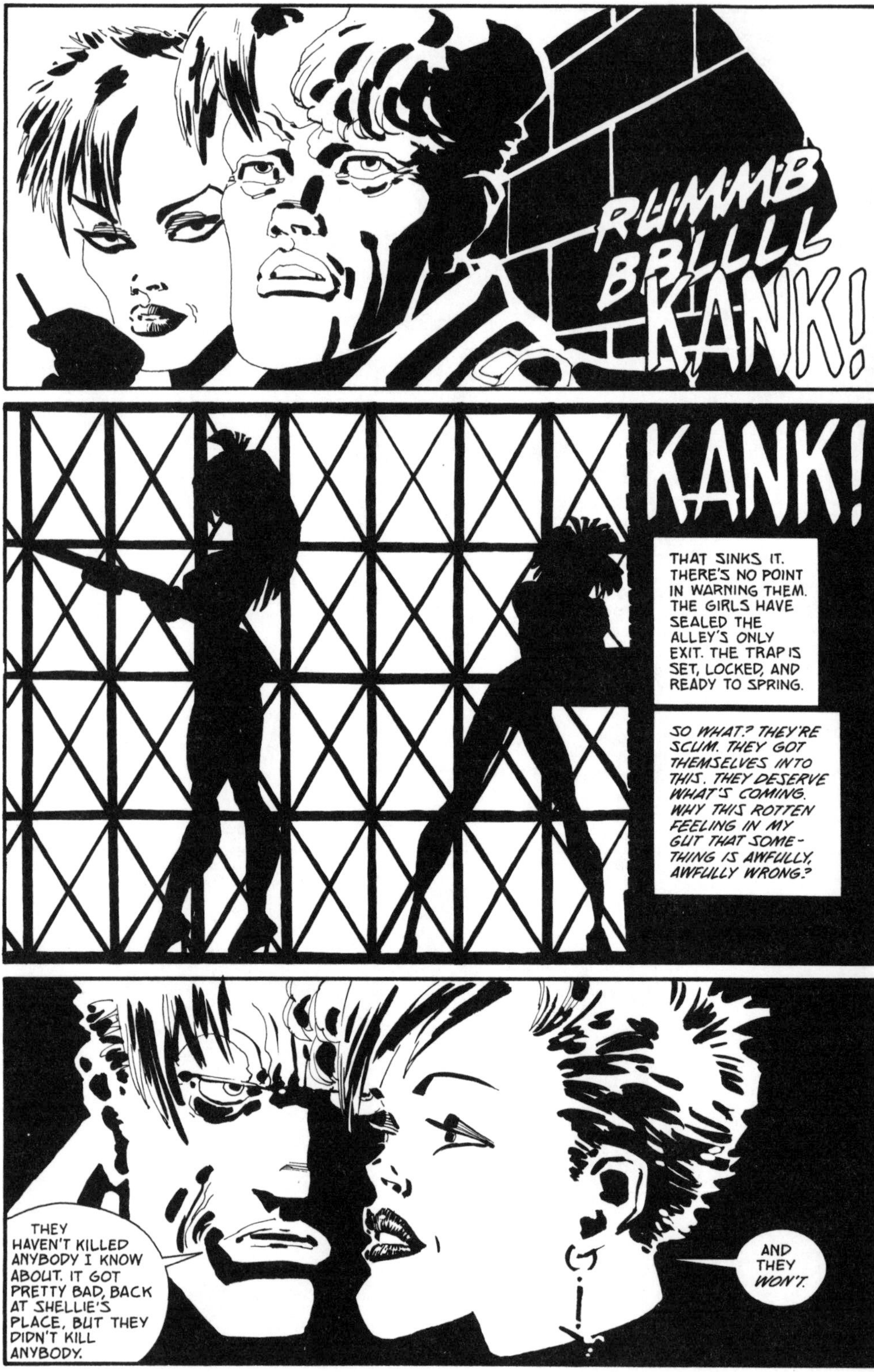

RUMMB
BBLLLL
KANK!
KANK!
THAT SINKS IT. THERE'S NO POINT IN WARNING THEM. THE GIRLS HAVE SEALED THE ALLEY'S ONLY EXIT. THE TRAP IS SET, LOCKED, AND READY TO SPRING.
SO WHAT? THEY'RE SCUM. THEY GOT THEMSELVES INTO THIS. THEY DESERVE WHAT'S COMING. WHY THIS ROTTEN FEELING IN MY GUT THAT SOMETHING IS AWFULLY, AWFULLY WRONG?
THEY HAVEN'T KILLED ANYBODY I KNOW ABOUT. IT GOT PRETTY BAD, BACK AT SHELLIE'S PLACE, BUT THEY DIDN'T KILL ANYBODY.
AND THEY *WON'T.*

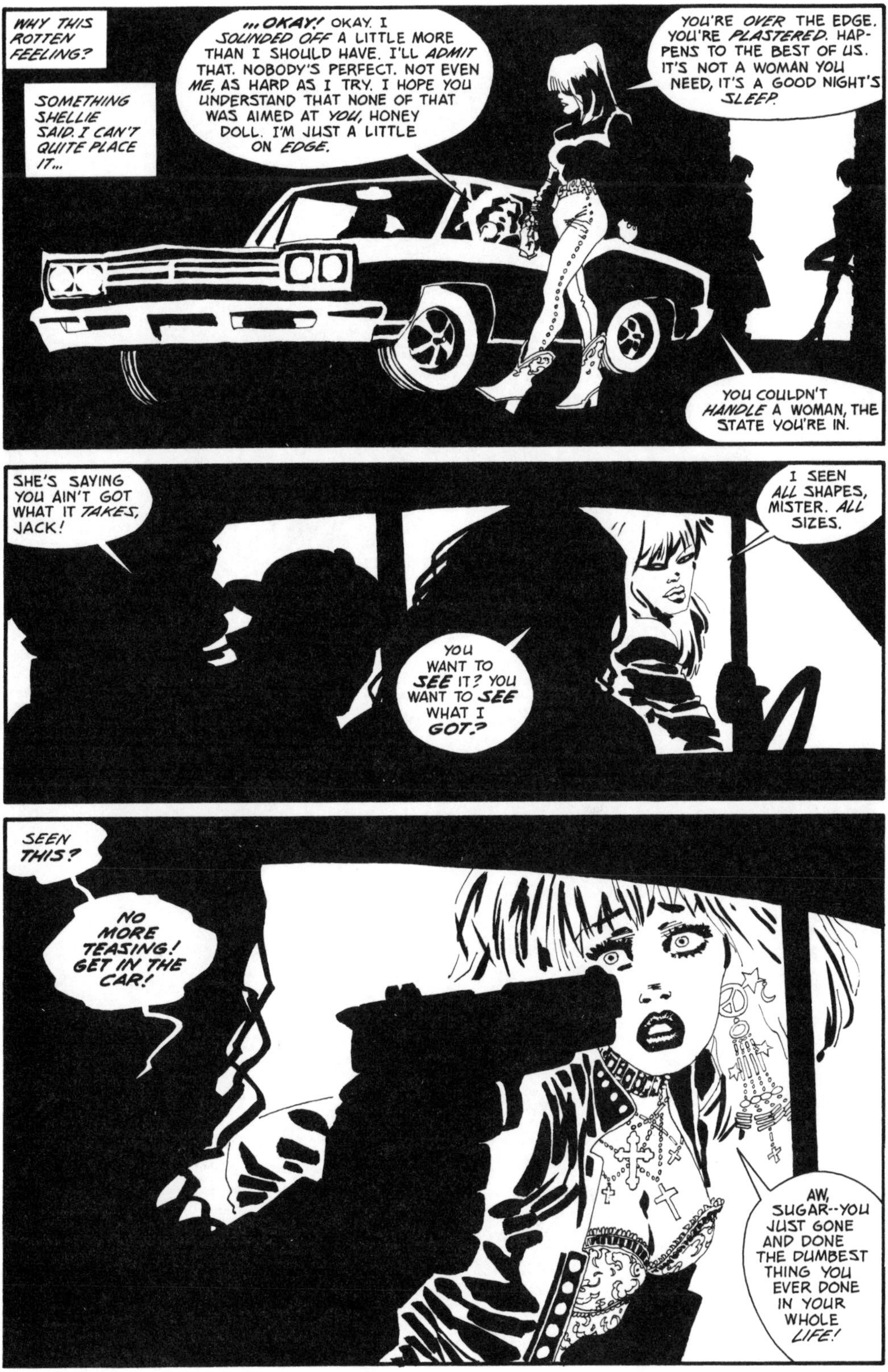
WHY THIS ROTTEN FEELING?
SOMETHING SHELLIE SAID. I CAN'T QUITE PLACE IT...
...OKAY! OKAY. I SOUNDED OFF A LITTLE MORE THAN I SHOULD HAVE. I'LL ADMIT THAT. NOBODY'S PERFECT. NOT EVEN ME, AS HARD AS I TRY. I HOPE YOU UNDERSTAND THAT NONE OF THAT WAS AIMED AT YOU, HONEY DOLL. I'M JUST A LITTLE ON EDGE.
YOU'RE OVER THE EDGE. YOU'RE PLASTERED. HAPPENS TO THE BEST OF US. IT'S NOT A WOMAN YOU NEED, IT'S A GOOD NIGHT'S SLEEP.
YOU COULDN'T HANDLE A WOMAN, THE STATE YOU'RE IN.
SHE'S SAYING YOU AIN'T GOT WHAT IT TAKES, JACK!
I SEEN ALL SHAPES, MISTER. ALL SIZES.
YOU WANT TO SEE IT? YOU WANT TO SEE WHAT I GOT?
SEEN THIS?
NO MORE TEASING! GET IN THE CAR!
AW, SUGAR--YOU JUST GONE AND DONE THE DUMBEST THING YOU EVER DONE IN YOUR WHOLE LIFE!

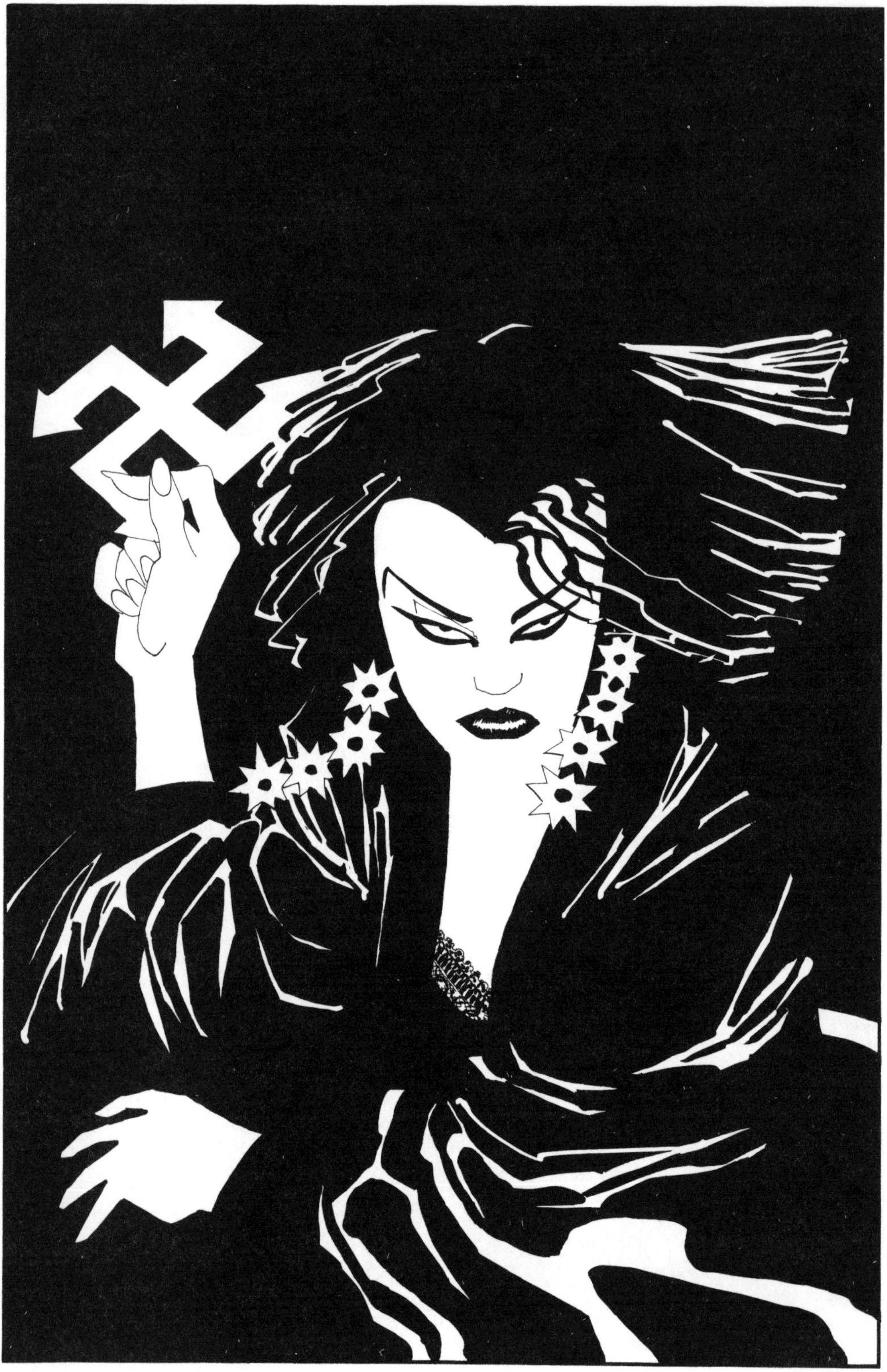

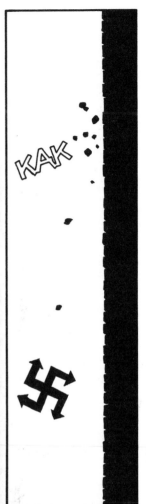

KAK

CHUNK!!

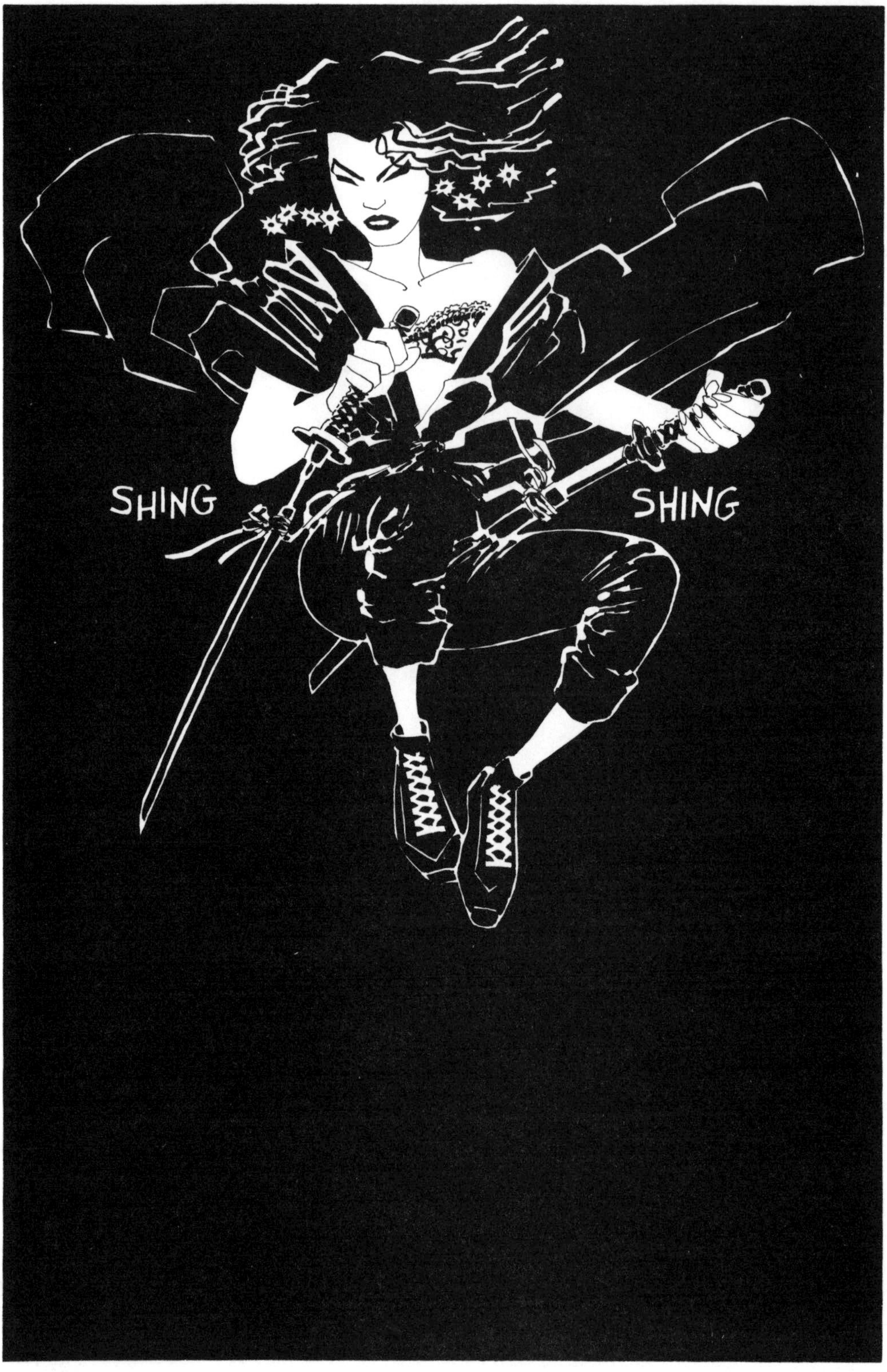
SHING
SHING

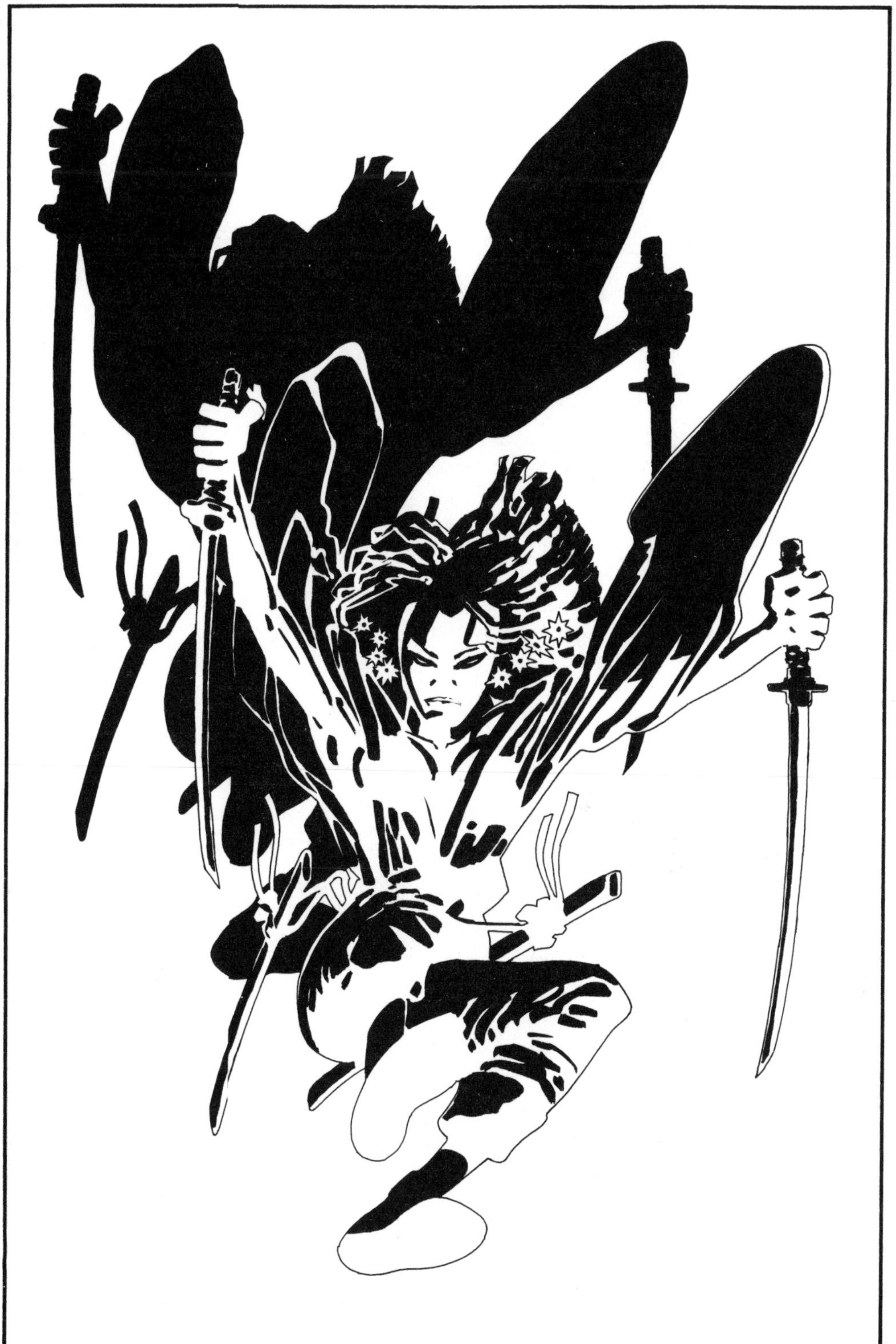

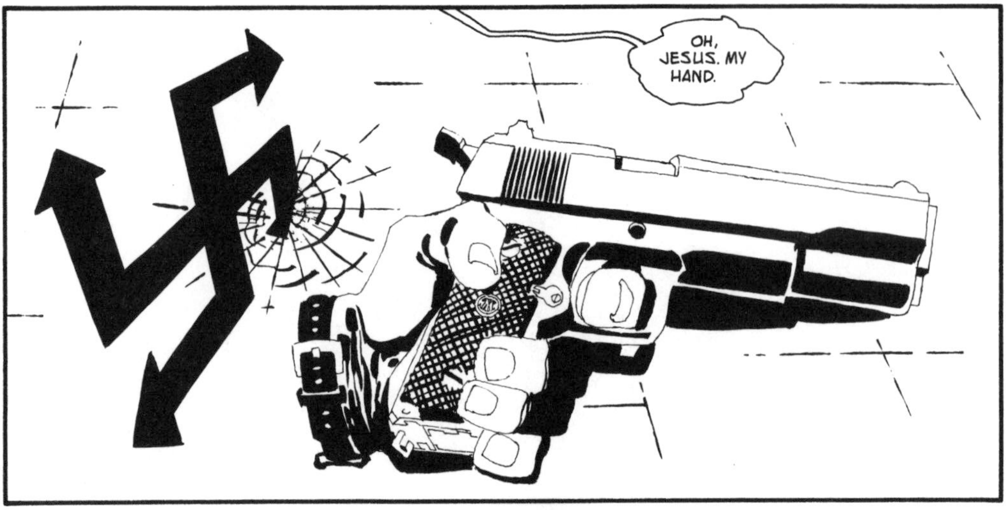
OH, JESUS. MY HAND.

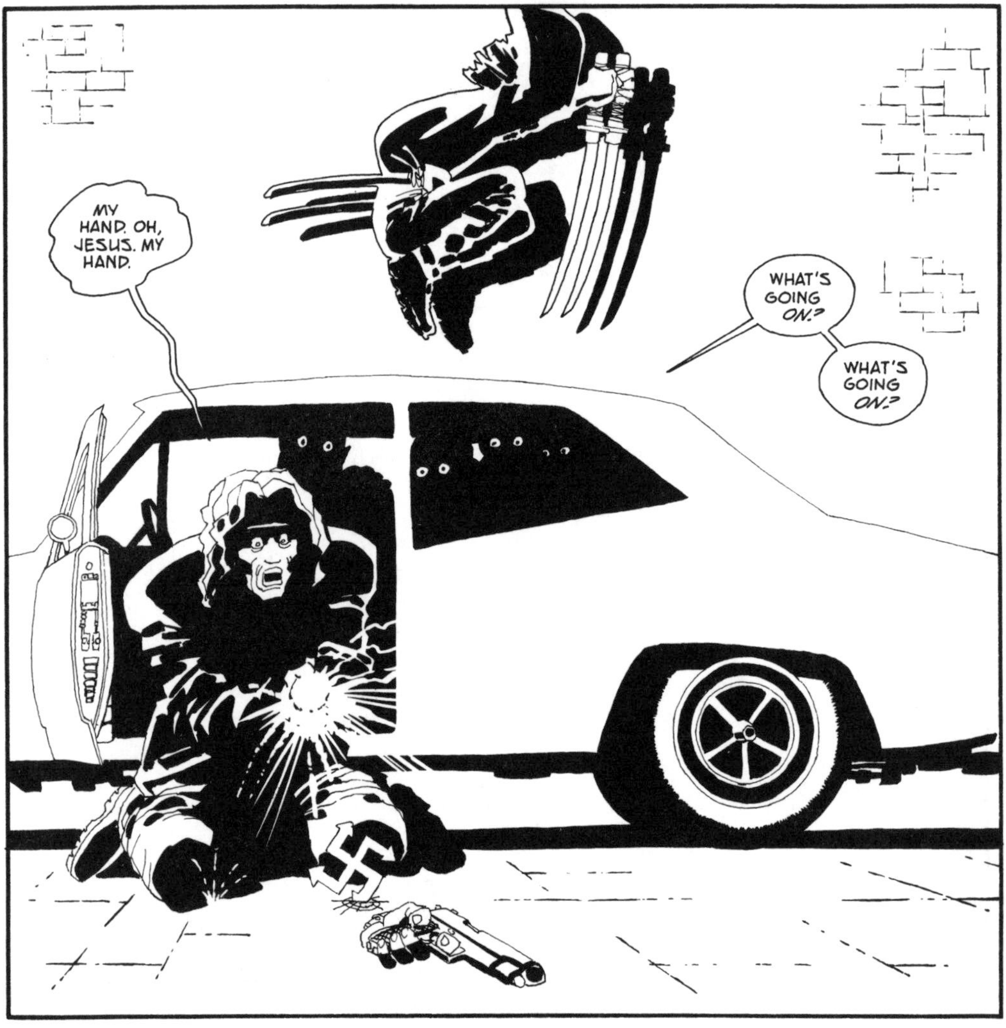
MY HAND. OH, JESUS. MY HAND.
WHAT'S GOING *ON?*
WHAT'S GOING *ON?*

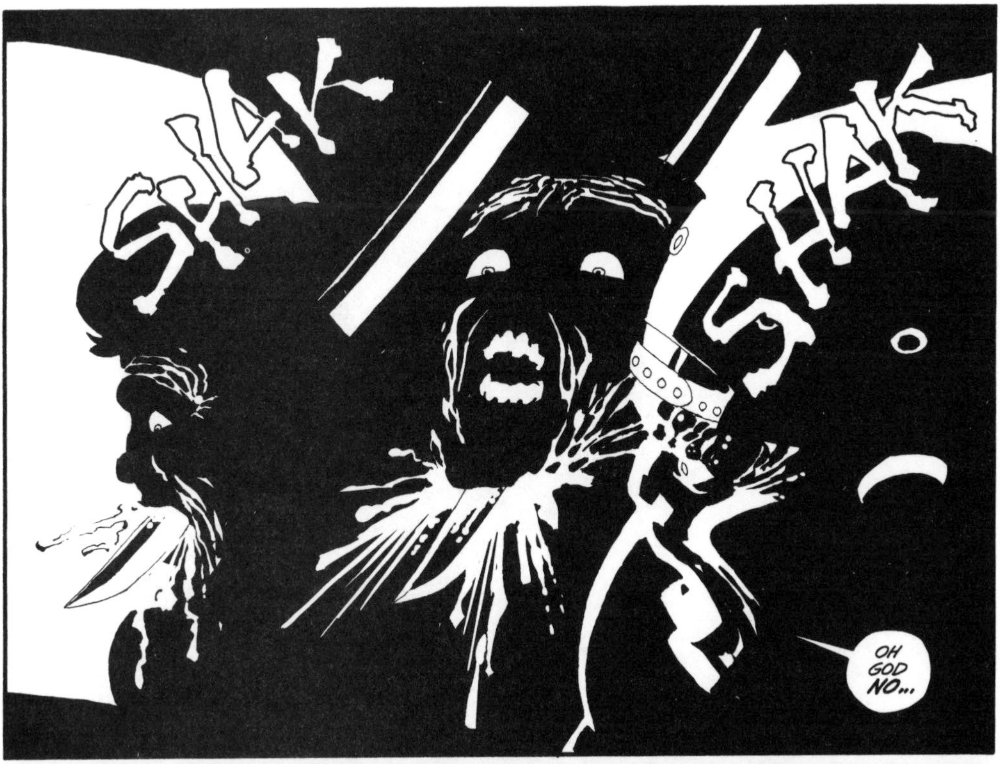
SHAK
SHAK
OH GOD NO...

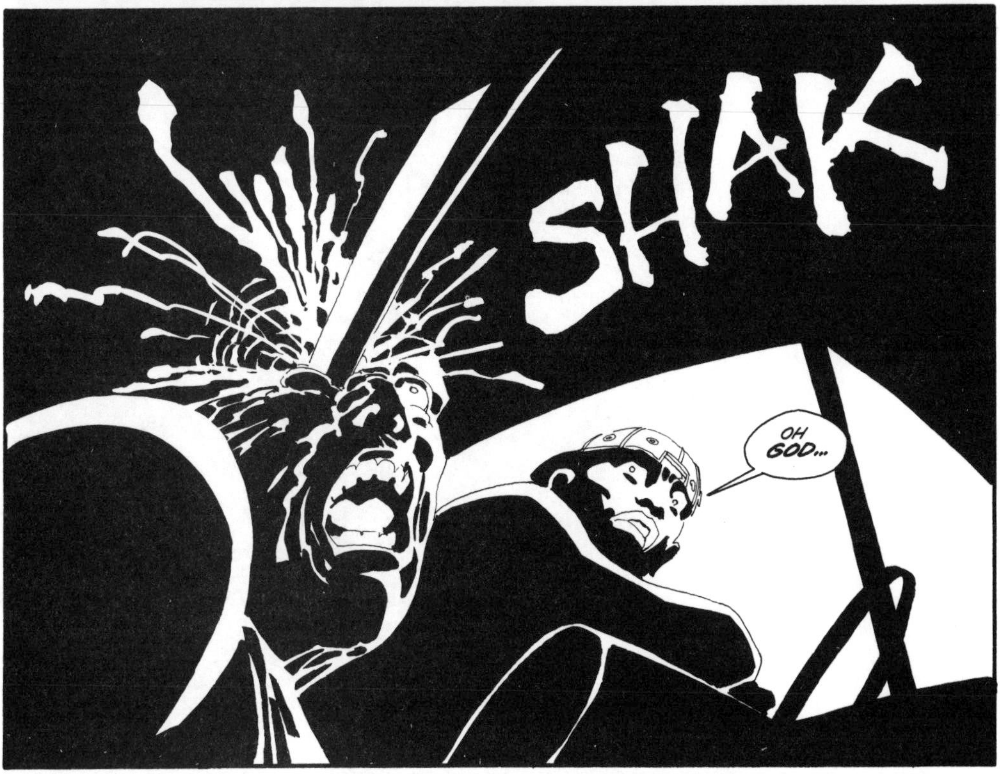
SHAK
OH GOD...

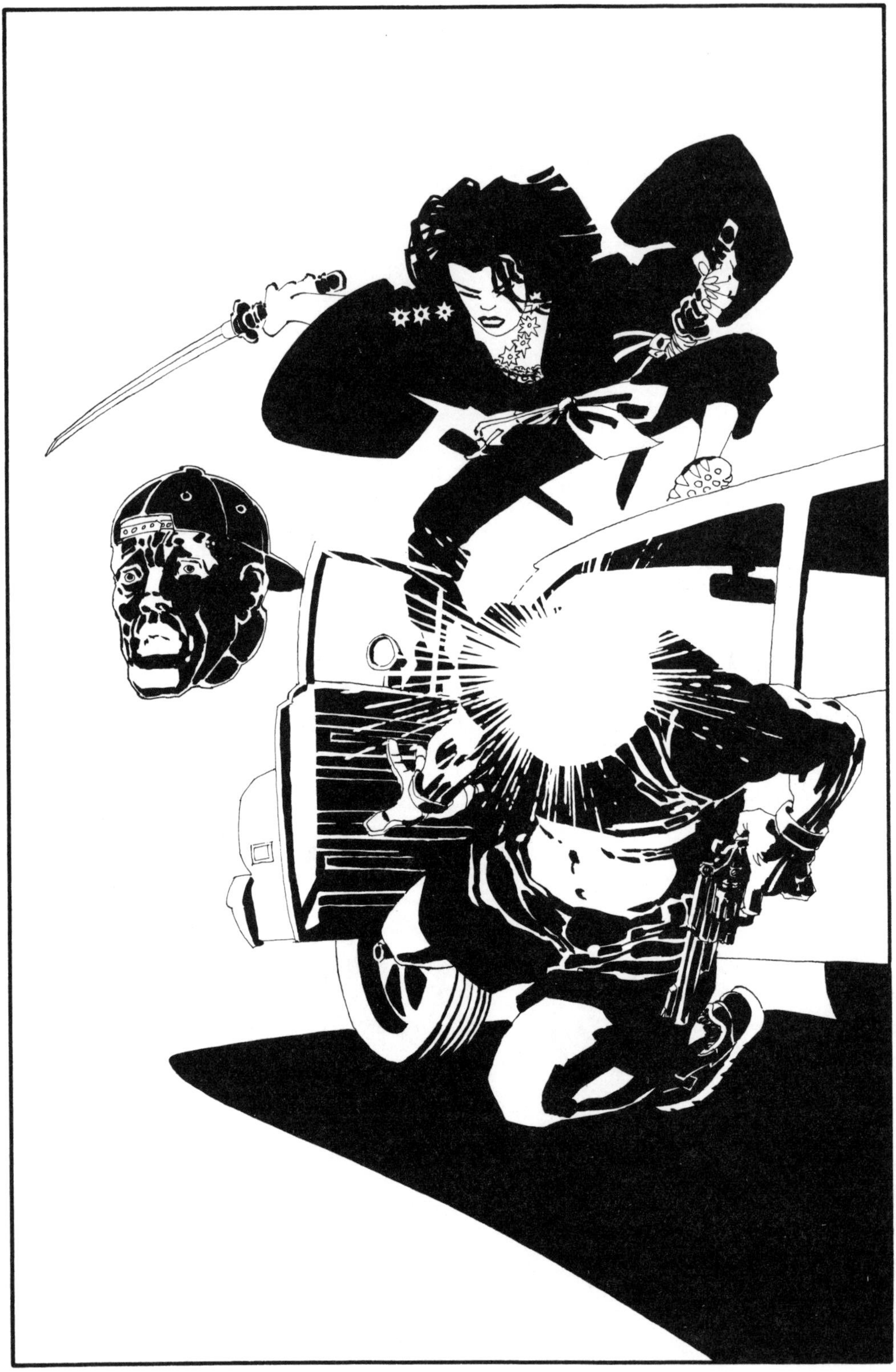

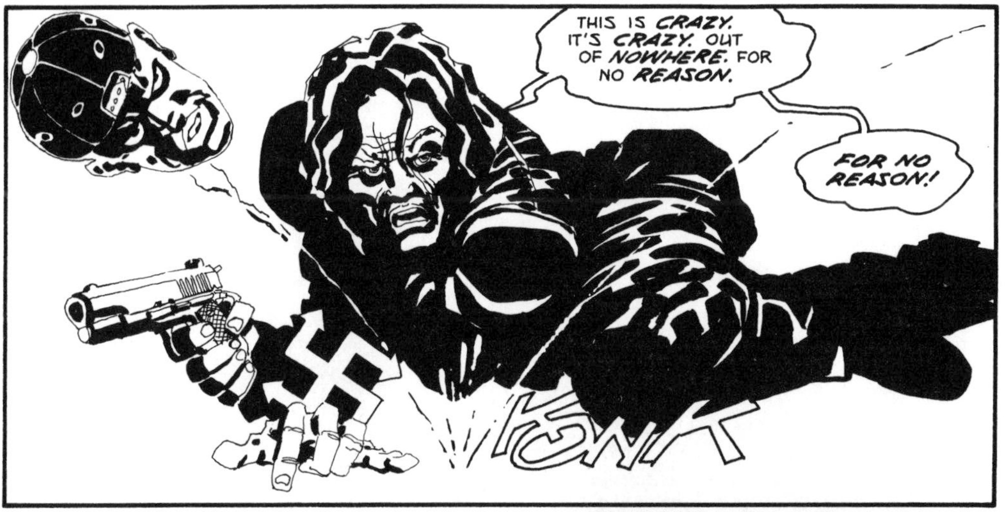
THIS IS CRAZY. IT'S CRAZY. OUT OF NOWHERE. FOR NO REASON.
FOR NO REASON!
YONK

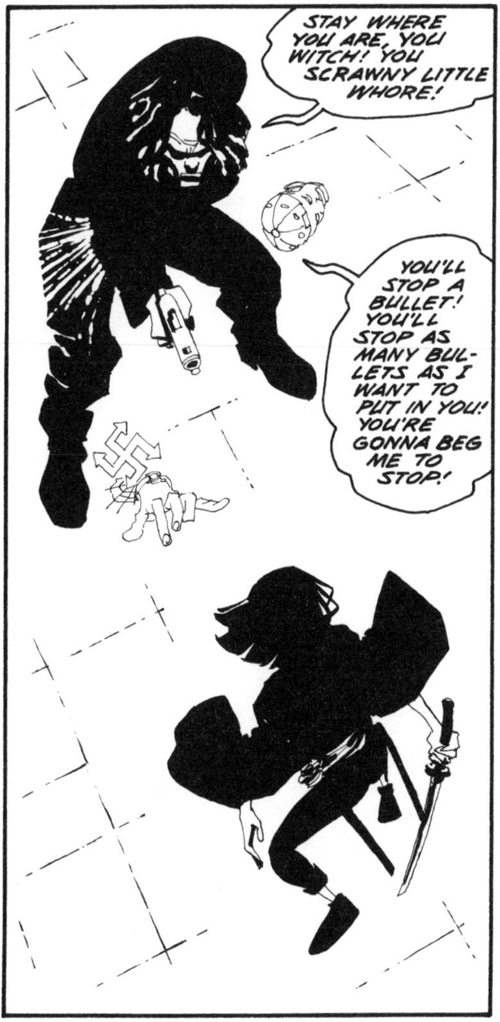
STAY WHERE YOU ARE, YOU WITCH! YOU SCRAWNY LITTLE WHORE!
YOU'LL STOP A BULLET! YOU'LL STOP AS MANY BULLETS AS I WANT TO PUT IN YOU! YOU'RE GONNA BEG ME TO STOP!

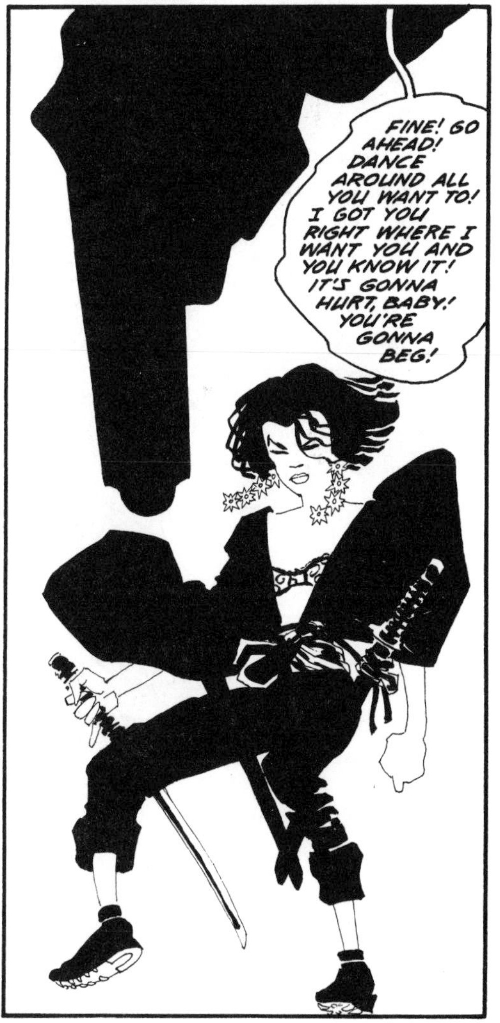
FINE! GO AHEAD! DANCE AROUND ALL YOU WANT TO! I GOT YOU RIGHT WHERE I WANT YOU AND YOU KNOW IT! IT'S GONNA HURT, BABY! YOU'RE GONNA BEG!

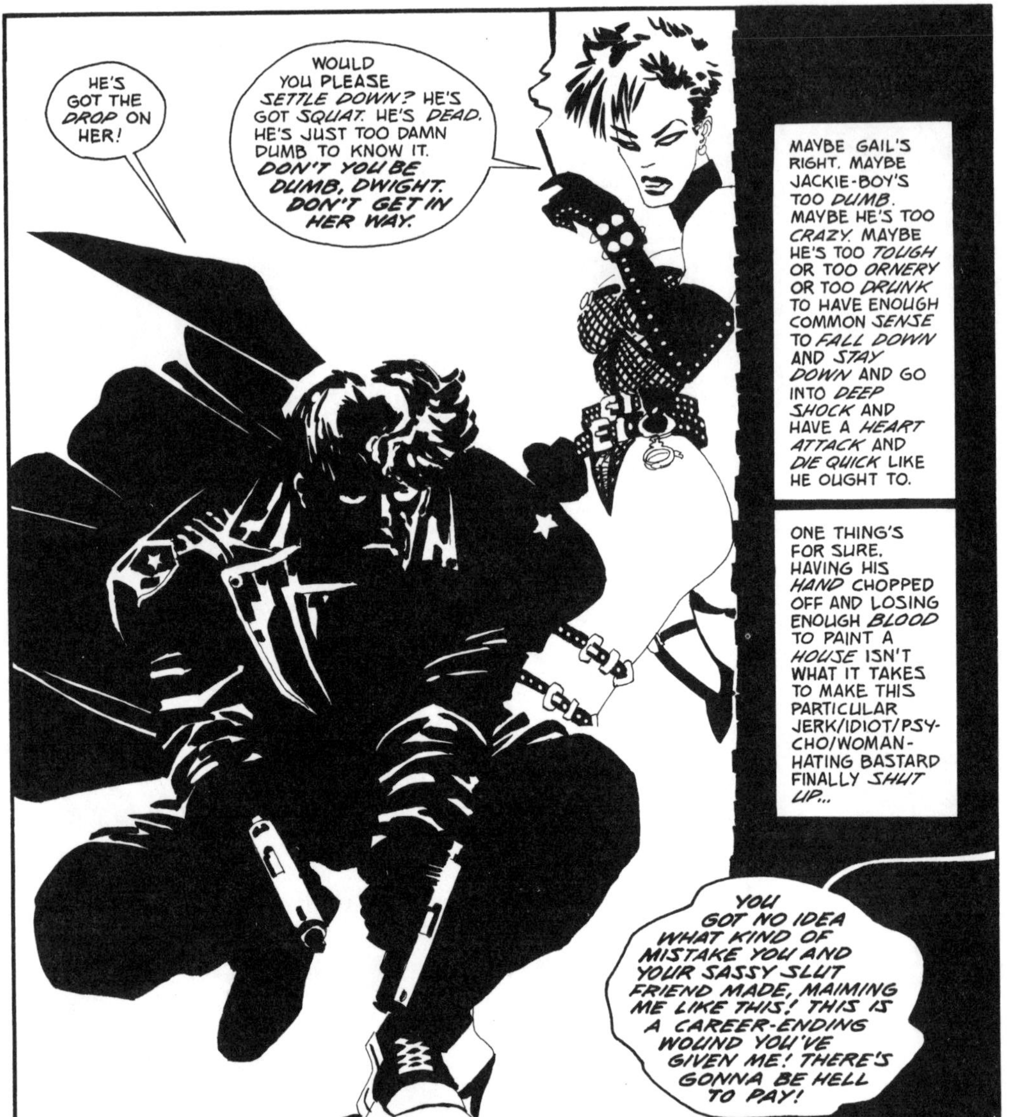
HE'S GOT THE DROP ON HER!
WOULD YOU PLEASE SETTLE DOWN? HE'S GOT SQUAT. HE'S DEAD. HE'S JUST TOO DAMN DUMB TO KNOW IT. DON'T YOU BE DUMB, DWIGHT. DON'T GET IN HER WAY.
MAYBE GAIL'S RIGHT. MAYBE JACKIE-BOY'S TOO DUMB. MAYBE HE'S TOO CRAZY. MAYBE HE'S TOO TOUGH OR TOO ORNERY OR TOO DRUNK TO HAVE ENOUGH COMMON SENSE TO FALL DOWN AND STAY DOWN AND GO INTO DEEP SHOCK AND HAVE A HEART ATTACK AND DIE QUICK LIKE HE OUGHT TO.
ONE THING'S FOR SURE. HAVING HIS HAND CHOPPED OFF AND LOSING ENOUGH BLOOD TO PAINT A HOUSE ISN'T WHAT IT TAKES TO MAKE THIS PARTICULAR JERK/IDIOT/PSY-CHO/WOMAN-HATING BASTARD FINALLY SHUT UP...
YOU GOT NO IDEA WHAT KIND OF MISTAKE YOU AND YOUR SASSY SLUT FRIEND MADE, MAIMING ME LIKE THIS! THIS IS A CAREER-ENDING WOUND YOU'VE GIVEN ME! THERE'S GONNA BE HELL TO PAY!

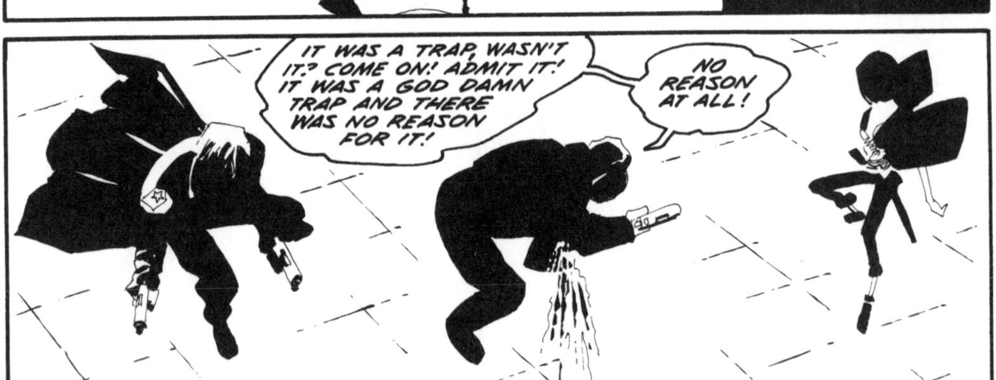
IT WAS A TRAP, WASN'T IT? COME ON! ADMIT IT! IT WAS A GOD DAMN TRAP AND THERE WAS NO REASON FOR IT!
NO REASON AT ALL!

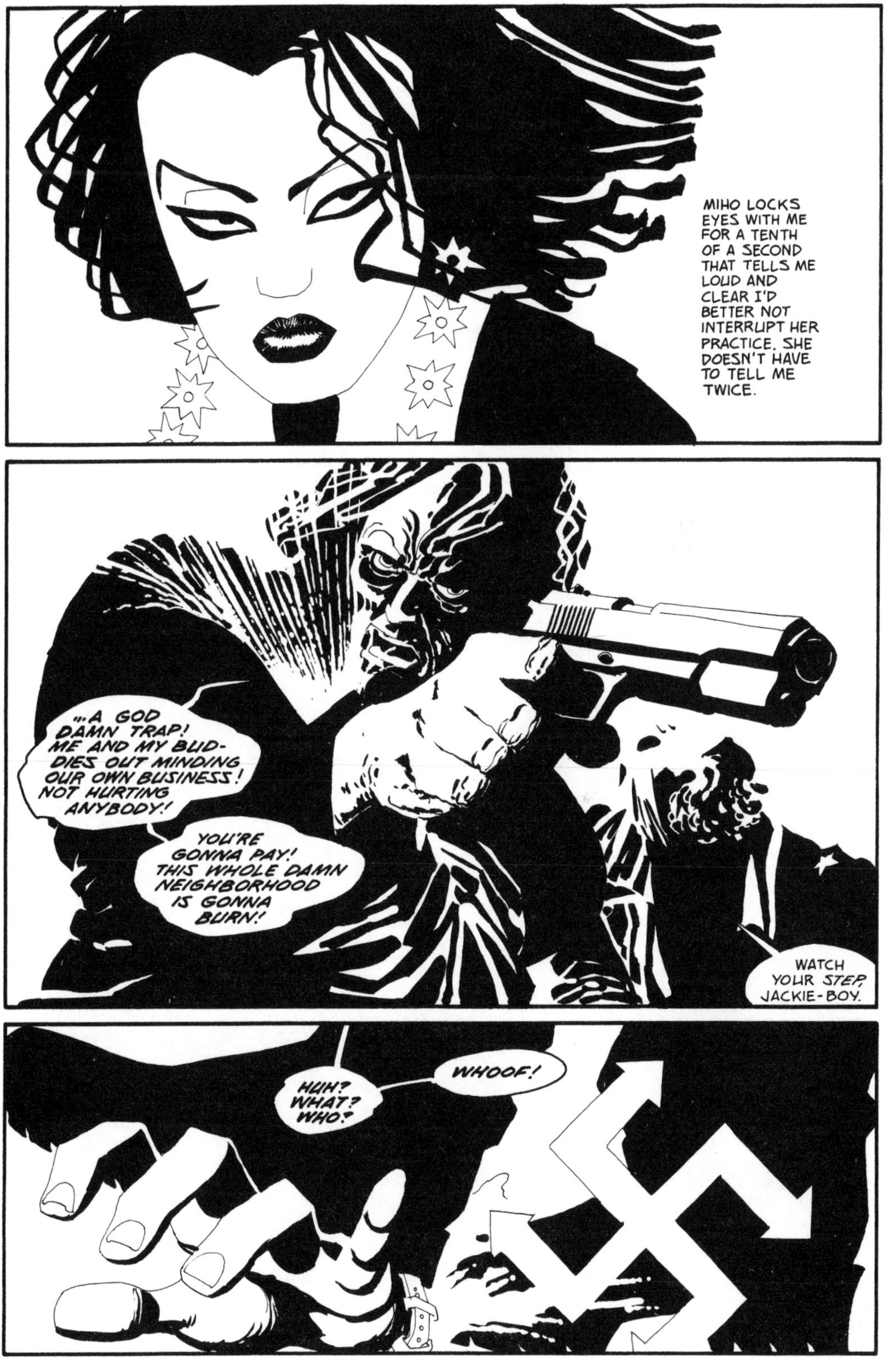
MIHO LOCKS EYES WITH ME FOR A TENTH OF A SECOND THAT TELLS ME LOUD AND CLEAR I'D BETTER NOT INTERRUPT HER PRACTICE. SHE DOESN'T HAVE TO TELL ME TWICE.
...A GOD DAMN TRAP! ME AND MY BUDDIES OUT MINDING OUR OWN BUSINESS! NOT HURTING ANYBODY!
YOU'RE GONNA PAY! THIS WHOLE DAMN NEIGHBORHOOD IS GONNA BURN!
WATCH YOUR STEP, JACKIE-BOY.
HUH? WHAT? WHO?
WHOOF!

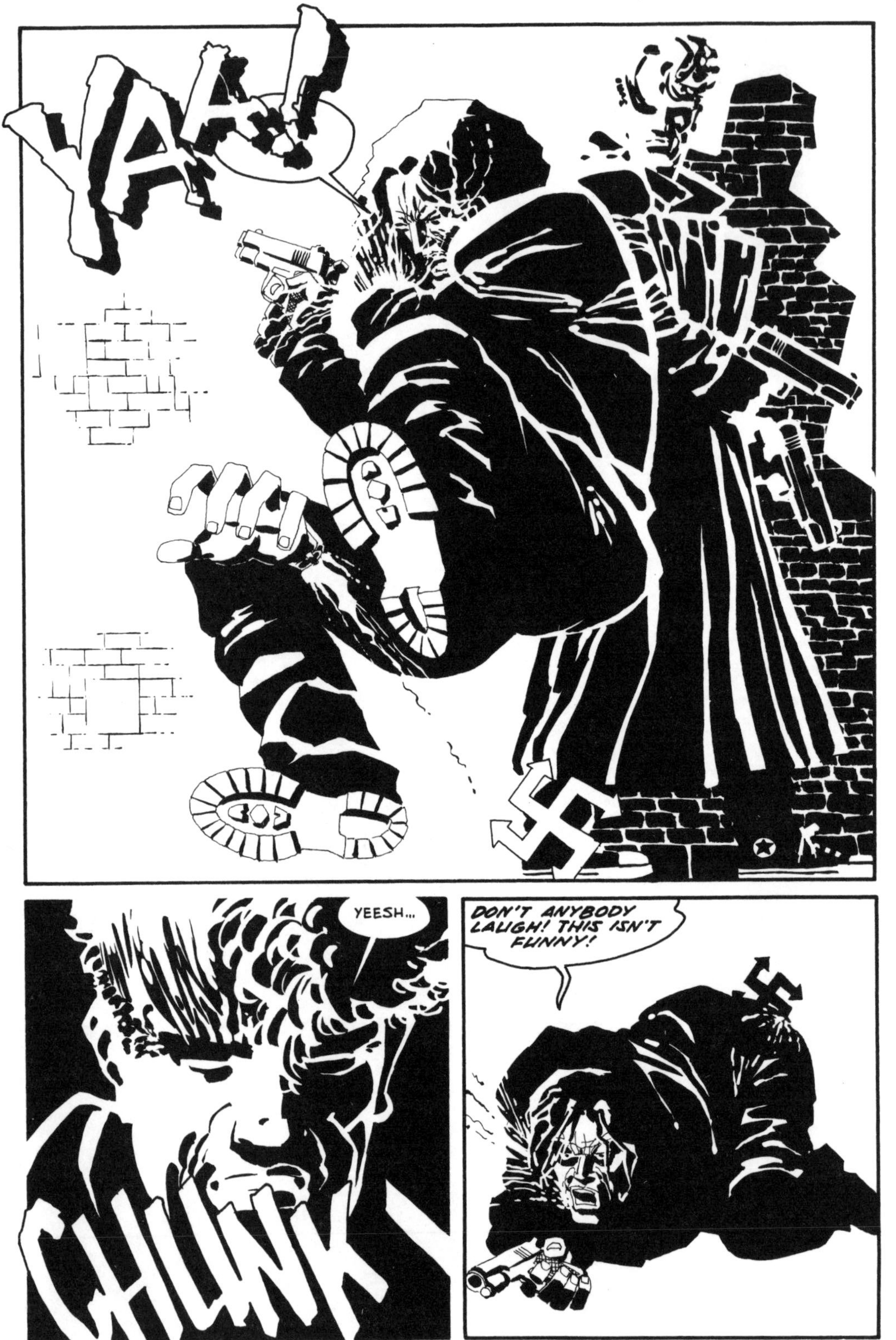
YAA!
YEESH...
CHUNK
DON'T ANYBODY LAUGH! THIS ISN'T FUNNY!

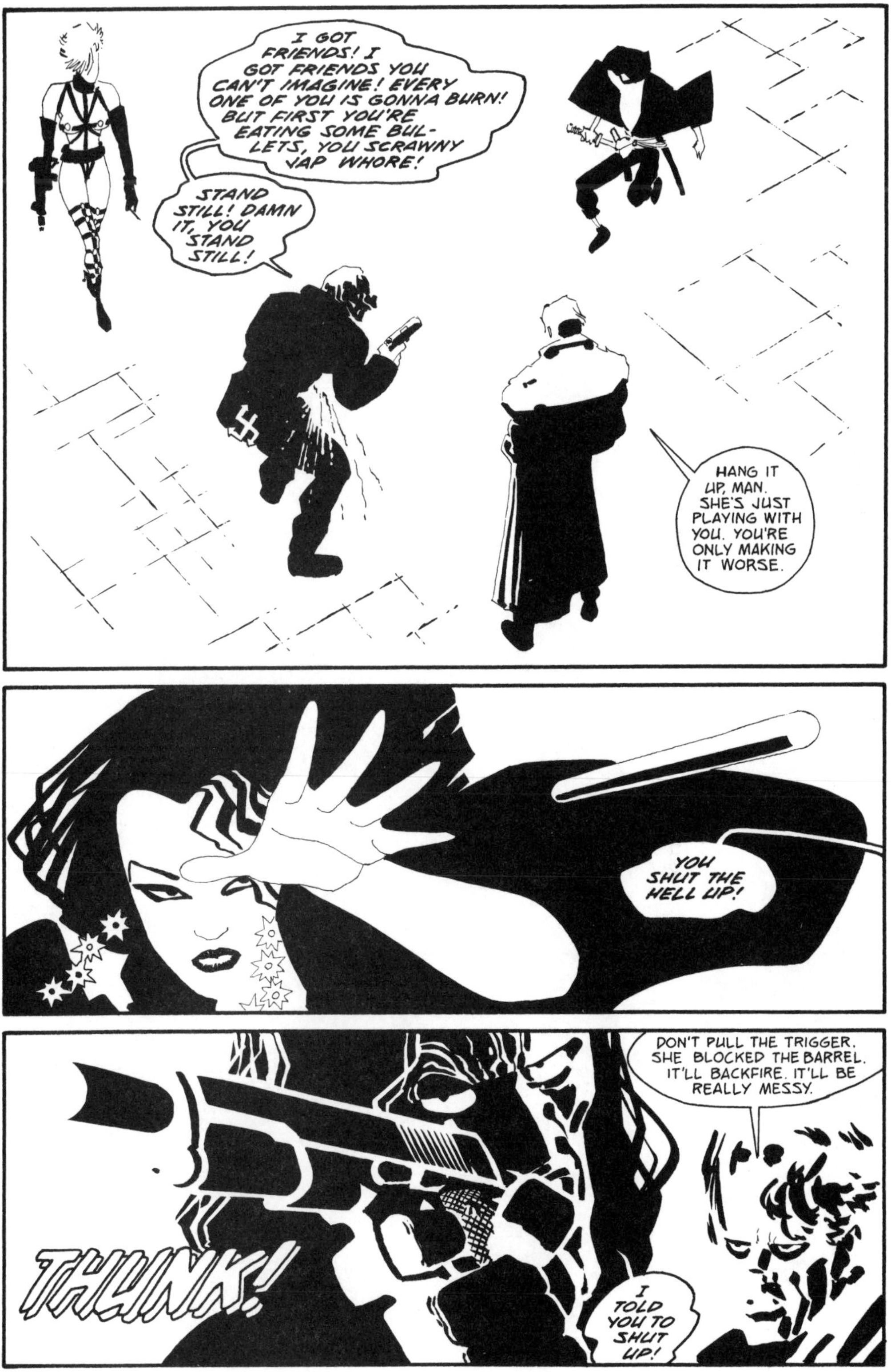
I GOT FRIENDS! I GOT FRIENDS YOU CAN'T IMAGINE! EVERY ONE OF YOU IS GONNA BURN! BUT FIRST YOU'RE EATING SOME BUL-LETS, YOU SCRAWNY JAP WHORE!
STAND STILL! DAMN IT, YOU STAND STILL!
HANG IT UP, MAN. SHE'S JUST PLAYING WITH YOU. YOU'RE ONLY MAKING IT WORSE.
YOU SHUT THE HELL UP!
DON'T PULL THE TRIGGER. SHE BLOCKED THE BARREL. IT'LL BACKFIRE. IT'LL BE REALLY MESSY.
THUNK!
I TOLD YOU TO SHUT UP!

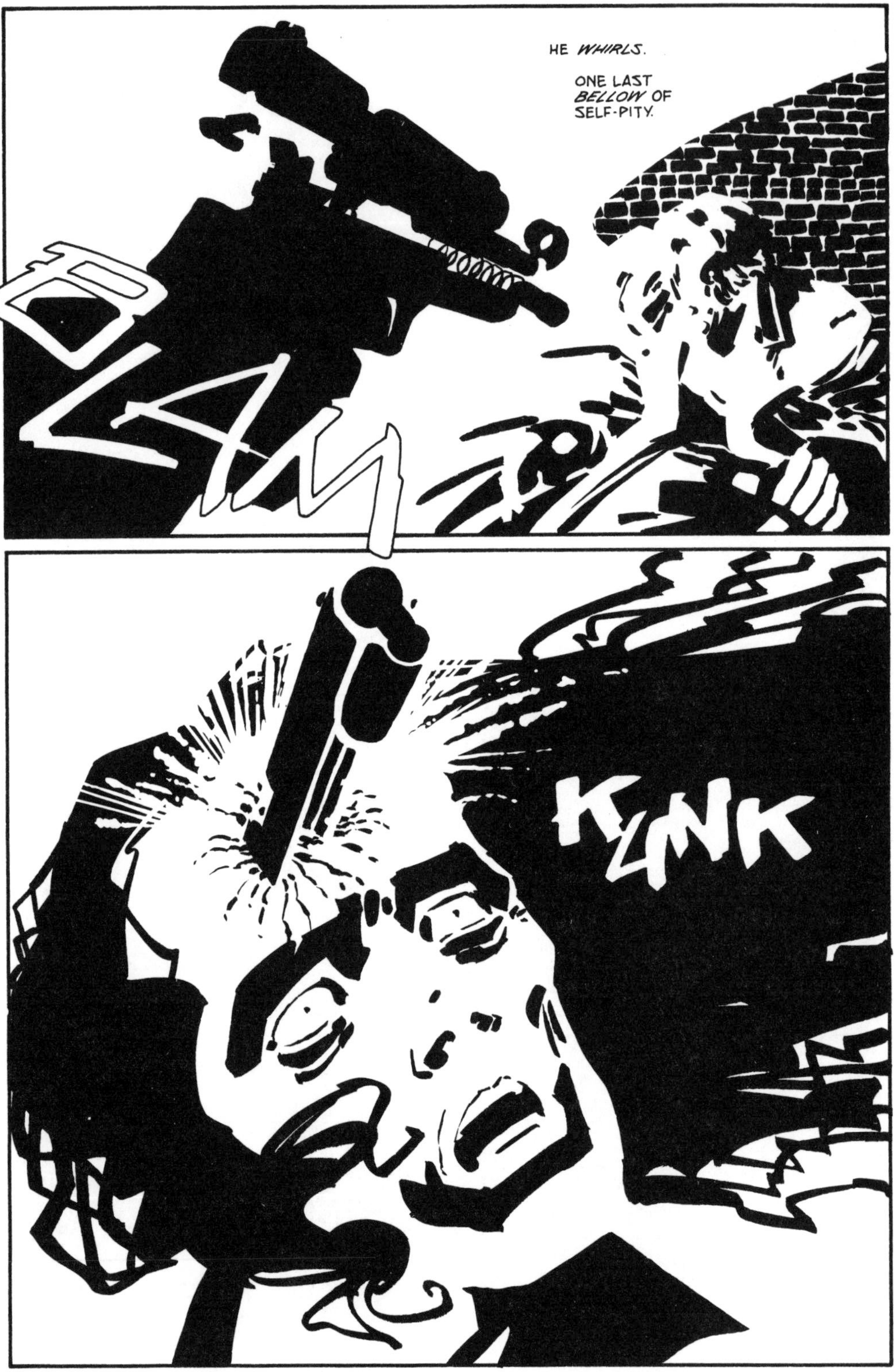
HE *WHIRLS*.
ONE LAST *BELLOW* OF SELF-PITY.
BLAM

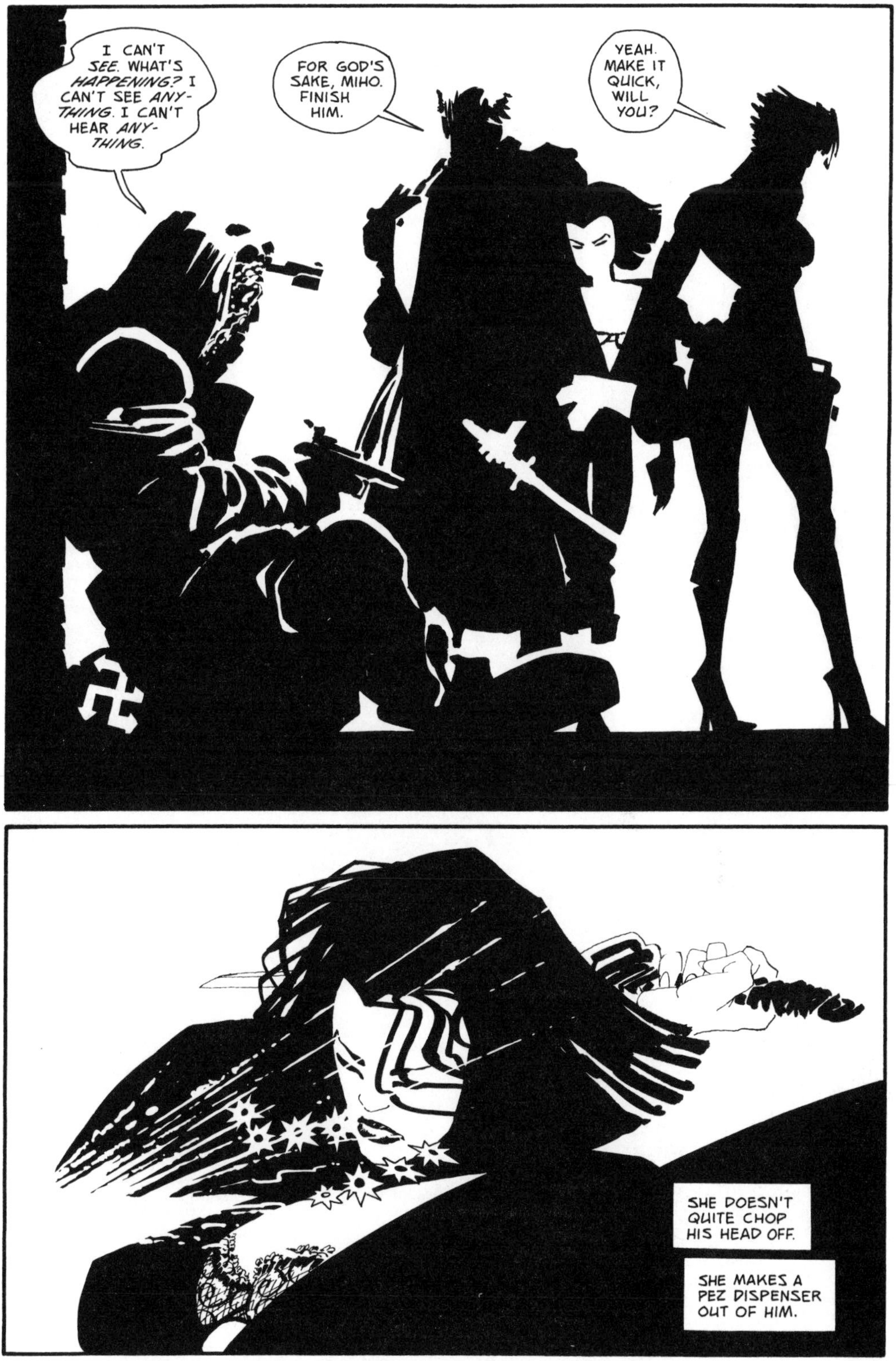
I CAN'T *SEE*. WHAT'S *HAPPENING?* I CAN'T SEE *ANY-THING*. I CAN'T HEAR *ANY-THING*.
FOR GOD'S SAKE, MIHO. FINISH HIM.
YEAH. MAKE IT QUICK, WILL YOU?
SHE DOESN'T QUITE CHOP HIS HEAD OFF.
SHE MAKES A PEZ DISPENSER OUT OF HIM.

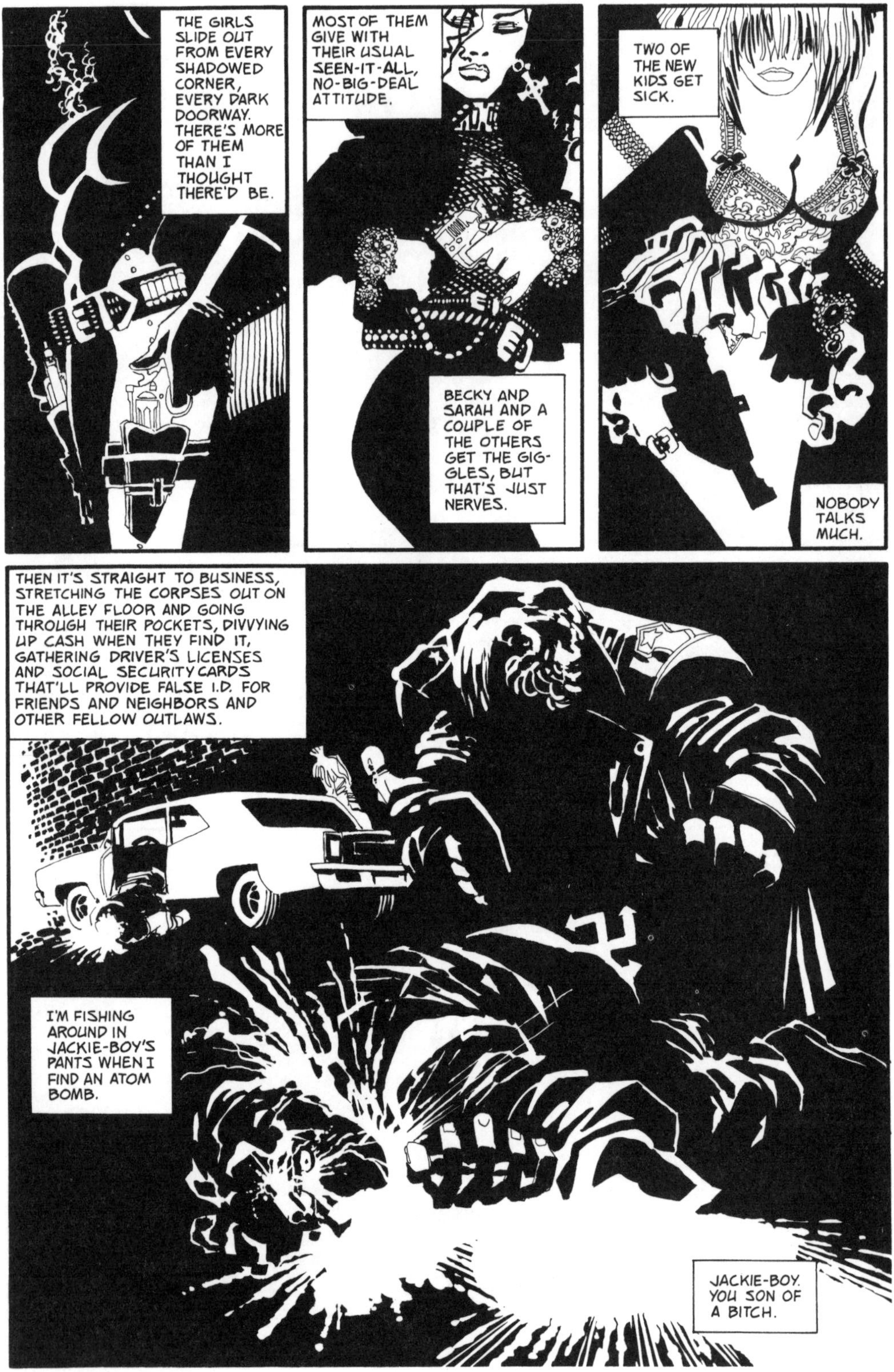
THE GIRLS SLIDE OUT FROM EVERY SHADOWED CORNER, EVERY DARK DOORWAY. THERE'S MORE OF THEM THAN I THOUGHT THERE'D BE.
MOST OF THEM GIVE WITH THEIR USUAL SEEN-IT-ALL, NO-BIG-DEAL ATTITUDE.
BECKY AND SARAH AND A COUPLE OF THE OTHERS GET THE GIG-GLES, BUT THAT'S JUST NERVES.
TWO OF THE NEW KIDS GET SICK.
NOBODY TALKS MUCH.
THEN IT'S STRAIGHT TO BUSINESS, STRETCHING THE CORPSES OUT ON THE ALLEY FLOOR AND GOING THROUGH THEIR POCKETS, DIVVYING UP CASH WHEN THEY FIND IT, GATHERING DRIVER'S LICENSES AND SOCIAL SECURITY CARDS THAT'LL PROVIDE FALSE I.D. FOR FRIENDS AND NEIGHBORS AND OTHER FELLOW OUTLAWS.
I'M FISHING AROUND IN JACKIE-BOY'S PANTS WHEN I FIND AN ATOM BOMB.
JACKIE-BOY. YOU SON OF A BITCH.

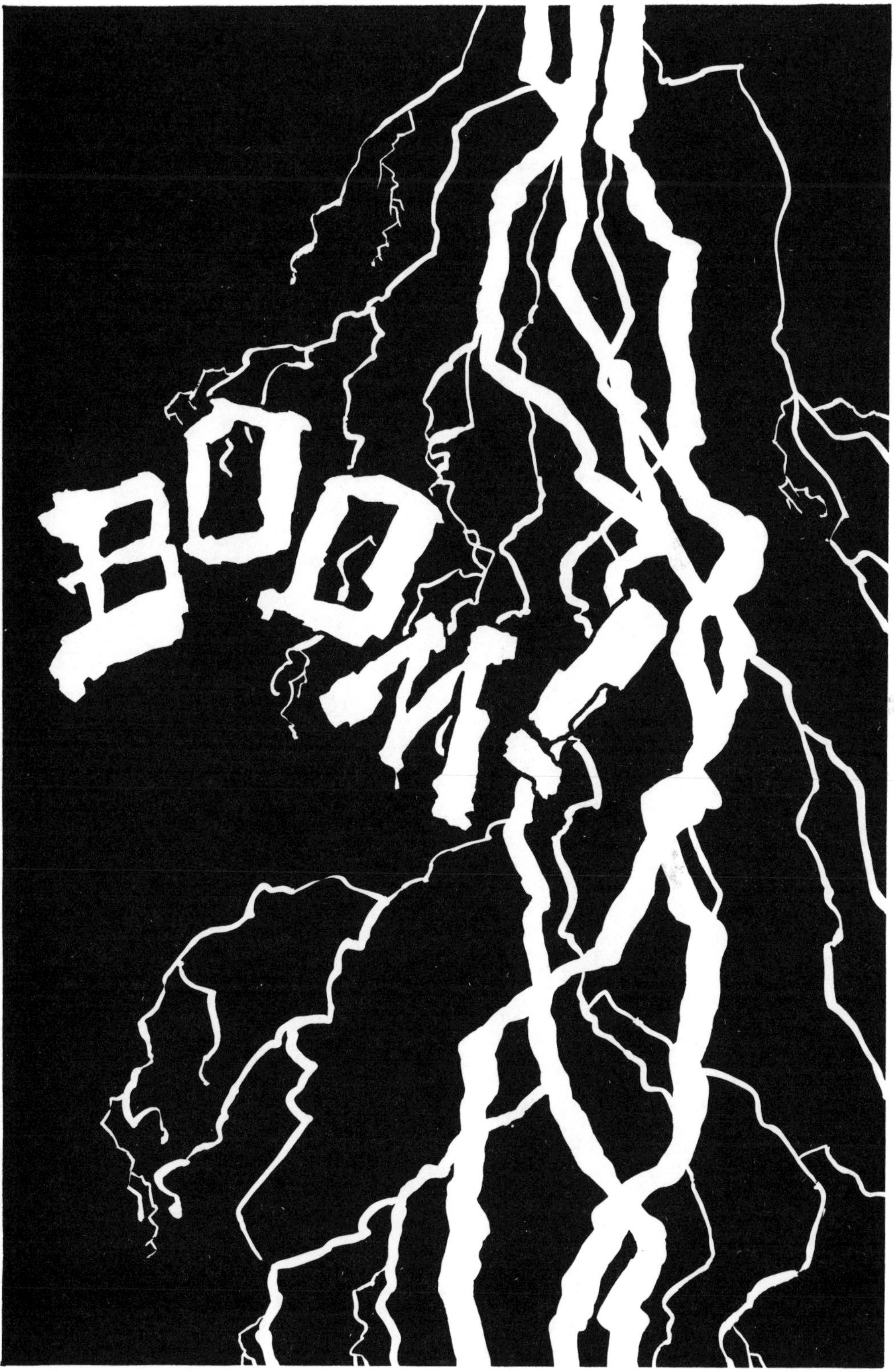
BOOM!

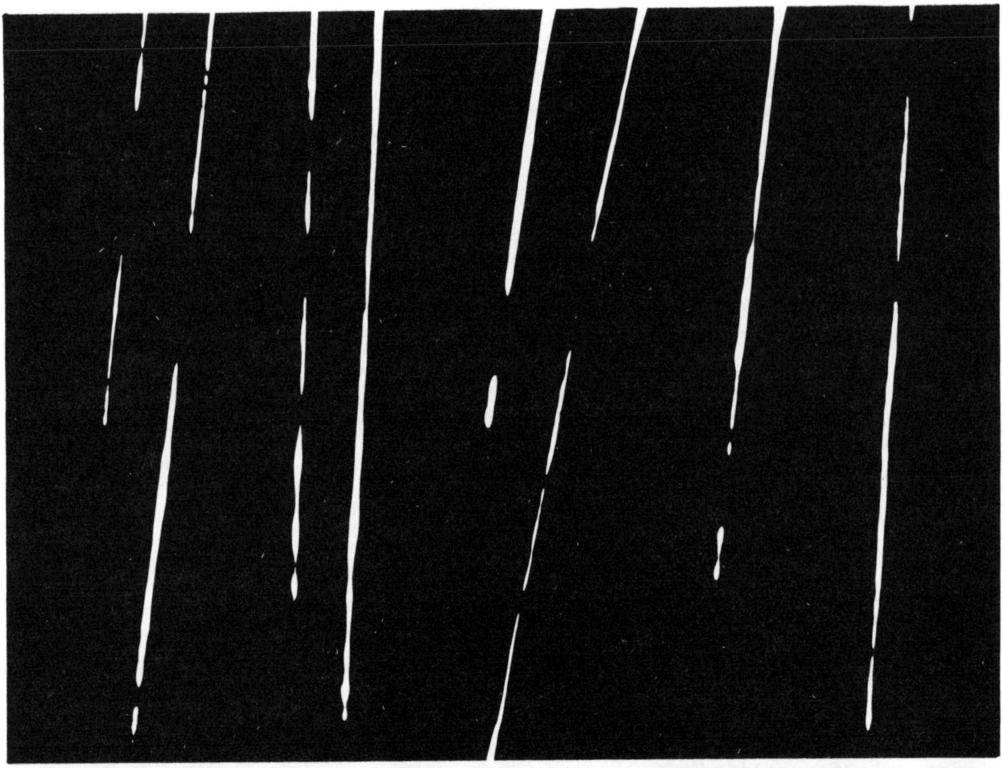

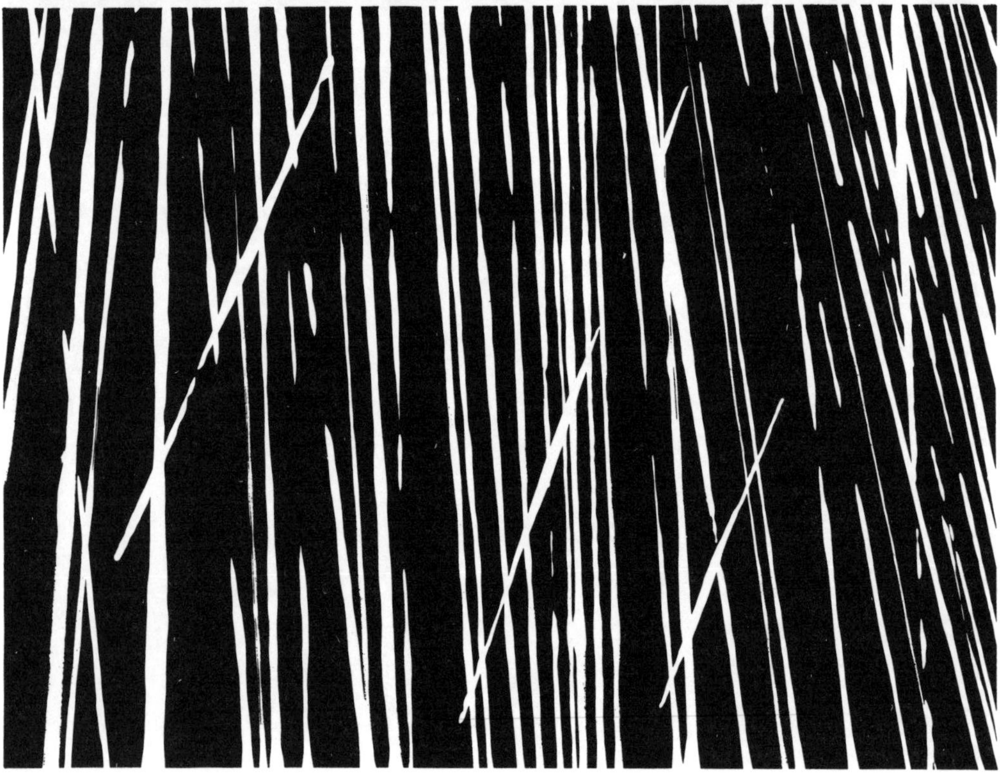

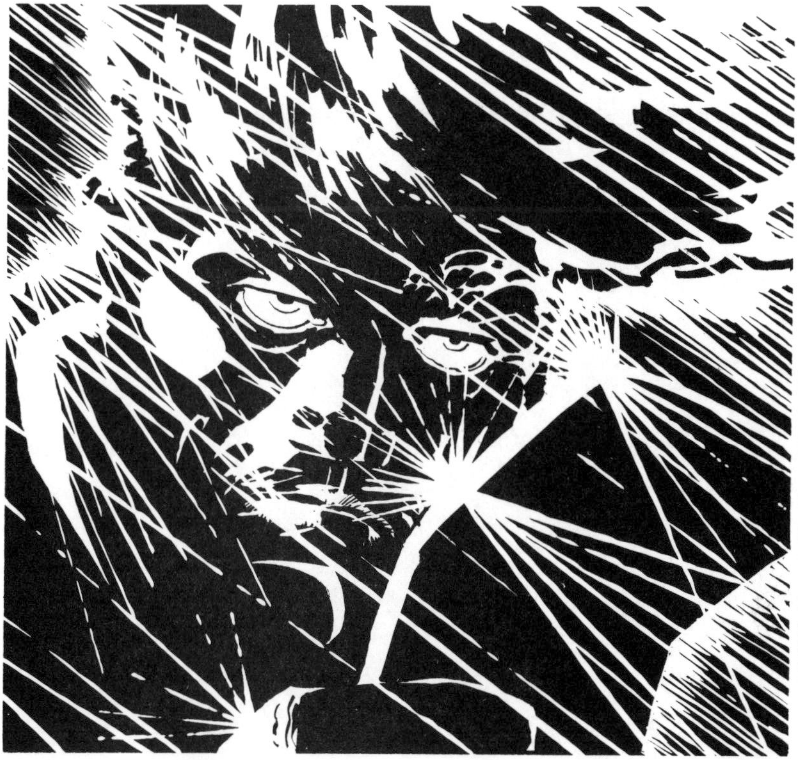

THE ATOM BOMB ISN'T THE FIRST THING I FIND ON HIM. IT TAKES ME A WHILE TO GET TO IT. HE DOESN'T KEEP IT IN HIS WALLET AND HIS WALLET KEEPS ME BUSY FOR A WHILE. IT'S PACKED. MASTERCARD. DISCOVER. PLATINUM AMERICAN EXPRESS. SNAPSHOTS OF TWO ADORABLE STRAWBERRY BLONDE GIRLS WHO MUST BE HIS KIDS. AN A.T.M. RECEIPT WRAPPED AROUND NEARLY THREE HUNDRED BUCKS' WORTH OF TWENTIES THAT I'M NOT TOO PROUD TO STUFF INTO MY OWN POCKETS.

IT ISN'T UNTIL I FEEL A LUMP UNDER HIS BELT THAT I FIND THE ATOM BOMB.

I RUN MY THUMB ACROSS ITS SCULPTED SURFACE FOR I DON'T KNOW HOW LONG.

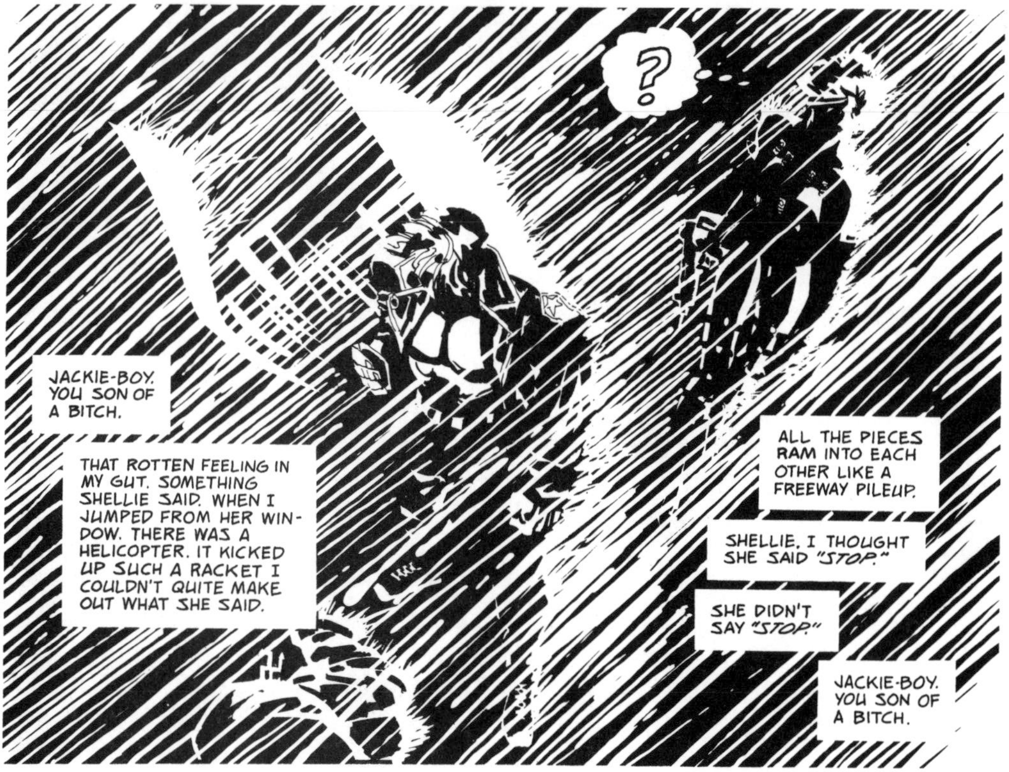
?
JACKIE-BOY. YOU SON OF A BITCH.
THAT ROTTEN FEELING IN MY GUT. SOMETHING SHELLIE SAID. WHEN I JUMPED FROM HER WINDOW. THERE WAS A HELICOPTER. IT KICKED UP SUCH A RACKET I COULDN'T QUITE MAKE OUT WHAT SHE SAID.
ALL THE PIECES RAM INTO EACH OTHER LIKE A FREEWAY PILEUP.
SHELLIE. I THOUGHT SHE SAID "STOP."
SHE DIDN'T SAY "STOP."
JACKIE-BOY. YOU SON OF A BITCH.

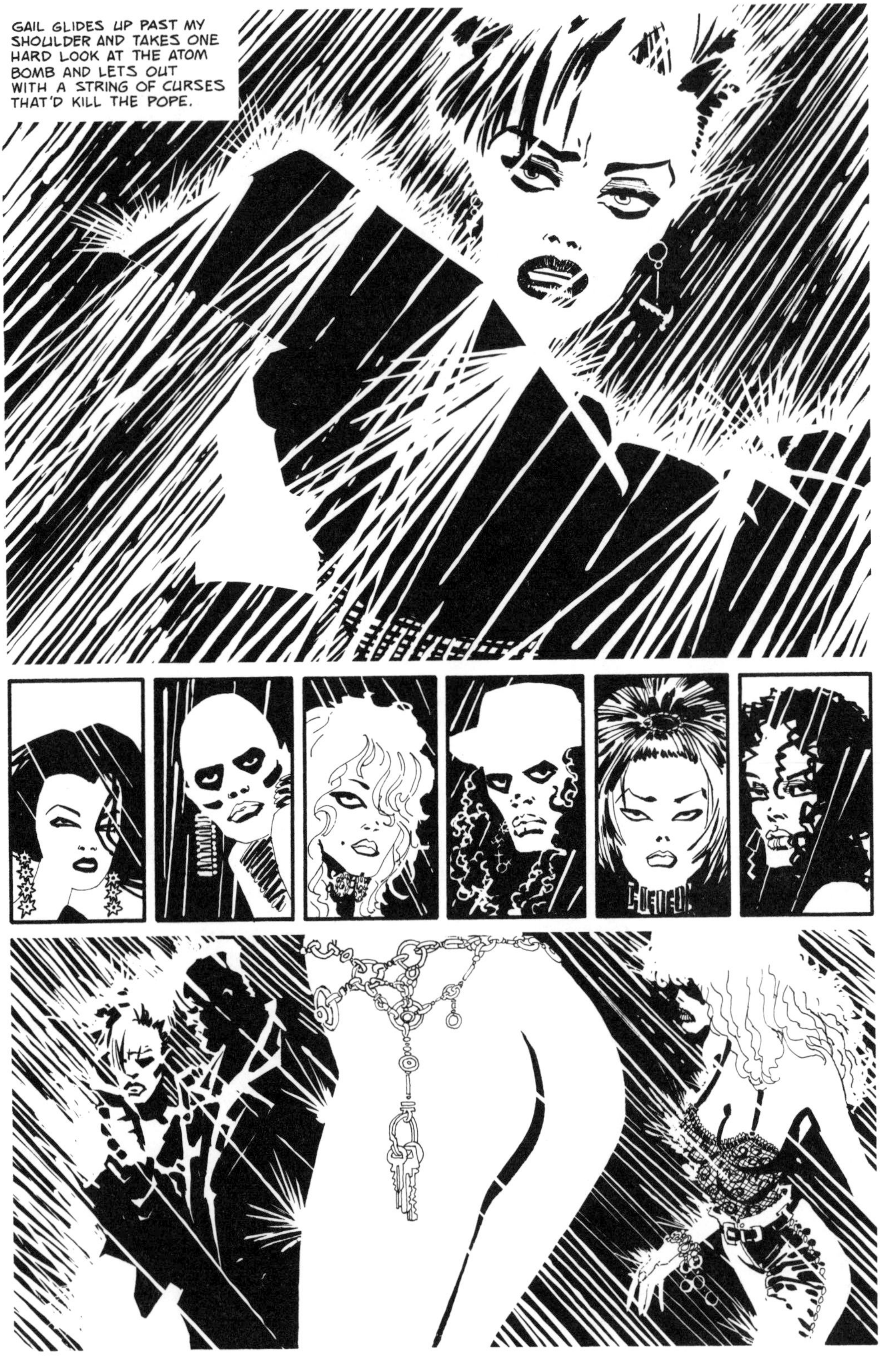
GAIL GLIDES UP PAST MY SHOULDER AND TAKES ONE HARD LOOK AT THE ATOM BOMB AND LETS OUT WITH A STRING OF CURSES THAT'D KILL THE POPE.

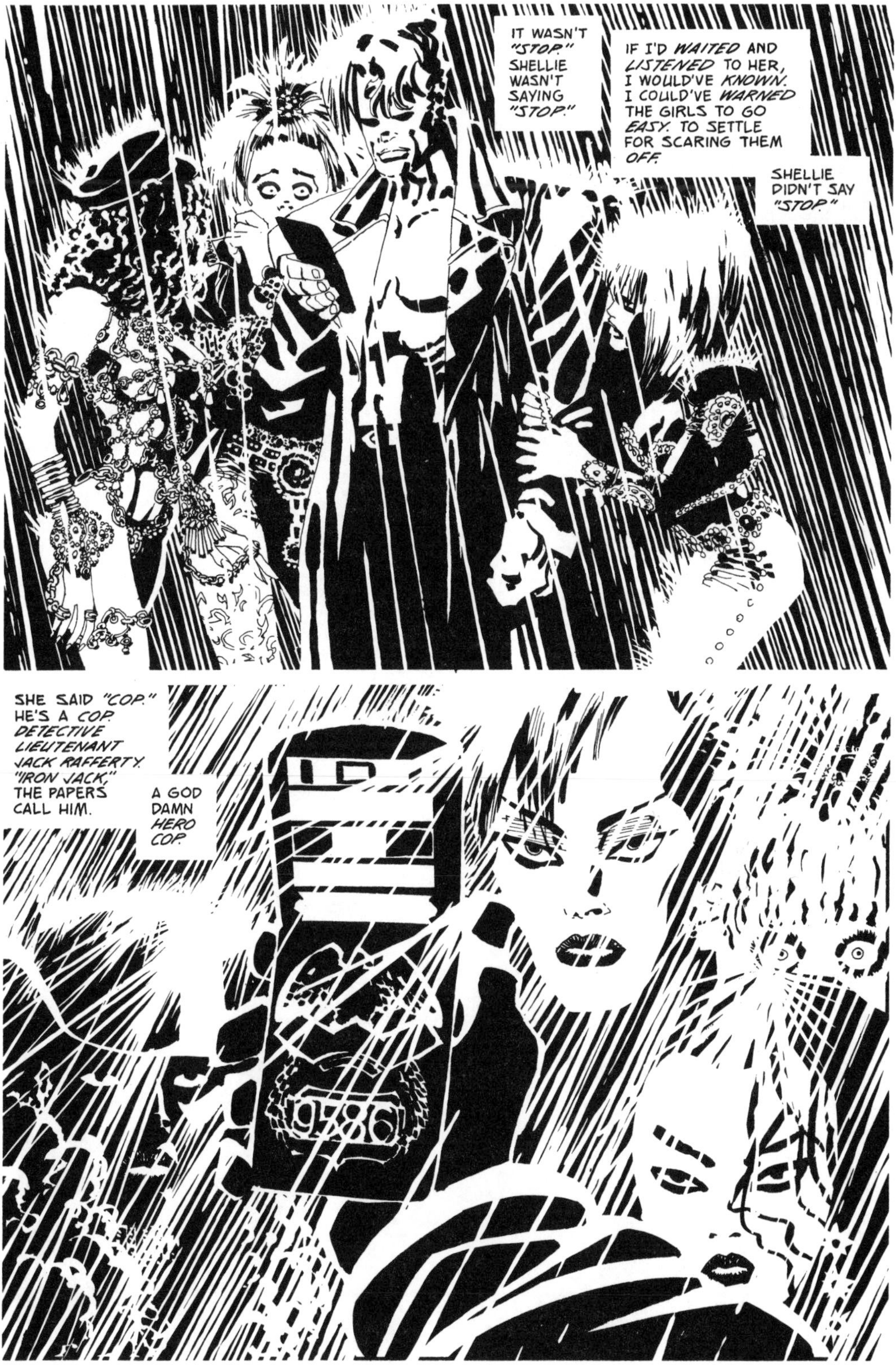
IT WASN'T "STOP." SHELLIE WASN'T SAYING "STOP."
IF I'D WAITED AND LISTENED TO HER, I WOULD'VE KNOWN. I COULD'VE WARNED THE GIRLS TO GO EASY. TO SETTLE FOR SCARING THEM OFF.
SHELLIE DIDN'T SAY "STOP."
SHE SAID "COP." HE'S A COP. DETECTIVE LIEUTENANT JACK RAFFERTY. "IRON JACK," THE PAPERS CALL HIM.
A GOD DAMN HERO COP.
9786

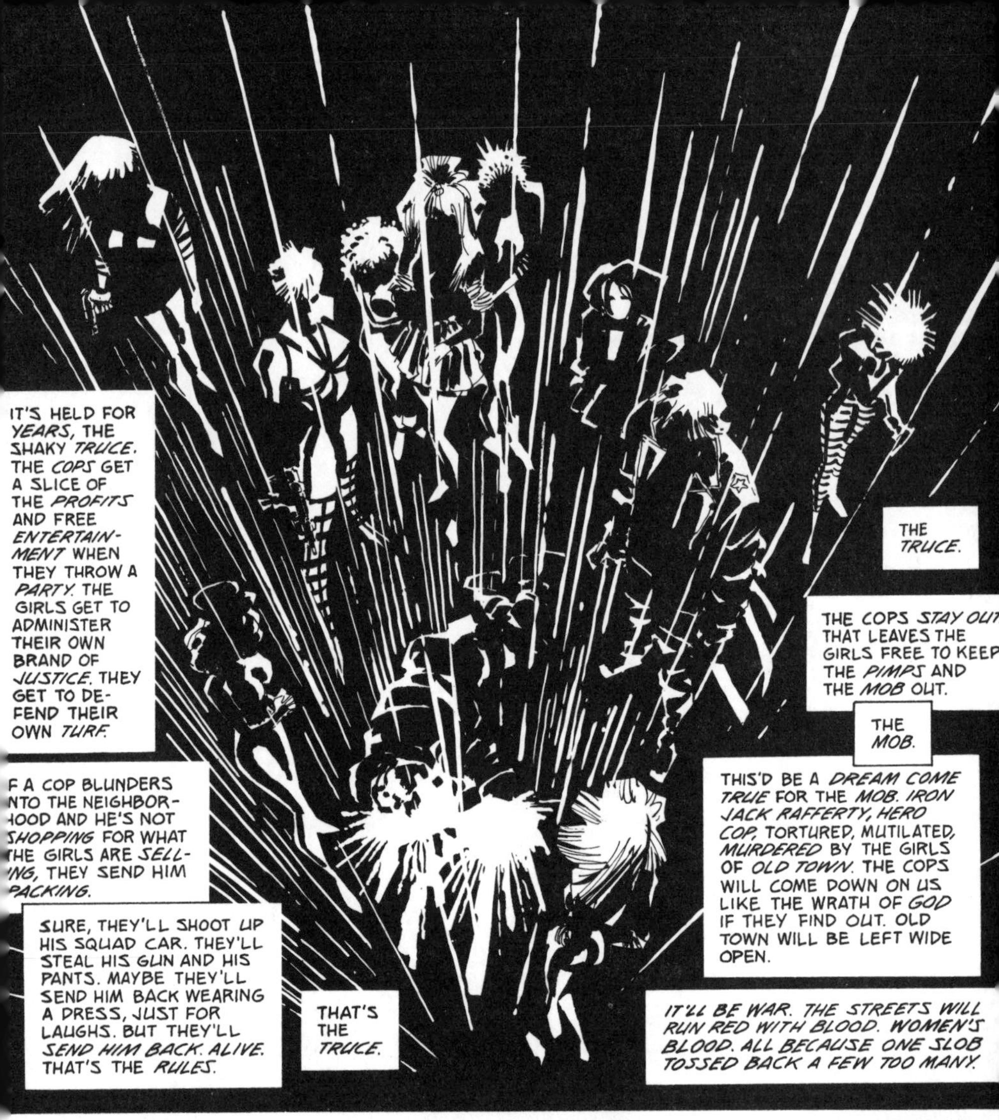
IT'S HELD FOR YEARS, THE SHAKY TRUCE. THE COPS GET A SLICE OF THE PROFITS AND FREE ENTERTAIN-MENT WHEN THEY THROW A PARTY. THE GIRLS GET TO ADMINISTER THEIR OWN BRAND OF JUSTICE. THEY GET TO DE-FEND THEIR OWN TURF.
F A COP BLUNDERS NTO THE NEIGHBOR-HOOD AND HE'S NOT SHOPPING FOR WHAT THE GIRLS ARE SELL-NG, THEY SEND HIM PACKING.
SURE, THEY'LL SHOOT UP HIS SQUAD CAR. THEY'LL STEAL HIS GUN AND HIS PANTS. MAYBE THEY'LL SEND HIM BACK WEARING A DRESS, JUST FOR LAUGHS. BUT THEY'LL SEND HIM BACK. ALIVE. THAT'S THE RULES.
THAT'S THE TRUCE.
THE TRUCE.
THE COPS STAY OUT. THAT LEAVES THE GIRLS FREE TO KEEP THE PIMPS AND THE MOB OUT.
THE MOB.
THIS'D BE A DREAM COME TRUE FOR THE MOB. IRON JACK RAFFERTY, HERO COP, TORTURED, MUTILATED, MURDERED BY THE GIRLS OF OLD TOWN. THE COPS WILL COME DOWN ON US LIKE THE WRATH OF GOD IF THEY FIND OUT. OLD TOWN WILL BE LEFT WIDE OPEN.
IT'LL BE WAR. THE STREETS WILL RUN RED WITH BLOOD. WOMEN'S BLOOD. ALL BECAUSE ONE SLOB TOSSED BACK A FEW TOO MANY.
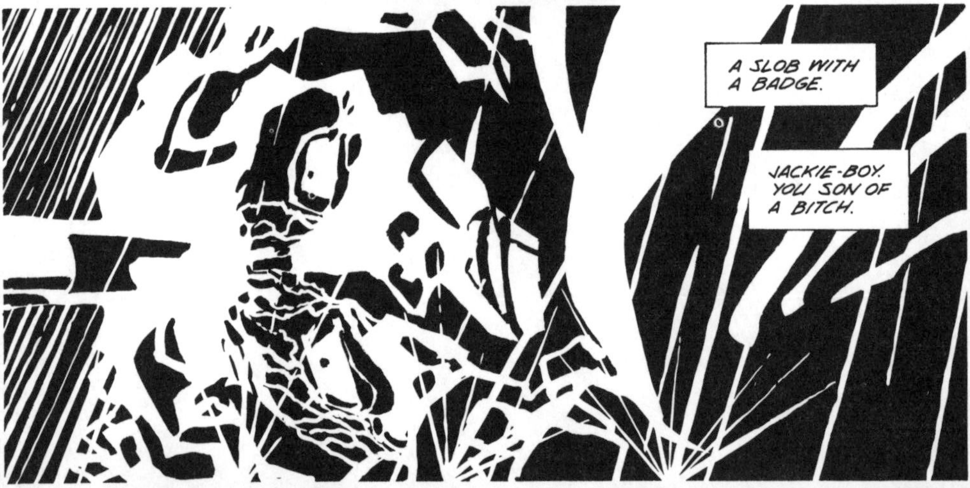
A SLOB WITH A BADGE.
JACKIE-BOY. YOU SON OF A BITCH.

CHAPTER THREE

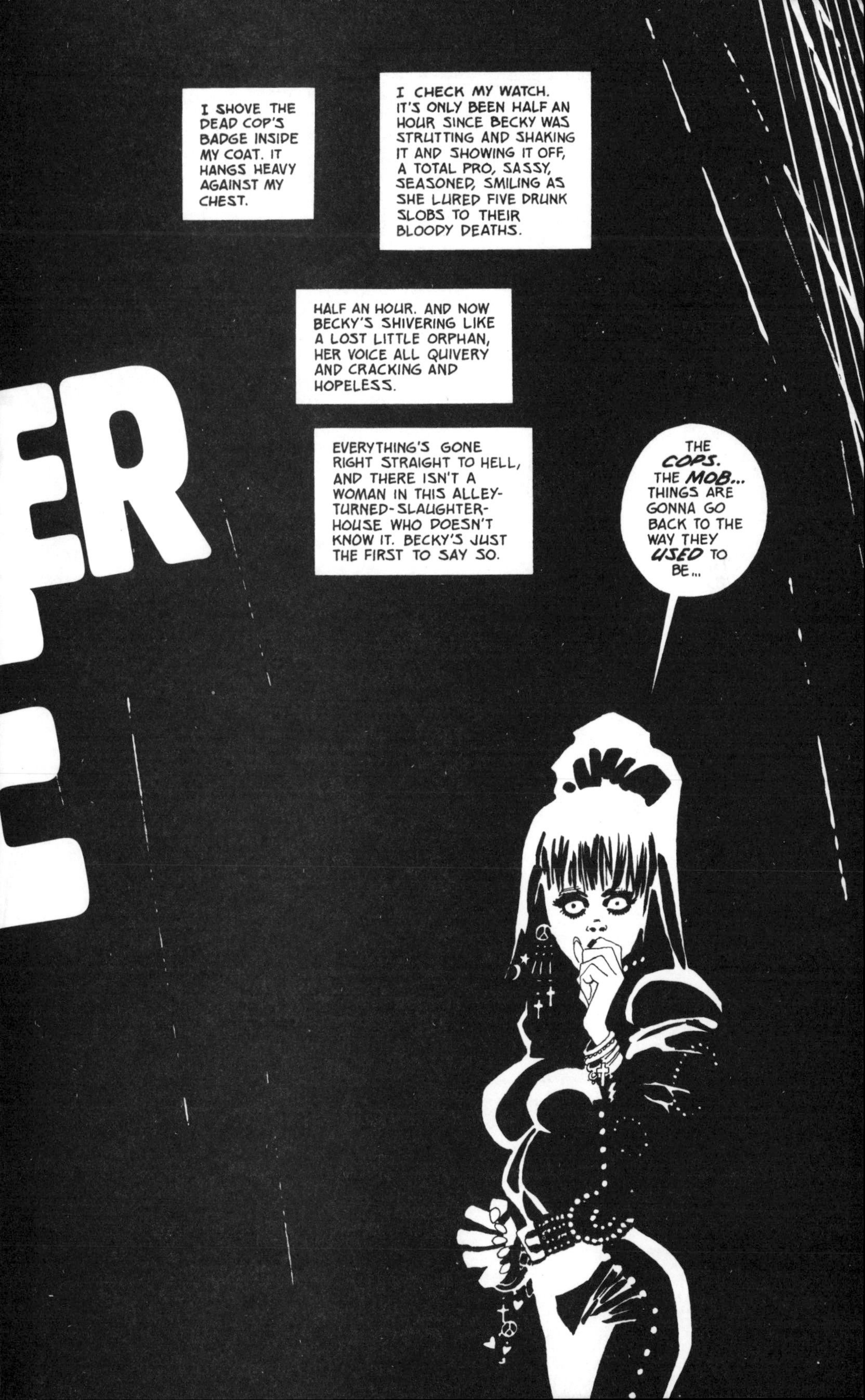
I SHOVE THE DEAD COP'S BADGE INSIDE MY COAT. IT HANGS HEAVY AGAINST MY CHEST.
I CHECK MY WATCH. IT'S ONLY BEEN HALF AN HOUR SINCE BECKY WAS STRUTTING AND SHAKING IT AND SHOWING IT OFF, A TOTAL PRO, SASSY, SEASONED, SMILING AS SHE LURED FIVE DRUNK SLOBS TO THEIR BLOODY DEATHS.
HALF AN HOUR. AND NOW BECKY'S SHIVERING LIKE A LOST LITTLE ORPHAN, HER VOICE ALL QUIVERY AND CRACKING AND HOPELESS.
EVERYTHING'S GONE RIGHT STRAIGHT TO HELL, AND THERE ISN'T A WOMAN IN THIS ALLEY-TURNED-SLAUGHTERHOUSE WHO DOESN'T KNOW IT. BECKY'S JUST THE FIRST TO SAY SO.
THE *COPS.* THE *MOB...* THINGS ARE GONNA GO BACK TO THE WAY THEY *USED* TO BE...

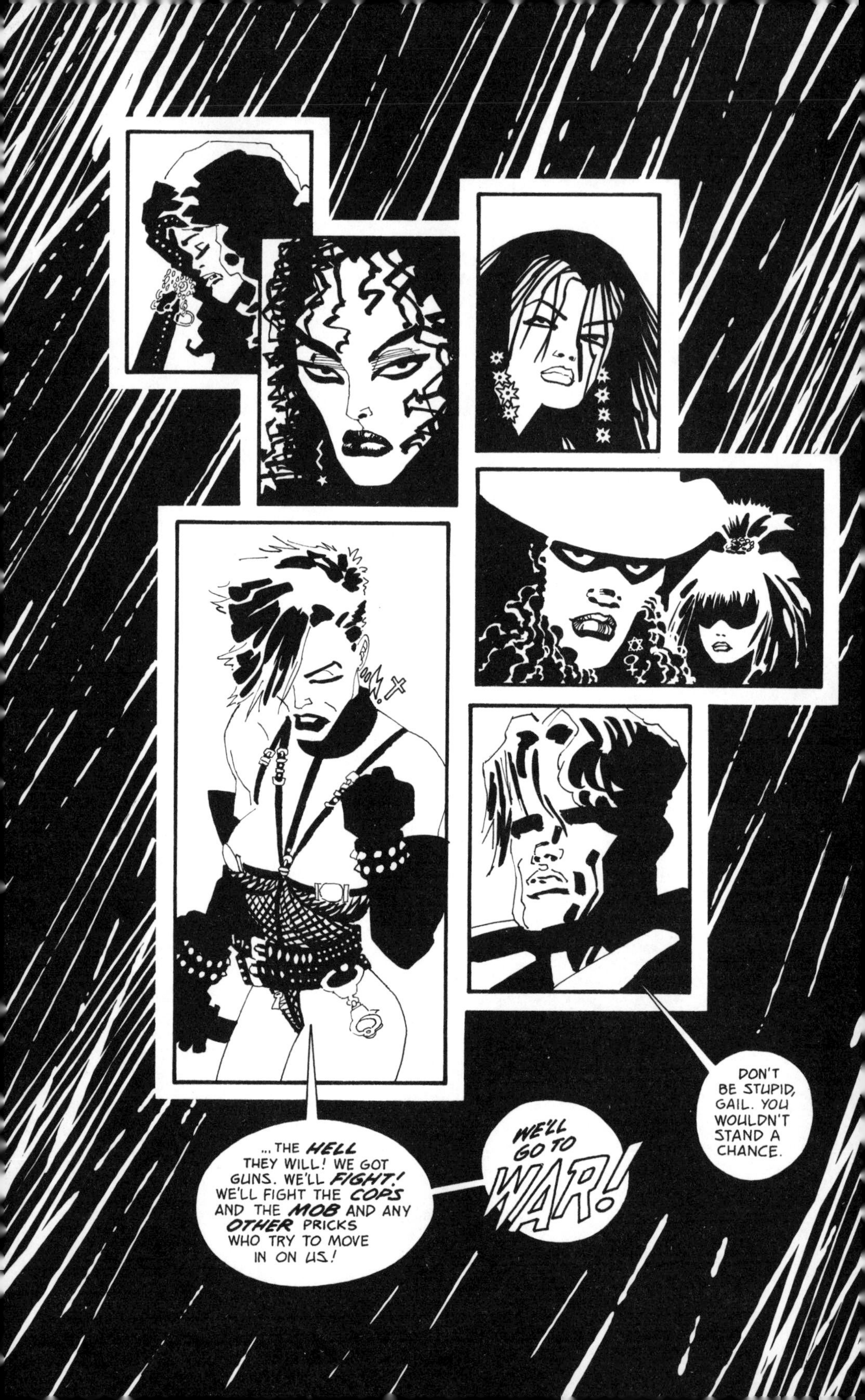

...THE HELL THEY WILL! WE GOT GUNS. WE'LL FIGHT! WE'LL FIGHT THE COPS AND THE MOB AND ANY OTHER PRICKS WHO TRY TO MOVE IN ON US!
WE'LL GO TO WAR!
DON'T BE STUPID, GAIL. YOU WOULDN'T STAND A CHANCE.

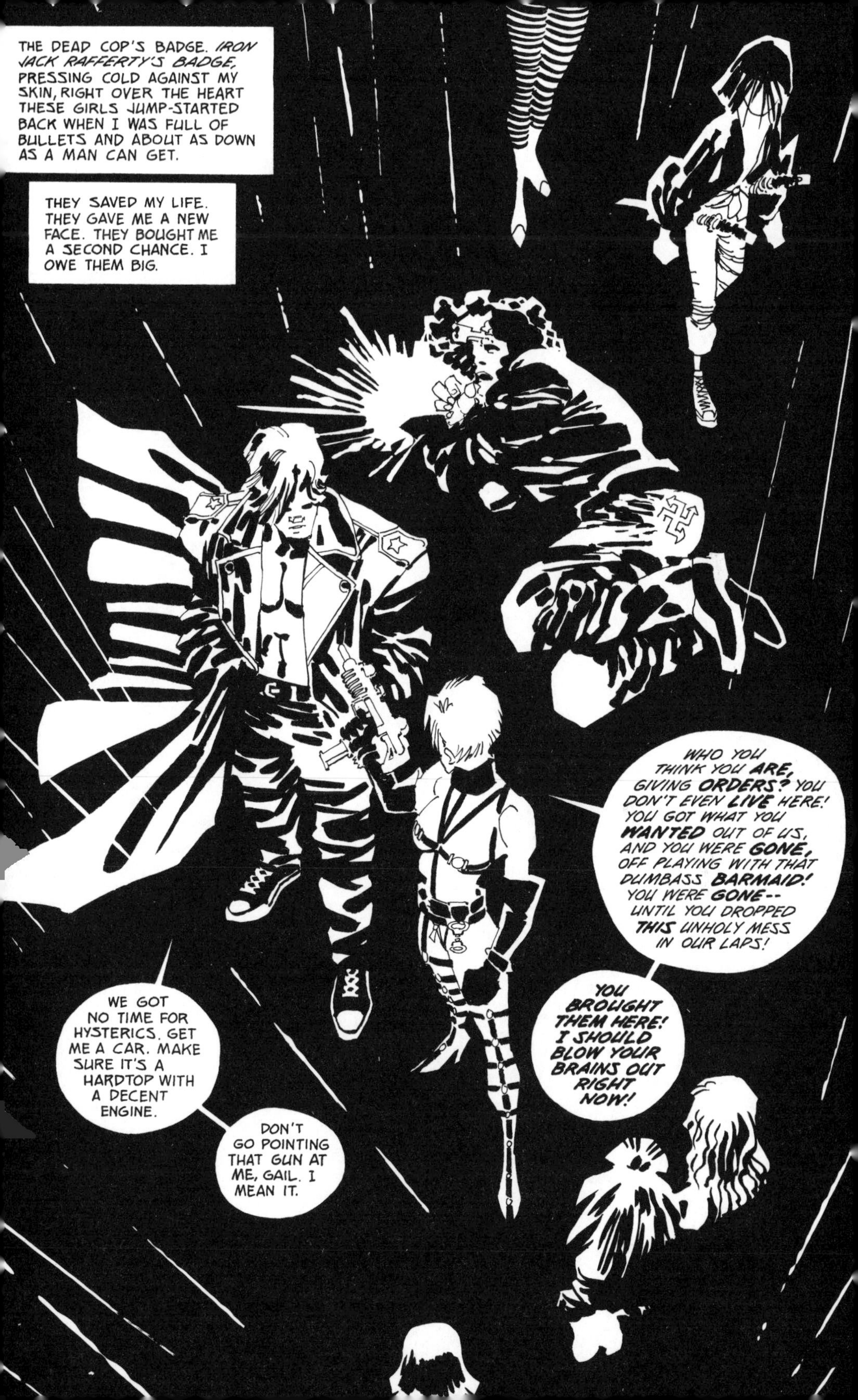
THE DEAD COP'S BADGE. *IRON JACK RAFFERTY'S BADGE,* PRESSING COLD AGAINST MY SKIN, RIGHT OVER THE HEART THESE GIRLS JUMP-STARTED BACK WHEN I WAS FULL OF BULLETS AND ABOUT AS DOWN AS A MAN CAN GET.
THEY SAVED MY LIFE. THEY GAVE ME A NEW FACE. THEY BOUGHT ME A SECOND CHANCE. I OWE THEM BIG.
WHO YOU THINK YOU **ARE,** GIVING **ORDERS?** YOU DON'T EVEN **LIVE** HERE! YOU GOT WHAT YOU **WANTED** OUT OF US, AND YOU WERE **GONE,** OFF PLAYING WITH THAT DUMBASS **BARMAID!** YOU WERE **GONE**-- UNTIL YOU DROPPED **THIS** UNHOLY MESS IN OUR LAPS!
YOU BROUGHT THEM HERE! I SHOULD BLOW YOUR BRAINS OUT RIGHT NOW!
WE GOT NO TIME FOR HYSTERICS. GET ME A CAR. MAKE SURE IT'S A HARDTOP WITH A DECENT ENGINE.
DON'T GO POINTING THAT GUN AT ME, GAIL. I MEAN IT.

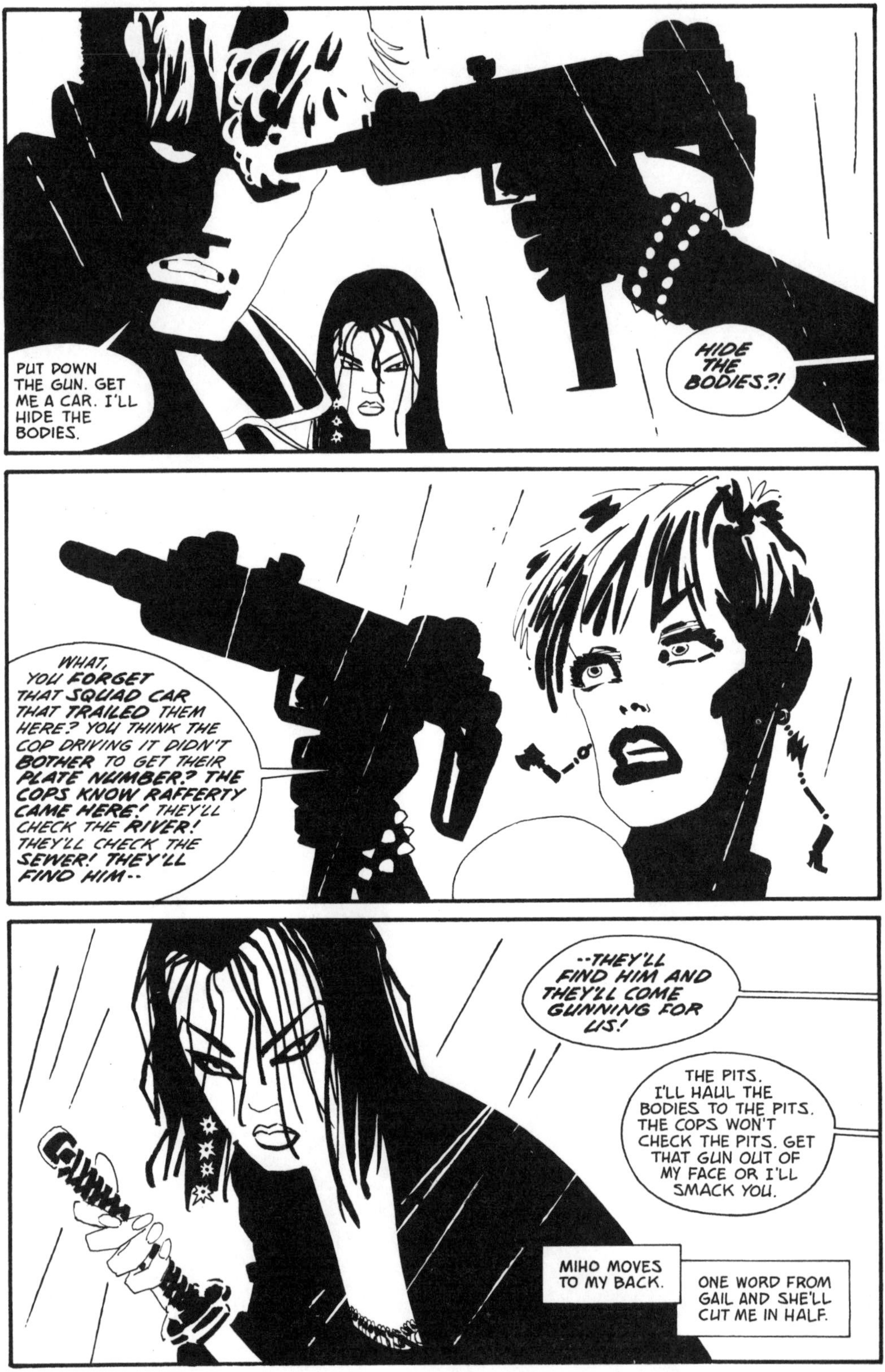
PUT DOWN THE GUN. GET ME A CAR. I'LL HIDE THE BODIES.
HIDE THE BODIES?!
WHAT, YOU FORGET THAT SQUAD CAR THAT TRAILED THEM HERE? YOU THINK THE COP DRIVING IT DIDN'T BOTHER TO GET THEIR PLATE NUMBER? THE COPS KNOW RAFFERTY CAME HERE! THEY'LL CHECK THE RIVER! THEY'LL CHECK THE SEWER! THEY'LL FIND HIM--
--THEY'LL FIND HIM AND THEY'LL COME GUNNING FOR US!
THE PITS. I'LL HAUL THE BODIES TO THE PITS. THE COPS WON'T CHECK THE PITS. GET THAT GUN OUT OF MY FACE OR I'LL SMACK YOU.
MIHO MOVES TO MY BACK.
ONE WORD FROM GAIL AND SHE'LL CUT ME IN HALF.

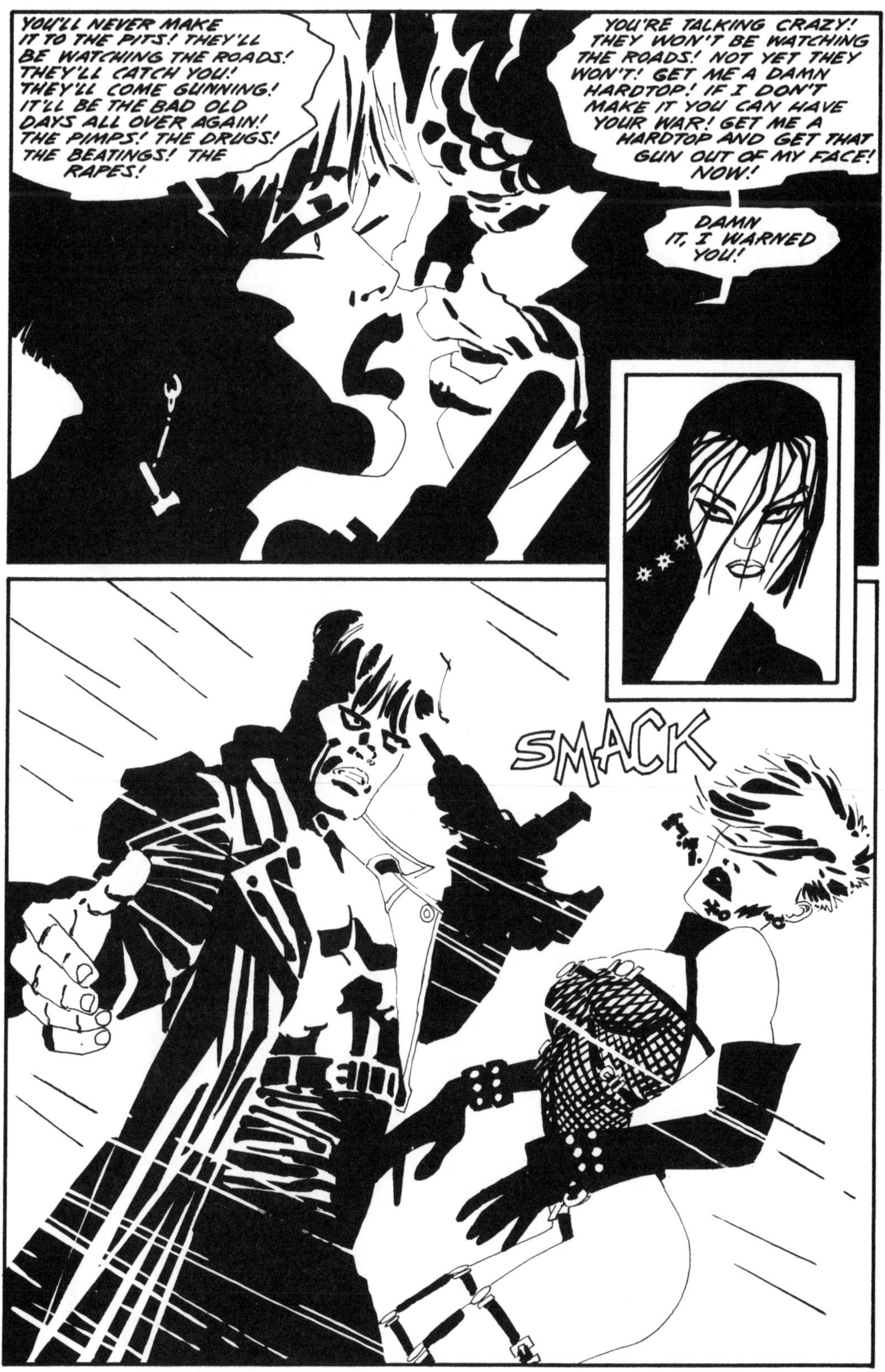
YOU'LL NEVER MAKE IT TO THE PITS! THEY'LL BE WATCHING THE ROADS! THEY'LL CATCH YOU! THEY'LL COME GUNNING! IT'LL BE THE BAD OLD DAYS ALL OVER AGAIN! THE PIMPS! THE DRUGS! THE BEATINGS! THE RAPES!
YOU'RE TALKING CRAZY! THEY WON'T BE WATCHING THE ROADS! NOT YET THEY WON'T! GET ME A DAMN HARDTOP! IF I DON'T MAKE IT YOU CAN HAVE YOUR WAR! GET ME A HARDTOP AND GET THAT GUN OUT OF MY FACE! NOW!
DAMN IT, I WARNED YOU!
SMACK

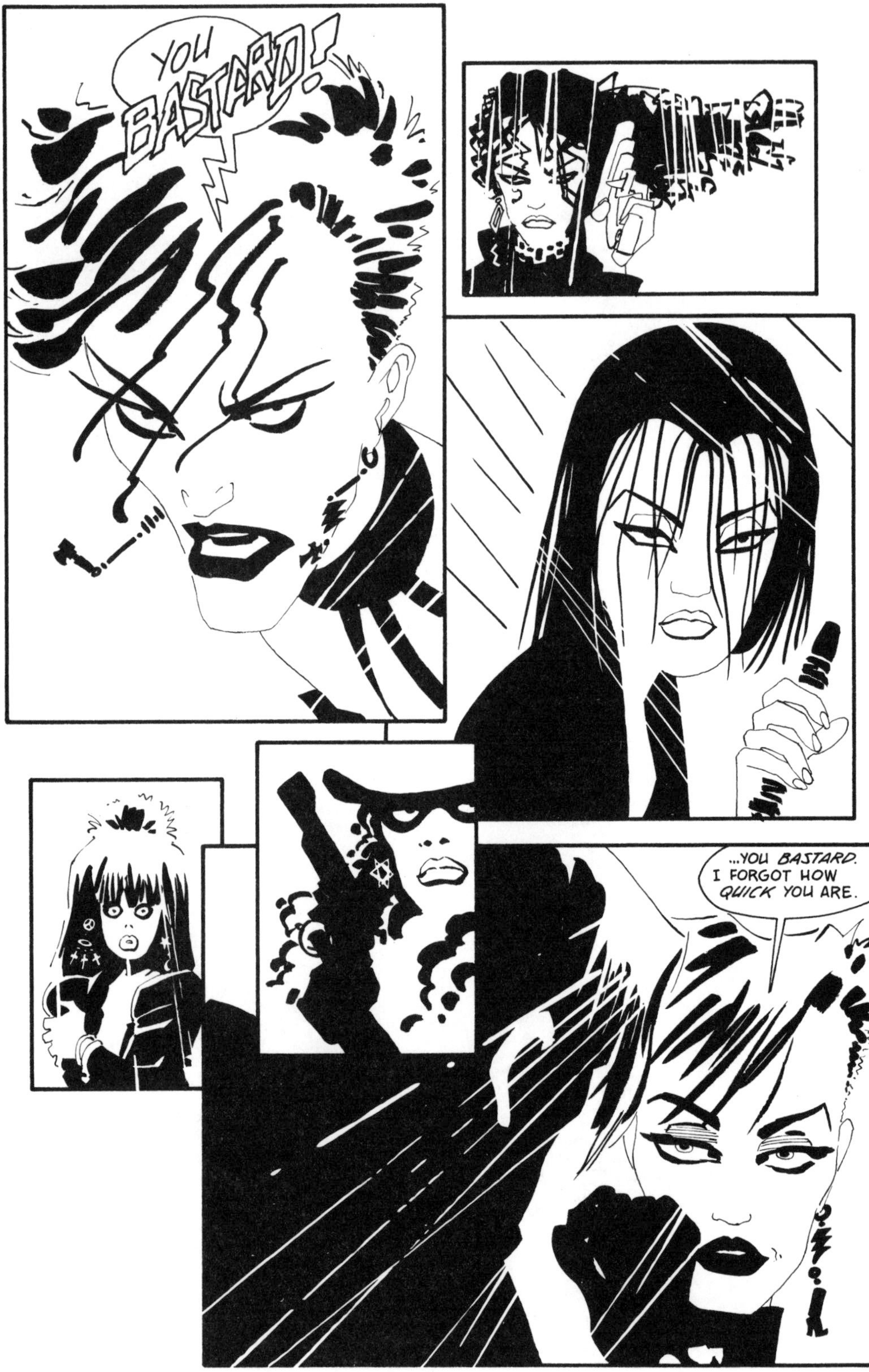
YOU BASTARD!
...YOU BASTARD. I FORGOT HOW QUICK YOU ARE.

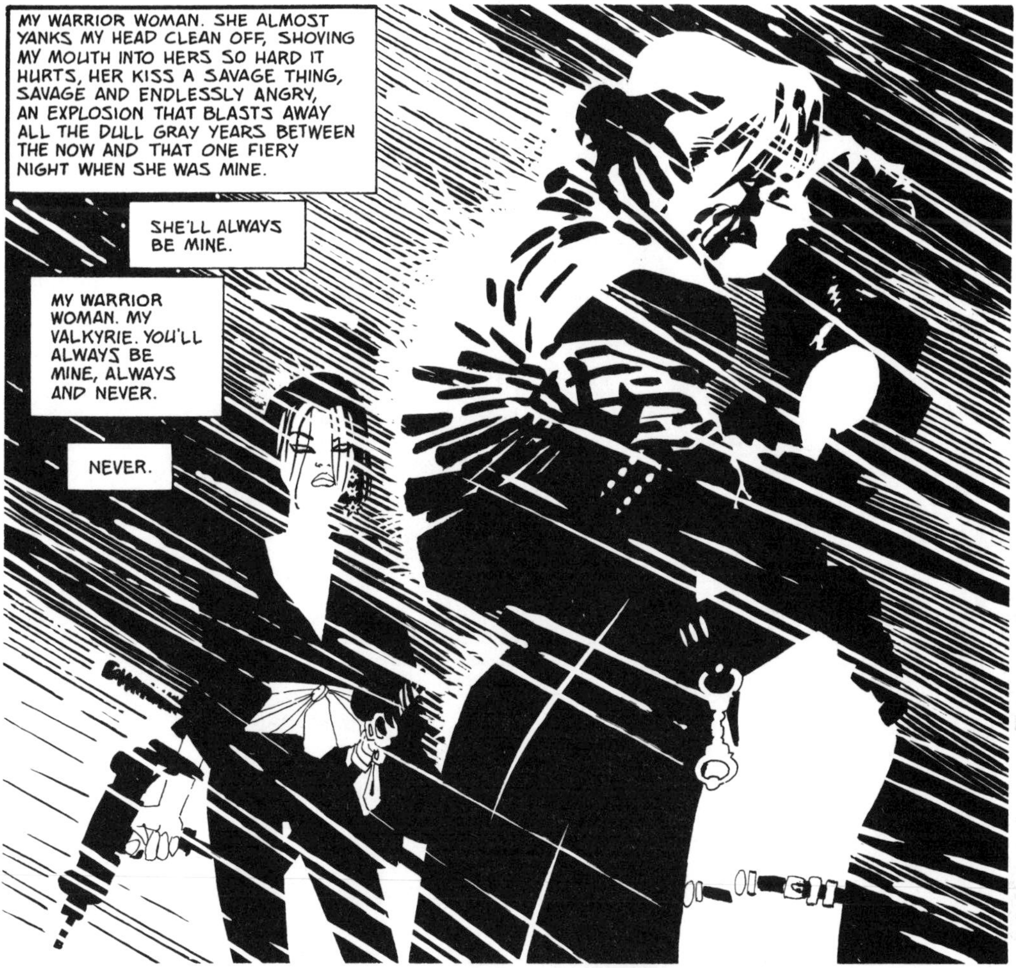
MY WARRIOR WOMAN. SHE ALMOST YANKS MY HEAD CLEAN OFF, SHOVING MY MOUTH INTO HERS SO HARD IT HURTS, HER KISS A SAVAGE THING, SAVAGE AND ENDLESSLY ANGRY, AN EXPLOSION THAT BLASTS AWAY ALL THE DULL GRAY YEARS BETWEEN THE NOW AND THAT ONE FIERY NIGHT WHEN SHE WAS MINE.
SHE'LL ALWAYS BE MINE.
MY WARRIOR WOMAN. MY VALKYRIE. YOU'LL ALWAYS BE MINE, ALWAYS AND NEVER.
NEVER.

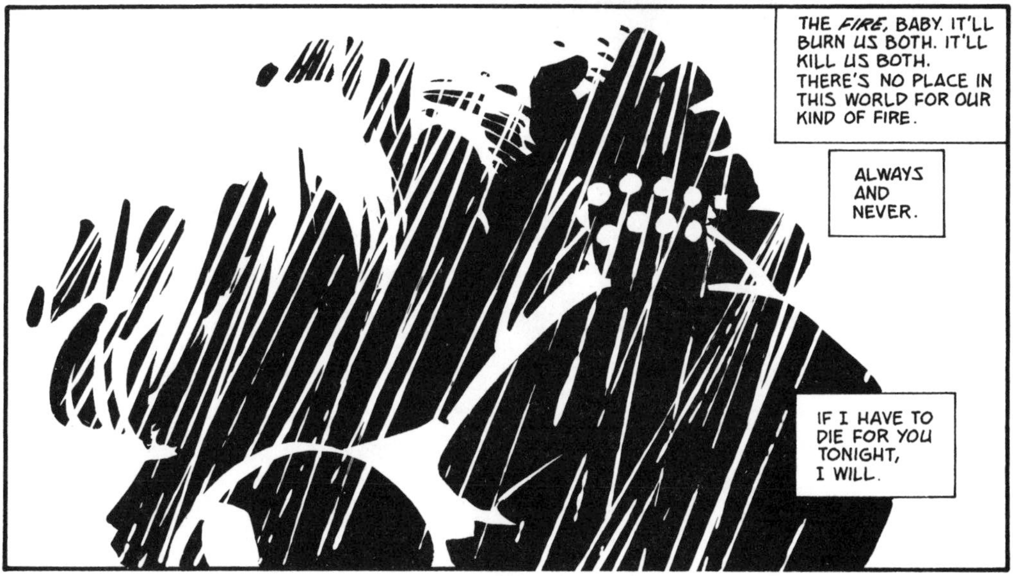
THE *FIRE*, BABY. IT'LL BURN US BOTH. IT'LL KILL US BOTH. THERE'S NO PLACE IN THIS WORLD FOR OUR KIND OF FIRE.
ALWAYS AND NEVER.
IF I HAVE TO DIE FOR YOU TONIGHT, I WILL.

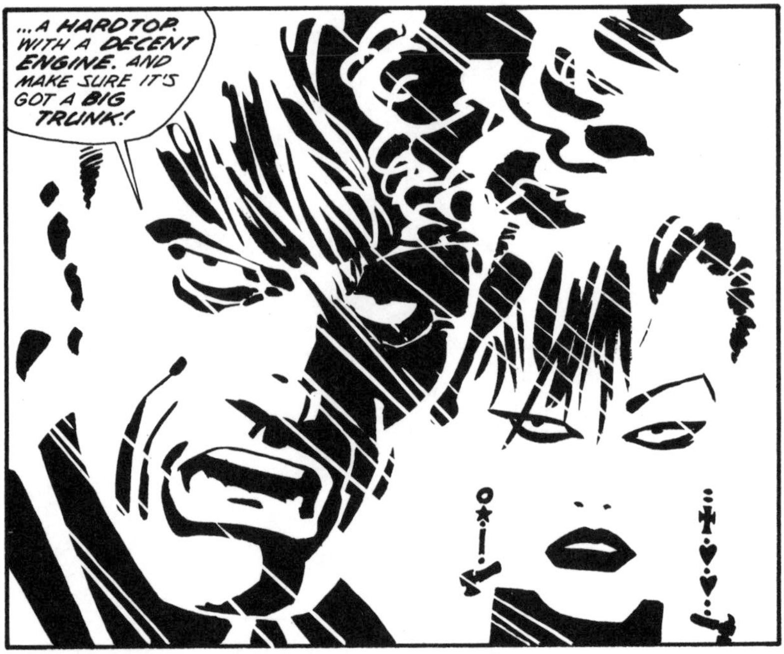
...A HARDTOP. WITH A DECENT ENGINE. AND MAKE SURE IT'S GOT A BIG TRUNK!

I'D RATHER TAKE MY CADDY, BUT THE SAME COP WHO FOLLOWED RAFFERTY MIGHT'VE GOTTEN MY PLATE NUMBER, TOO. BESIDES, MY CADDY'S TOP IS BROKEN AND I HAVEN'T HAD THE CASH TO GET THE PARTS I NEED TO FIX IT AND I'D BE SURE TO GET PULLED OVER, DRIVING ALL THE WAY TO THE PITS IN THE RAIN WITH THE TOP DOWN.

THE WHOLE TIME I'M GIVING ORDERS, GAIL'S EYES ARE BURNING INTO THE BACK OF MY SKULL LIKE A PAIR OF LASER BEAMS. SHE DOESN'T SAY A WORD. IF THAT KISS WAS OUR LAST GOODBYE IT WAS A DAMN GOOD ONE AND WE'D BOTH JUST AS SOON LEAVE IT THAT WAY.

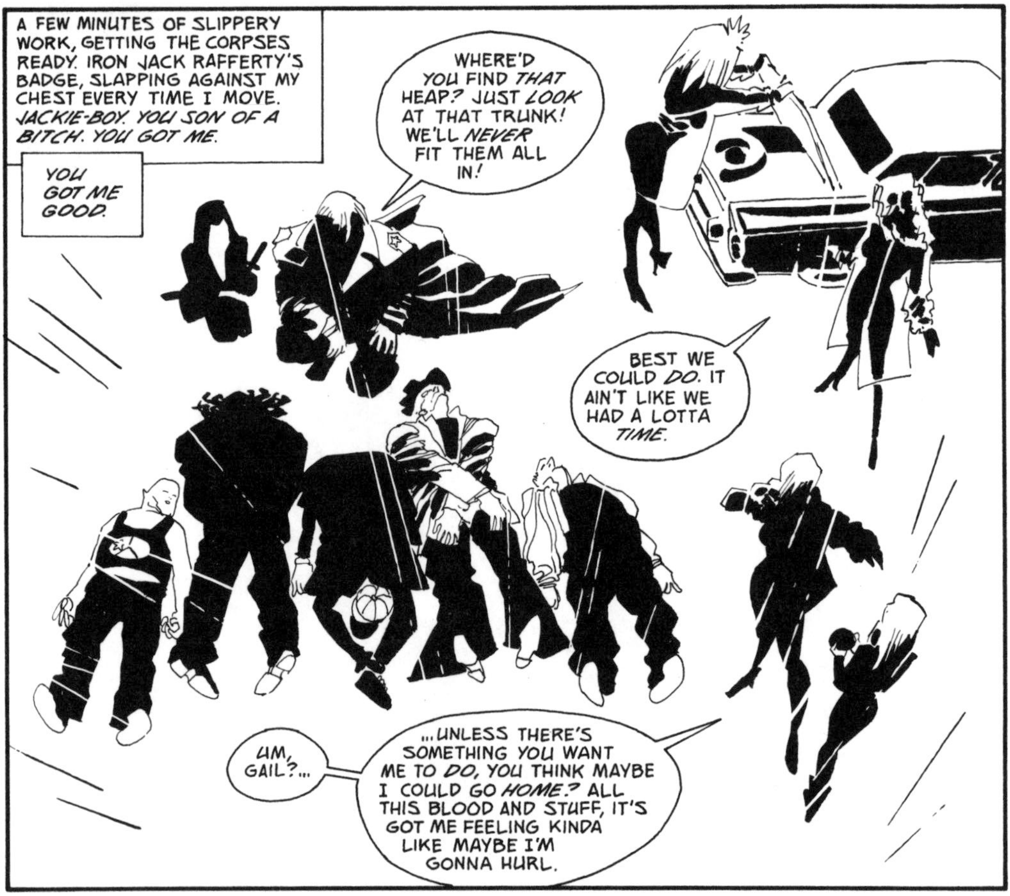
A FEW MINUTES OF SLIPPERY WORK, GETTING THE CORPSES READY. IRON JACK RAFFERTY'S BADGE, SLAPPING AGAINST MY CHEST EVERY TIME I MOVE. JACKIE-BOY. YOU SON OF A BITCH. YOU GOT ME.
YOU GOT ME GOOD.
WHERE'D YOU FIND THAT HEAP? JUST LOOK AT THAT TRUNK! WE'LL NEVER FIT THEM ALL IN!
BEST WE COULD DO. IT AIN'T LIKE WE HAD A LOTTA TIME.
UM, GAIL?...
...UNLESS THERE'S SOMETHING YOU WANT ME TO DO, YOU THINK MAYBE I COULD GO HOME? ALL THIS BLOOD AND STUFF, IT'S GOT ME FEELING KINDA LIKE MAYBE I'M GONNA HURL.

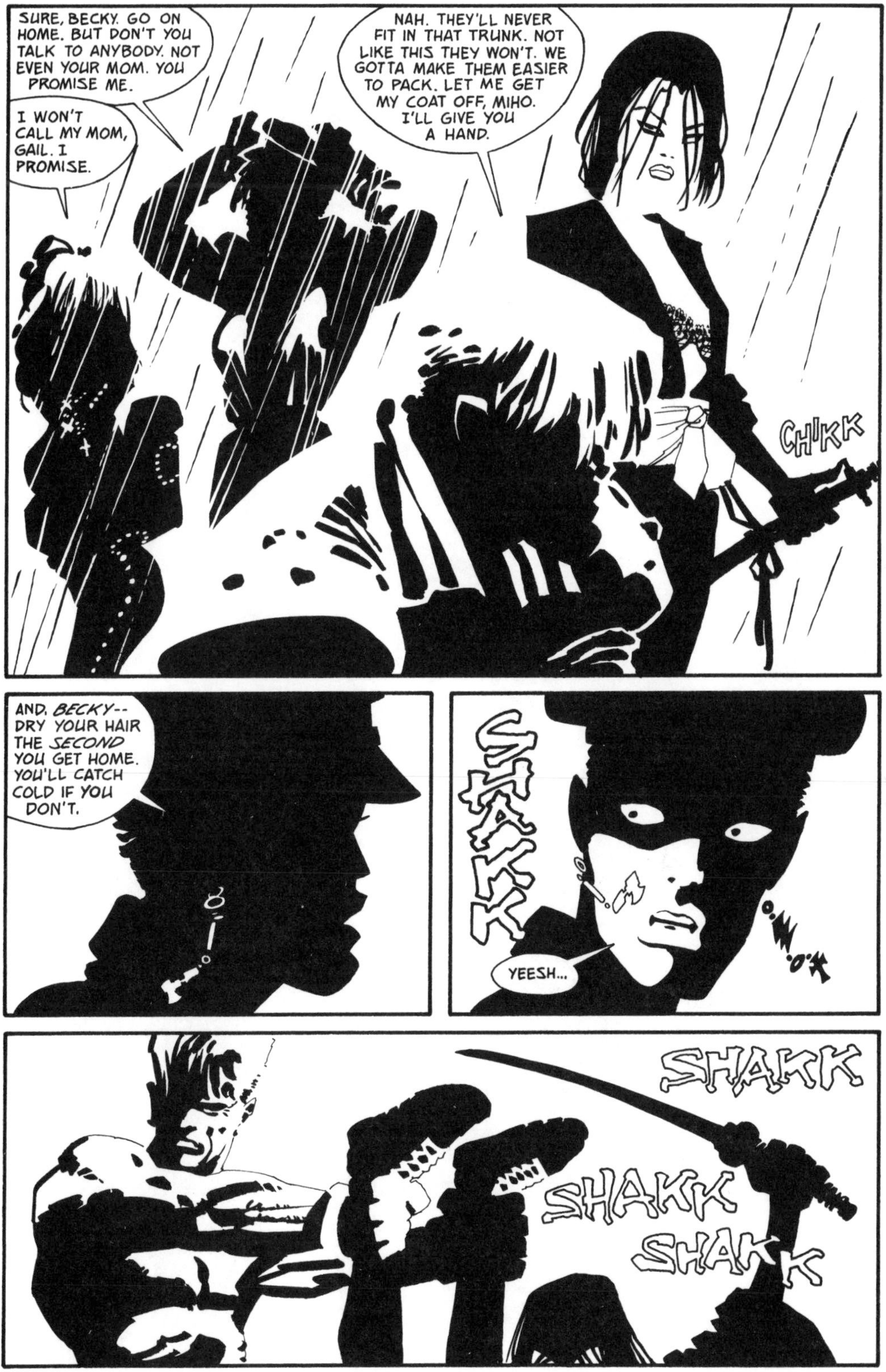
SURE, BECKY. GO ON HOME. BUT DON'T YOU TALK TO ANYBODY. NOT EVEN YOUR MOM. YOU PROMISE ME.
I WON'T CALL MY MOM, GAIL. I PROMISE.
NAH. THEY'LL NEVER FIT IN THAT TRUNK. NOT LIKE THIS THEY WON'T. WE GOTTA MAKE THEM EASIER TO PACK. LET ME GET MY COAT OFF, MIHO. I'LL GIVE YOU A HAND.
CHIKK
AND, BECKY-- DRY YOUR HAIR THE SECOND YOU GET HOME. YOU'LL CATCH COLD IF YOU DON'T.
SHAKK
YEESH...
SHAKK
SHAKK
SHAKK

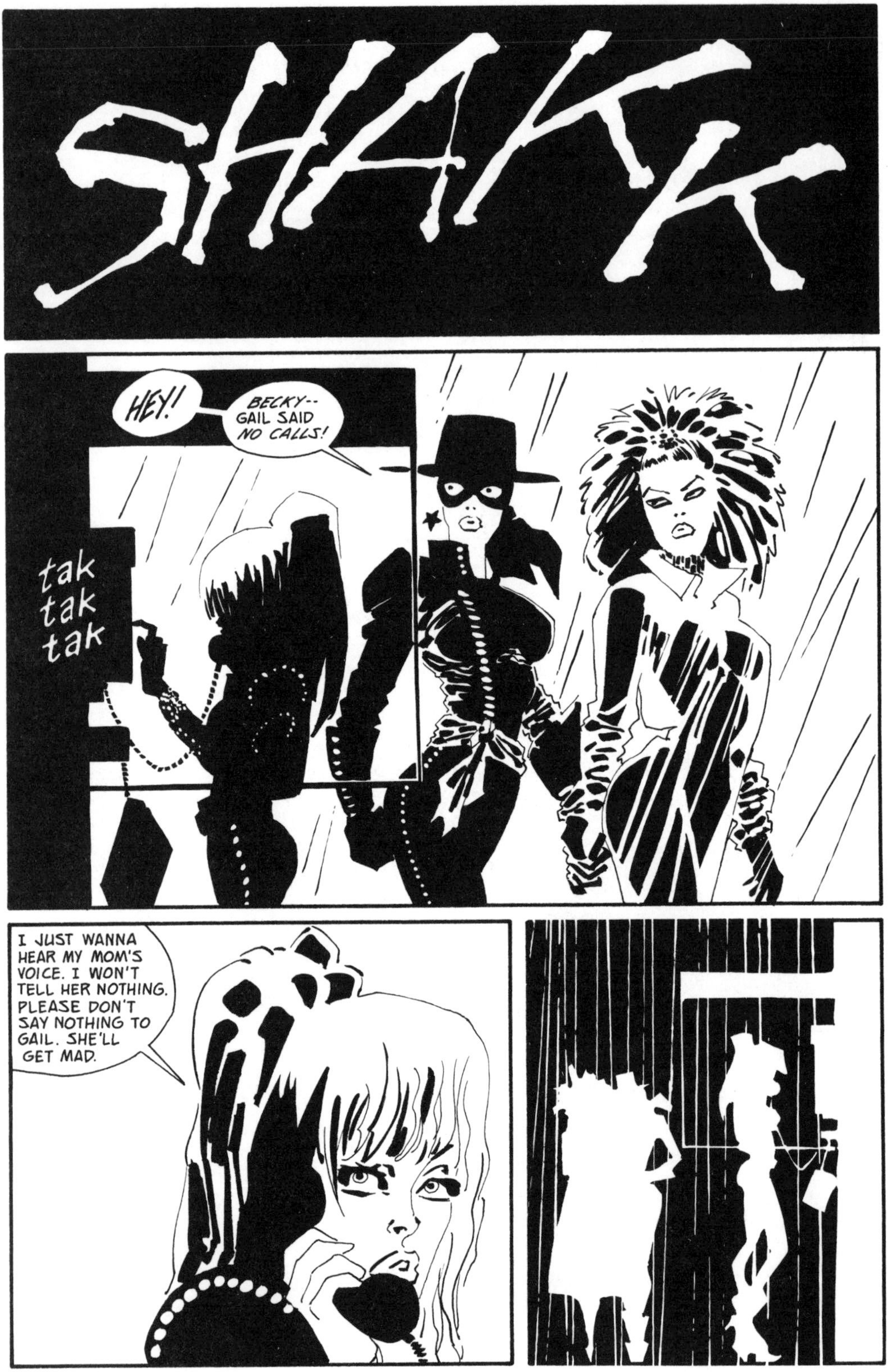
SHAKK
HEY!
BECKY-- GAIL SAID NO CALLS!
tak tak tak
I JUST WANNA HEAR MY MOM'S VOICE. I WON'T TELL HER NOTHING. PLEASE DON'T SAY NOTHING TO GAIL. SHE'LL GET MAD.

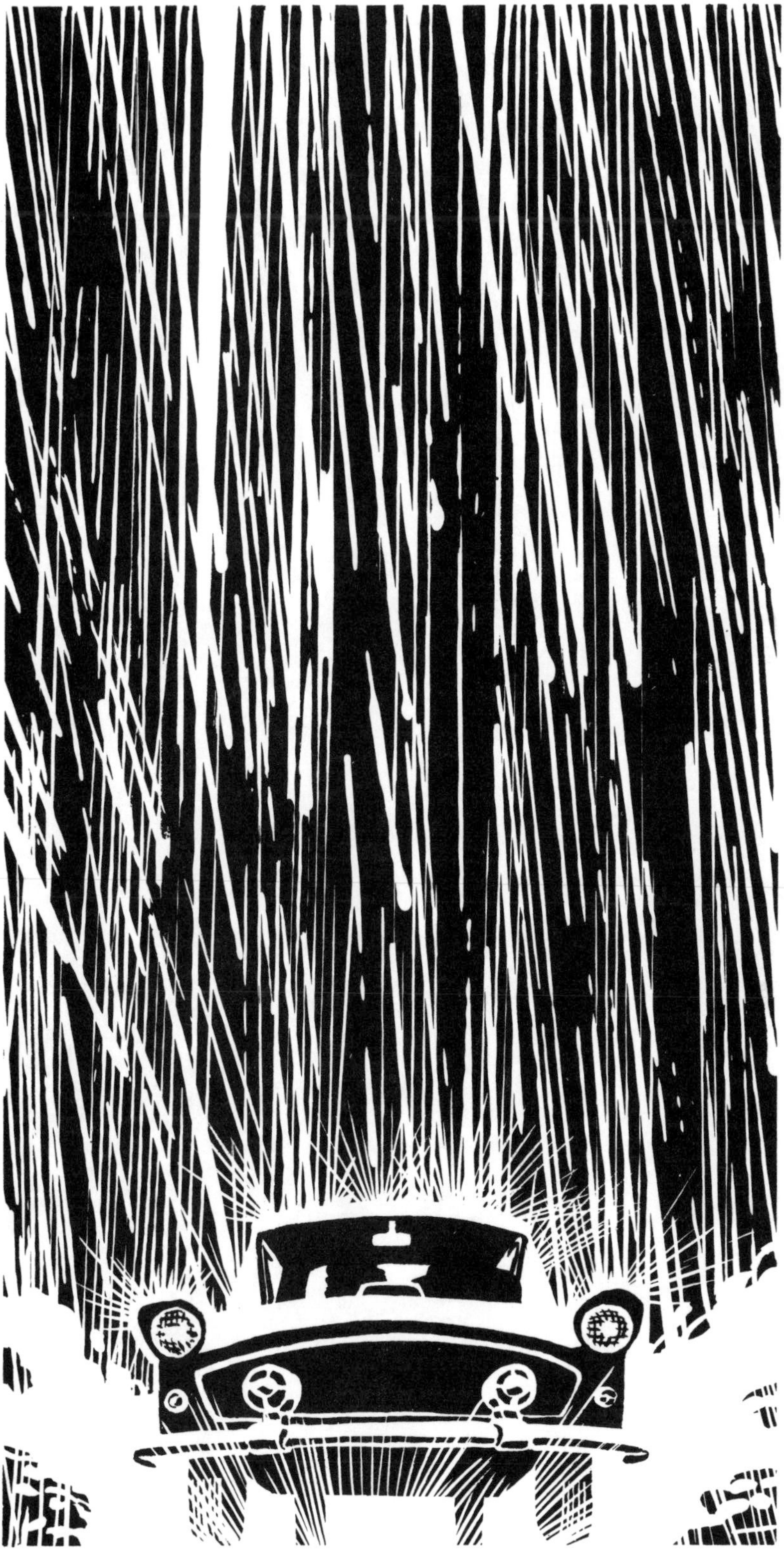

DIZZY DAMES. WHAT WERE THEY *THINKING*, STICKING ME WITH A BEAT-UP BUCKET OF BOLTS LIKE THIS? SOMEBODY OUGHTTA TAKE IT OUT BACK AND *SHOOT* IT. IT'D BE A *MERCY.*

A FEW YEARS BEFORE I WAS *BORN*, THIS T-BIRD MUST'VE BEEN A PRETTY SWEET SET OF WHEELS. BUT IT'S BEEN AROUND A FEW TOO MANY BLOCKS A FEW TOO MANY TIMES AND WHOEVER OWNED IT OBVIOUSLY DIDN'T INDULGE IN LUXURIES LIKE THE OCCASIONAL TUNE-UP OR OIL CHANGE. THE ENGINE JERKS AND FARTS LIKE AN OLD MAN ON A BAD DIET. THE STEERING MECHANISM'S GOT TERMINAL ARTHRITIS. THE SUSPENSION MAKES EVERY POTHOLE AN ADVENTURE. THE LEFT REAR TIRE IS AS SOFT AS A ROTTEN BANANA AND IF THAT'S A SLOW LEAK I'M GOOD AND SCREWED. I HAD TO CHUCK THE SPARE TO MAKE ROOM FOR ALL THE NEATLY CHOPPED BODY PARTS WE PACKED IN THE TRUNK.

MAYBE FIVE BLOCKS OUT I HAPPEN TO GLANCE DOWN AT THE GAS GAUGE. WHAT I SEE GETS ME POUNDING MY FISTS AGAINST THE STEERING WHEEL LIKE SOME LUNATIC. I CURSE OUT EVERY GIRL WHO EVER WORKED OLD TOWN AND EVERY RELATIVE ANY OF THEM EVER HAD.

HOW THE HELL AM I SUPPOSED TO MAKE IT ALL THE WAY TO THE PITS AND BACK ON LESS THAN AN EIGHTH OF A TANK?

DIZZY DAMES! DIZZY, SCARED, STUPID DAMES! YOU COULDN'T BOTHER TO FILL THE GOD DAMN GAS TANK?

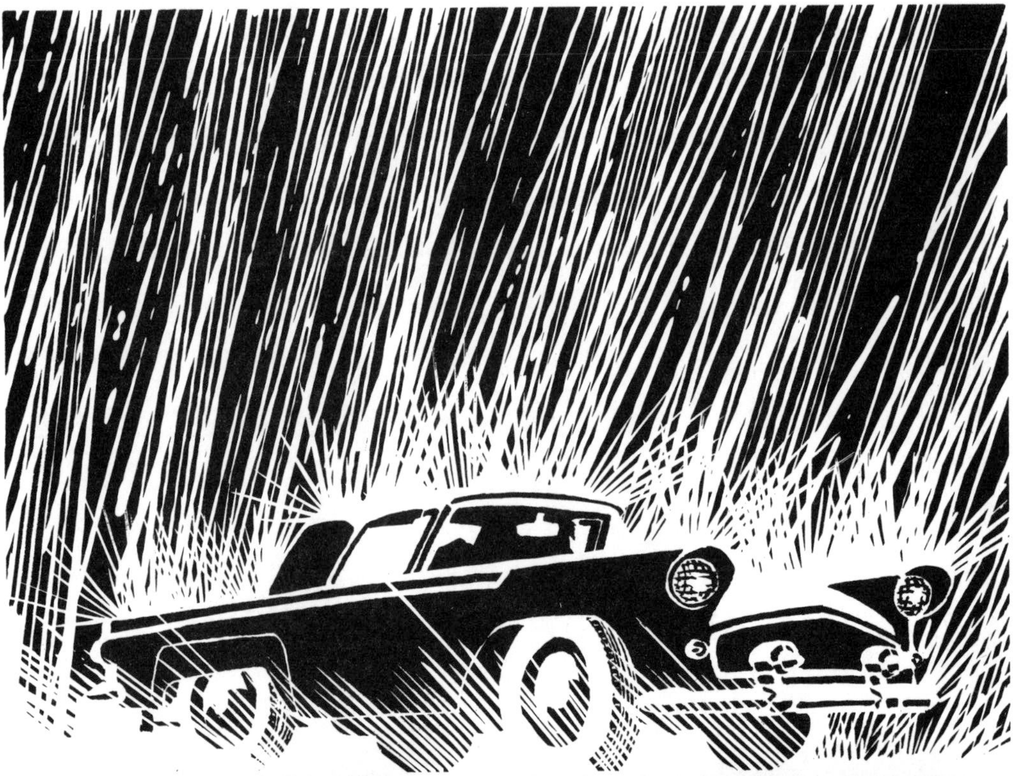

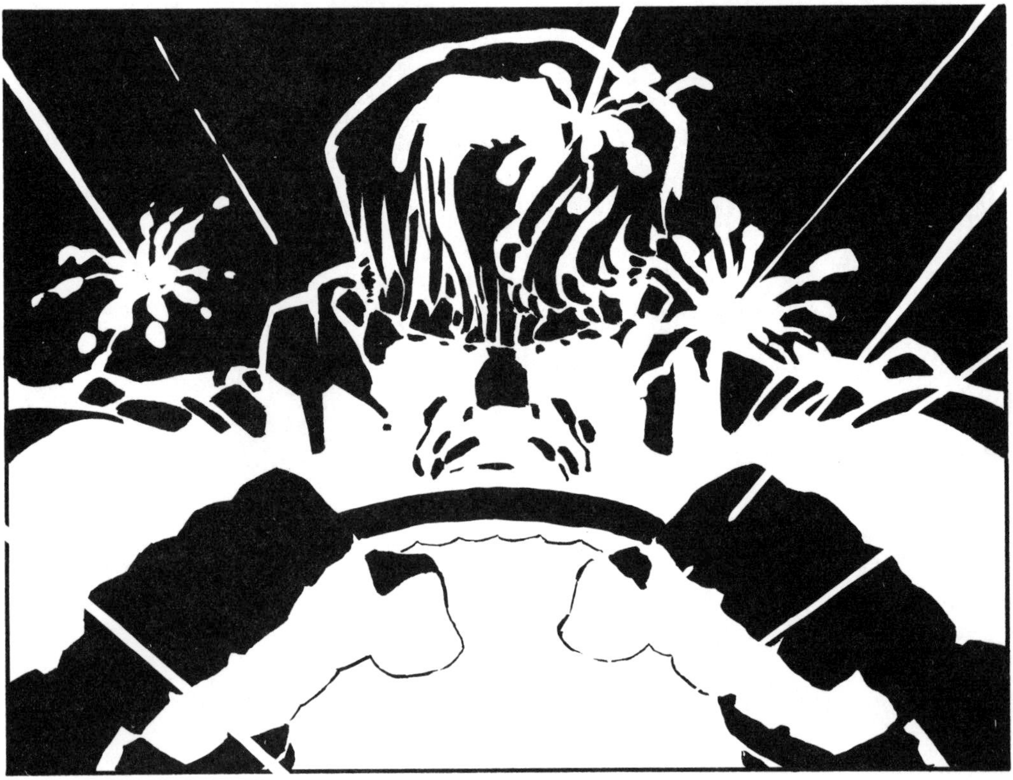

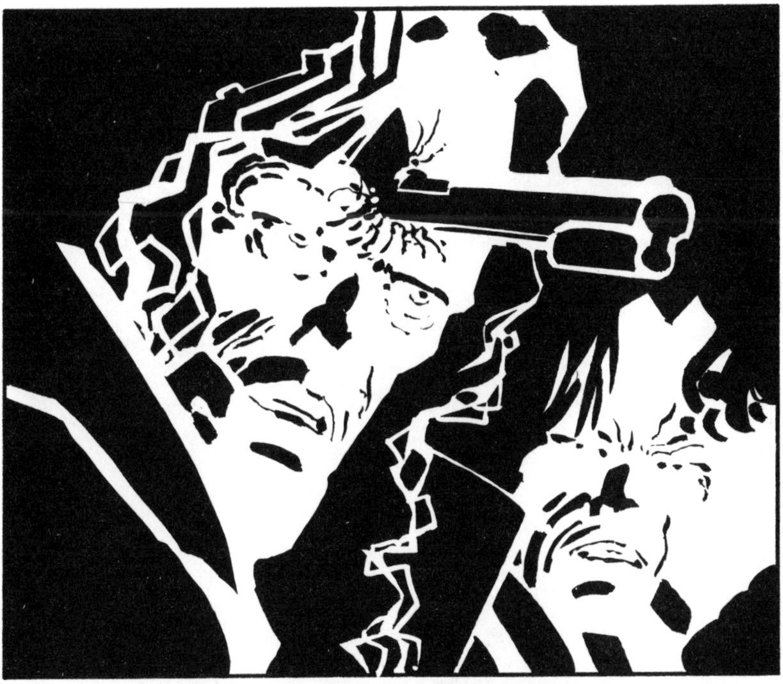

SETTLE DOWN. GET RATTLED AND YOU'RE NO USE TO ANYBODY. BREATHE STEADY. BREATHE DEEP. ALL YOU NEED IS LUCK. A LOT OF LUCK. GREAT, BIG, FAT GOBS OF LUCK. AN ACT OF GOD WOULDN'T HURT A BIT.

I CAN'T STOP FOR GAS. I CAN'T STOP FOR ANYTHING. I CAN'T GET STOPPED FOR ANYTHING.

NOT WHILE I'M HAULING HUNDREDS OF POUNDS OF THE WRONG KIND OF MEAT.

NOT WITH THE PASSENGER I'VE GOT RIDING SHOTGUN.

MY FELLOW TRAVELER.

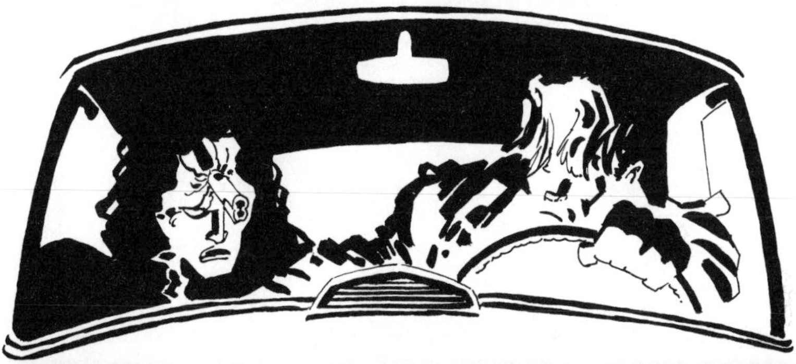

WE RAN OUT OF ROOM. WE WERE BARELY ABLE TO GET THE TRUNK TO STAY CLOSED AS IT WAS, WE'D PACKED IT SO TIGHT. TWO OF THE GIRLS HAD TO SIT ON THE LID BEFORE I COULD GET THE LOCK TO CATCH.

AND THERE WAS JACKIE-BOY, LEFT OVER.

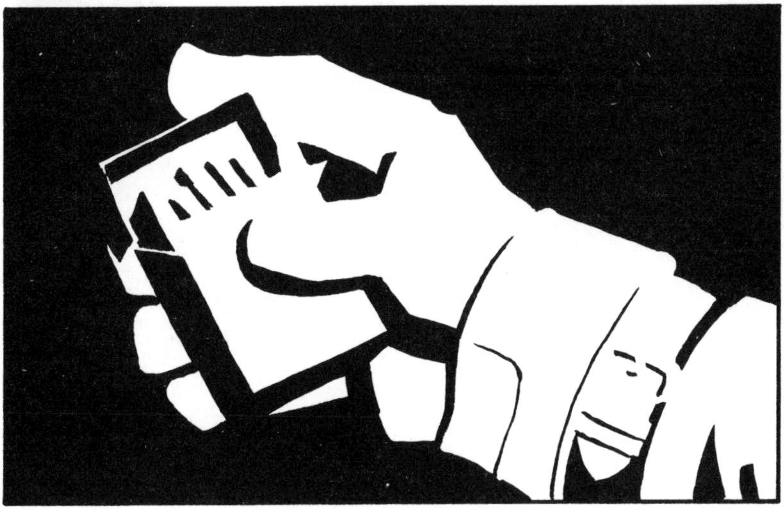

IF THIS HEAP WAS A FOUR-SEATER, WE COULD'VE TOSSED HIM IN THE BACK. BUT THERE WASN'T ANYTHING WE COULD DO BUT PILE HIM IN RIGHT NEXT TO ME, OUT WHERE ANYBODY WHO CARES TO LOOK WILL SEE HIM.

GO AHEAD. HELP YOURSELF TO ONE OF HIS CIGARETTES. IT'LL HELP.

GO AHEAD. IT'LL HELP.

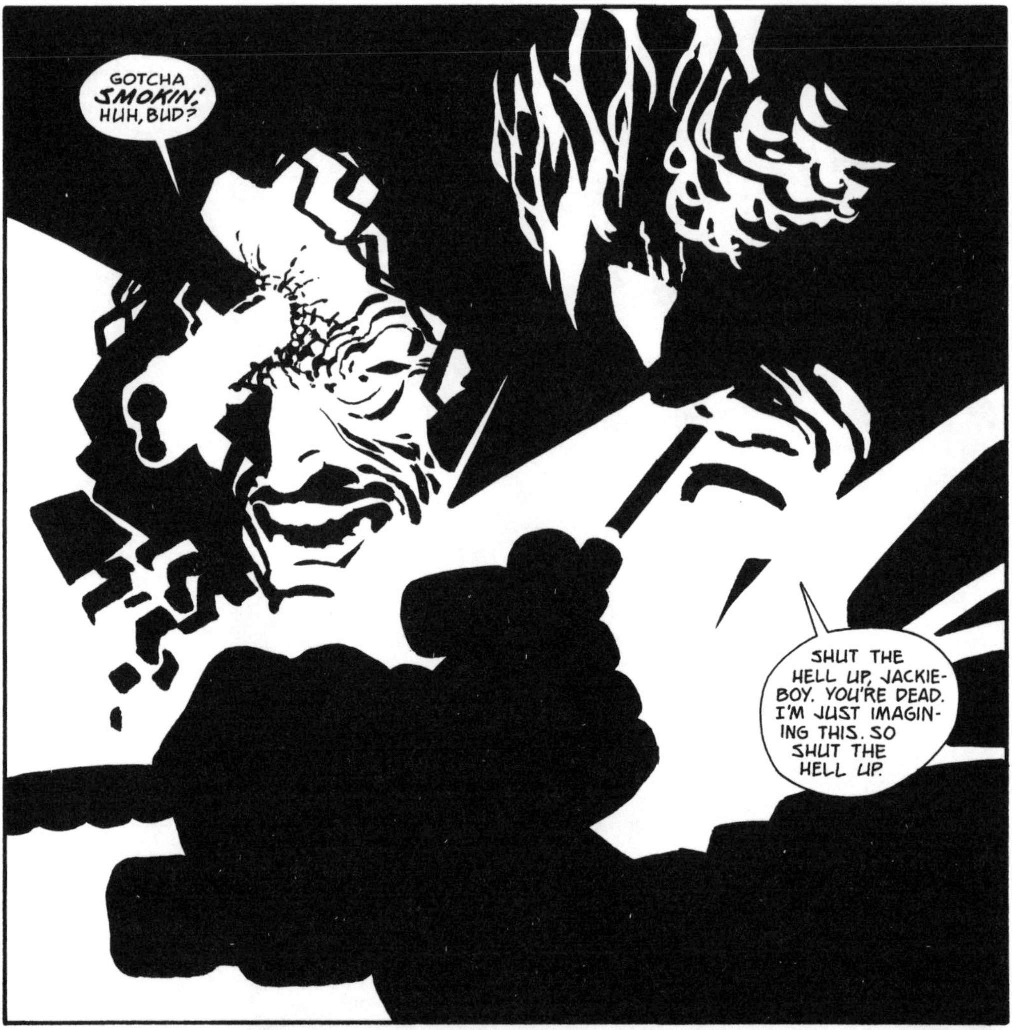
GOTCHA SMOKIN'. HUH, BUD?
SHUT THE HELL UP, JACKIE-BOY. YOU'RE DEAD. I'M JUST IMAGINING THIS. SO SHUT THE HELL UP.

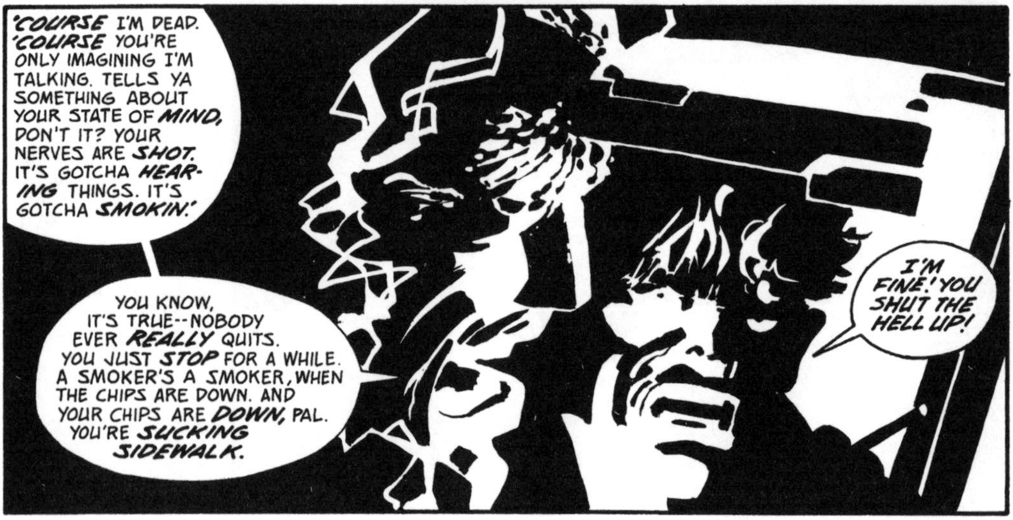
'COURSE I'M DEAD. 'COURSE YOU'RE ONLY IMAGINING I'M TALKING. TELLS YA SOMETHING ABOUT YOUR STATE OF MIND, DON'T IT? YOUR NERVES ARE SHOT. IT'S GOTCHA HEARING THINGS. IT'S GOTCHA SMOKIN'.
YOU KNOW, IT'S TRUE--NOBODY EVER REALLY QUITS. YOU JUST STOP FOR A WHILE. A SMOKER'S A SMOKER, WHEN THE CHIPS ARE DOWN. AND YOUR CHIPS ARE DOWN, PAL. YOU'RE SUCKING SIDEWALK.
I'M FINE! YOU SHUT THE HELL UP!

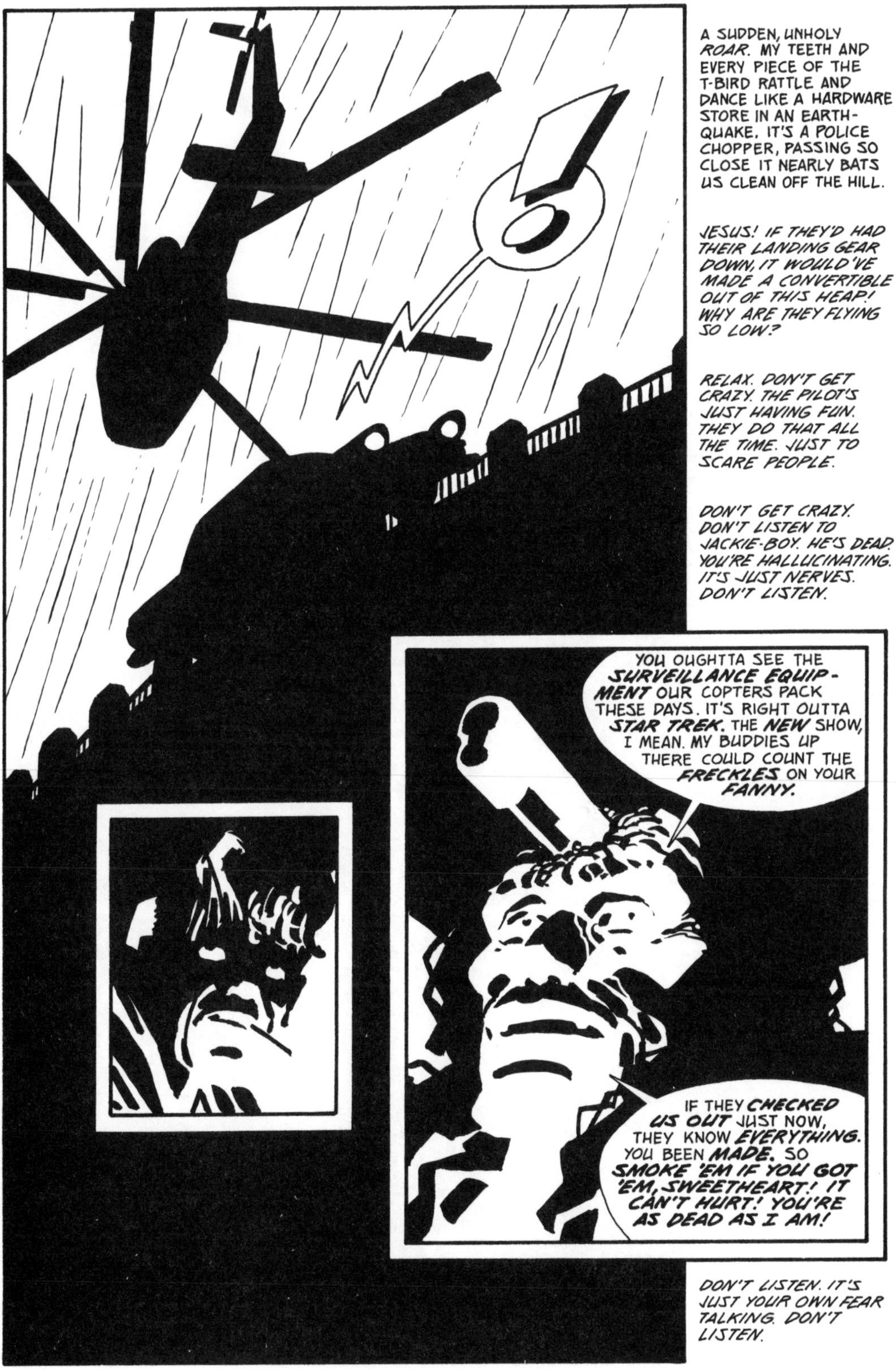
A SUDDEN, UNHOLY ROAR. MY TEETH AND EVERY PIECE OF THE T-BIRD RATTLE AND DANCE LIKE A HARDWARE STORE IN AN EARTH-QUAKE. IT'S A POLICE CHOPPER, PASSING SO CLOSE IT NEARLY BATS US CLEAN OFF THE HILL.
JESUS! IF THEY'D HAD THEIR LANDING GEAR DOWN, IT WOULD'VE MADE A CONVERTIBLE OUT OF THIS HEAP! WHY ARE THEY FLYING SO LOW?
RELAX. DON'T GET CRAZY. THE PILOT'S JUST HAVING FUN. THEY DO THAT ALL THE TIME. JUST TO SCARE PEOPLE.
DON'T GET CRAZY. DON'T LISTEN TO JACKIE-BOY. HE'S DEAD. YOU'RE HALLUCINATING. IT'S JUST NERVES. DON'T LISTEN.
YOU OUGHTTA SEE THE SURVEILLANCE EQUIPMENT OUR COPTERS PACK THESE DAYS. IT'S RIGHT OUTTA STAR TREK. THE NEW SHOW, I MEAN. MY BUDDIES UP THERE COULD COUNT THE FRECKLES ON YOUR FANNY.
IF THEY CHECKED US OUT JUST NOW, THEY KNOW EVERYTHING. YOU BEEN MADE. SO SMOKE 'EM IF YOU GOT 'EM, SWEETHEART! IT CAN'T HURT! YOU'RE AS DEAD AS I AM!
DON'T LISTEN. IT'S JUST YOUR OWN FEAR TALKING. DON'T LISTEN.

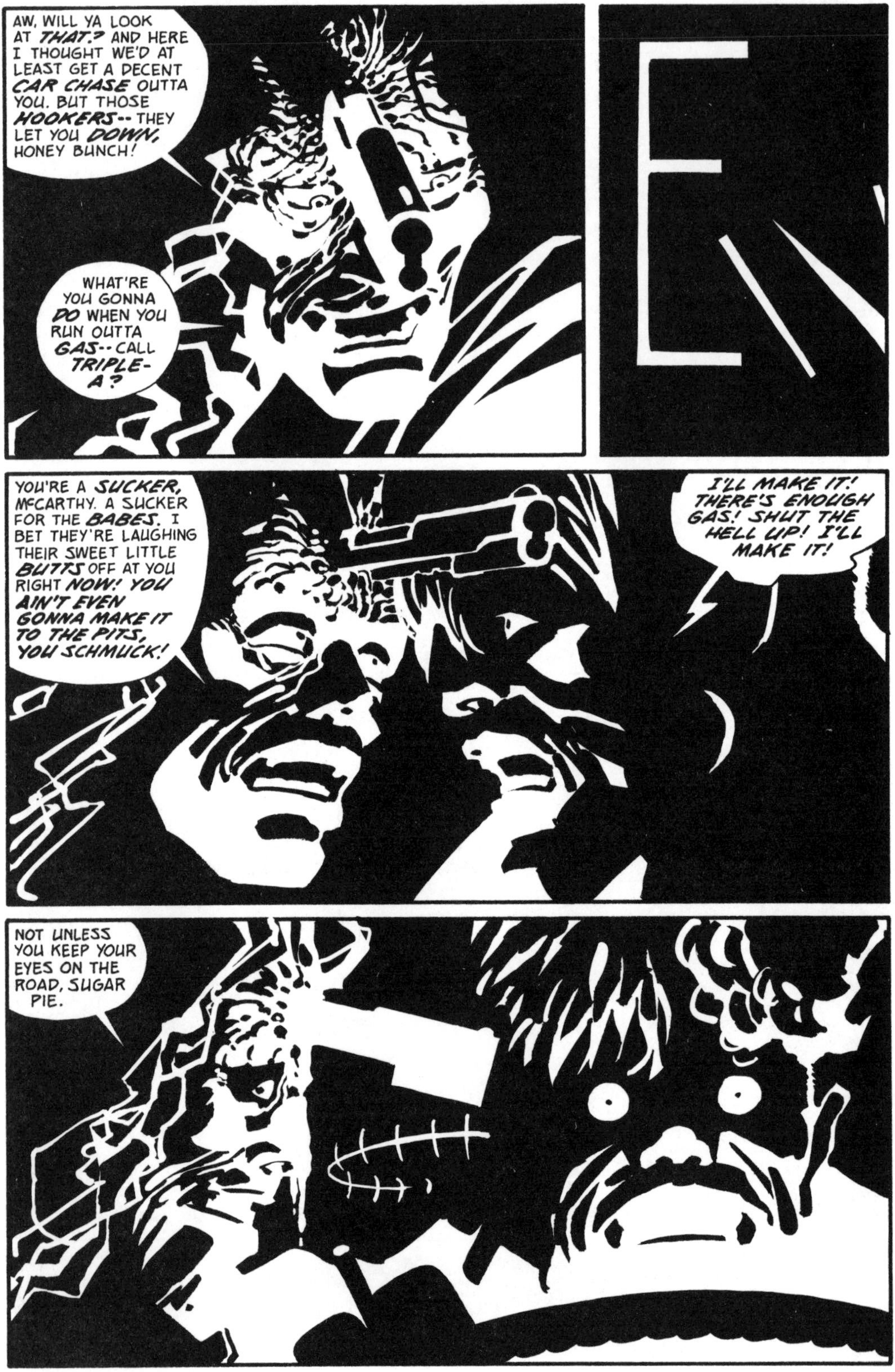
AW, WILL YA LOOK AT THAT? AND HERE I THOUGHT WE'D AT LEAST GET A DECENT CAR CHASE OUTTA YOU. BUT THOSE HOOKERS-- THEY LET YOU DOWN, HONEY BUNCH!
WHAT'RE YOU GONNA DO WHEN YOU RUN OUTTA GAS-- CALL TRIPLE-A?
YOU'RE A SUCKER, McCARTHY. A SUCKER FOR THE BABES. I BET THEY'RE LAUGHING THEIR SWEET LITTLE BUTTS OFF AT YOU RIGHT NOW! YOU AIN'T EVEN GONNA MAKE IT TO THE PITS, YOU SCHMUCK!
I'LL MAKE IT! THERE'S ENOUGH GAS! SHUT THE HELL UP! I'LL MAKE IT!
NOT UNLESS YOU KEEP YOUR EYES ON THE ROAD, SUGAR PIE.

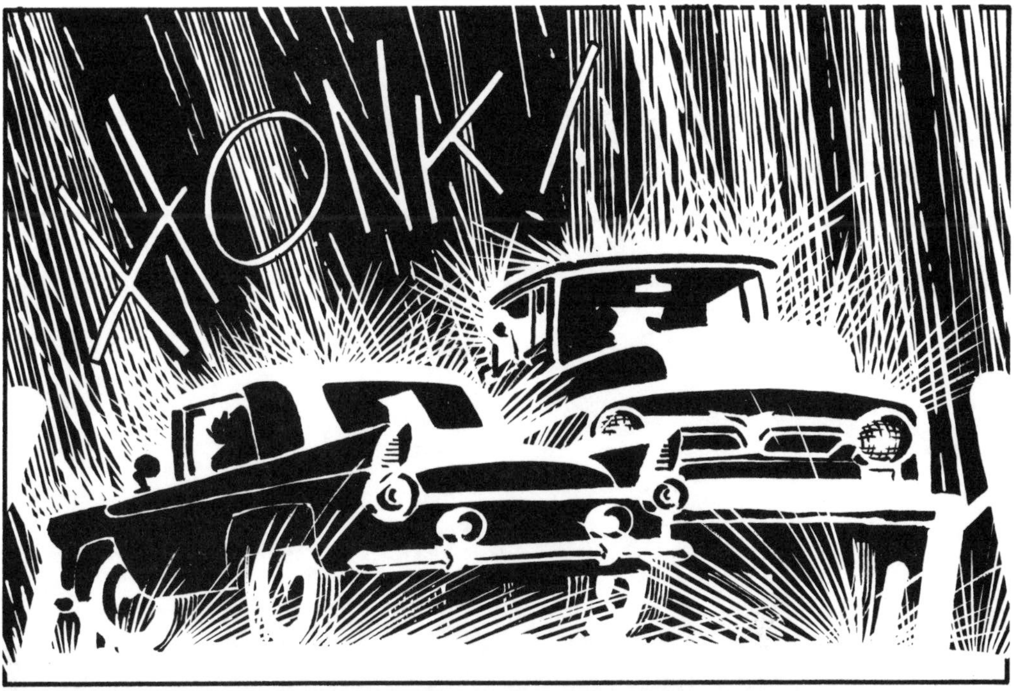
HONK!

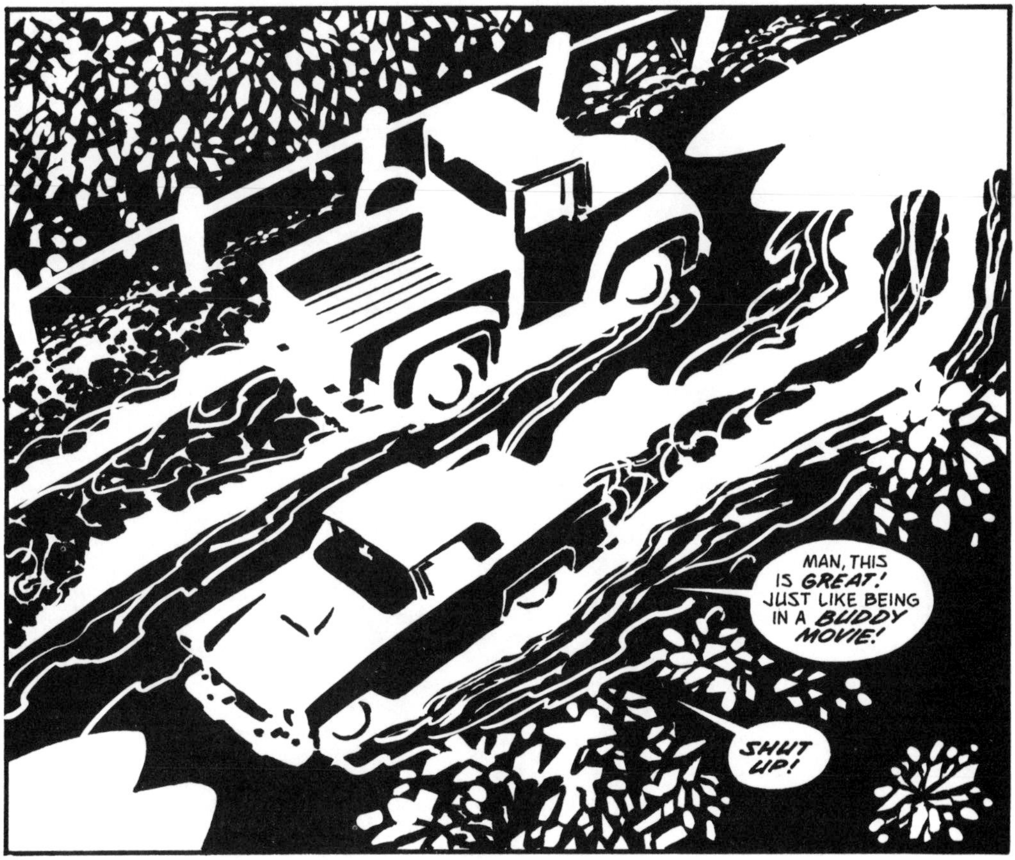
MAN, THIS IS GREAT! JUST LIKE BEING IN A BUDDY MOVIE!
SHUT UP!

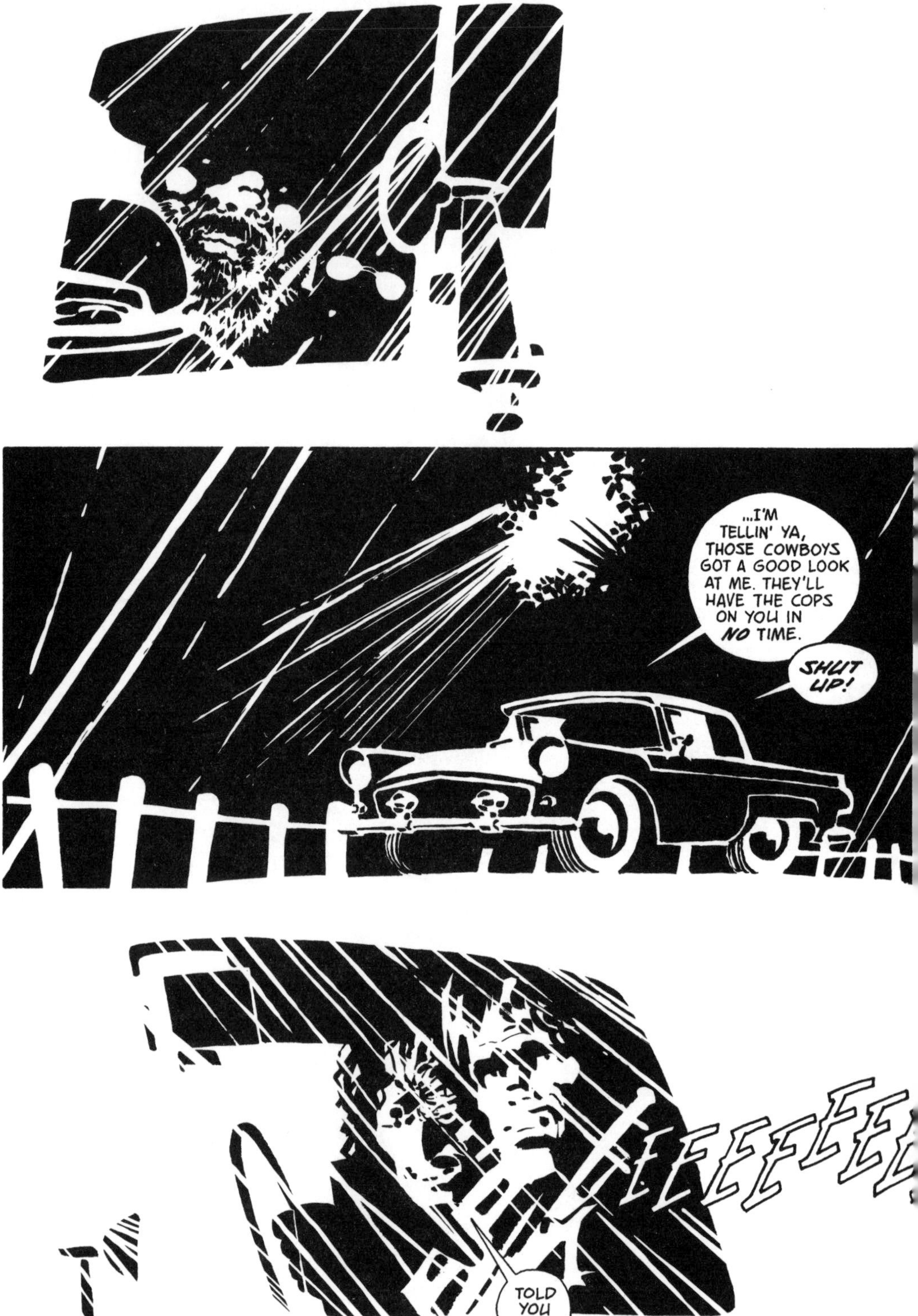

...I'M TELLIN' YA, THOSE COWBOYS GOT A GOOD LOOK AT ME. THEY'LL HAVE THE COPS ON YOU IN *NO* TIME.
SHUT UP!
TOLD YOU SO.

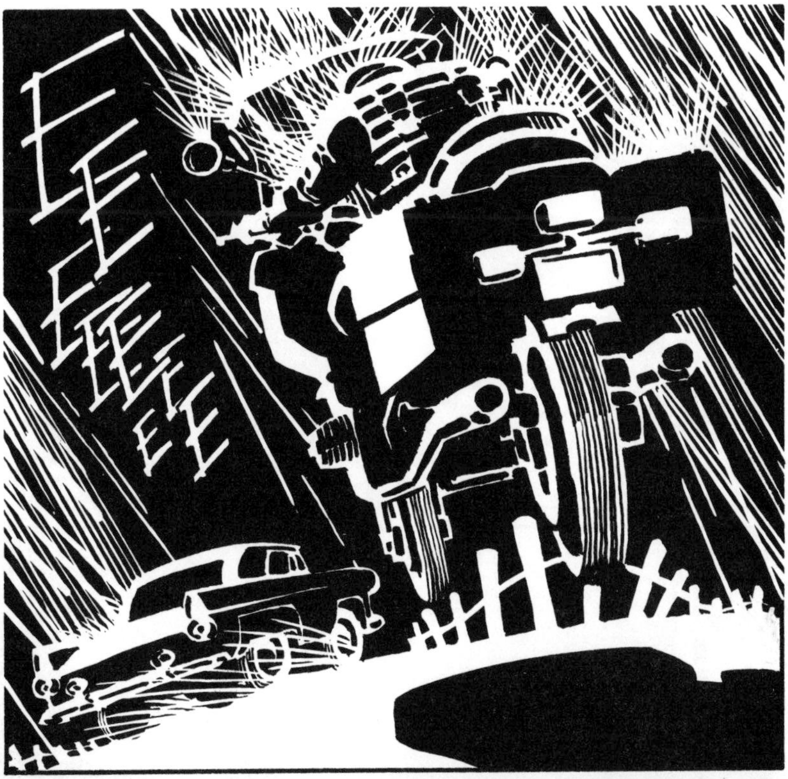

*"I MAY BE DEAD," HOWLS JACKIE-BOY, "I MAY BE DEAD, BUT YOU ARE **SCREWED!** YOU ARE **DOWN!** YOU ARE **OUT!** YOU ARE **FINISHED!** STICK A **FORK** IN IT! YOU'RE **COOKED!** YOU'RE **GONE!** YOU'RE **DEAD!** YOU'RE SWIRLING AROUND THE BOTTOM OF THE BOWL AND NOSE-DIVING DOWN THE **PIPE!** IT'S **OVER!** YOU'RE **FLUSHED!"***

THIS TIME I CAN'T BRING MYSELF TO TELL HIM TO SHUT UP. SURE HE'S AN ASSHOLE. SURE HE'S DEAD. SURE I'M JUST IMAGINING THAT HE'S TALKING TO ME. NONE OF THAT STOPS THE BASTARD FROM BEING ABSOLUTELY RIGHT ABOUT EVERYTHING HE'S SAYING.

THIS COP WANTS ME AND I DON'T HAVE A PRAYER OF OUT-RUNNING HIM. NOT IN THIS HEAP.

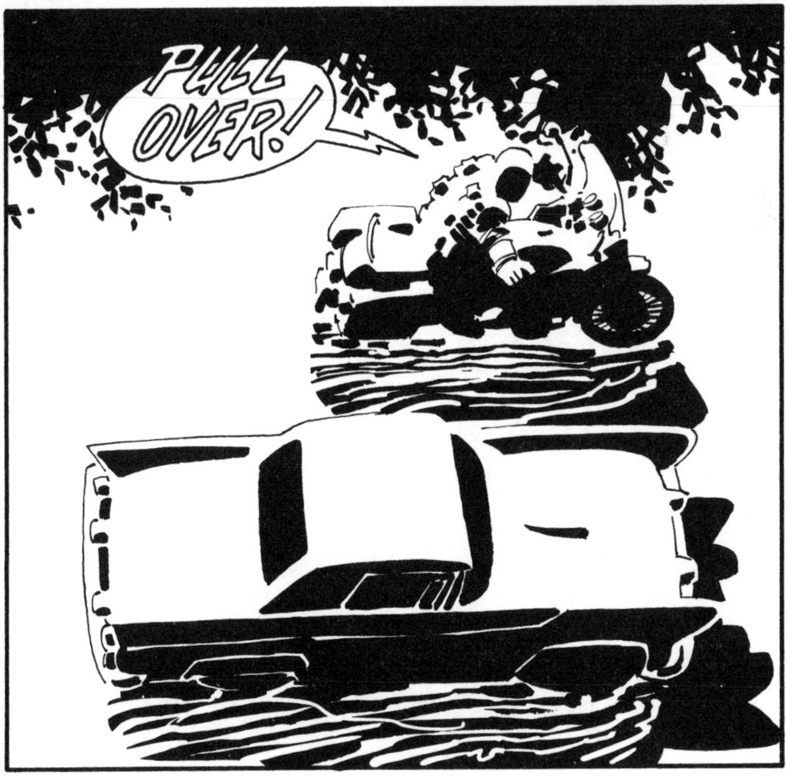
PULL OVER!

THE ONLY QUESTION LEFT IS WHETHER I'M GONNA KILL HIM OR NOT.

IT'S A TOUGH CALL. FOR ALL I KNOW, THIS COP IS AS HONEST AS THE DAY IS LONG. FOR ALL I KNOW HE'S A PRINCE AMONG MEN, A SAINT IN THE MAKING. OR MAYBE HE'S JUST A REGULAR GUY, A WORKING STIFF WITH A MORTGAGE AND A WIFE AND A PILE OF KIDS.

MY HANDS MOVE ALL ON THEIR OWN, SLIDING ONE OF MY GUNS TO MY LAP AND THUMBING BACK THE HAMMER.

I DON'T KNOW WHAT TO DO.

I DON'T KNOW WHAT TO DO.

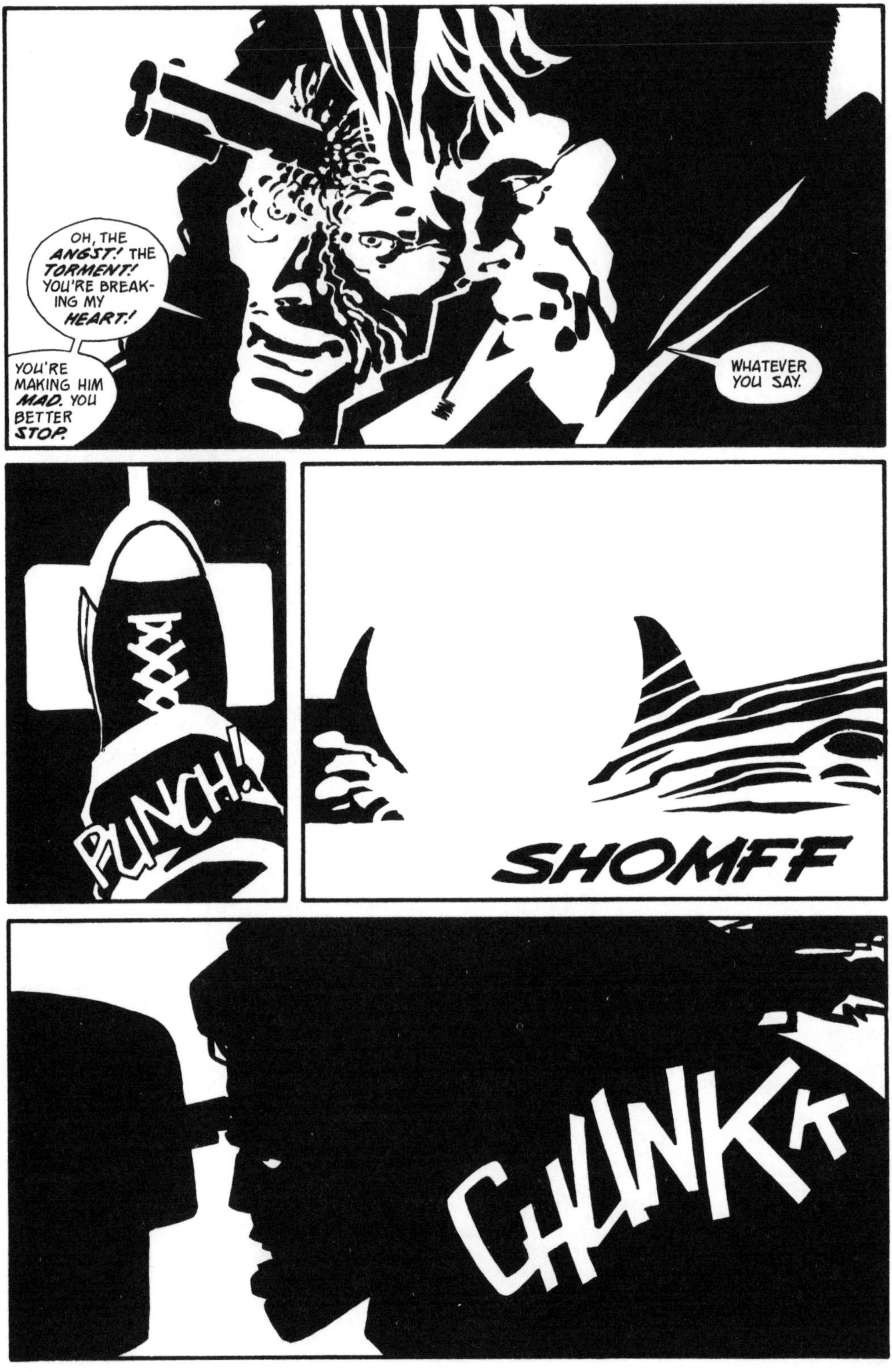
OH, THE ANGST! THE TORMENT! YOU'RE BREAKING MY HEART!
YOU'RE MAKING HIM MAD. YOU BETTER STOP.
WHATEVER YOU SAY.
PUNCH!
SHOMFF
CHUNK

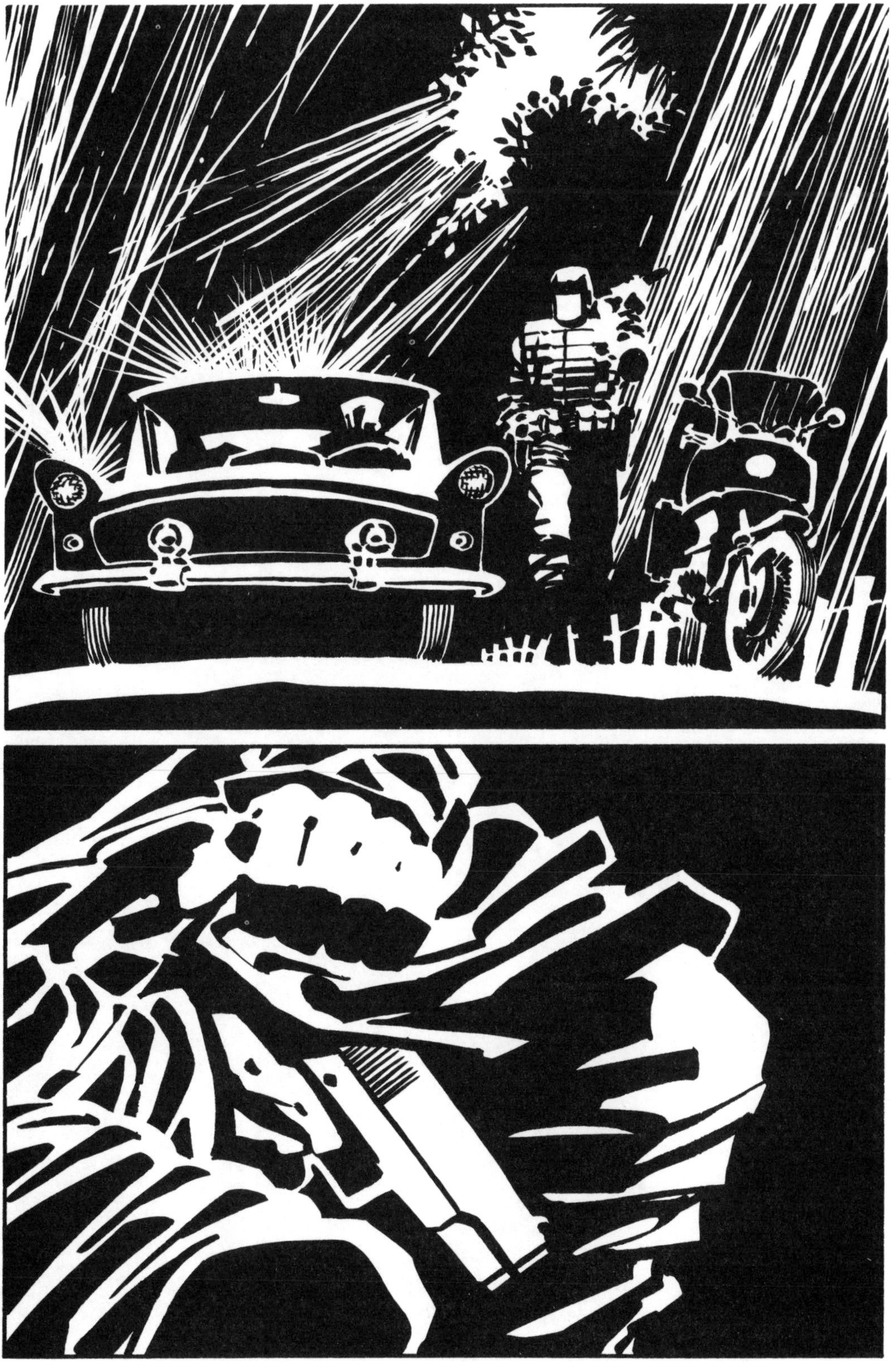

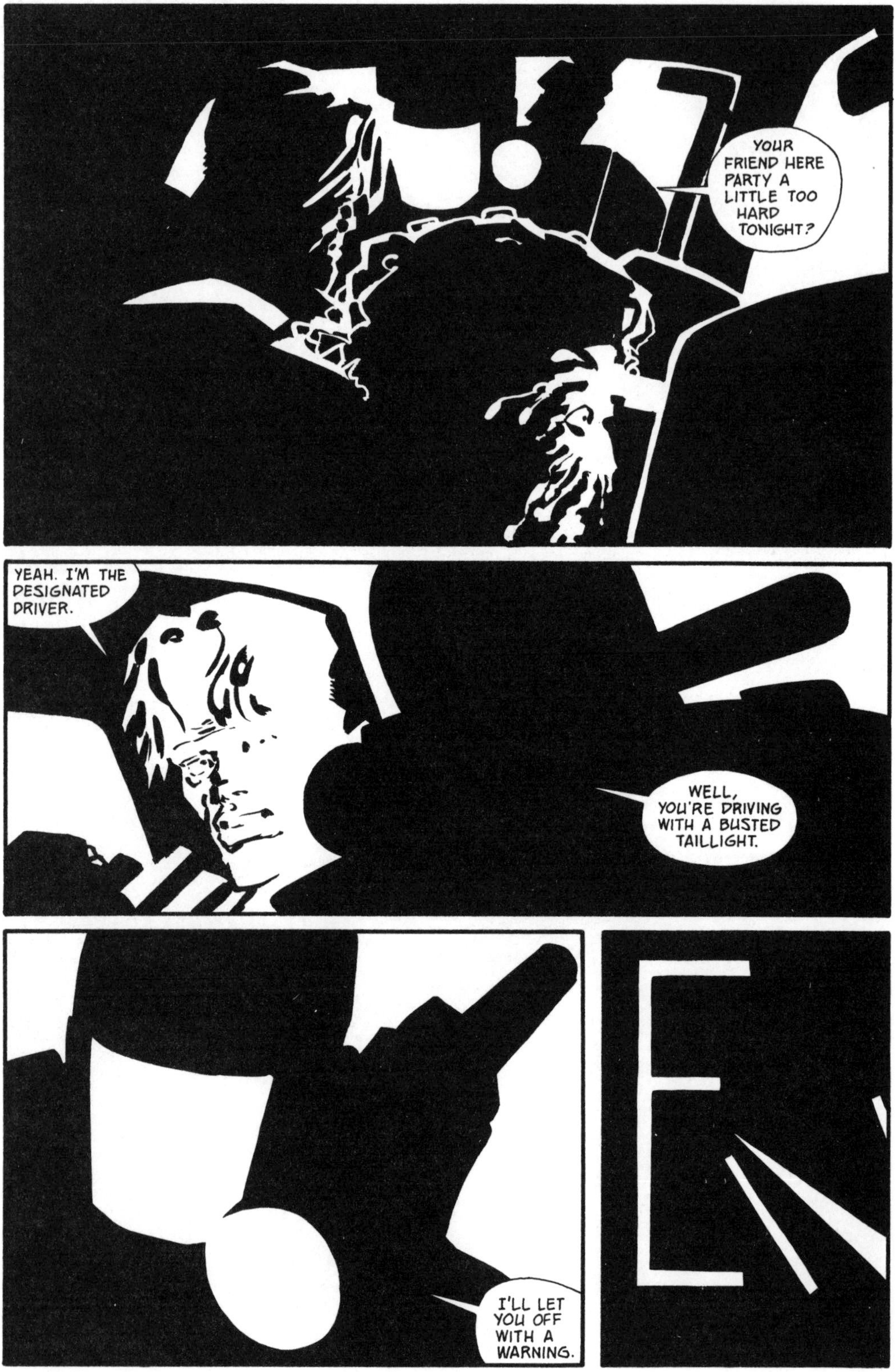
YOUR FRIEND HERE PARTY A LITTLE TOO HARD TONIGHT?
YEAH. I'M THE DESIGNATED DRIVER.
WELL, YOU'RE DRIVING WITH A BUSTED TAILLIGHT.
I'LL LET YOU OFF WITH A WARNING.

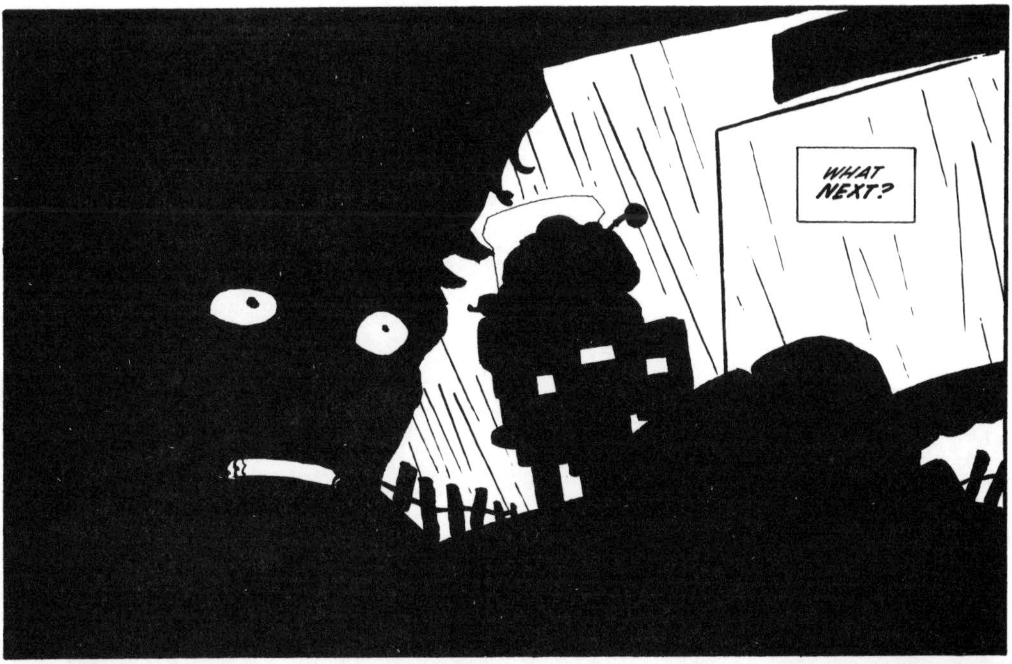
WHAT NEXT?

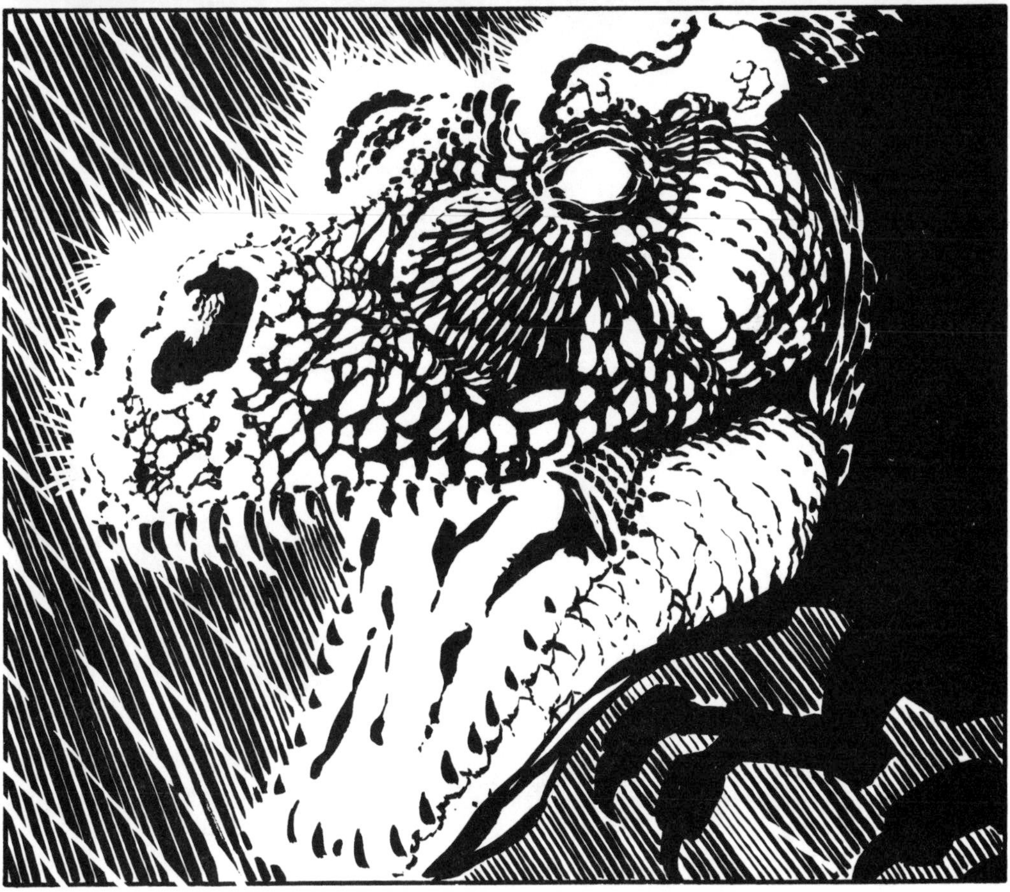

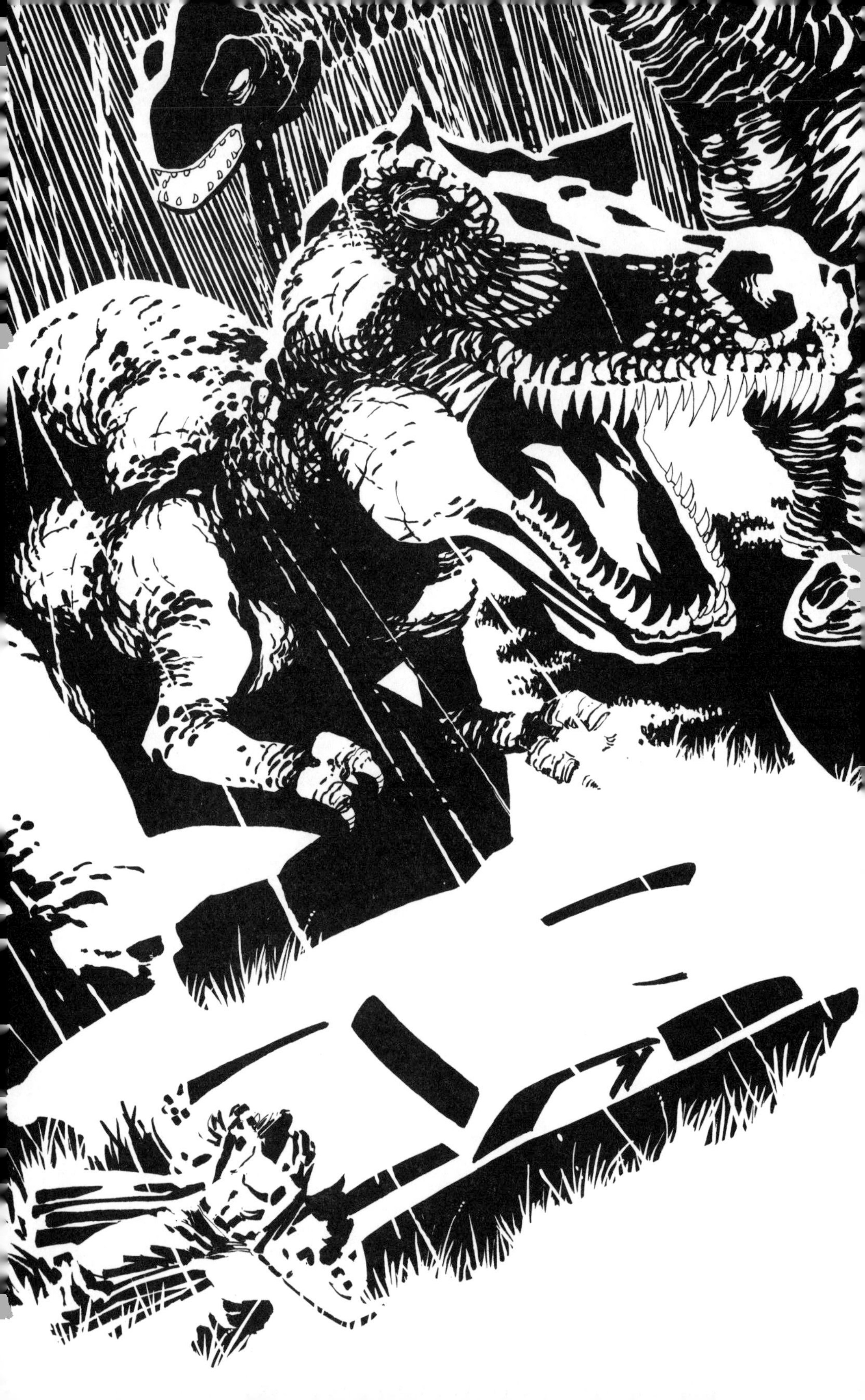

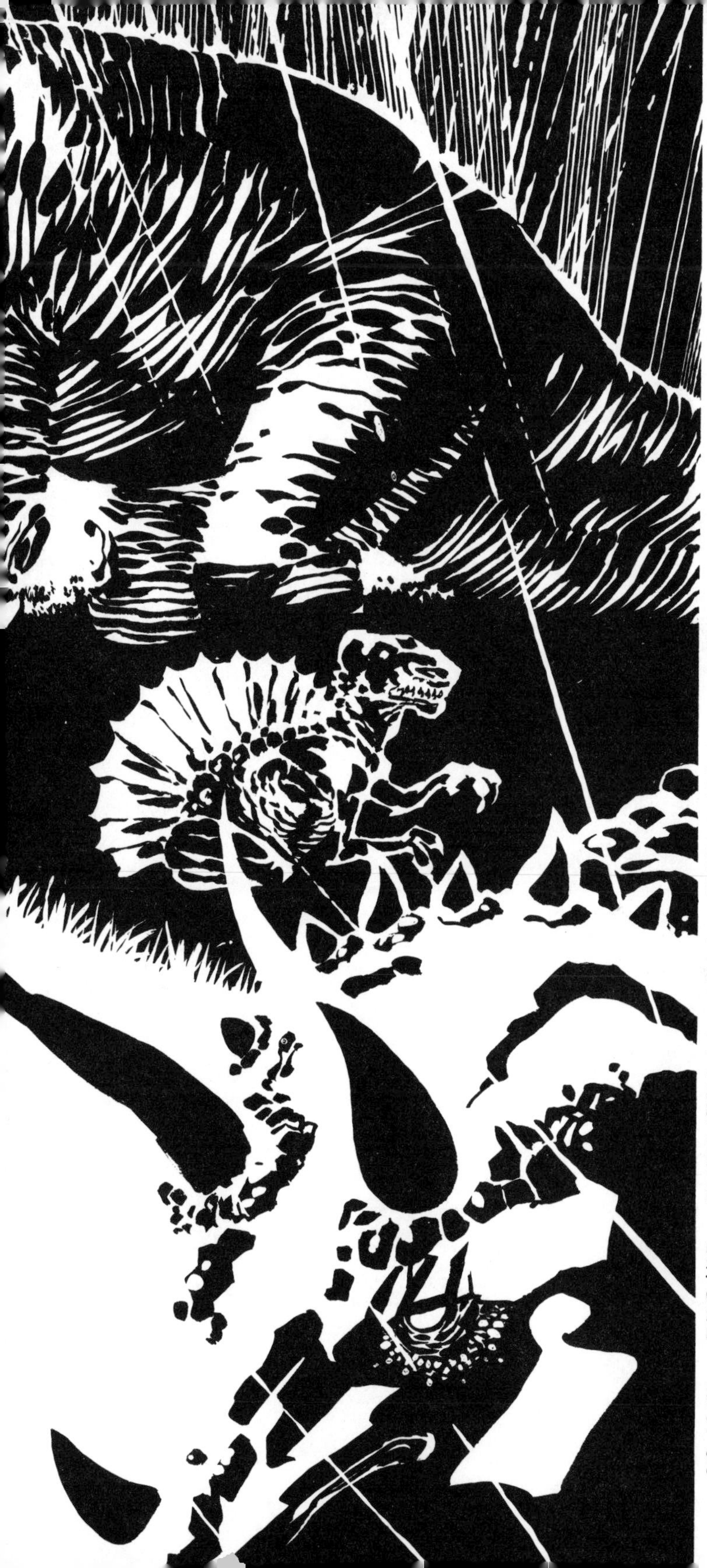

THE TANK GOES DRY A QUARTER MILE FROM THE PITS. I SHOVE THE T-BIRD THE REST OF THE WAY.

A COUPLE MILLION YEARS AGO, THE *SANTA YOLANDA TAR PITS* TRAPPED SOME OF THE DUMBER RESIDENTS OF THE NEIGHBORHOOD, PRESERVING THE SKELETONS OF *CAVE MEN* AND *WOOLLY MAMMOTHS* AND A *SABER-TOOTHED TIGER* OR TWO. MORE RECENTLY, THE COUNTY TURNED THE PITS INTO A *THEME PARK* AND FOUND OUT THE GOOP COULD SUCK IN *MONEY,* TOO. TURNS OUT THE *TOURISTS* DIDN'T TURN OUT IN DROVES TO SEE BIG BLACK *PUDDLES* AND A BUNCH OF OLD *BONES.* THEY TRIED DRESSING UP REAL ANIMALS, BUT WATCHING DRUGGED TIGERS STAGGER AROUND WEARING FALSE TEETH JUST MADE PEOPLE FEEL DEPRESSED.

THEN A BIG-BUDGET *DINOSAUR MOVIE* CAUSED A SENSATION, SO THE COUNTY DUMPED A FEW MILLION TAX DOLLARS MORE INTO THE PITS, PUTTING UP ALL THESE STATUES. BUSINESS PICKED UP JUST SWELL-- UNTIL A RAILING BROKE AND SOMEBODY'S GRANDMOTHER FELL IN AND HAD A HEART ATTACK BEFORE THEY COULD PULL HER OUT. A WANNA-BE PHOTOGRAPHER TOOK PICTURES. THE NEXT MORNING THAT THRASHING OLD WOMAN MADE THE FRONT PAGE OF EVERY NEWSPAPER IN THE COUNTRY. THERE WAS NOTHING LEFT TO DO BUT SWALLOW THE COST AND SHUT THE PLACE DOWN.

HIGH-SCHOOLERS SNEAK IN HERE ALL THE TIME WHEN THE WEATHER'S GOOD. IT'S NO TROUBLE FINDING A HOLE IN THE FENCE.

A FEW MINUTES MORE WORK AND IT'LL ALL BE OVER. I'LL CATCH A TRAIN OUT OF SACRED OAKS AND GO HOME AND CALL IT A NIGHT.

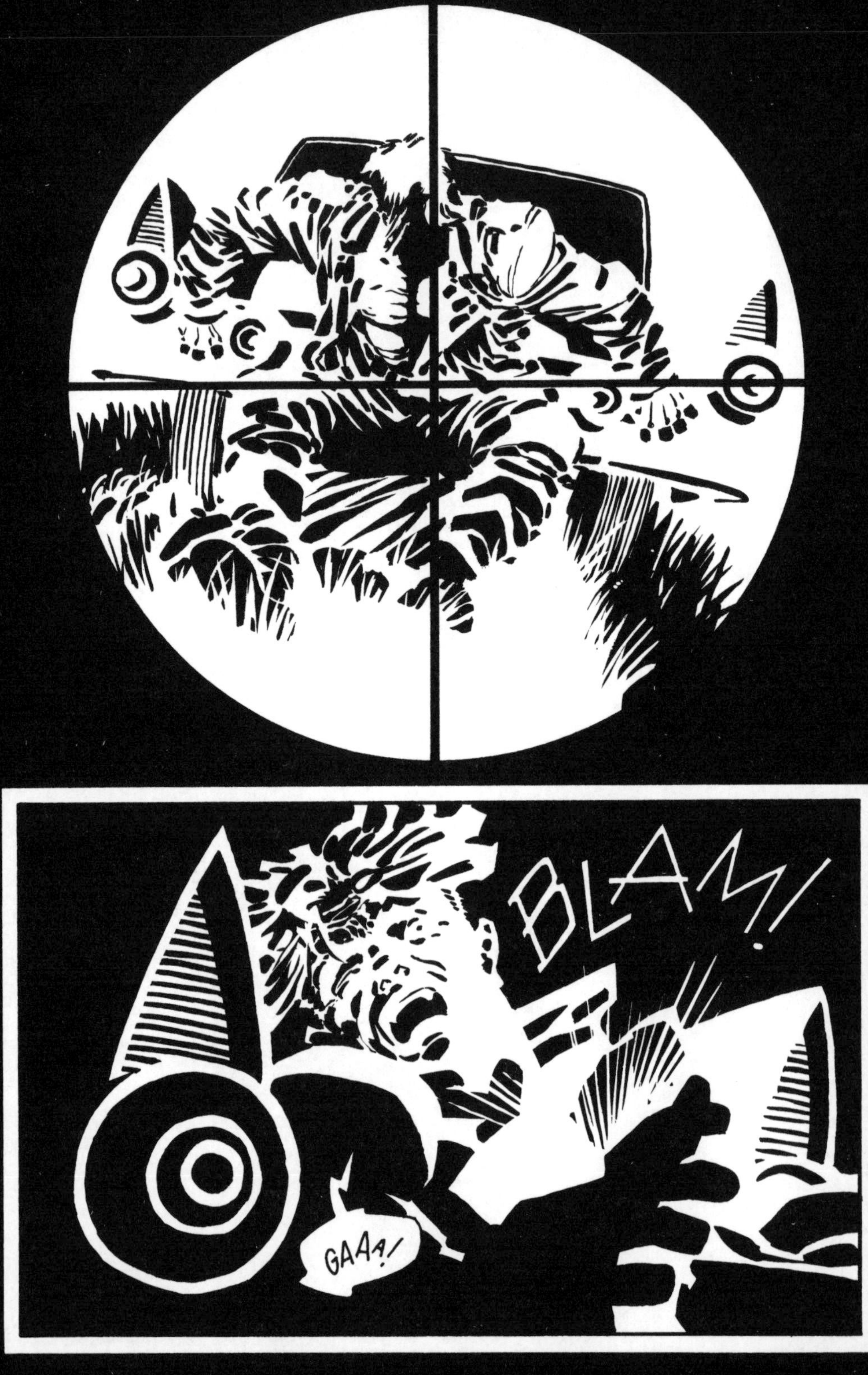
BLAM!
GAAA!

CHAPTER

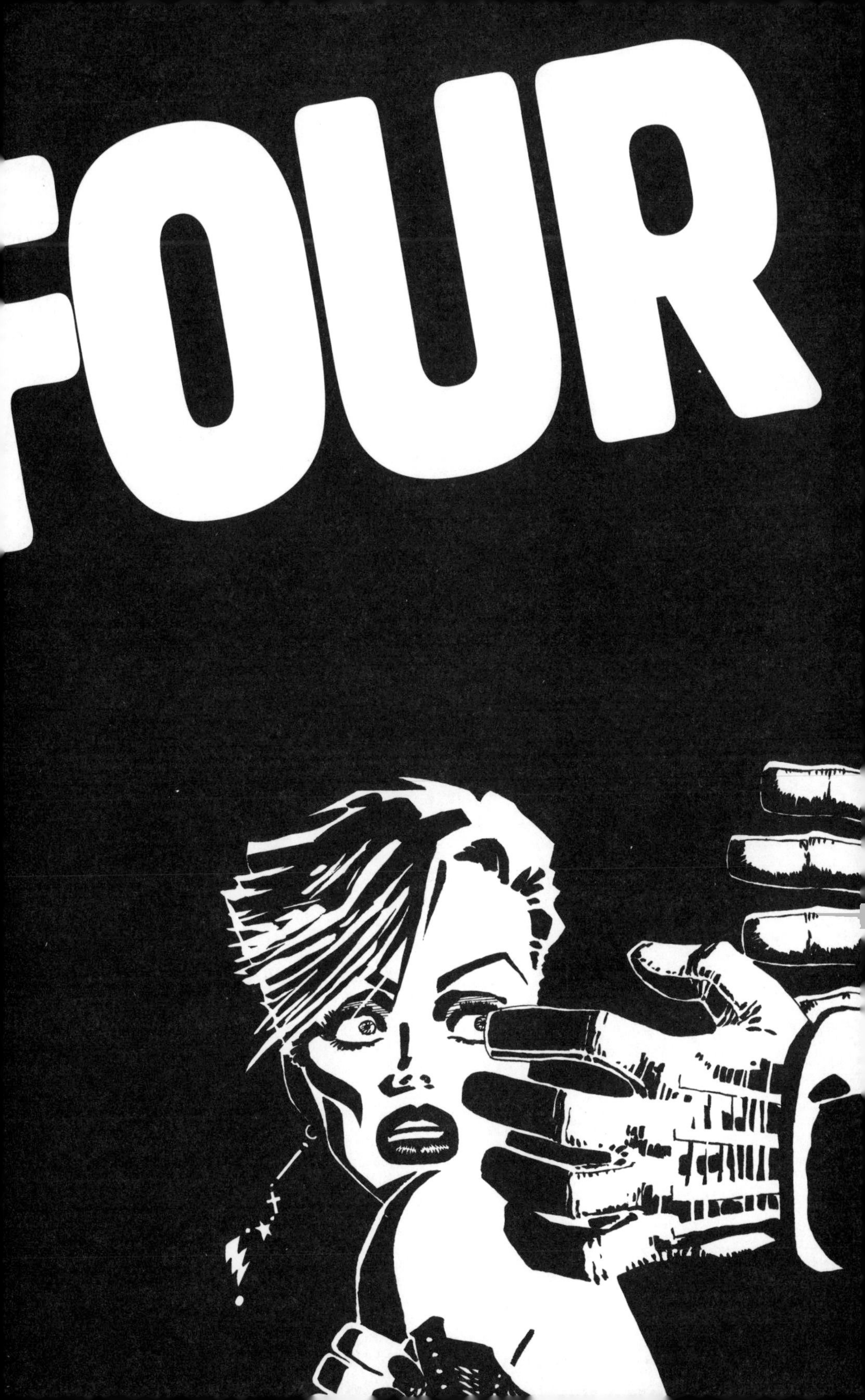
FOUR

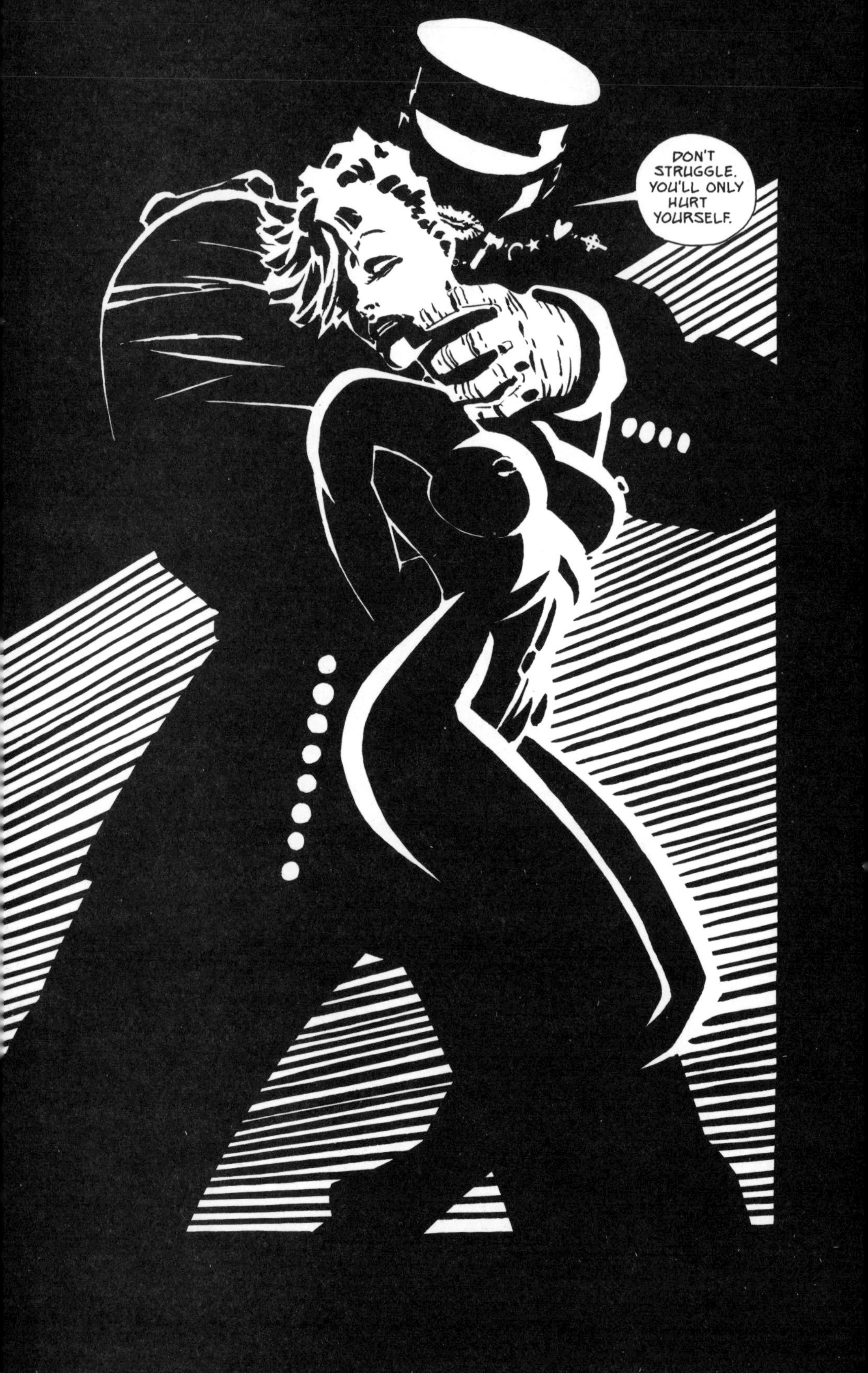
DON'T STRUGGLE. YOU'LL ONLY HURT YOURSELF.

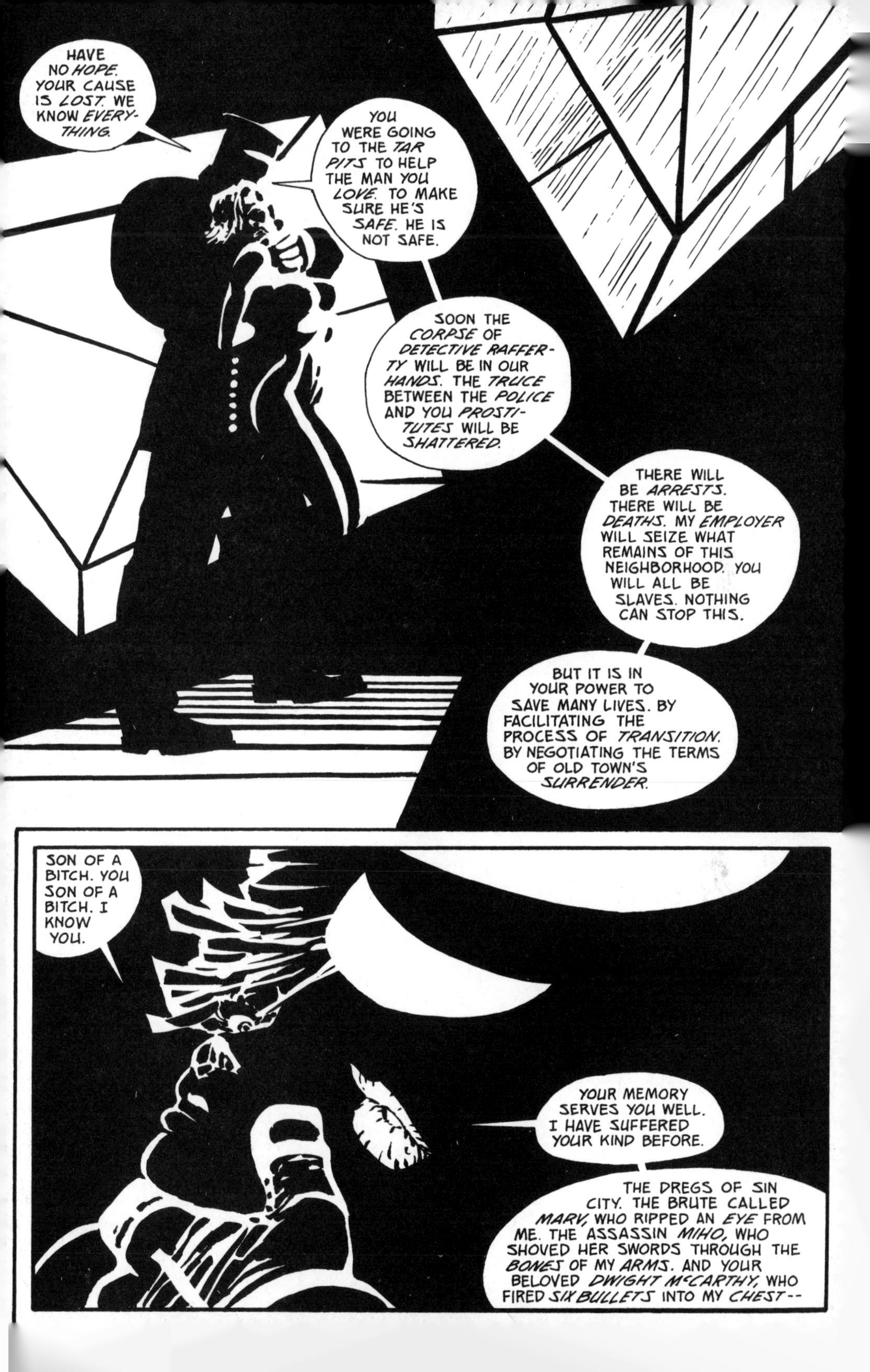
HAVE NO HOPE. YOUR CAUSE IS LOST. WE KNOW EVERYTHING.
YOU WERE GOING TO THE TAR PITS TO HELP THE MAN YOU LOVE. TO MAKE SURE HE'S SAFE. HE IS NOT SAFE.
SOON THE CORPSE OF DETECTIVE RAFFERTY WILL BE IN OUR HANDS. THE TRUCE BETWEEN THE POLICE AND YOU PROSTITUTES WILL BE SHATTERED.
THERE WILL BE ARRESTS. THERE WILL BE DEATHS. MY EMPLOYER WILL SEIZE WHAT REMAINS OF THIS NEIGHBORHOOD. YOU WILL ALL BE SLAVES. NOTHING CAN STOP THIS.
BUT IT IS IN YOUR POWER TO SAVE MANY LIVES. BY FACILITATING THE PROCESS OF TRANSITION. BY NEGOTIATING THE TERMS OF OLD TOWN'S SURRENDER.
SON OF A BITCH. YOU SON OF A BITCH. I KNOW YOU.
YOUR MEMORY SERVES YOU WELL. I HAVE SUFFERED YOUR KIND BEFORE.
THE DREGS OF SIN CITY. THE BRUTE CALLED MARV, WHO RIPPED AN EYE FROM ME. THE ASSASSIN MIHO, WHO SHOVED HER SWORDS THROUGH THE BONES OF MY ARMS. AND YOUR BELOVED DWIGHT McCARTHY, WHO FIRED SIX BULLETS INTO MY CHEST--

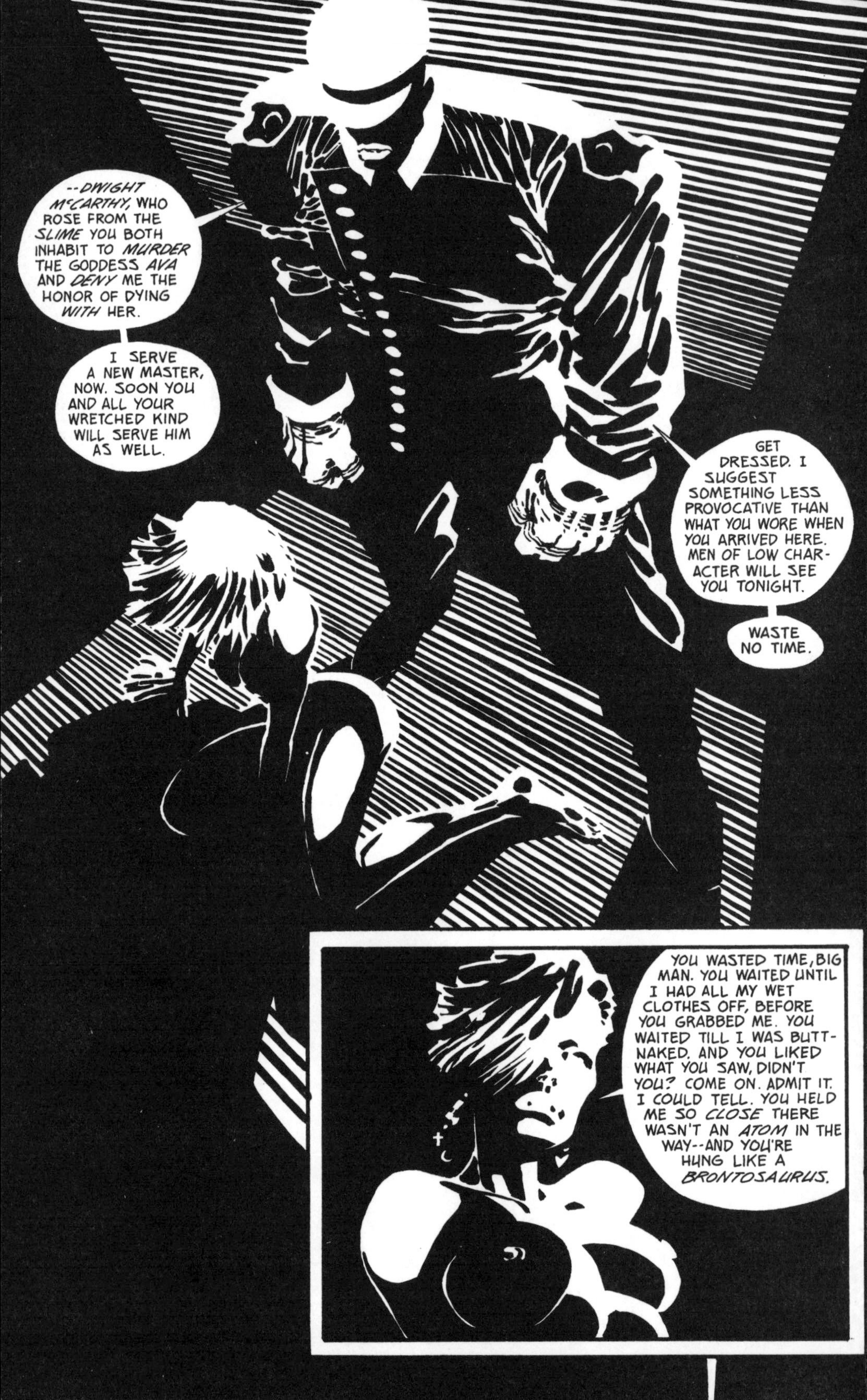
--DWIGHT McCARTHY, WHO ROSE FROM THE SLIME YOU BOTH INHABIT TO MURDER THE GODDESS AVA AND DENY ME THE HONOR OF DYING WITH HER.
I SERVE A NEW MASTER, NOW. SOON YOU AND ALL YOUR WRETCHED KIND WILL SERVE HIM AS WELL.
GET DRESSED. I SUGGEST SOMETHING LESS PROVOCATIVE THAN WHAT YOU WORE WHEN YOU ARRIVED HERE. MEN OF LOW CHARACTER WILL SEE YOU TONIGHT.
WASTE NO TIME.
YOU WASTED TIME, BIG MAN. YOU WAITED UNTIL I HAD ALL MY WET CLOTHES OFF, BEFORE YOU GRABBED ME. YOU WAITED TILL I WAS BUTT-NAKED. AND YOU LIKED WHAT YOU SAW, DIDN'T YOU? COME ON. ADMIT IT. I COULD TELL. YOU HELD ME SO CLOSE THERE WASN'T AN ATOM IN THE WAY--AND YOU'RE HUNG LIKE A BRONTOSAURUS.

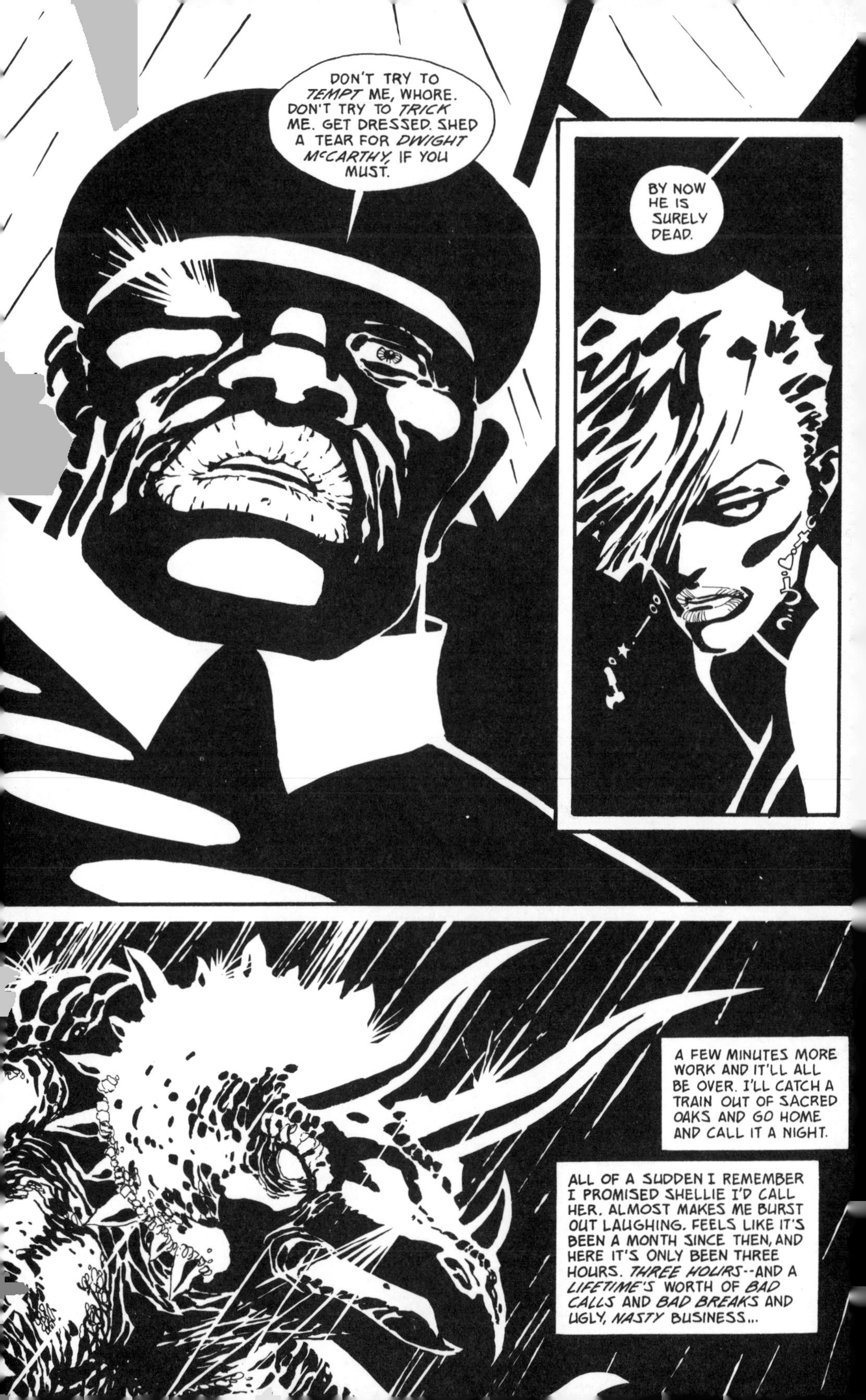
DON'T TRY TO TEMPT ME, WHORE. DON'T TRY TO TRICK ME. GET DRESSED. SHED A TEAR FOR DWIGHT McCARTHY, IF YOU MUST.
BY NOW HE IS SURELY DEAD.
A FEW MINUTES MORE WORK AND IT'LL ALL BE OVER. I'LL CATCH A TRAIN OUT OF SACRED OAKS AND GO HOME AND CALL IT A NIGHT.
ALL OF A SUDDEN I REMEMBER I PROMISED SHELLIE I'D CALL HER. ALMOST MAKES ME BURST OUT LAUGHING. FEELS LIKE IT'S BEEN A MONTH SINCE THEN, AND HERE IT'S ONLY BEEN THREE HOURS. THREE HOURS--AND A LIFETIME'S WORTH OF BAD CALLS AND BAD BREAKS AND UGLY, NASTY BUSINESS...

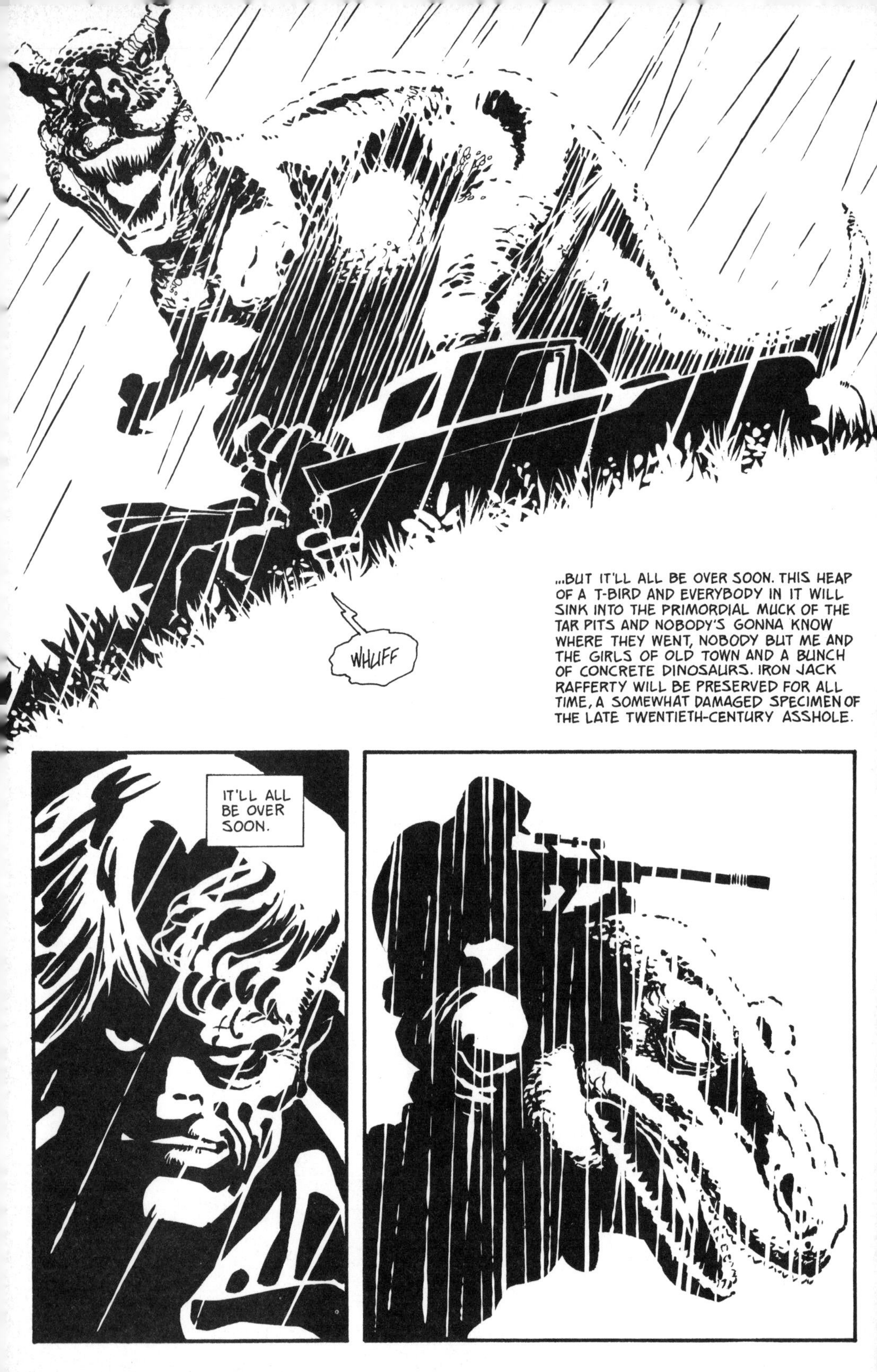
...BUT IT'LL ALL BE OVER SOON. THIS HEAP OF A T-BIRD AND EVERYBODY IN IT WILL SINK INTO THE PRIMORDIAL MUCK OF THE TAR PITS AND NOBODY'S GONNA KNOW WHERE THEY WENT, NOBODY BUT ME AND THE GIRLS OF OLD TOWN AND A BUNCH OF CONCRETE DINOSAURS. IRON JACK RAFFERTY WILL BE PRESERVED FOR ALL TIME, A SOMEWHAT DAMAGED SPECIMEN OF THE LATE TWENTIETH-CENTURY ASSHOLE.
WHUFF
IT'LL ALL BE OVER SOON.

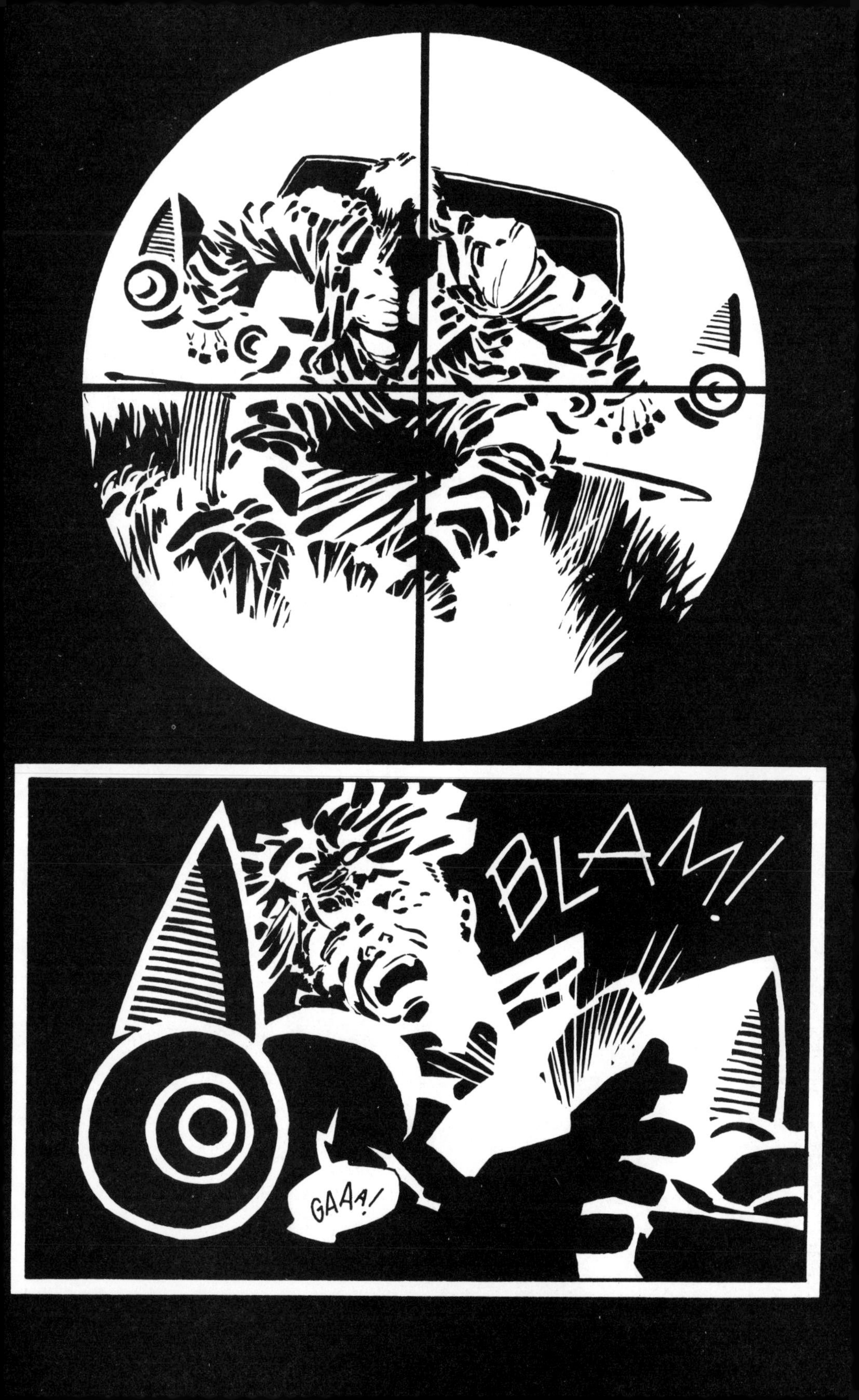
BLAM!
GAAA!

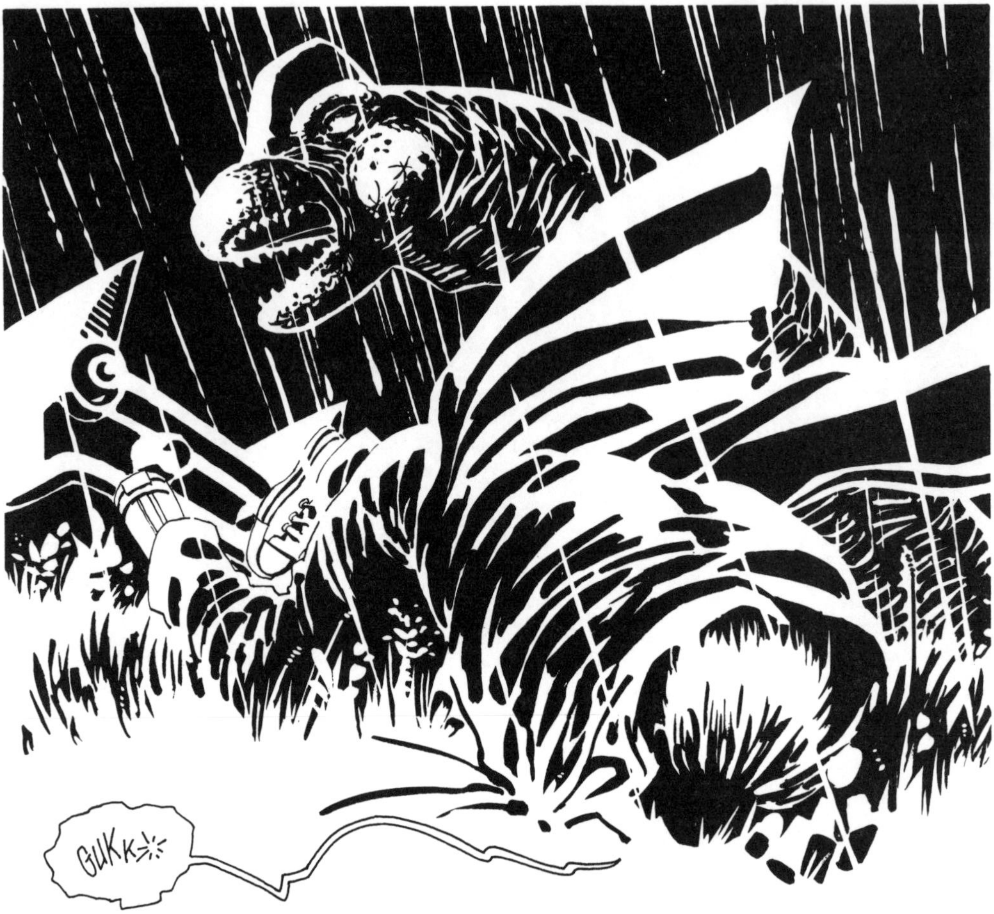
GUKK

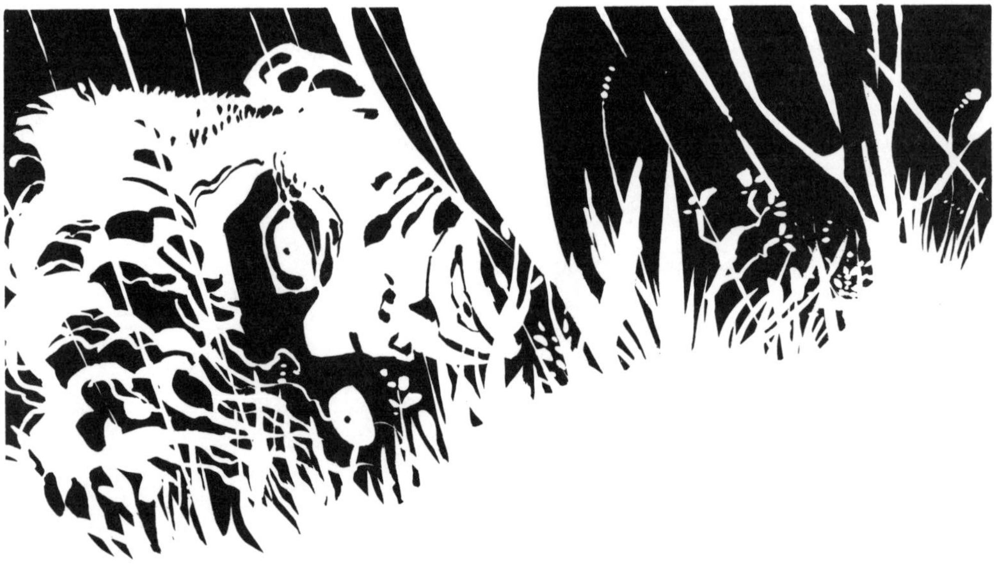

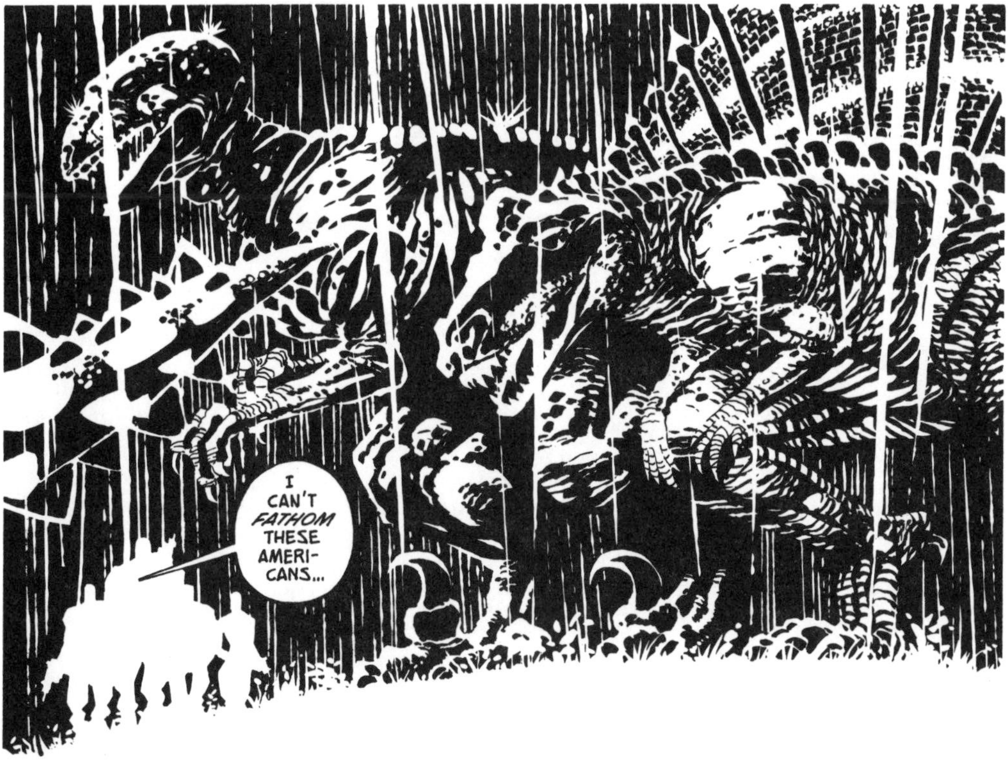
I CAN'T FATHOM THESE AMERI-CANS...

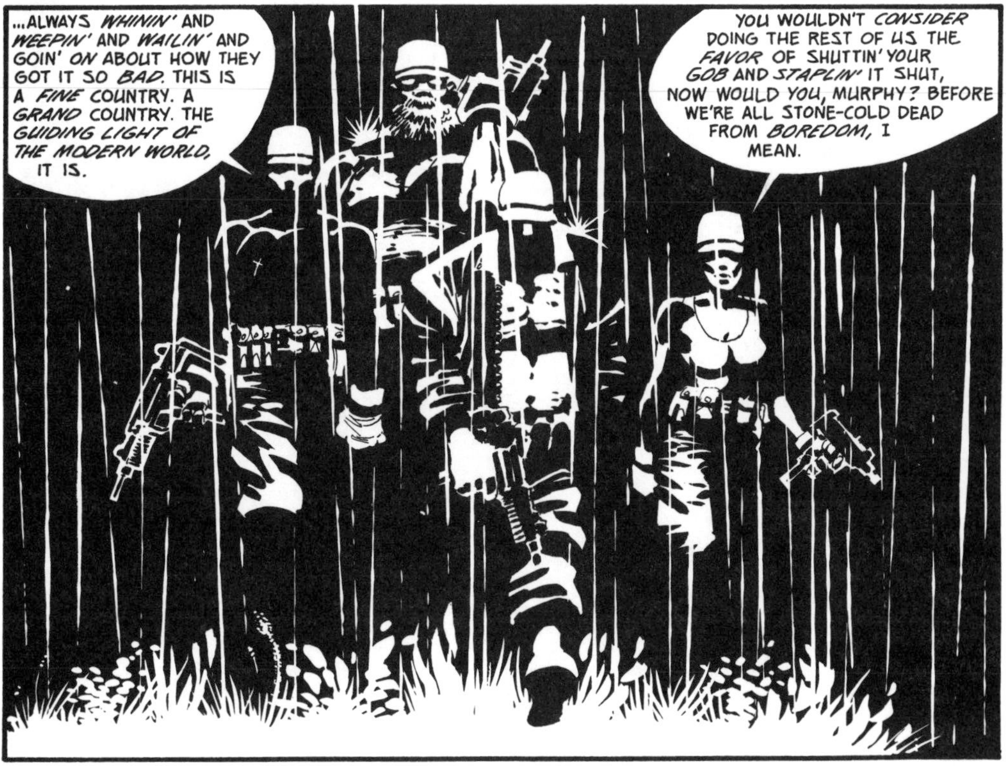
...ALWAYS WHININ' AND WEEPIN' AND WAILIN' AND GOIN' ON ABOUT HOW THEY GOT IT SO BAD. THIS IS A FINE COUNTRY. A GRAND COUNTRY. THE GUIDING LIGHT OF THE MODERN WORLD, IT IS.
YOU WOULDN'T CONSIDER DOING THE REST OF US THE FAVOR OF SHUTTIN' YOUR GOB AND STAPLIN' IT SHUT, NOW WOULD YOU, MURPHY? BEFORE WE'RE ALL STONE-COLD DEAD FROM BOREDOM, I MEAN.

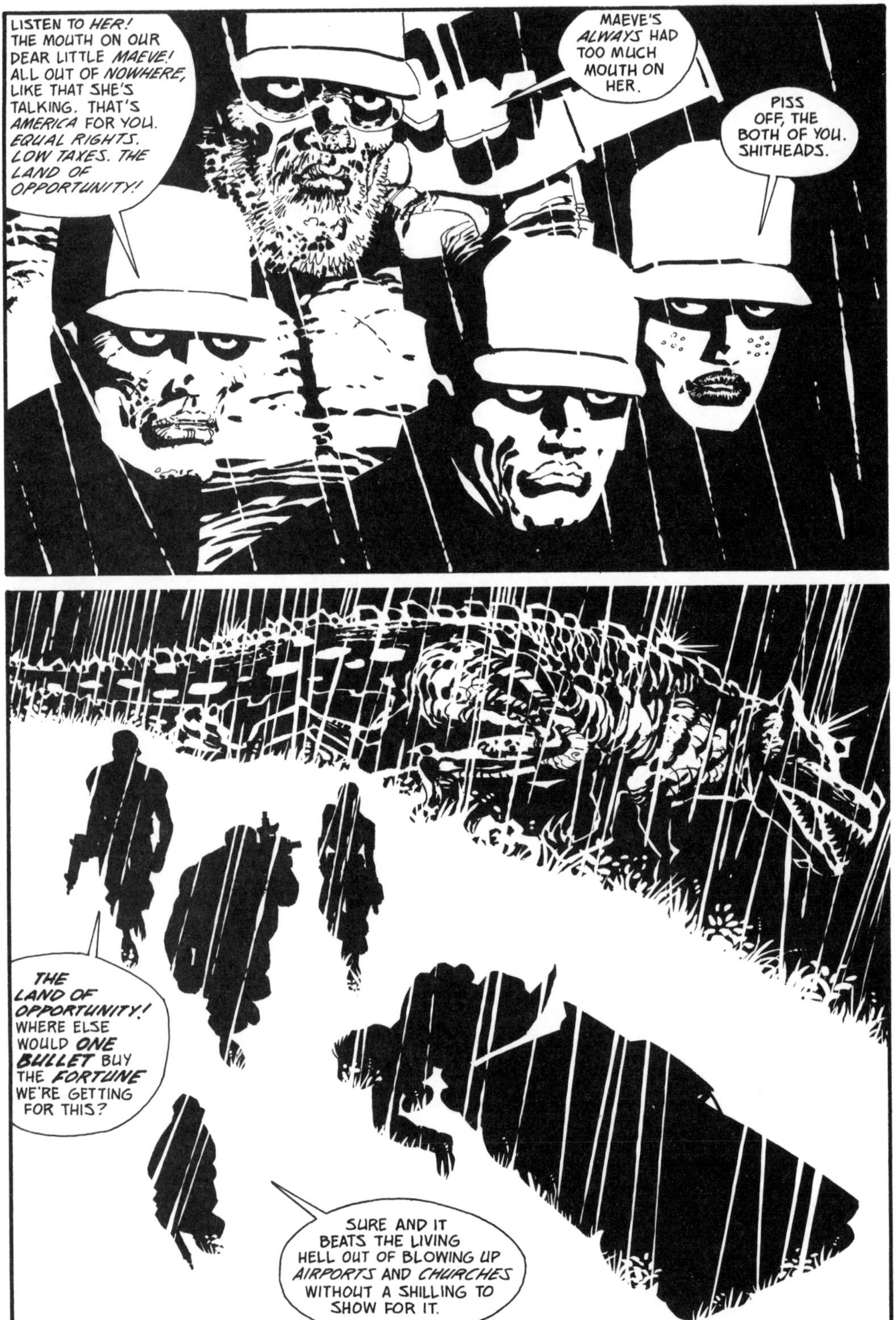
LISTEN TO HER! THE MOUTH ON OUR DEAR LITTLE MAEVE! ALL OUT OF NOWHERE, LIKE THAT SHE'S TALKING. THAT'S AMERICA FOR YOU. EQUAL RIGHTS. LOW TAXES. THE LAND OF OPPORTUNITY!
MAEVE'S ALWAYS HAD TOO MUCH MOUTH ON HER.
PISS OFF, THE BOTH OF YOU. SHITHEADS.
THE LAND OF OPPORTUNITY! WHERE ELSE WOULD ONE BULLET BUY THE FORTUNE WE'RE GETTING FOR THIS?
SURE AND IT BEATS THE LIVING HELL OUT OF BLOWING UP AIRPORTS AND CHURCHES WITHOUT A SHILLING TO SHOW FOR IT.

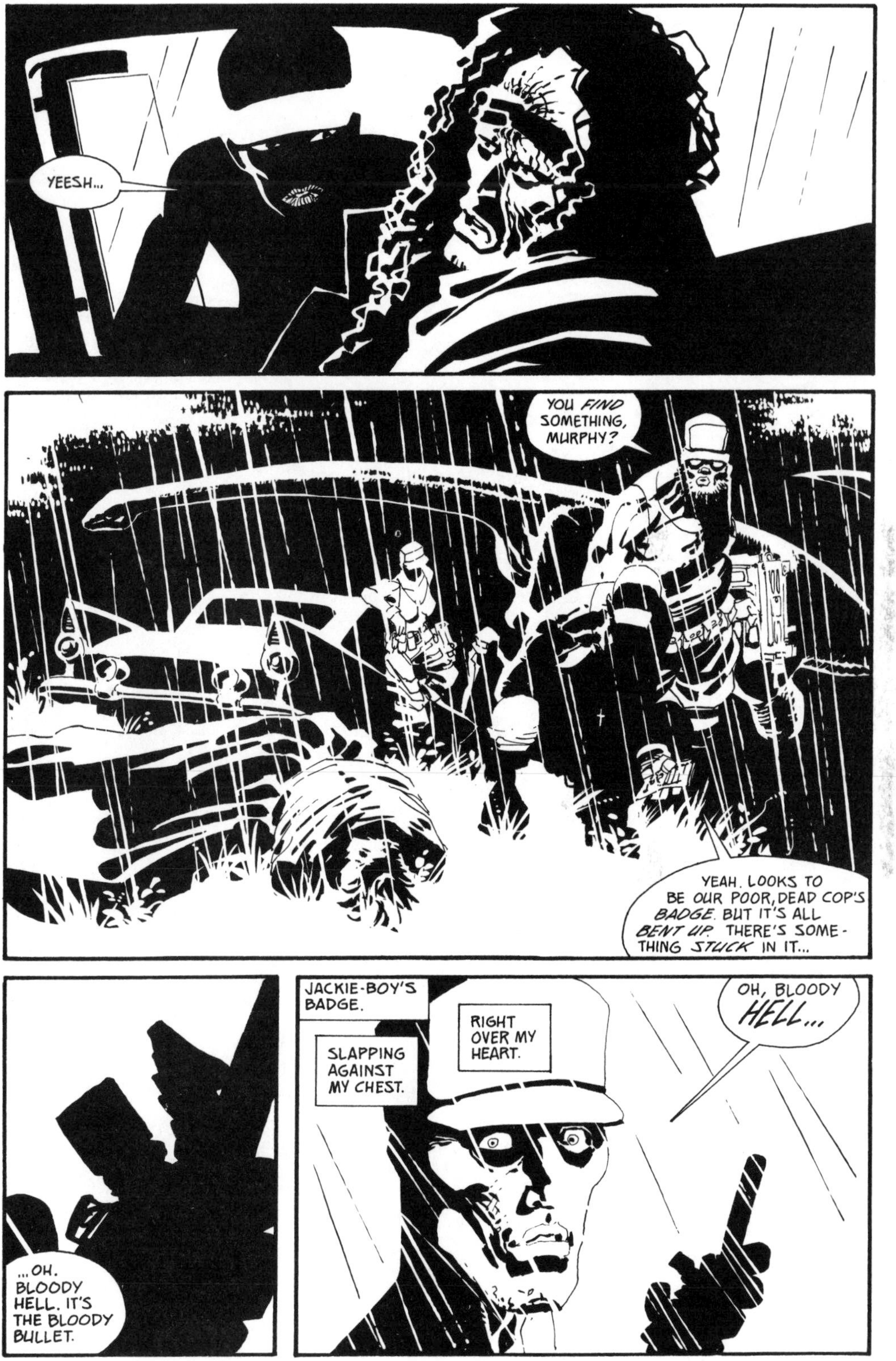
YEESH...
YOU FIND SOMETHING, MURPHY?
YEAH. LOOKS TO BE OUR POOR, DEAD COP'S BADGE. BUT IT'S ALL BENT UP. THERE'S SOMETHING STUCK IN IT...
...OH. BLOODY HELL. IT'S THE BLOODY BULLET.
JACKIE-BOY'S BADGE.
SLAPPING AGAINST MY CHEST.
RIGHT OVER MY HEART.
OH, BLOODY HELL...

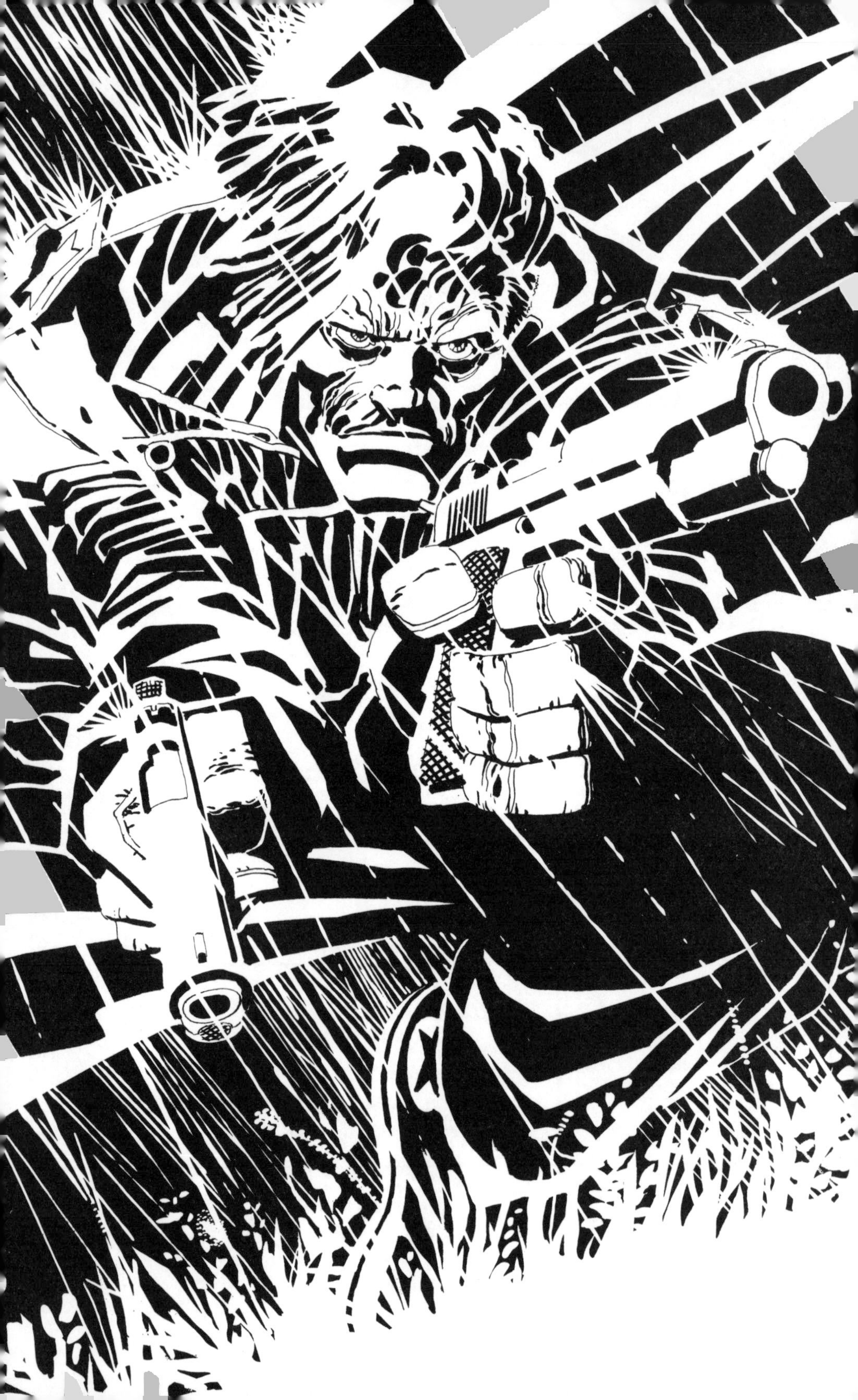

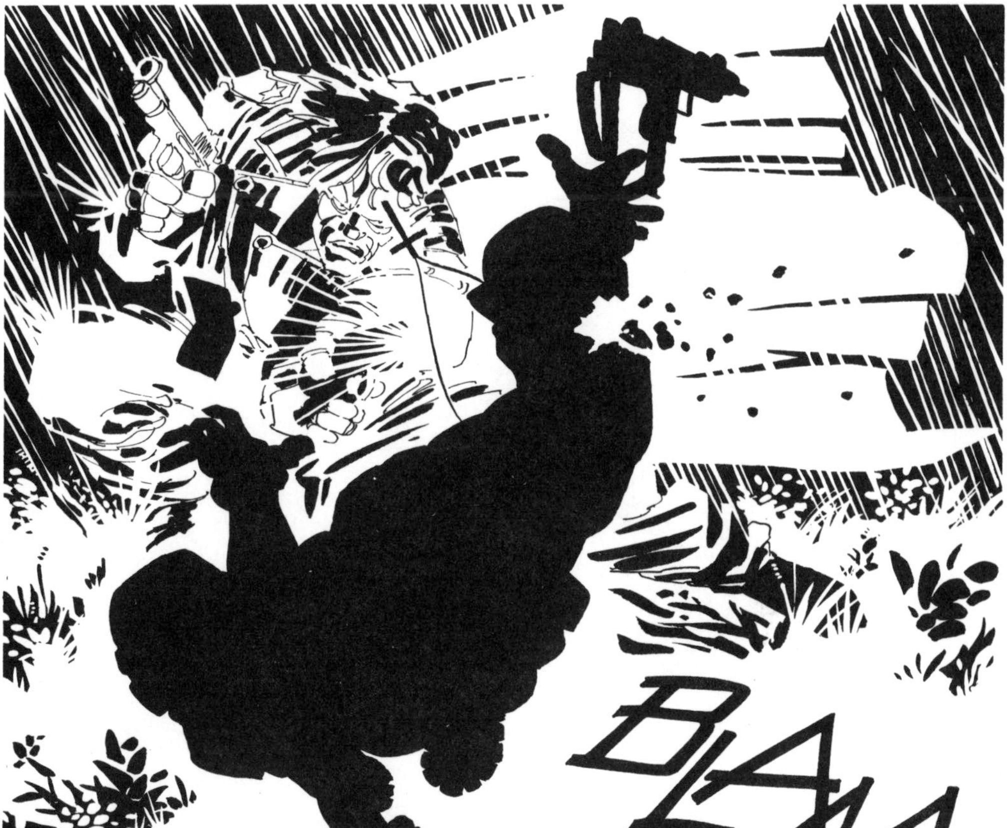
BLAM

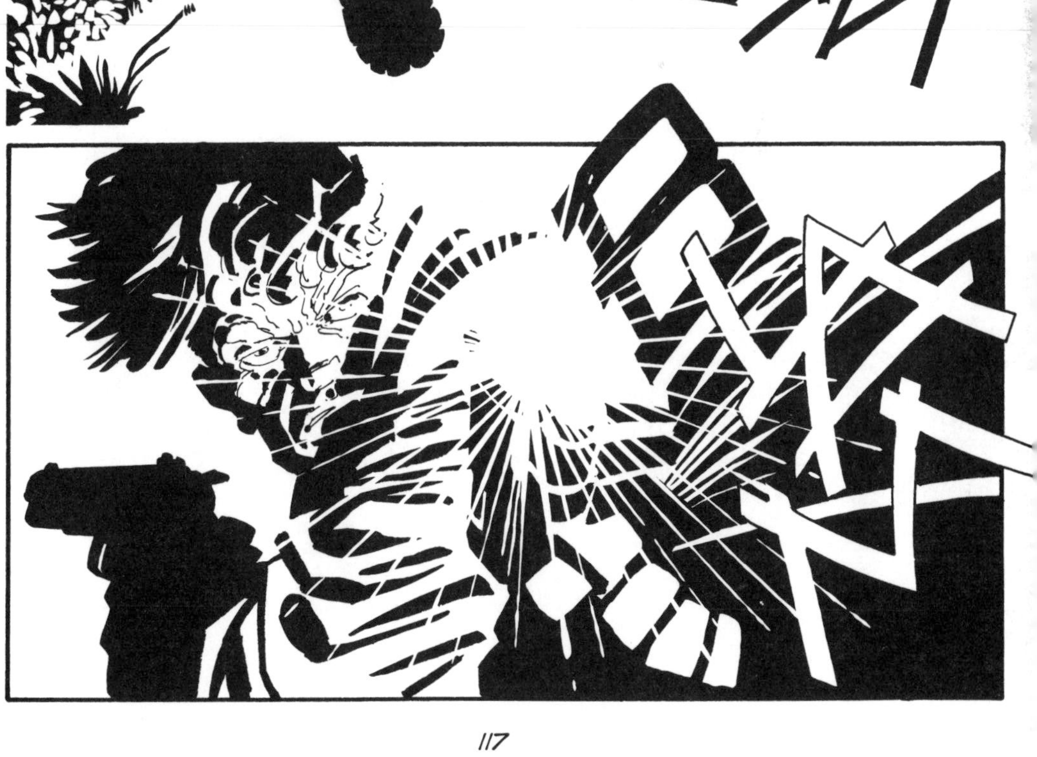

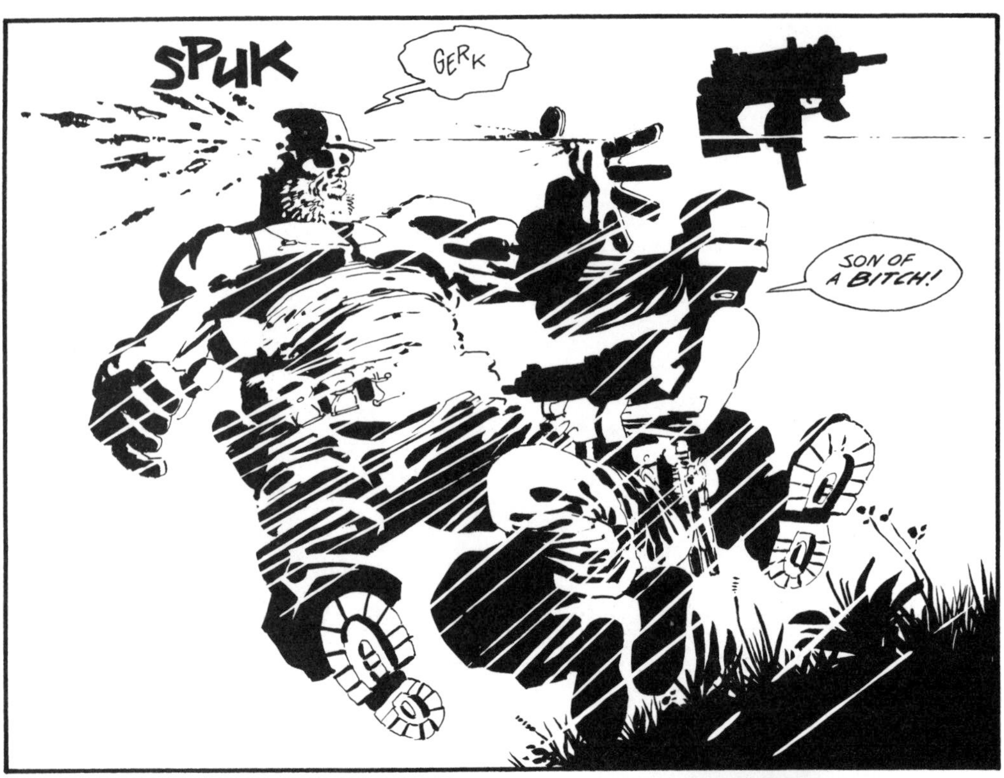
SPUK
GERK
SON OF A BITCH!

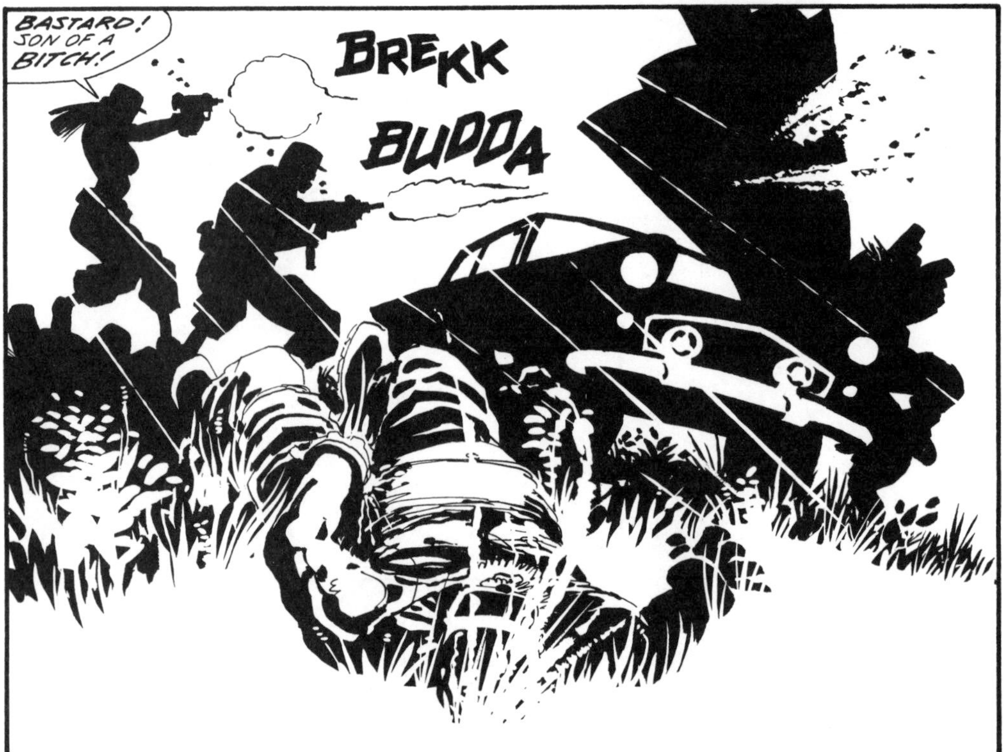
BASTARD! SON OF A BITCH!
BREKK
BUDDA

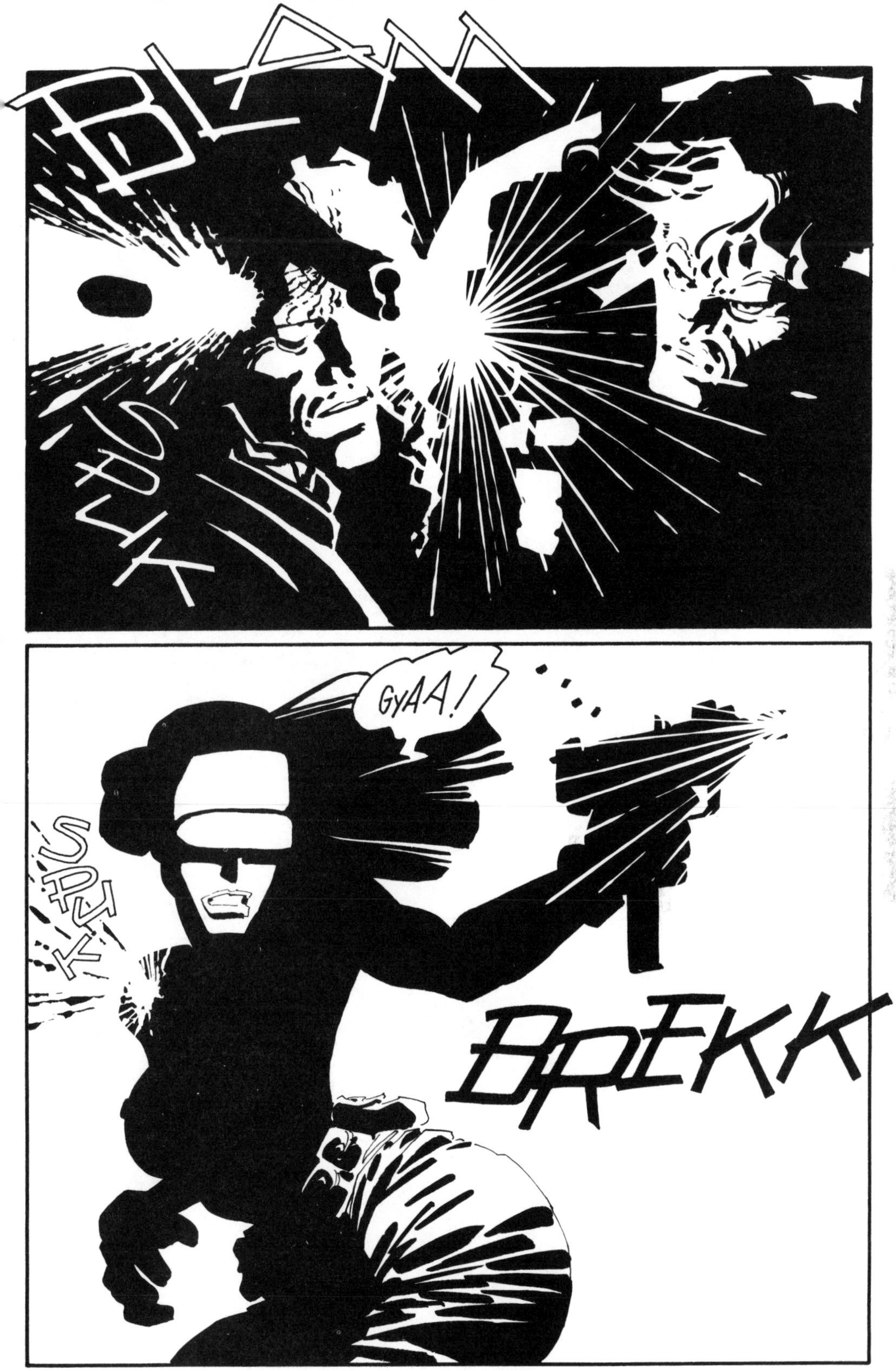
BLAM
GYAA!
SPUK
BREKK

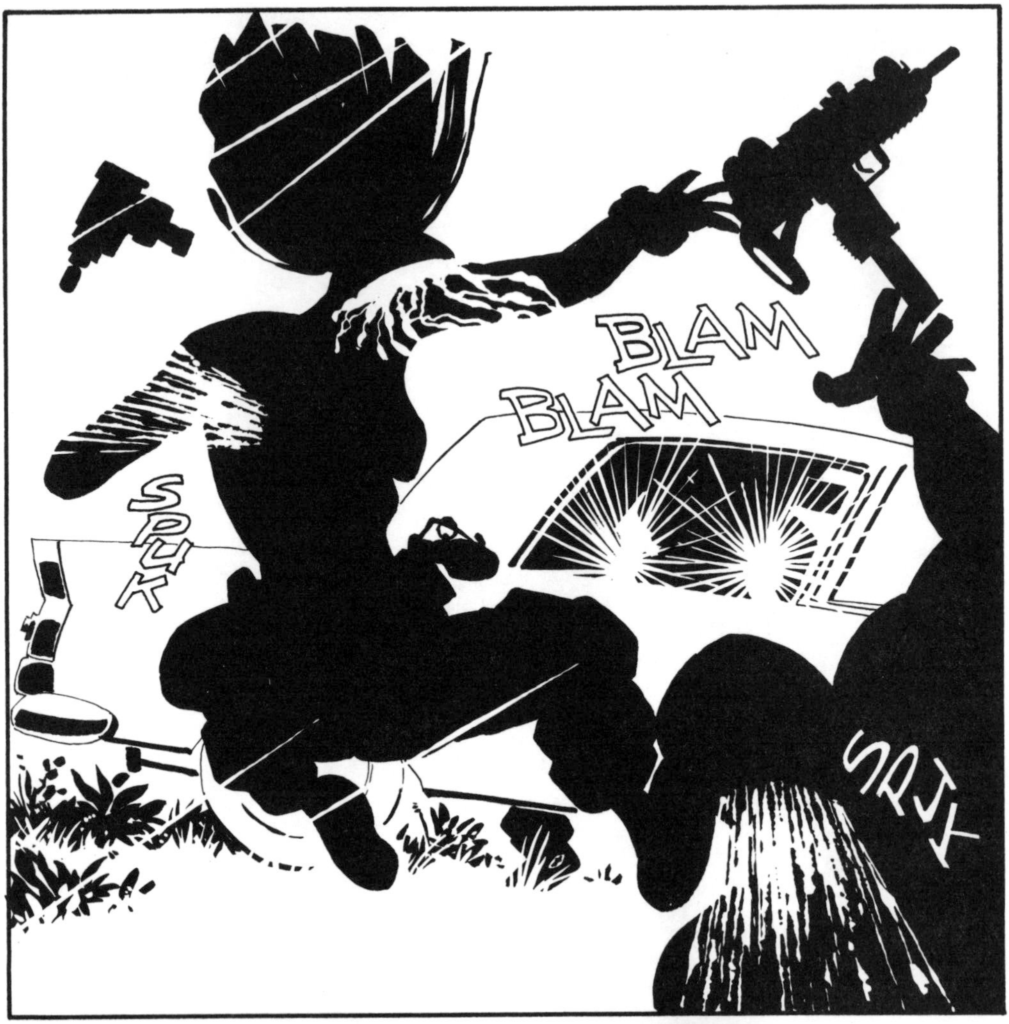
SPUK
BLAM
BLAM

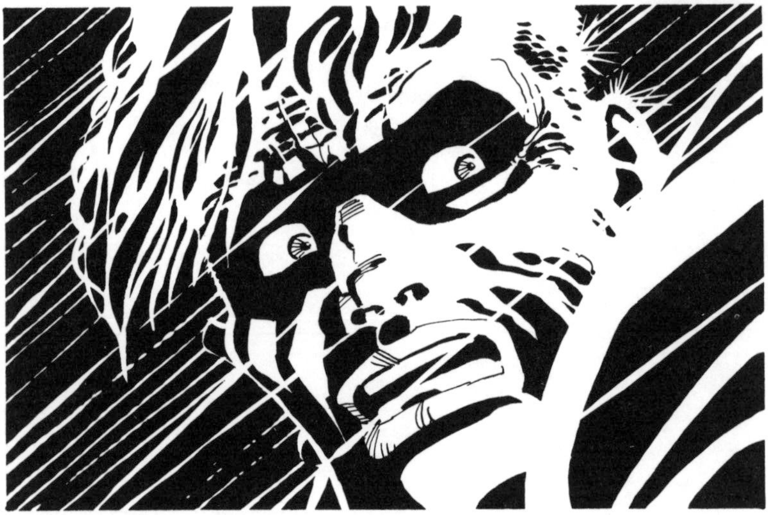

I GULP DOWN THE BILE IN MY THROAT AND TELL MY STOMACH THERE'S NOTHING IN IT TO THROW UP WITH.

THEY WEREN'T COPS, THESE FOUR. THEY WERE MERCENARIES, RENTED TERRORISTS. AND IF THEY WERE HIRED BY WHO I THINK THEY WERE, THE BAD TIMES HAVEN'T EVEN STARTED YET.

SOMETHING HEAVY SOFT-LANDS IN THE GRASS, NOT FOUR YARDS AWAY.

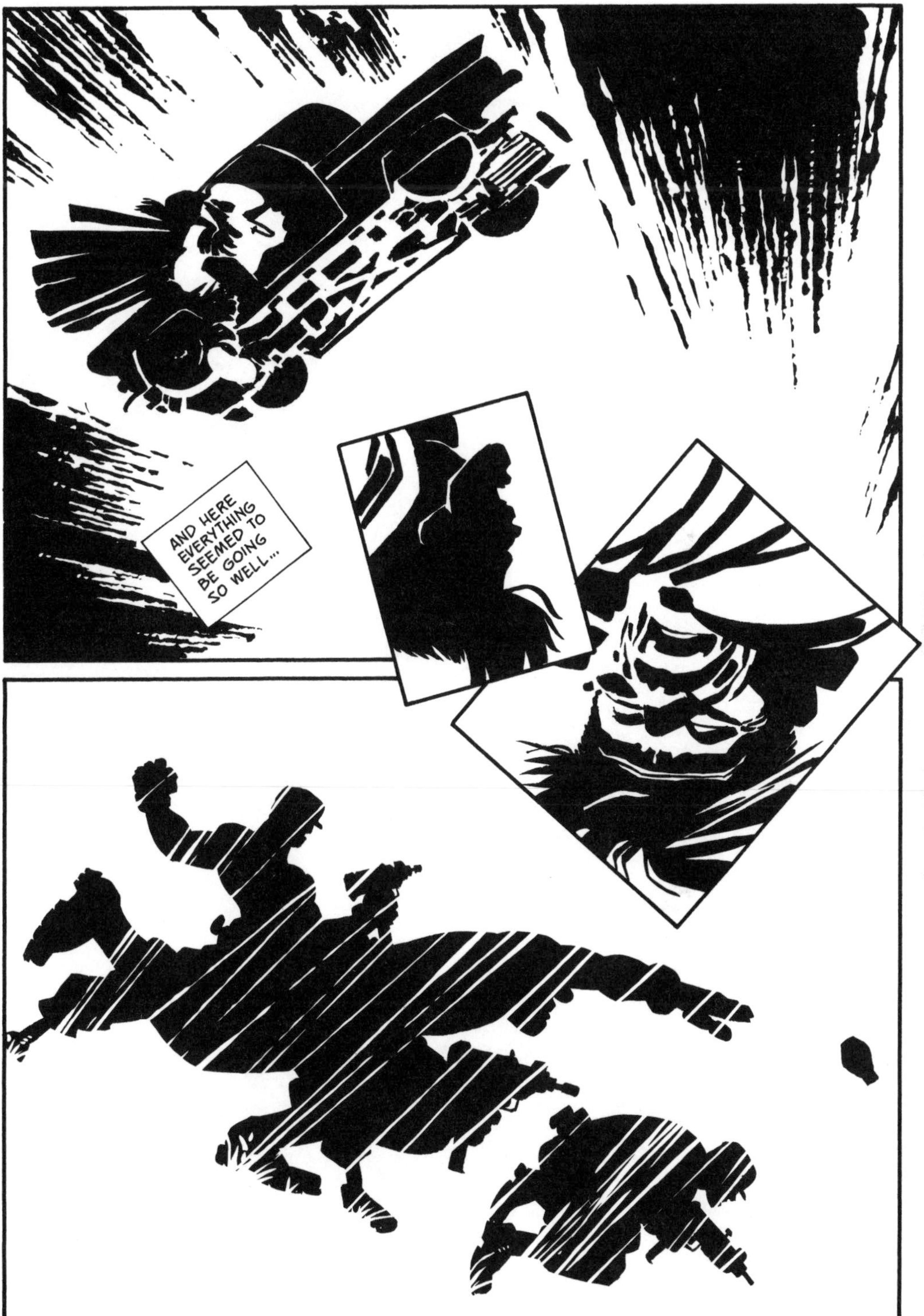
AND HERE EVERYTHING SEEMED TO BE GOING SO WELL...

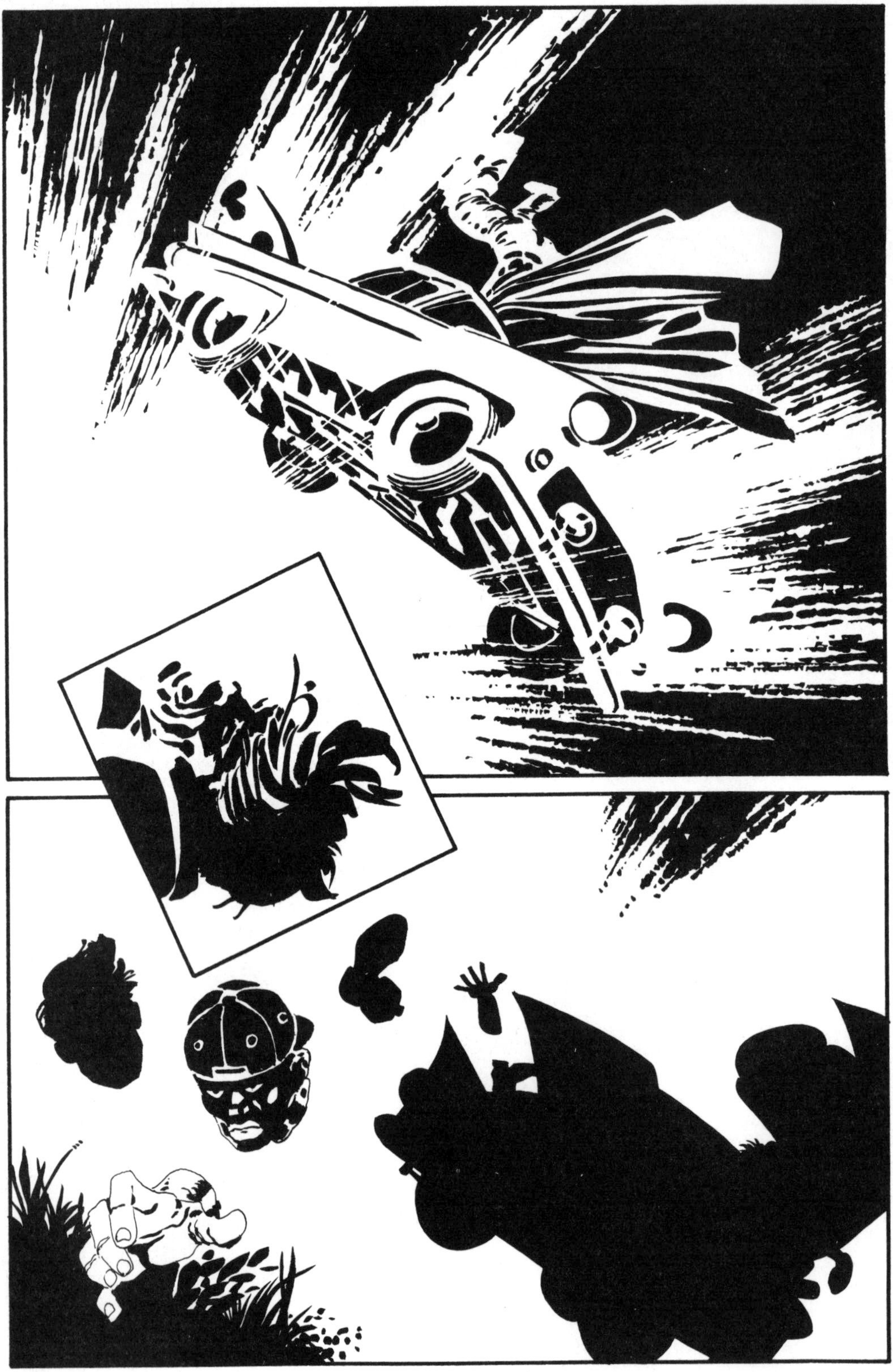

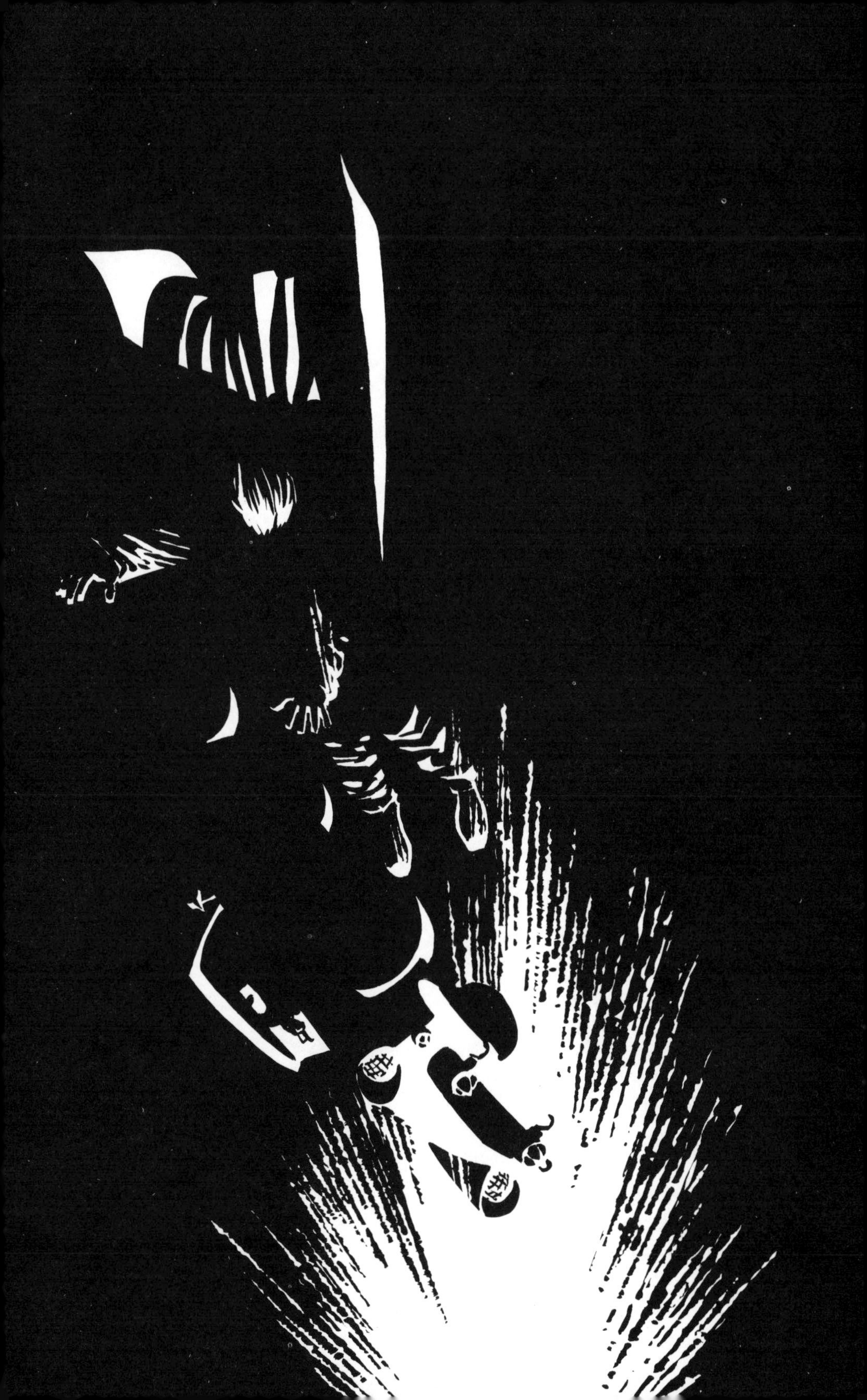

A *BLIP* OF NON-EXISTENCE, LIKE A TV SWITCHING STATIONS. THEN A *JACKHAMMER* WHERE MY *BRAIN* OUGHT TO BE. SCREECHING *DENTIST DRILLS* STUCK IN MY *EARS*.

FROM UNDER ALL THAT COME *VOICES*...

...SURE I GOT *HOLD* OF THIS COPPER WELL ENOUGH, RONNIE--BUT IT'S NOT LIKE I'M *HERCULES*, NOW IS IT? WE'D BE NEEDIN' US A FRIGGIN' *CRANE* TO PULL THE BASTARD OUTTA *THIS* SOUP.

IT'S NOT LIKE WE GOTTA DELIVER EVERY LAST *INCH* OF THE MAN, BRIAN.

YOU GOT A *POINT* THERE, RONNIE. LEND ME YOUR *KNIFE*.

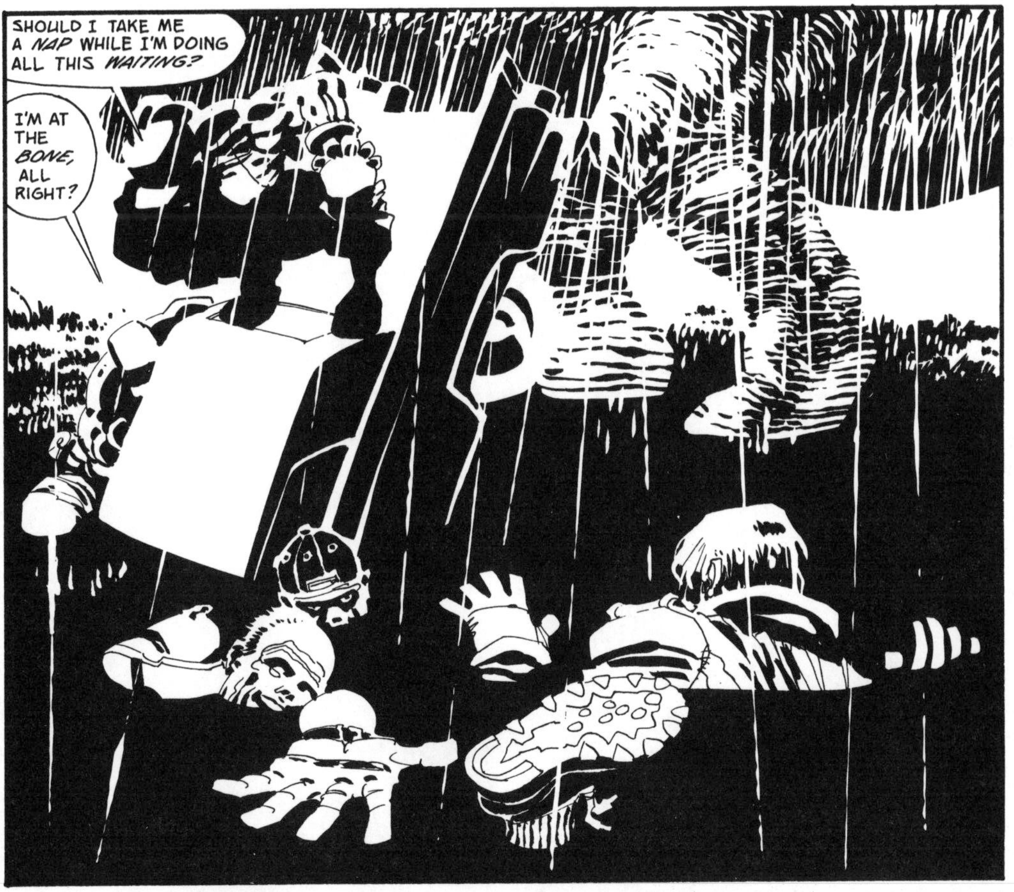
SHOULD I TAKE ME A NAP WHILE I'M DOING ALL THIS WAITING?
I'M AT THE BONE, ALL RIGHT?

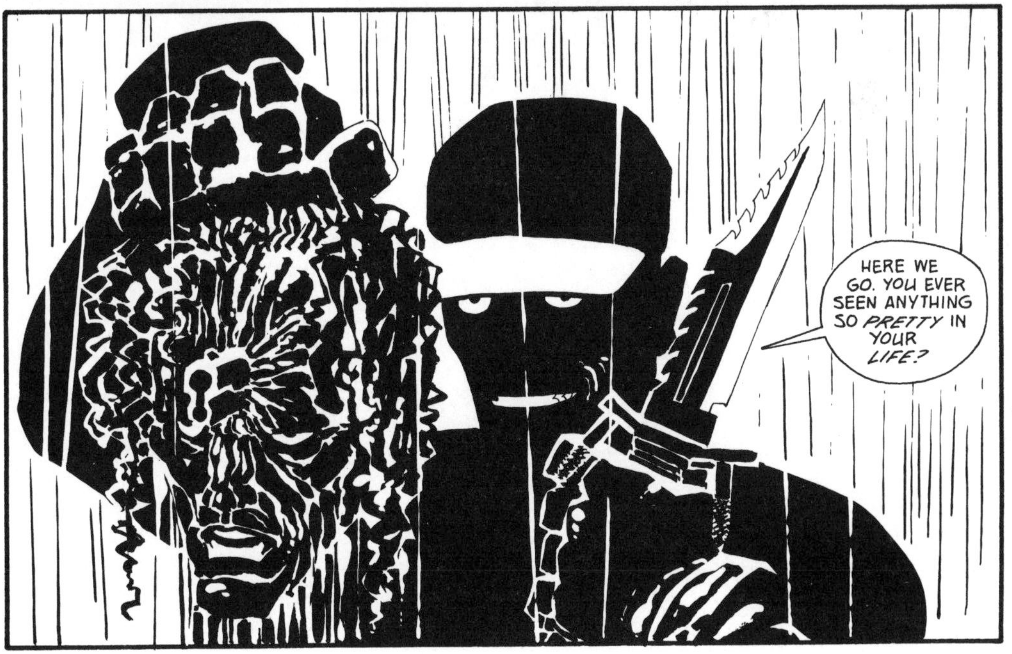
HERE WE GO. YOU EVER SEEN ANYTHING SO PRETTY IN YOUR LIFE?

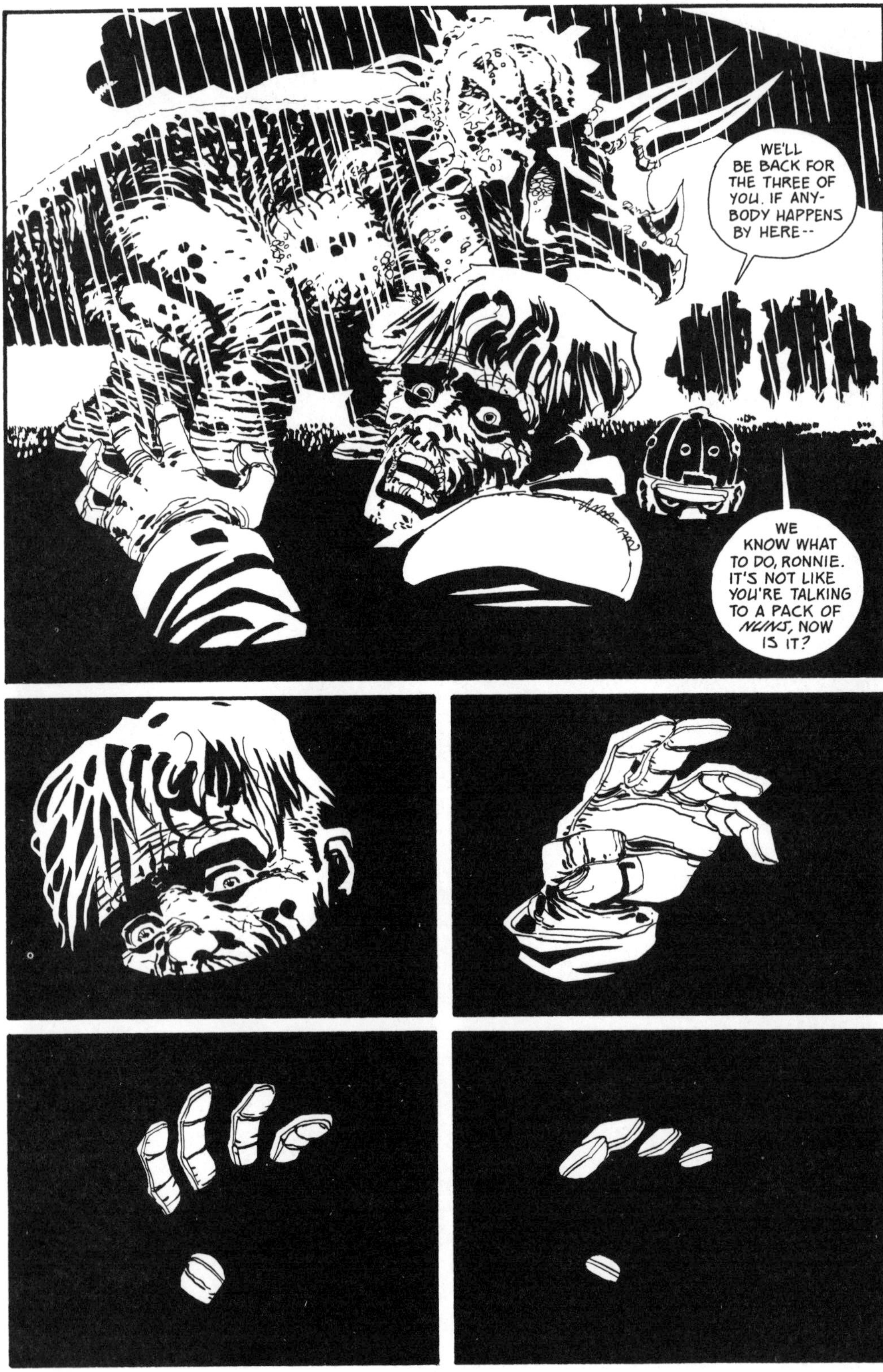
WE'LL BE BACK FOR THE THREE OF YOU. IF ANYBODY HAPPENS BY HERE--
WE KNOW WHAT TO DO, RONNIE. IT'S NOT LIKE YOU'RE TALKING TO A PACK OF NUNS, NOW IS IT?

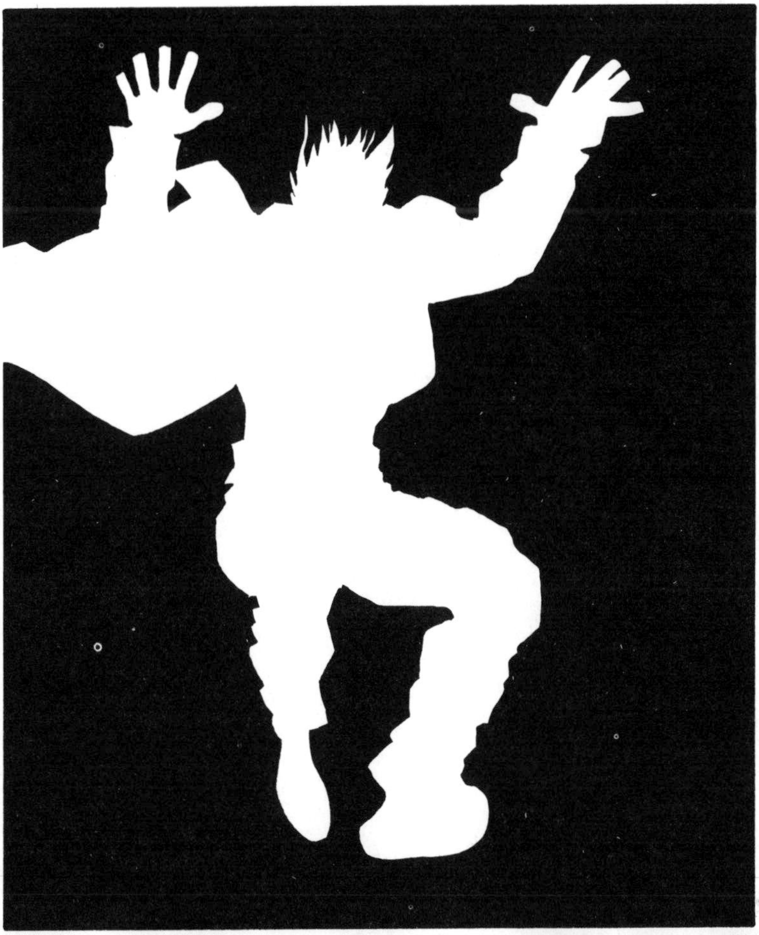

SILENCE, NOW. NO SOUND BUT JACKIE-BOY'S LAUGHTER AND I'M IMAGINING THAT.

NOTHING. NO SOUND. NO LIGHT. NO AIR TO BREATHE. ONLY THE BONE-DEEP COLD AND THE HORRID, OILY TAR-TASTE, CREEPING UP MY NOSTRILS, PRESSING AGAINST MY LIPS.

LET IT IN. LET IT FILL YOUR LUNGS. IT'S OVER. YOU'RE FINISHED. THE GIRLS ARE FINISHED. THEY WERE COUNTING ON YOU AND YOU BLEW IT.

LET IT IN. SUCK IT IN AND CHOKE ON IT AND DROWN IN IT AND DIE LIKE A MAN, NOT LIKE SOME SCARED LITTLE CATHOLIC BOY, THRASHING AND SNIVELING AND PRAYING TO JESUS.

LORD, I DON'T MIND DYING. NOT TOO AWFULLY MUCH I DON'T. BUT NOT LIKE THIS. I'M BEGGING YOU, LORD. DON'T LET ME DIE KNOWING I'M NOTHING BUT A JERK, A FAILURE, A LOSER, A COMPLETE AND TOTAL ASSHOLE.

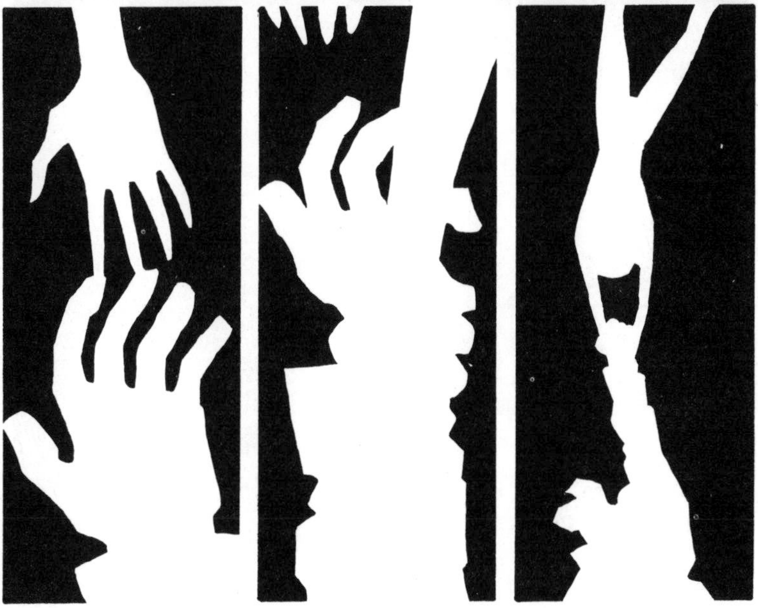

SKINNY, STEELY FINGERS AT MY WRIST.

MIHO.

NO, BABY. NO. IT'S TOO LATE. I'M DOWN TOO DEEP. YOU'RE ONLY KILLING YOURSELF.

A SUDDEN JERK UPWARD.

I'M DREAMING. IT'S IMPOSSIBLE.

IMPOSSIBLE.

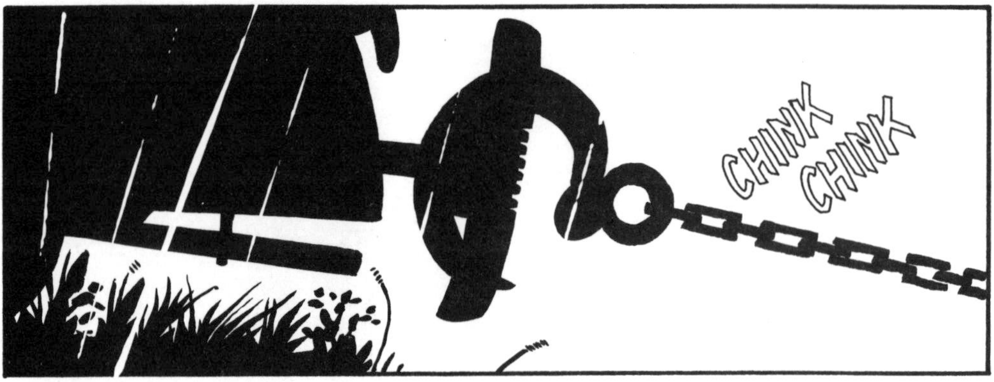
CHINK CHINK

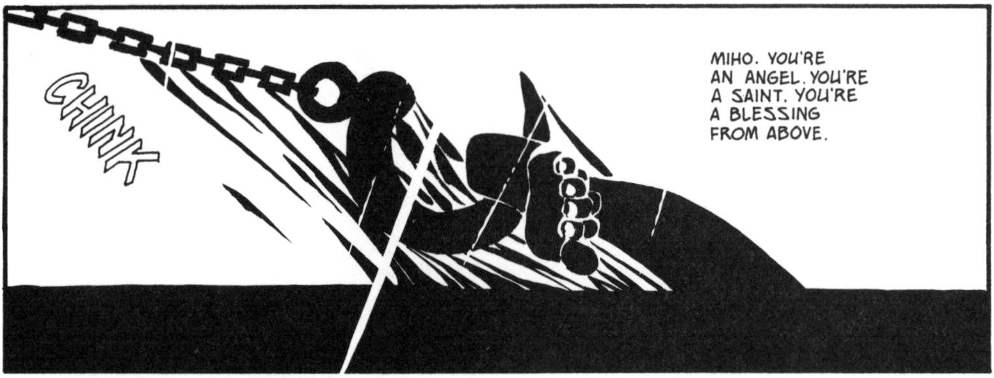
CHINK
MIHO. YOU'RE AN ANGEL. YOU'RE A SAINT. YOU'RE A BLESSING FROM ABOVE.

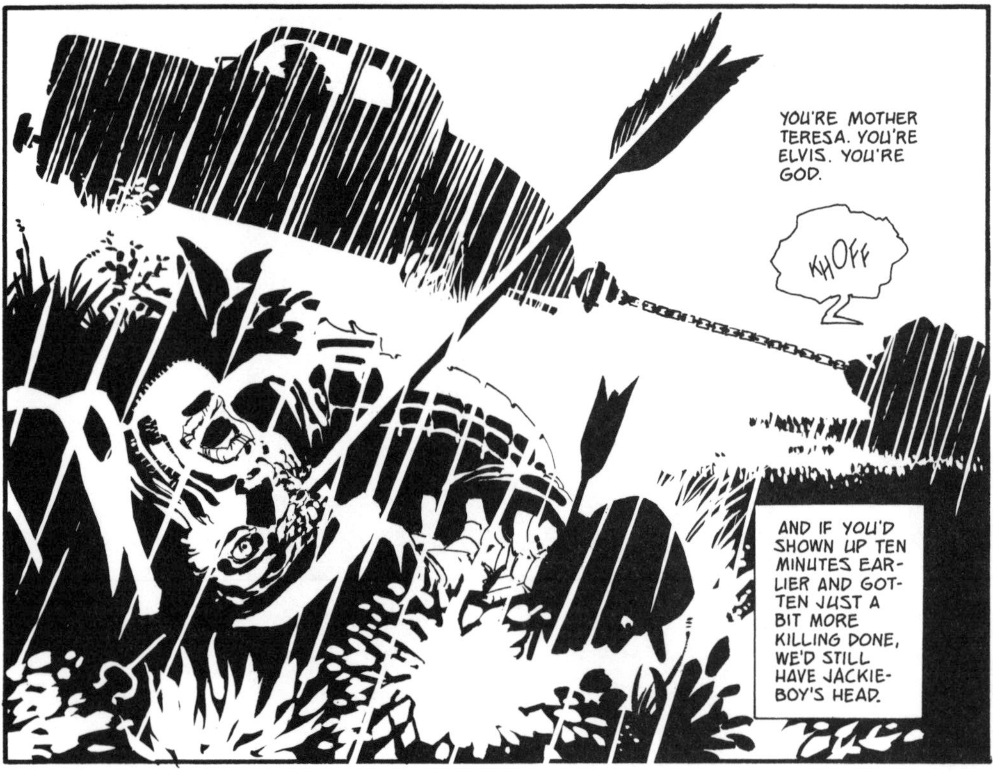
YOU'RE MOTHER TERESA. YOU'RE ELVIS. YOU'RE GOD.
KHOFF
AND IF YOU'D SHOWN UP TEN MINUTES EAR-LIER AND GOT-TEN JUST A BIT MORE KILLING DONE, WE'D STILL HAVE JACKIE-BOY'S HEAD.

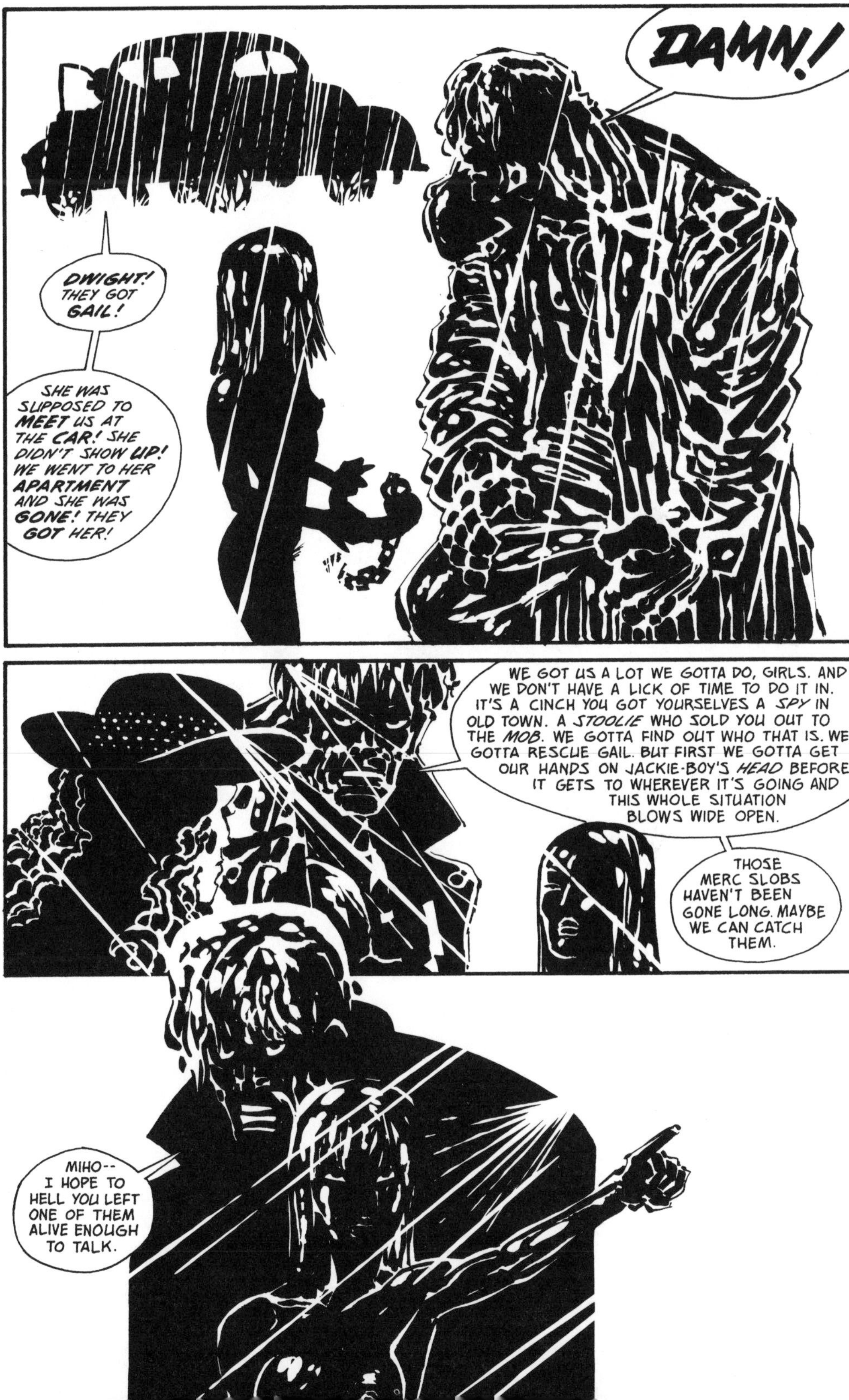
DAMN!
DWIGHT! THEY GOT GAIL!
SHE WAS SUPPOSED TO MEET US AT THE CAR! SHE DIDN'T SHOW UP! WE WENT TO HER APARTMENT AND SHE WAS GONE! THEY GOT HER!
WE GOT US A LOT WE GOTTA DO, GIRLS. AND WE DON'T HAVE A LICK OF TIME TO DO IT IN. IT'S A CINCH YOU GOT YOURSELVES A SPY IN OLD TOWN. A STOOLIE WHO SOLD YOU OUT TO THE MOB. WE GOTTA FIND OUT WHO THAT IS. WE GOTTA RESCUE GAIL. BUT FIRST WE GOTTA GET OUR HANDS ON JACKIE-BOY'S HEAD BEFORE IT GETS TO WHEREVER IT'S GOING AND THIS WHOLE SITUATION BLOWS WIDE OPEN.
THOSE MERC SLOBS HAVEN'T BEEN GONE LONG. MAYBE WE CAN CATCH THEM.
MIHO-- I HOPE TO HELL YOU LEFT ONE OF THEM ALIVE ENOUGH TO TALK.

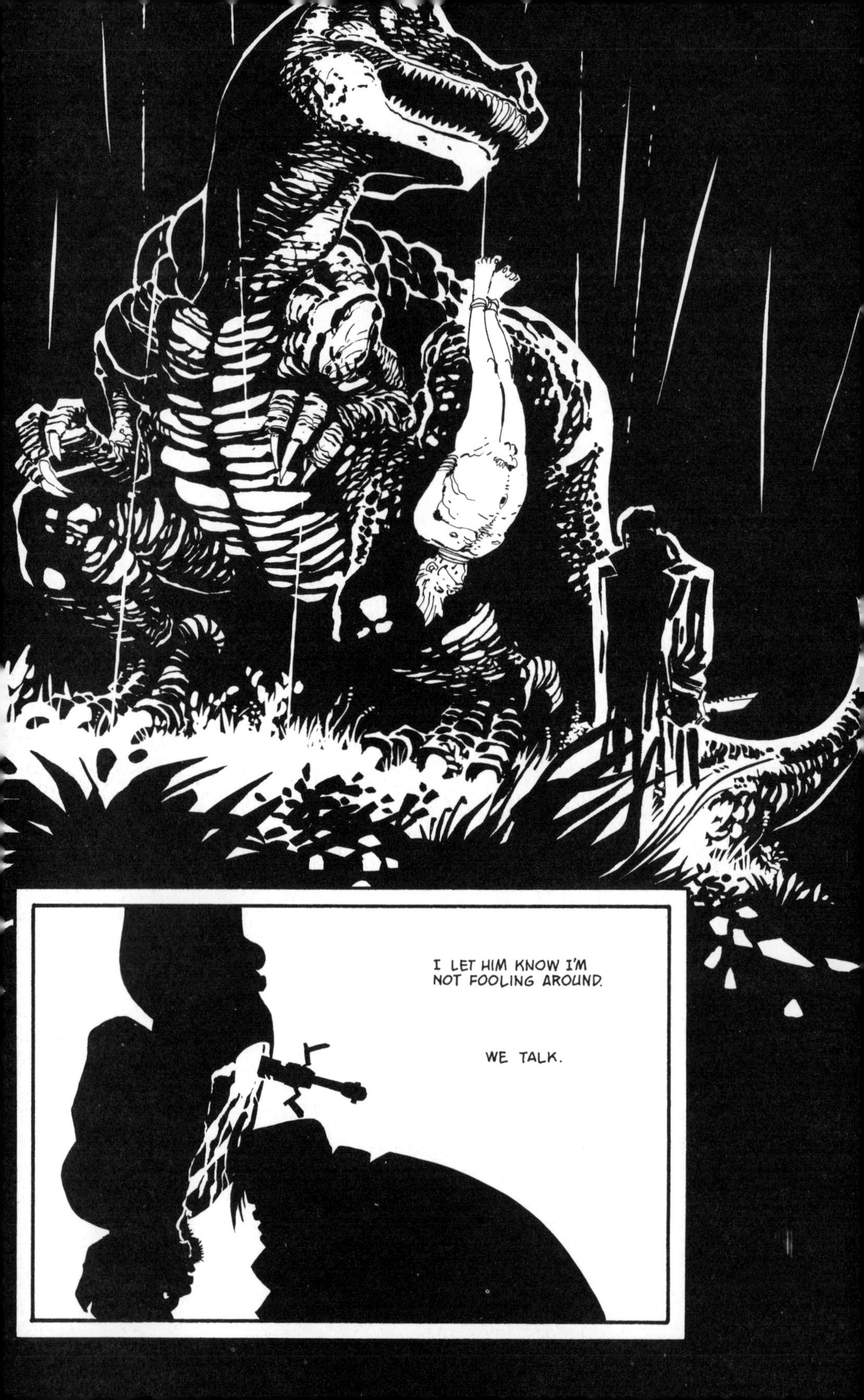
I LET HIM KNOW I'M NOT FOOLING AROUND.
WE TALK.

CHAPTER
FIVE

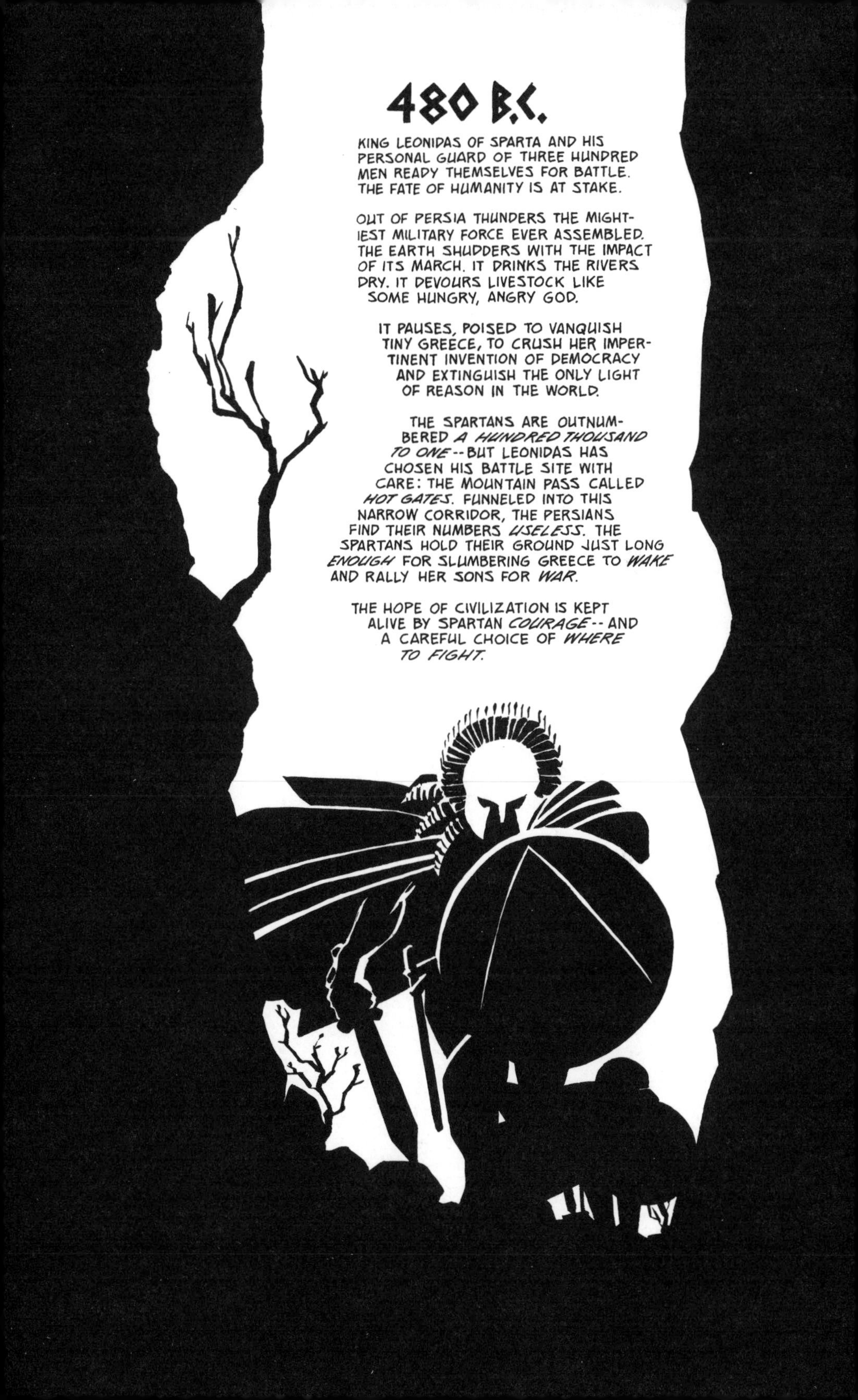
480 B.C.
KING LEONIDAS OF SPARTA AND HIS PERSONAL GUARD OF THREE HUNDRED MEN READY THEMSELVES FOR BATTLE. THE FATE OF HUMANITY IS AT STAKE.
OUT OF PERSIA THUNDERS THE MIGHTIEST MILITARY FORCE EVER ASSEMBLED. THE EARTH SHUDDERS WITH THE IMPACT OF ITS MARCH. IT DRINKS THE RIVERS DRY. IT DEVOURS LIVESTOCK LIKE SOME HUNGRY, ANGRY GOD.
IT PAUSES, POISED TO VANQUISH TINY GREECE, TO CRUSH HER IMPERTINENT INVENTION OF DEMOCRACY AND EXTINGUISH THE ONLY LIGHT OF REASON IN THE WORLD.
THE SPARTANS ARE OUTNUMBERED *A HUNDRED THOUSAND TO ONE*--BUT LEONIDAS HAS CHOSEN HIS BATTLE SITE WITH CARE: THE MOUNTAIN PASS CALLED *HOT GATES*. FUNNELED INTO THIS NARROW CORRIDOR, THE PERSIANS FIND THEIR NUMBERS *USELESS*. THE SPARTANS HOLD THEIR GROUND JUST LONG *ENOUGH* FOR SLUMBERING GREECE TO *WAKE* AND RALLY HER SONS FOR *WAR*.
THE HOPE OF CIVILIZATION IS KEPT ALIVE BY SPARTAN *COURAGE*--AND A CAREFUL CHOICE OF *WHERE TO FIGHT*.

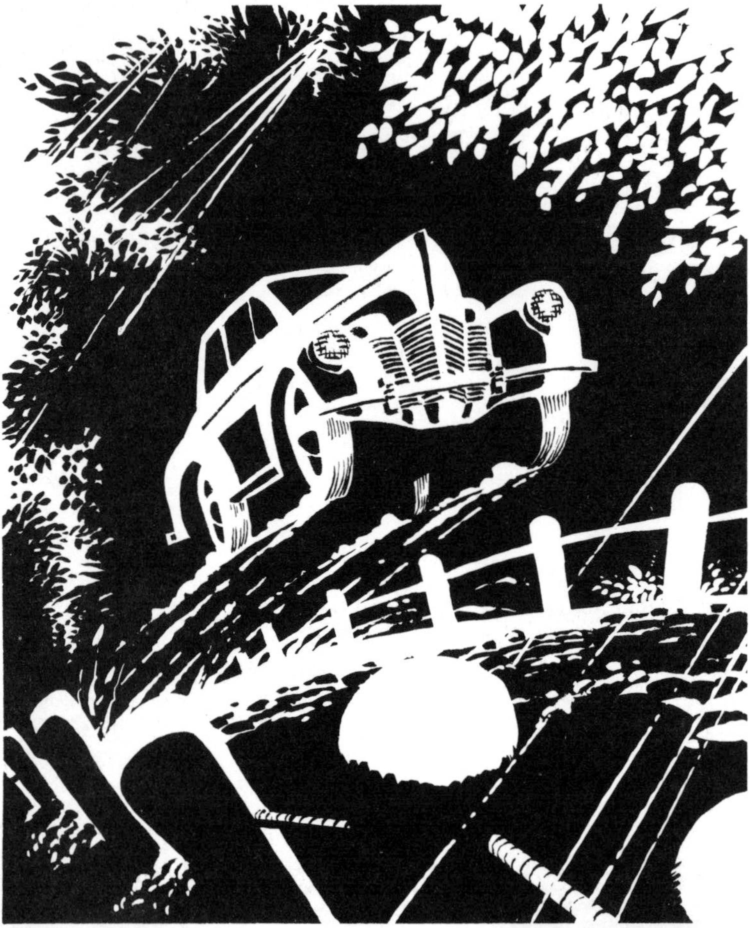

TWO MILLENNIA AND A WHOLE BUNCH OF CENTURIES LATER, I'M RATTLING AROUND IN THE CAB OF A BEAUTIFULLY RESTORED 1940 FORD COUPE AS IT SLIPS AND SLIDES AROUND MUDDY CORNERS AND ROCKETS ALONG THE STRAIGHT STRETCHES OF BARELY-THERE BACK ROADS THAT JUST ABOUT NOBODY'S USED SINCE THE OLD DAYS OF PROHIBITION AND BOOTLEGGERS. I'M DOING MY BEST TO KEEP MY STOMACH FROM JUMPING OUT OF MY MOUTH. I'M PRAYING THAT ME AND MY COMPANIONS CAN CATCH UP WITH A PAIR OF OUT-OF-WORK-IRISH-TERRORISTS-GONE-FREELANCE AND GET OUR HANDS ON THE SEVERED HEAD OF A MURDERED HERO COP BEFORE THE BASTARDS CAN DELIVER IT TO THE MOB.

MY COMPANIONS. DALLAS. MIHO. A HOOKER AND HER ASSASSIN PAL. NOBODY'D CALL THEM THE LAST HOPE OF CIVILIZATION, BUT THEY'RE MY FRIENDS AND YOU GOTTA STAND UP FOR YOUR FRIENDS.

I SUCK BACK THE DEAD COP'S CIGARETTES ONE AFTER ANOTHER, END TO END, NURSING A CHUNK OF HOT GRAVEL AT THE BASE OF MY THROAT AND TRYING TO CALM DOWN ENOUGH SO I CAN THINK STRAIGHT.

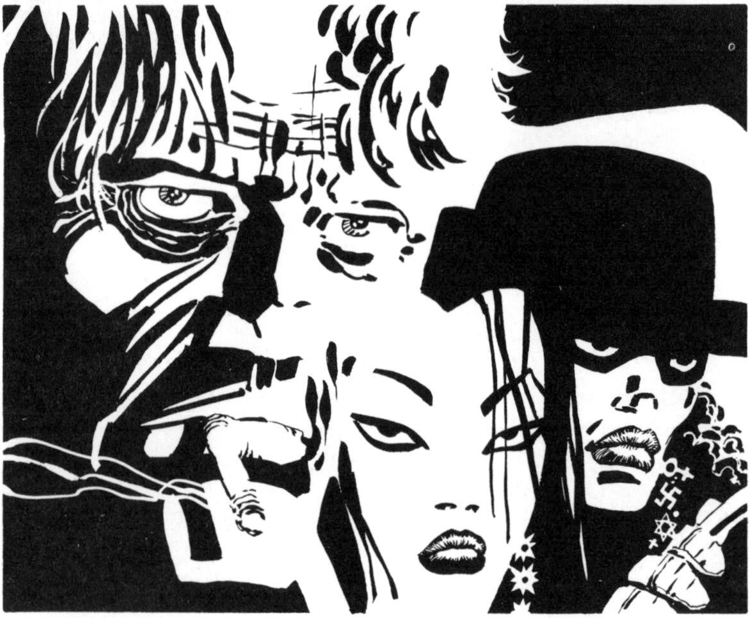

NO MORE FALSE MOVES. NO MORE DUMB MISTAKES. STAY SMART. STAY COOL. STAY STEADY. IT'S TIME TO PROVE TO YOUR FRIENDS THAT YOU'RE WORTH A DAMN.

YOU GOTTA STAND UP FOR YOUR FRIENDS. SOMETIMES THAT MEANS DYING. SOMETIMES IT MEANS KILLING A WHOLE LOT OF PEOPLE.

DALLAS FISHTAILS US ONTO AN ACCESS ROAD AND TORTURES HER OLD FORD ACROSS SCATTERED BRICKS AND PIPES AND POTHOLES BIG AS BATHTUBS.

NOW WE'LL SEE IF OUR LITTLE SHORT CUT'S GOTTEN US TO THE PROJECTS AHEAD OF THE OUT-OF-TOWNERS WE MEAN TO MURDER.

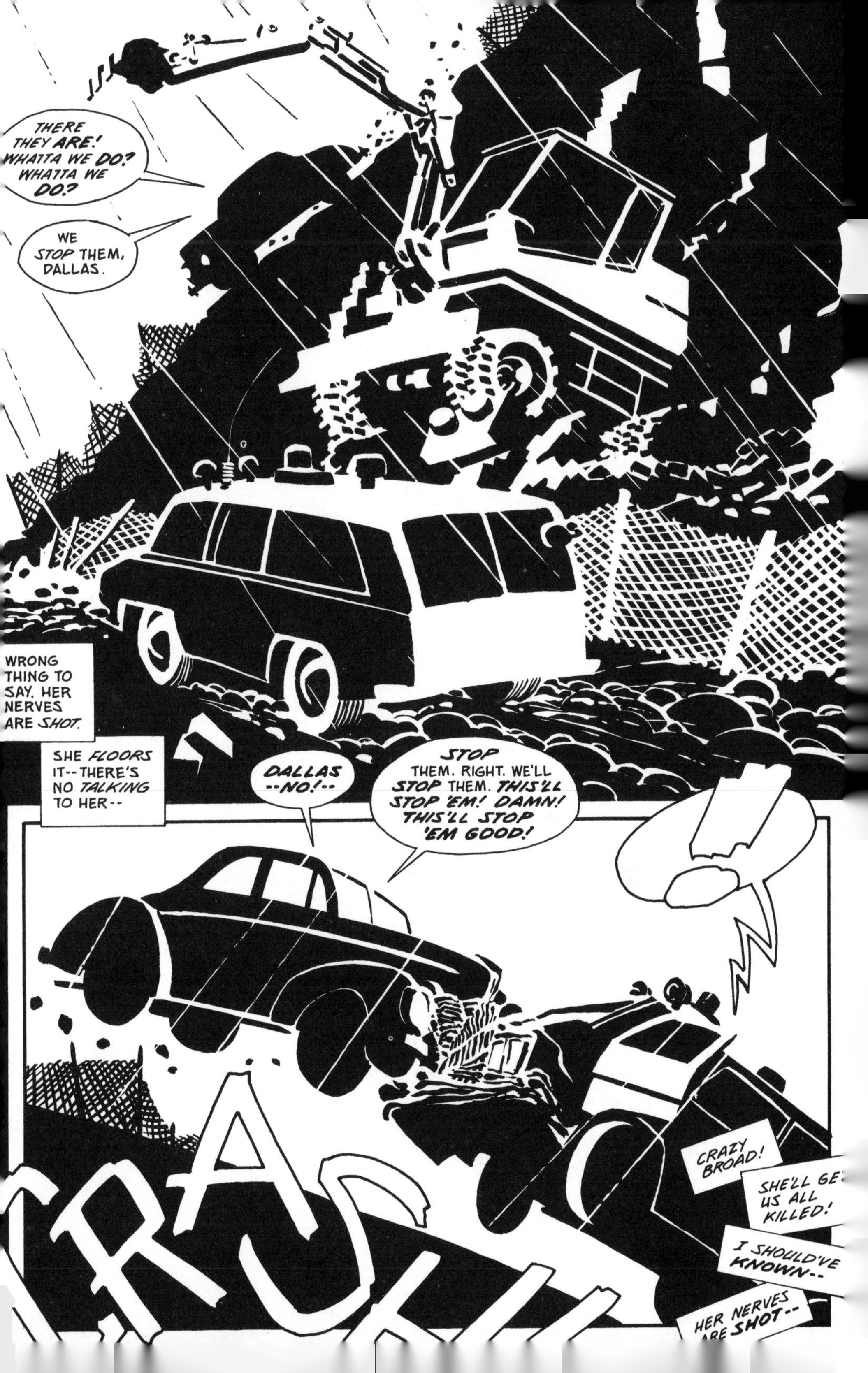
THERE THEY ARE! WHATTA WE DO? WHATTA WE DO?
WE STOP THEM, DALLAS.
WRONG THING TO SAY. HER NERVES ARE SHOT.
SHE FLOORS IT-- THERE'S NO TALKING TO HER--
DALLAS --NO!--
STOP THEM. RIGHT. WE'LL STOP THEM. THIS'LL STOP 'EM! DAMN! THIS'LL STOP 'EM GOOD!
CRASH
CRAZY BROAD!
SHE'LL GE
US ALL KILLED!
I SHOULD'VE KNOWN--
HER NERVES ARE SHOT--

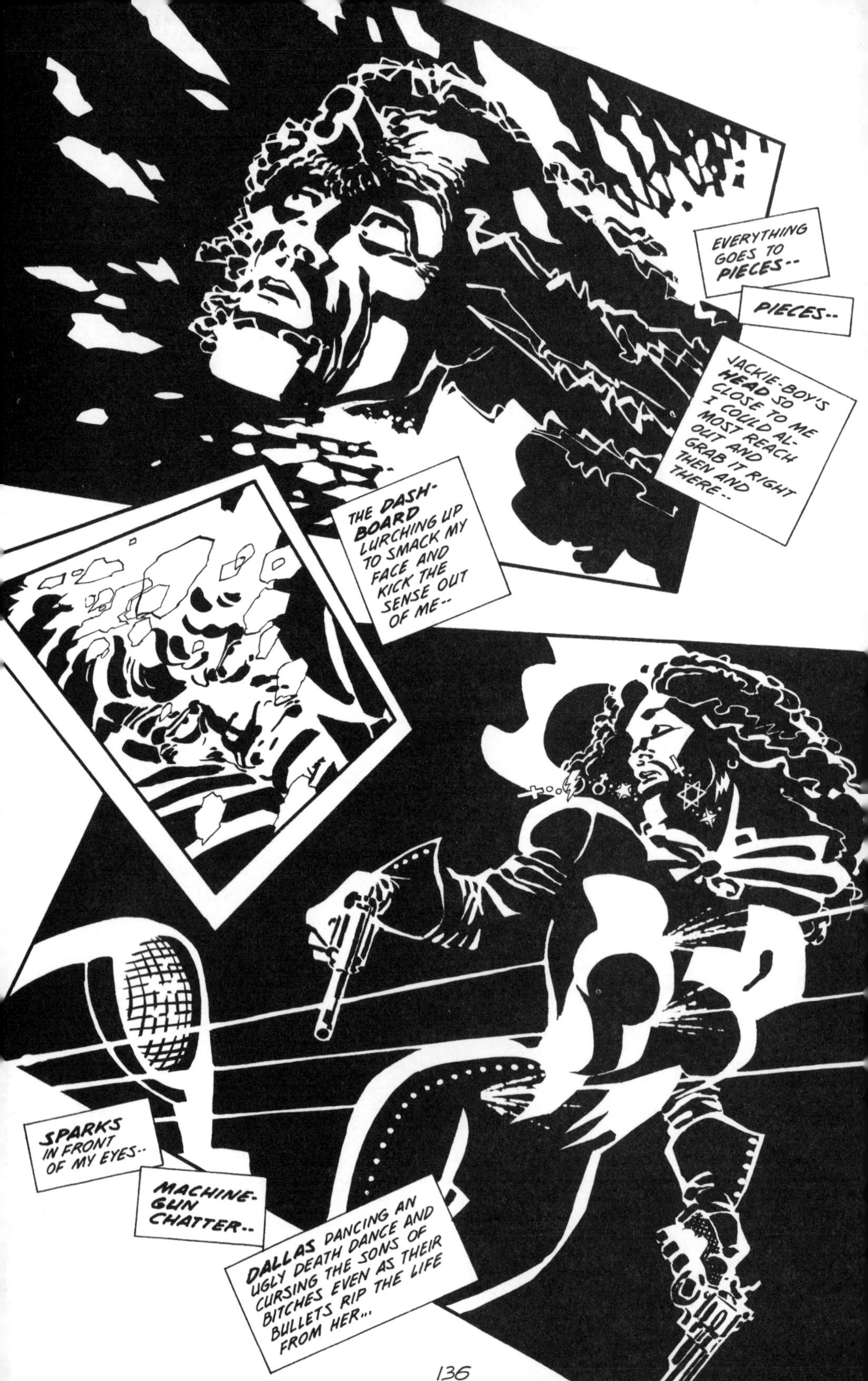
EVERYTHING GOES TO PIECES--
PIECES--
JACKIE-BOY'S HEAD SO CLOSE TO ME I COULD AL- MOST REACH OUT AND GRAB IT RIGHT THEN AND THERE--
THE DASH- BOARD LURCHING UP TO SMACK MY FACE AND KICK THE SENSE OUT OF ME--
SPARKS IN FRONT OF MY EYES--
MACHINE- GUN CHATTER--
DALLAS DANCING AN UGLY DEATH DANCE AND CURSING THE SONS OF BITCHES EVEN AS THEIR BULLETS RIP THE LIFE FROM HER...

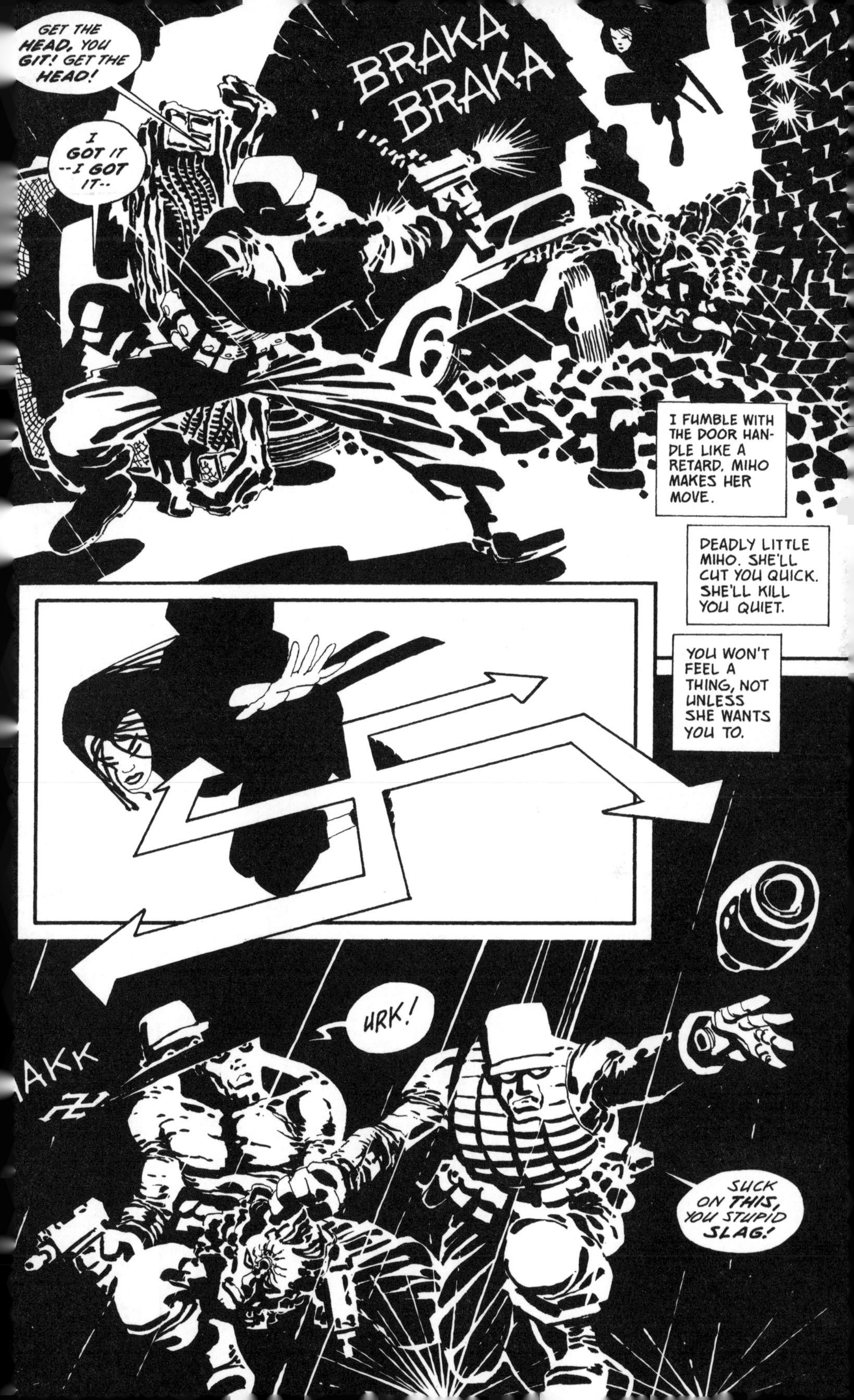
GET THE HEAD, YOU GIT! GET THE HEAD!
I GOT IT --I GOT IT--
BRAKA BRAKA
I FUMBLE WITH THE DOOR HANDLE LIKE A RETARD. MIHO MAKES HER MOVE.
DEADLY LITTLE MIHO. SHE'LL CUT YOU QUICK. SHE'LL KILL YOU QUIET.
YOU WON'T FEEL A THING, NOT UNLESS SHE WANTS YOU TO.
URK!
SUCK ON THIS, YOU STUPID SLAG!

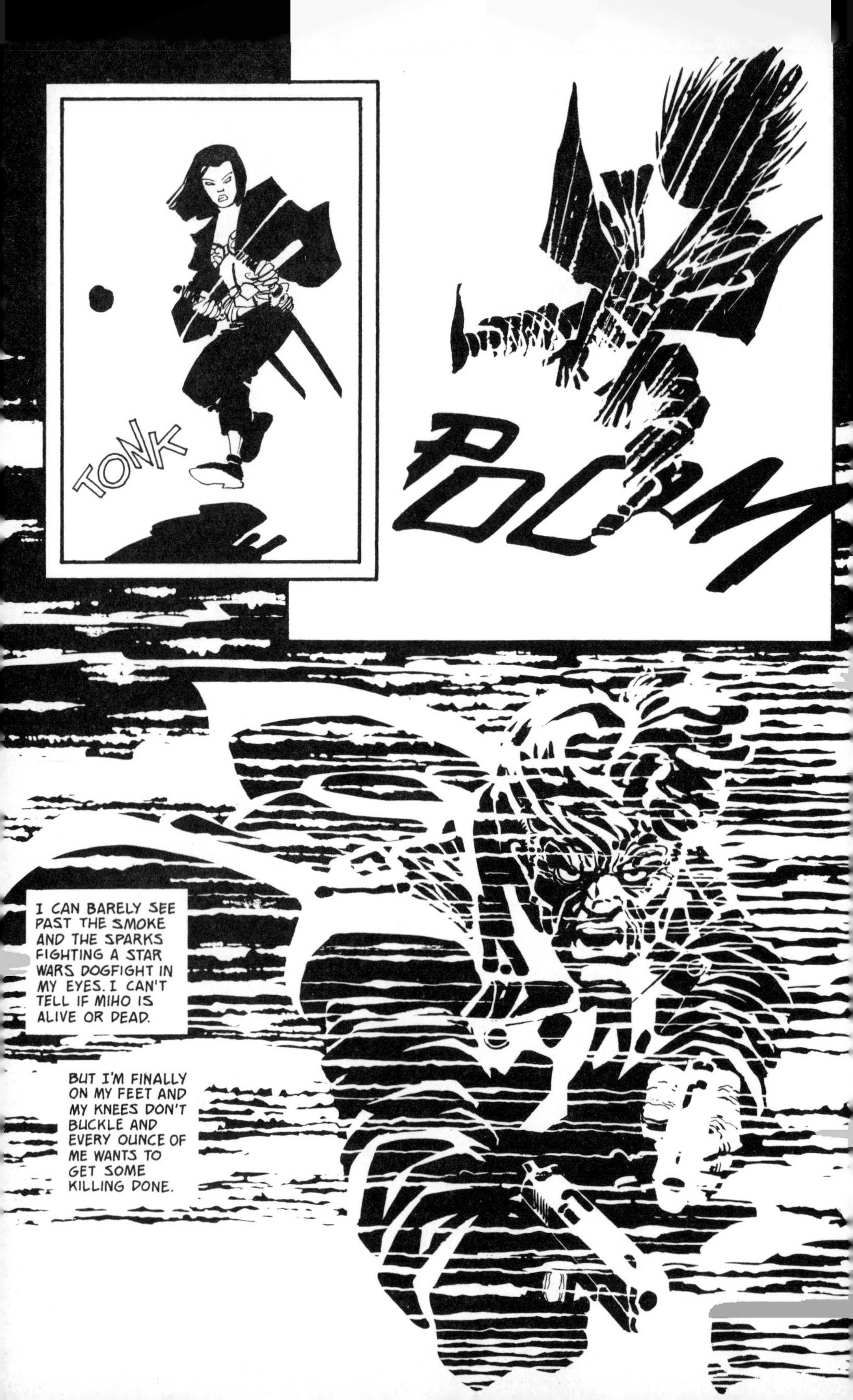
TONK
BOOM
I CAN BARELY SEE PAST THE SMOKE AND THE SPARKS FIGHTING A STAR WARS DOGFIGHT IN MY EYES. I CAN'T TELL IF MIHO IS ALIVE OR DEAD.
BUT I'M FINALLY ON MY FEET AND MY KNEES DON'T BUCKLE AND EVERY OUNCE OF ME WANTS TO GET SOME KILLING DONE.

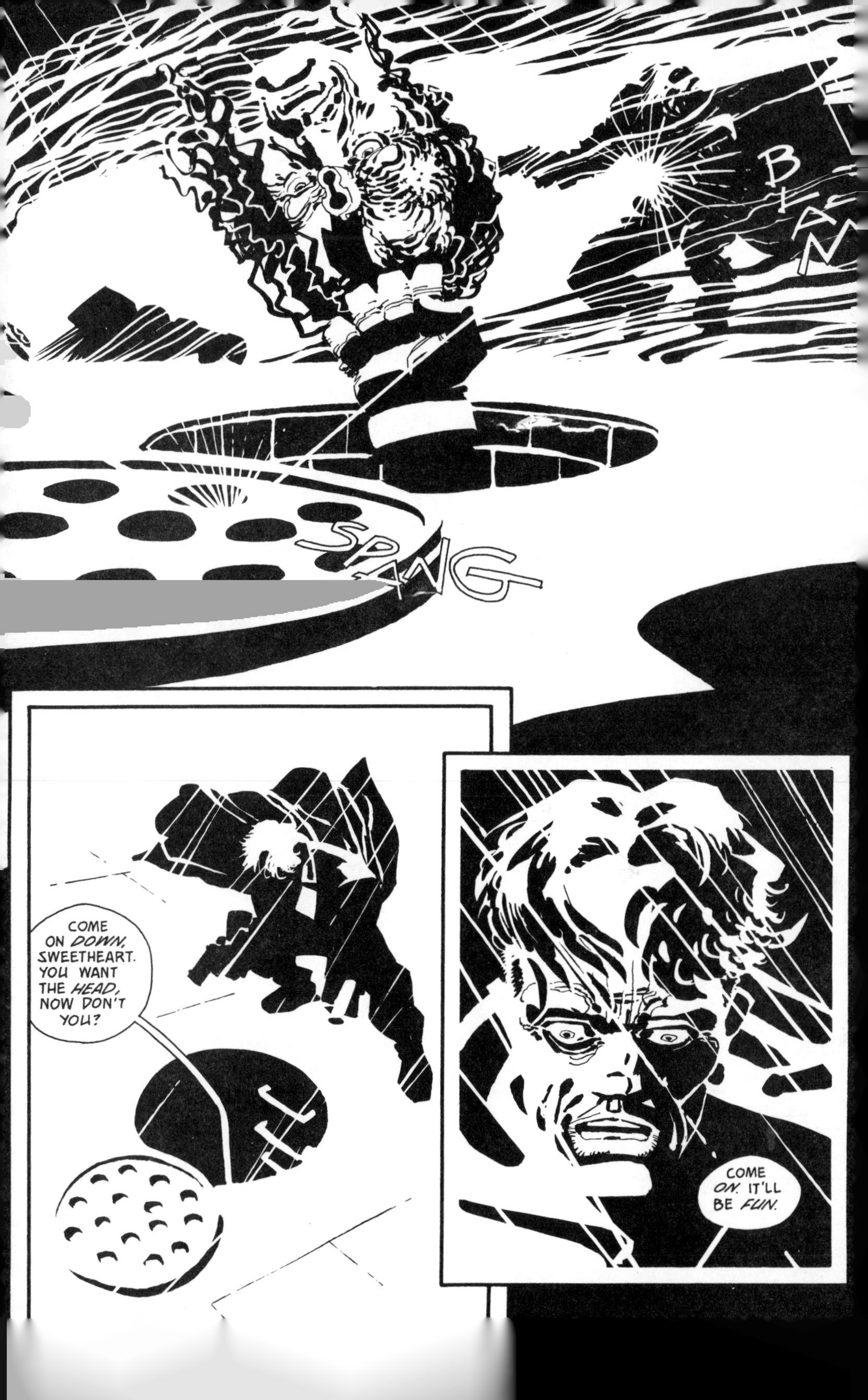
BLAM
SPANG
COME ON *DOWN*, SWEETHEART. YOU WANT THE *HEAD*, NOW DON'T YOU?
COME *ON*. IT'LL BE *FUN*.

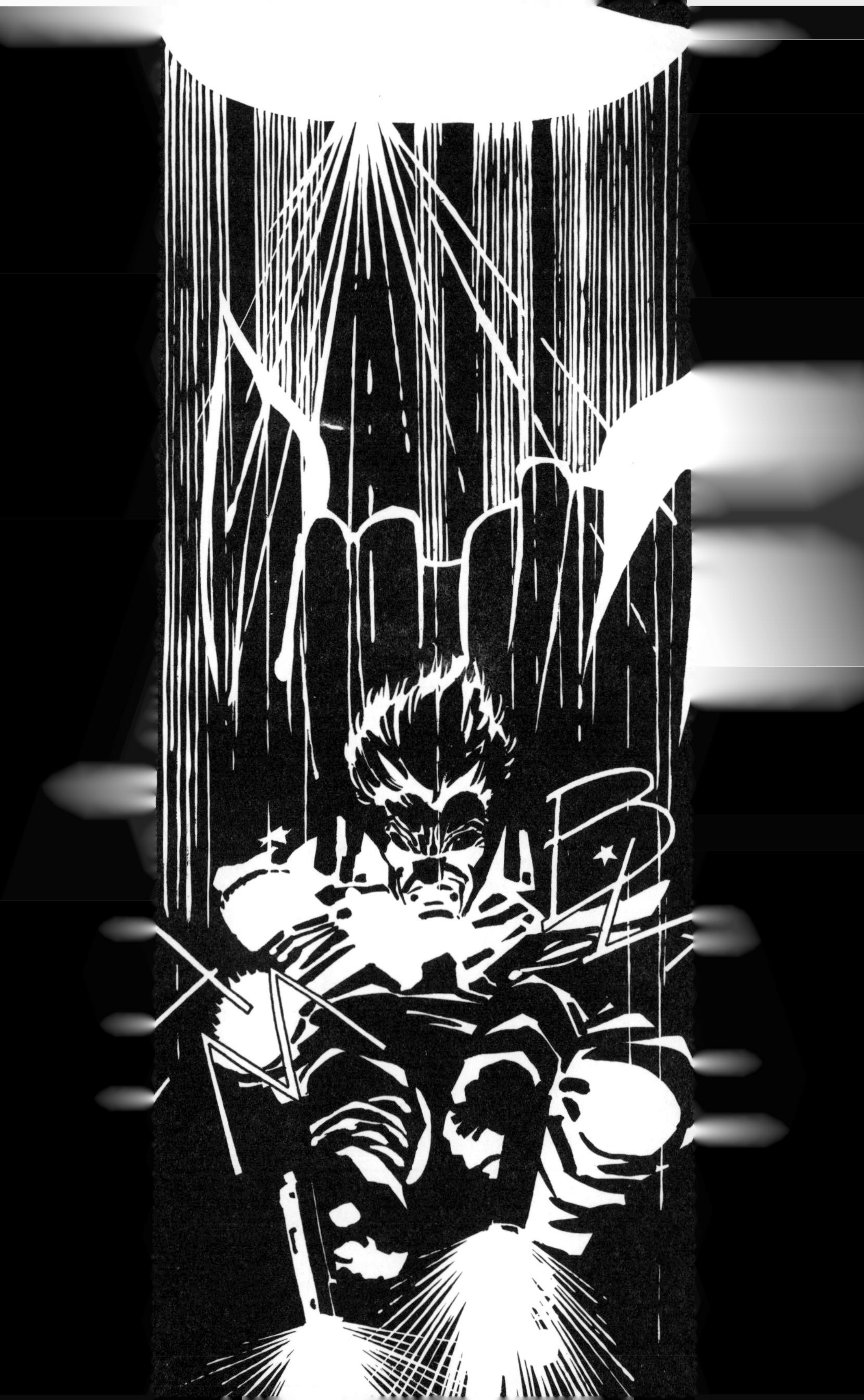

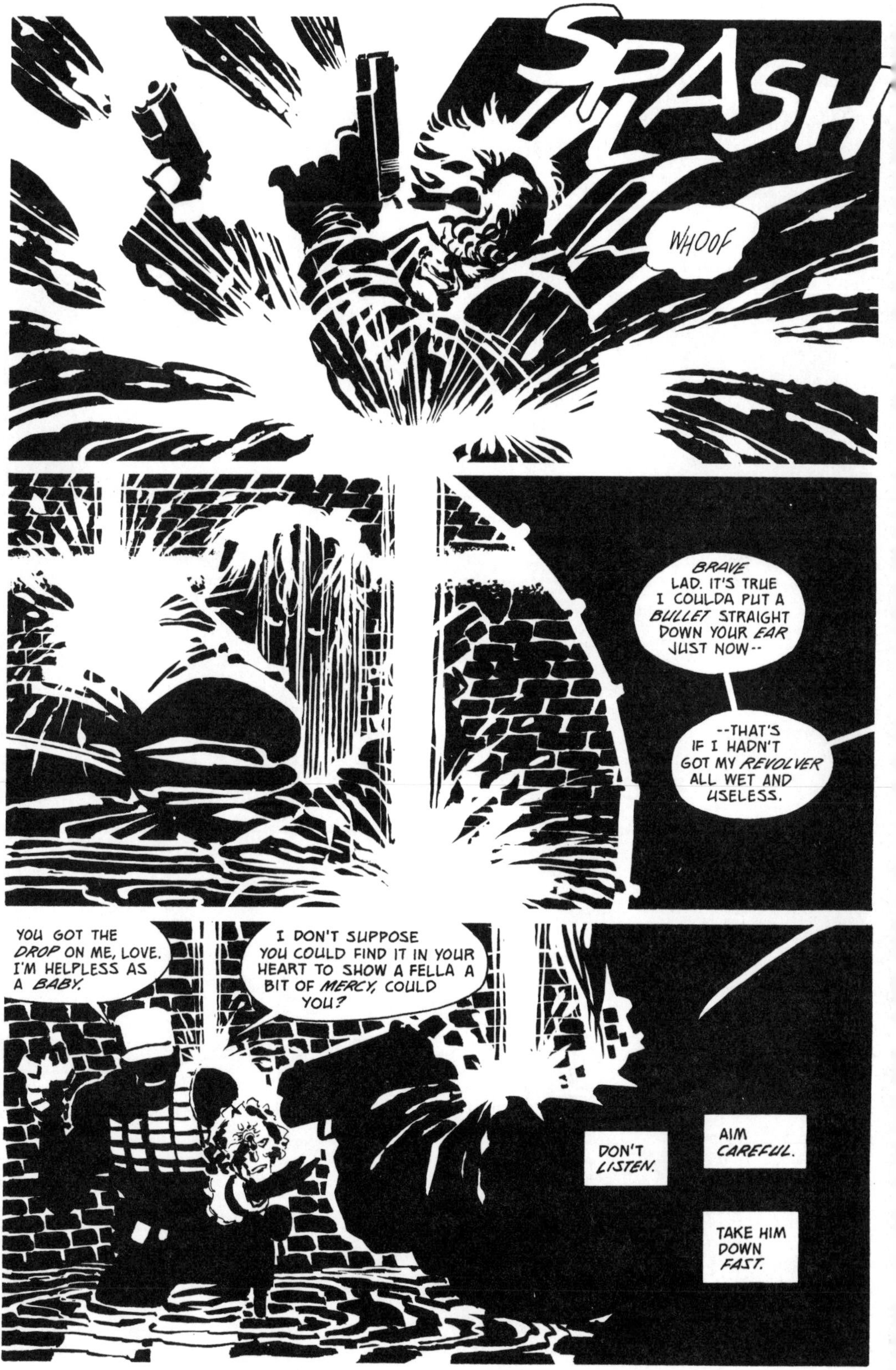

SPLASH
WHOOF
BRAVE LAD. IT'S TRUE I COULDA PUT A BULLET STRAIGHT DOWN YOUR EAR JUST NOW--
--THAT'S IF I HADN'T GOT MY REVOLVER ALL WET AND USELESS.
YOU GOT THE DROP ON ME, LOVE. I'M HELPLESS AS A BABY.
I DON'T SUPPOSE YOU COULD FIND IT IN YOUR HEART TO SHOW A FELLA A BIT OF MERCY, COULD YOU?
DON'T LISTEN.
AIM CAREFUL.
TAKE HIM DOWN FAST.

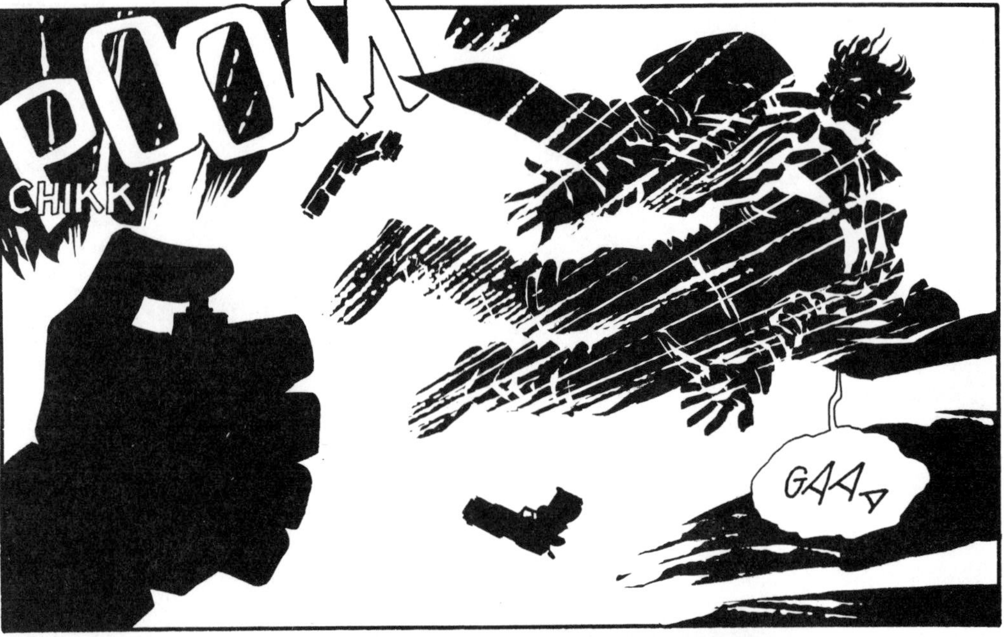
POOM
CHIKK
GAAA

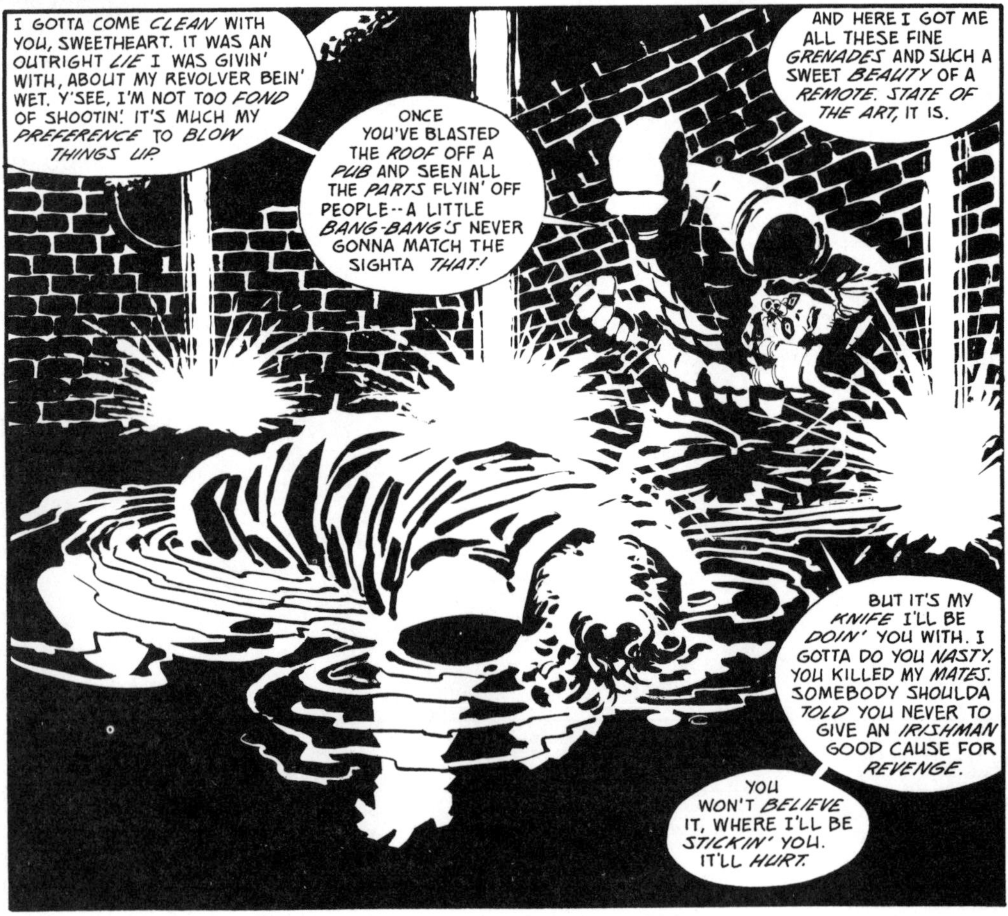
I GOTTA COME *CLEAN* WITH YOU, SWEETHEART. IT WAS AN OUTRIGHT *LIE* I WAS GIVIN' WITH, ABOUT MY REVOLVER BEIN' WET. Y'SEE, I'M NOT TOO *FOND* OF SHOOTIN'. IT'S MUCH MY *PREFERENCE* TO *BLOW* THINGS *UP*.
ONCE YOU'VE BLASTED THE *ROOF* OFF A *PUB* AND SEEN ALL THE *PARTS* FLYIN' OFF PEOPLE--A LITTLE *BANG-BANG'S* NEVER GONNA MATCH THE SIGHTA *THAT!*
AND HERE I GOT ME ALL THESE FINE *GRENADES* AND SUCH A SWEET *BEAUTY* OF A *REMOTE*. *STATE OF THE ART*, IT IS.
BUT IT'S MY *KNIFE* I'LL BE *DOIN'* YOU WITH. I GOTTA DO YOU *NASTY*. YOU KILLED MY *MATES*. SOMEBODY SHOULDA *TOLD* YOU NEVER TO GIVE AN *IRISHMAN* GOOD CAUSE FOR *REVENGE*.
YOU WON'T *BELIEVE* IT, WHERE I'LL BE *STICKIN'* YOU. IT'LL *HURT*.

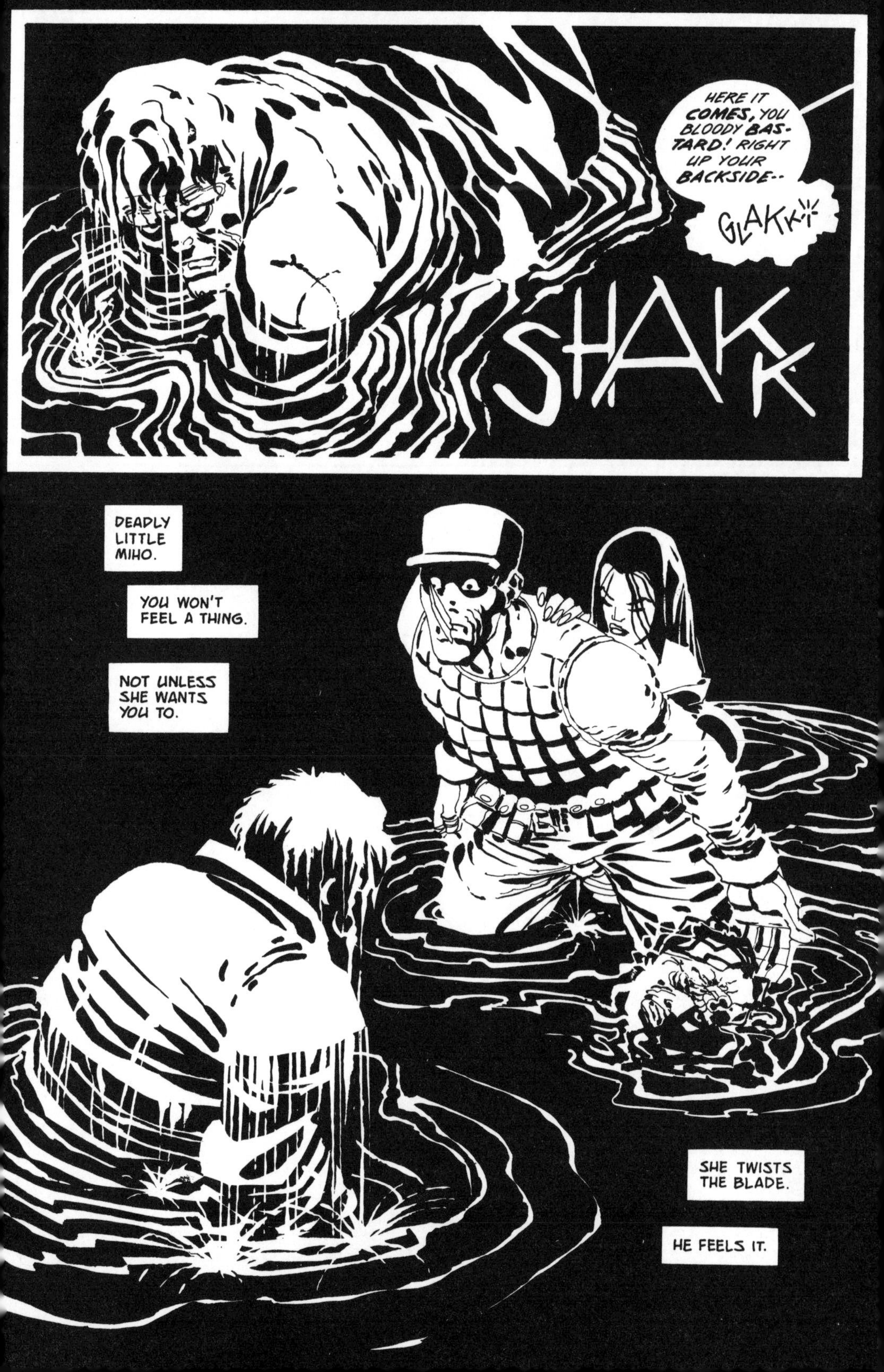
HERE IT COMES, YOU BLOODY BASTARD! RIGHT UP YOUR BACKSIDE--
GLAKK!
SHAKK
DEADLY LITTLE MIHO.
YOU WON'T FEEL A THING.
NOT UNLESS SHE WANTS YOU TO.
SHE TWISTS THE BLADE.
HE FEELS IT.

THE STORM KICKS UP A BIGGER FUSS THAN EVER. IT'S POUNDING, PUMMELING, DRENCH-YOU-TO-THE-BONE RAIN, DEAFENING, BLINDING, END-OF-THE-WORLD RAIN, THE KIND THAT DOESN'T HIT SIN CITY MORE THAN ONCE A YEAR.

I HATE THE RAIN. IT MAKES IT SO DAMN HARD TO THINK STRAIGHT.

I SHAKE THE SNOT OUT OF MY BRAIN AND THINK STRAIGHT ANYWAY. I GRAB POOR DALLAS'S CAR PHONE AND MAKE THE MOST IMPORTANT CALL OF MY LIFE. I TELL MIHO WHAT WE'RE GONNA DO AND HOW WE'RE GONNA DO IT.

FIRST WE GOTTA RESCUE GAIL. THEN COMES THE KILL, THE BIG, FAT KILL.

FOR A SECOND OR TWO THE WIND LAYS OFF AND I ALMOST THINK I HEAR A CRY, TINY, DISTANT, HELPLESS.

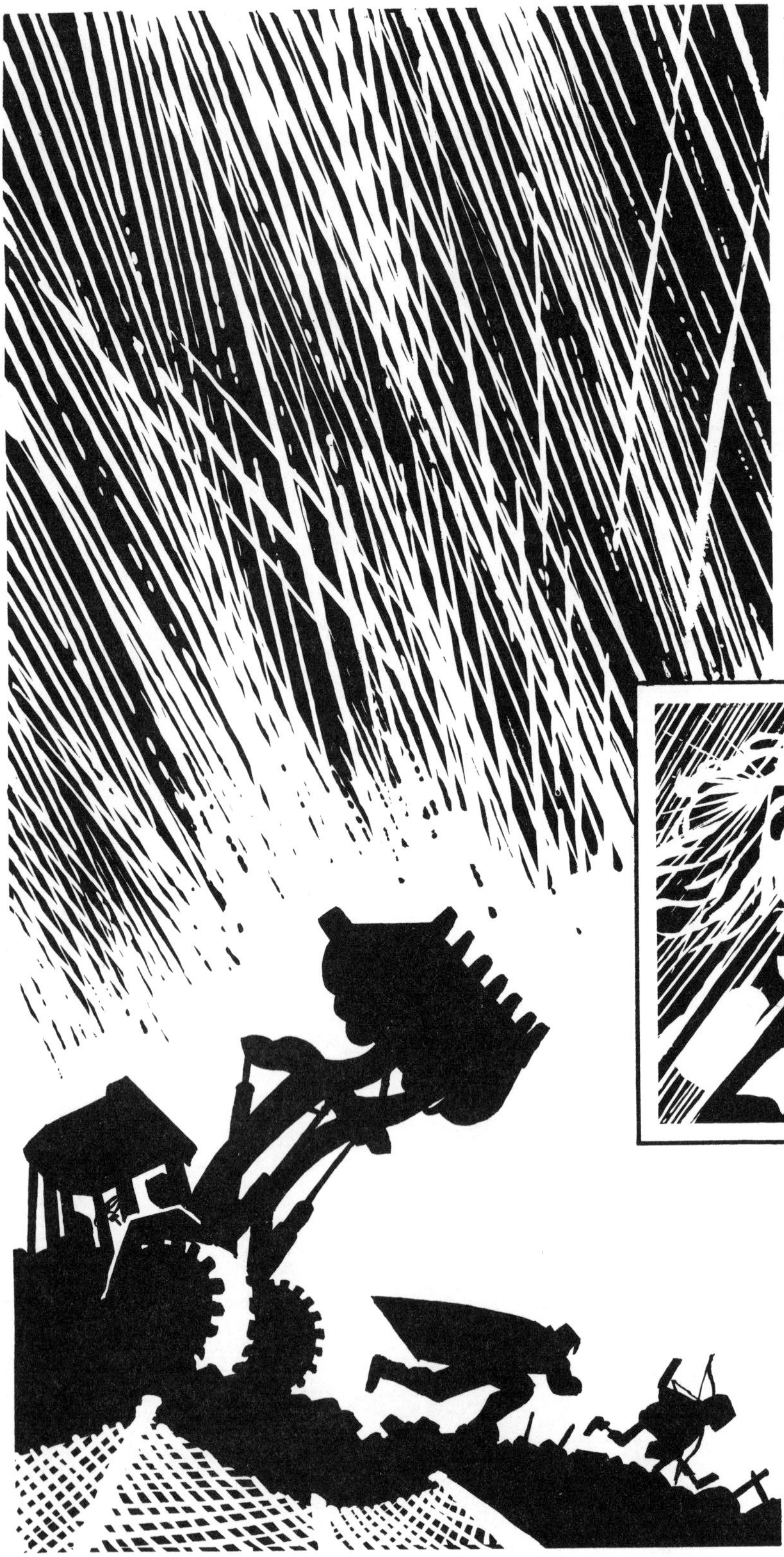

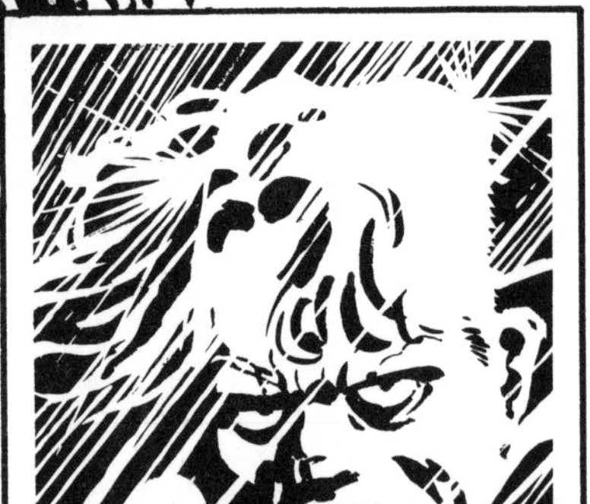

GAIL. BABY.

I HAVE TO WAIT.

I HAVE TO WAIT.

*I CAN ALMOST **HEAR** HER **SCREAM...***

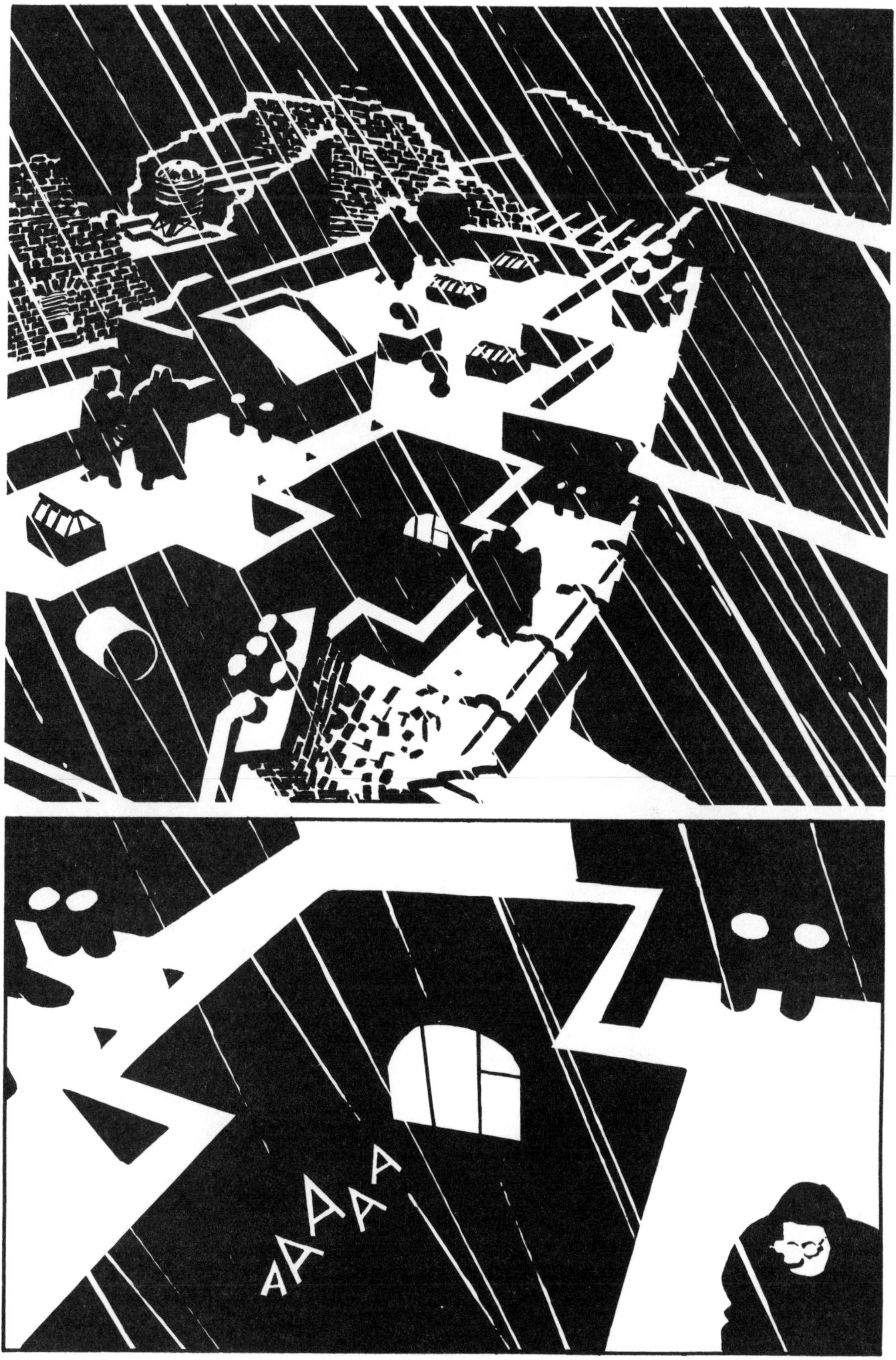
AAAAA

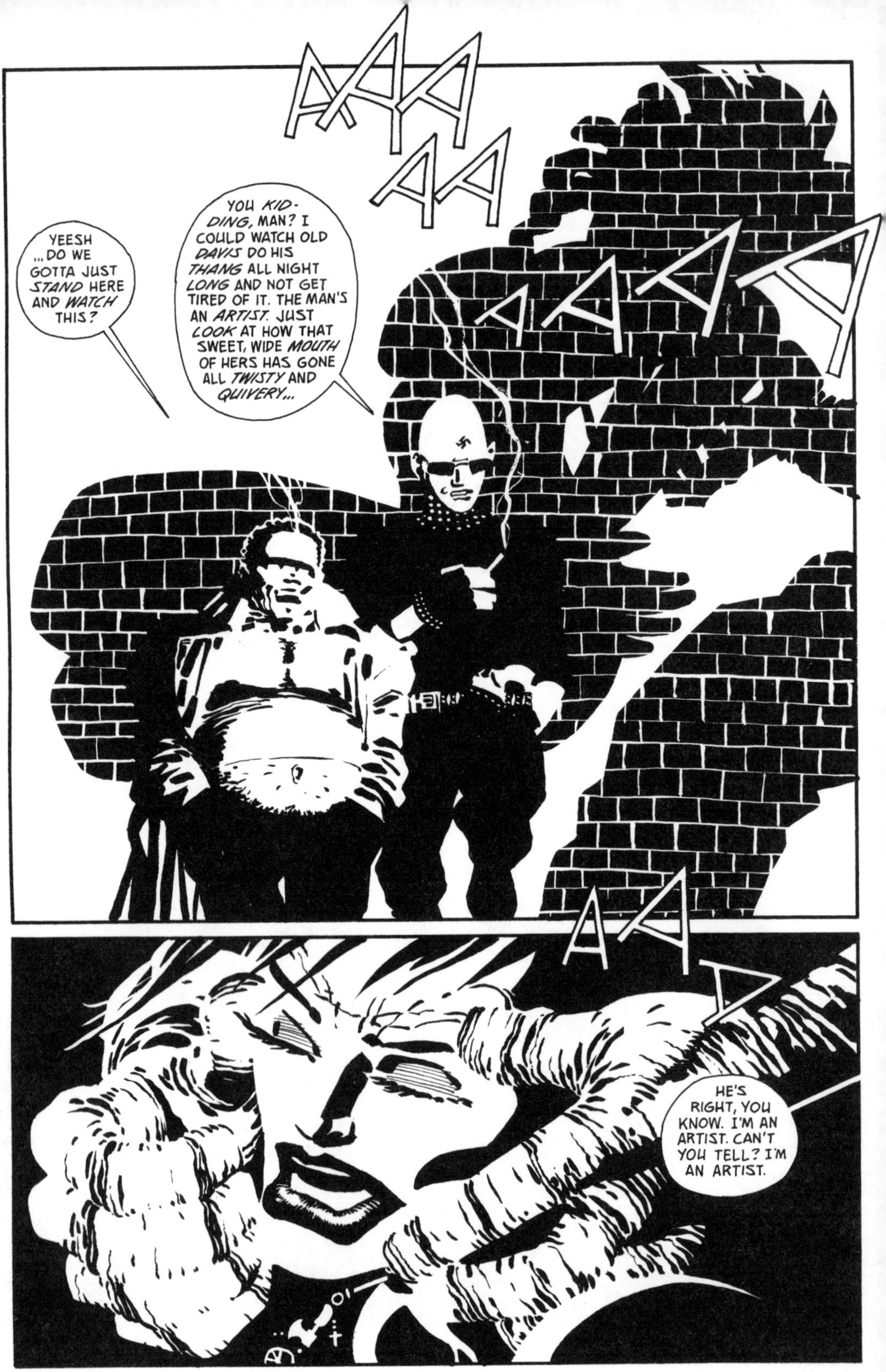
AAAAAA
YEESH ...DO WE GOTTA JUST STAND HERE AND WATCH THIS?
YOU KID-DING, MAN? I COULD WATCH OLD DAVIS DO HIS THANG ALL NIGHT LONG AND NOT GET TIRED OF IT. THE MAN'S AN ARTIST. JUST LOOK AT HOW THAT SWEET, WIDE MOUTH OF HERS HAS GONE ALL TWISTY AND QUIVERY...
AAAAA
AAA
HE'S RIGHT, YOU KNOW. I'M AN ARTIST. CAN'T YOU TELL? I'M AN ARTIST.

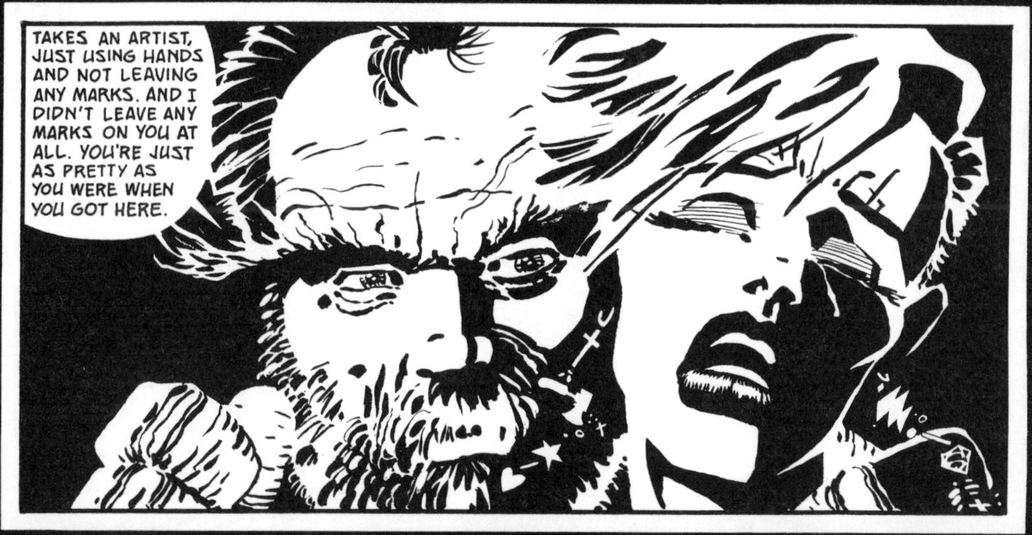
TAKES AN ARTIST, JUST USING HANDS AND NOT LEAVING ANY MARKS. AND I DIDN'T LEAVE ANY MARKS ON YOU AT ALL. YOU'RE JUST AS PRETTY AS YOU WERE WHEN YOU GOT HERE.

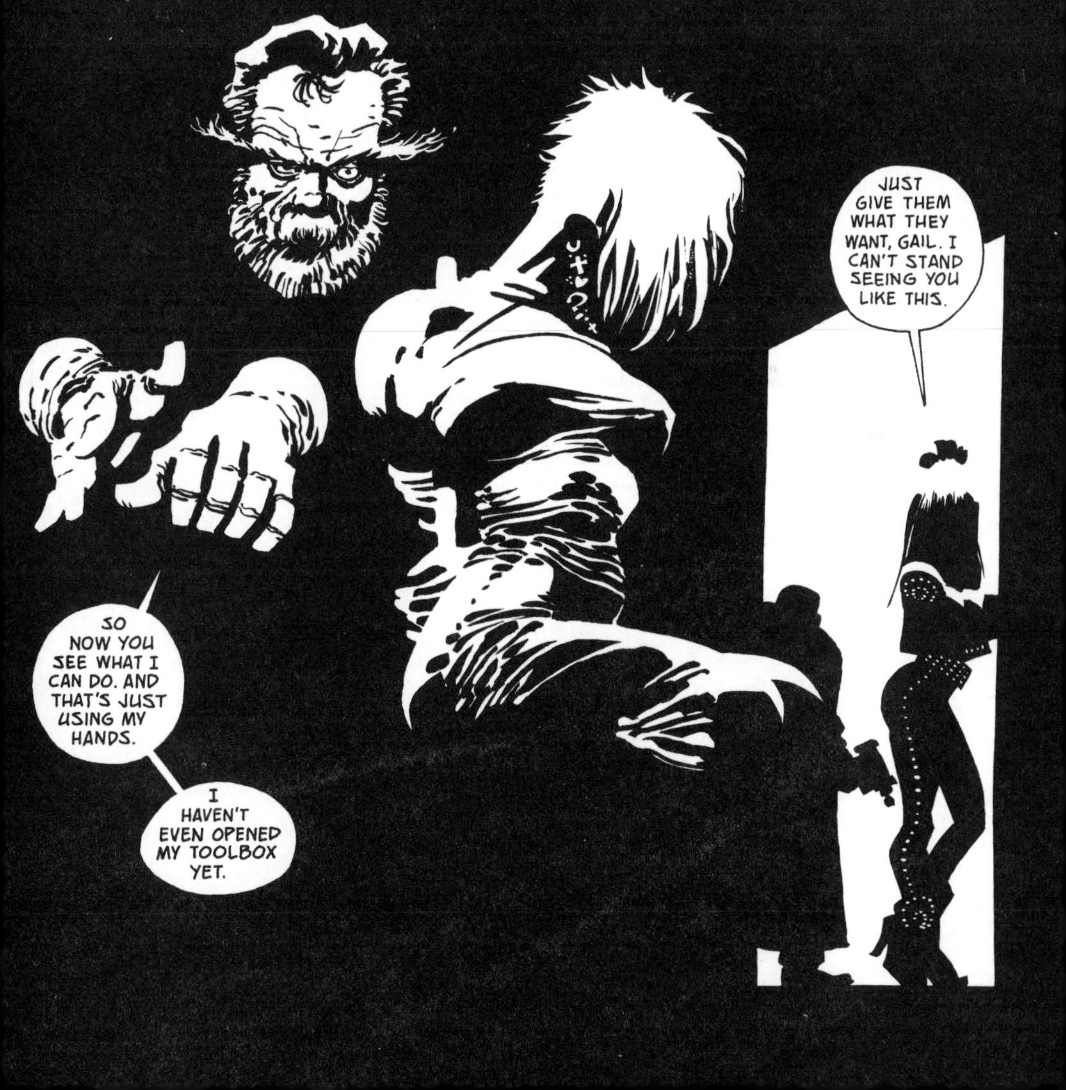
JUST GIVE THEM WHAT THEY WANT, GAIL. I CAN'T STAND SEEING YOU LIKE THIS.
SO NOW YOU SEE WHAT I CAN DO. AND THAT'S JUST USING MY HANDS.
I HAVEN'T EVEN OPENED MY TOOLBOX YET.

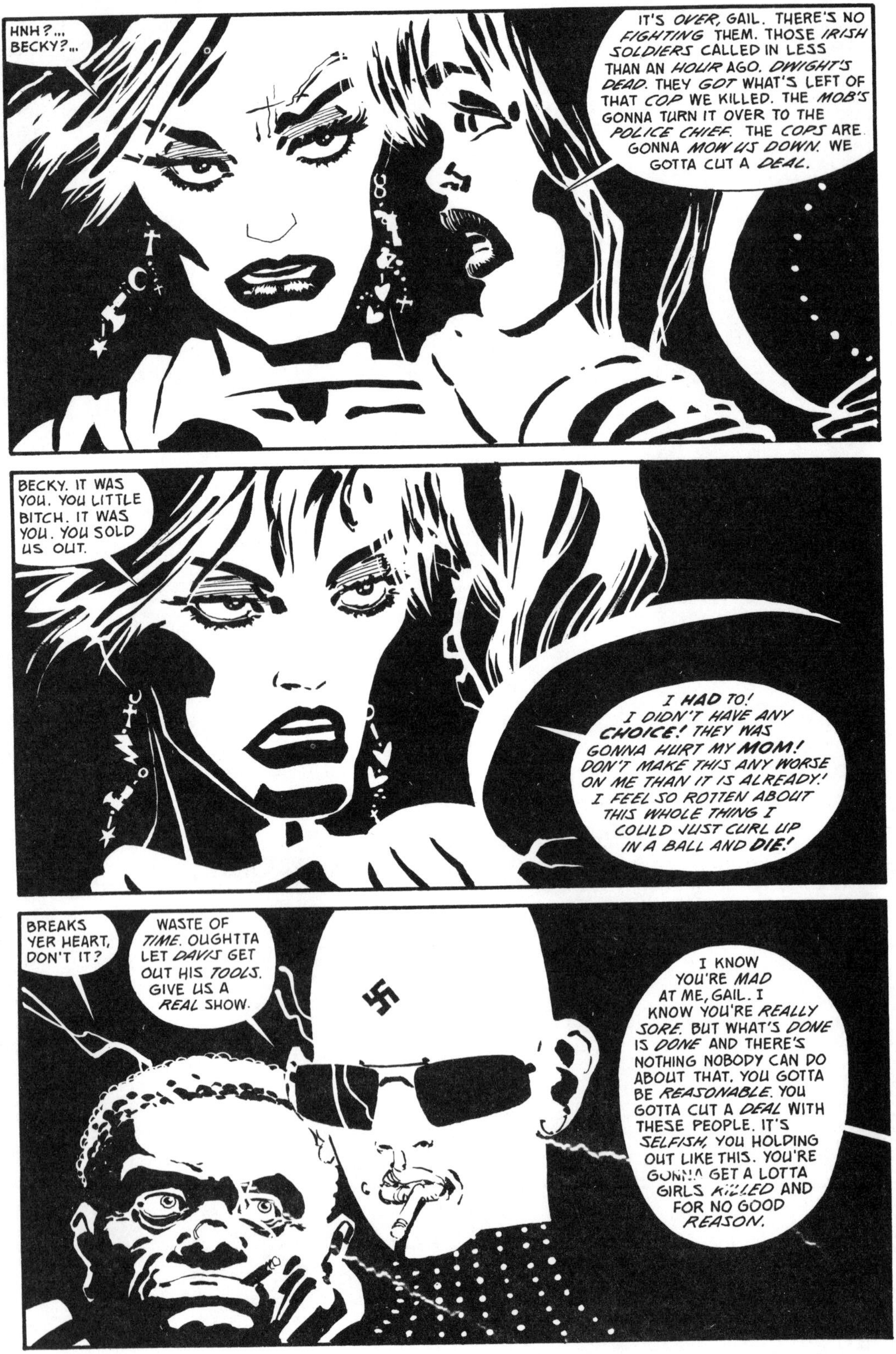
HNH?... BECKY?...
IT'S OVER, GAIL. THERE'S NO FIGHTING THEM. THOSE IRISH SOLDIERS CALLED IN LESS THAN AN HOUR AGO. DWIGHT'S DEAD. THEY GOT WHAT'S LEFT OF THAT COP WE KILLED. THE MOB'S GONNA TURN IT OVER TO THE POLICE CHIEF. THE COPS ARE GONNA MOW US DOWN. WE GOTTA CUT A DEAL.
BECKY. IT WAS YOU. YOU LITTLE BITCH. IT WAS YOU. YOU SOLD US OUT.
I HAD TO! I DIDN'T HAVE ANY CHOICE! THEY WAS GONNA HURT MY MOM! DON'T MAKE THIS ANY WORSE ON ME THAN IT IS ALREADY! I FEEL SO ROTTEN ABOUT THIS WHOLE THING I COULD JUST CURL UP IN A BALL AND DIE!
BREAKS YER HEART, DON'T IT?
WASTE OF TIME. OUGHTTA LET DAVIS GET OUT HIS TOOLS. GIVE US A REAL SHOW.
I KNOW YOU'RE MAD AT ME, GAIL. I KNOW YOU'RE REALLY SORE. BUT WHAT'S DONE IS DONE AND THERE'S NOTHING NOBODY CAN DO ABOUT THAT. YOU GOTTA BE REASONABLE. YOU GOTTA CUT A DEAL WITH THESE PEOPLE. IT'S SELFISH, YOU HOLDING OUT LIKE THIS. YOU'RE GONNA GET A LOTTA GIRLS KILLED AND FOR NO GOOD REASON.

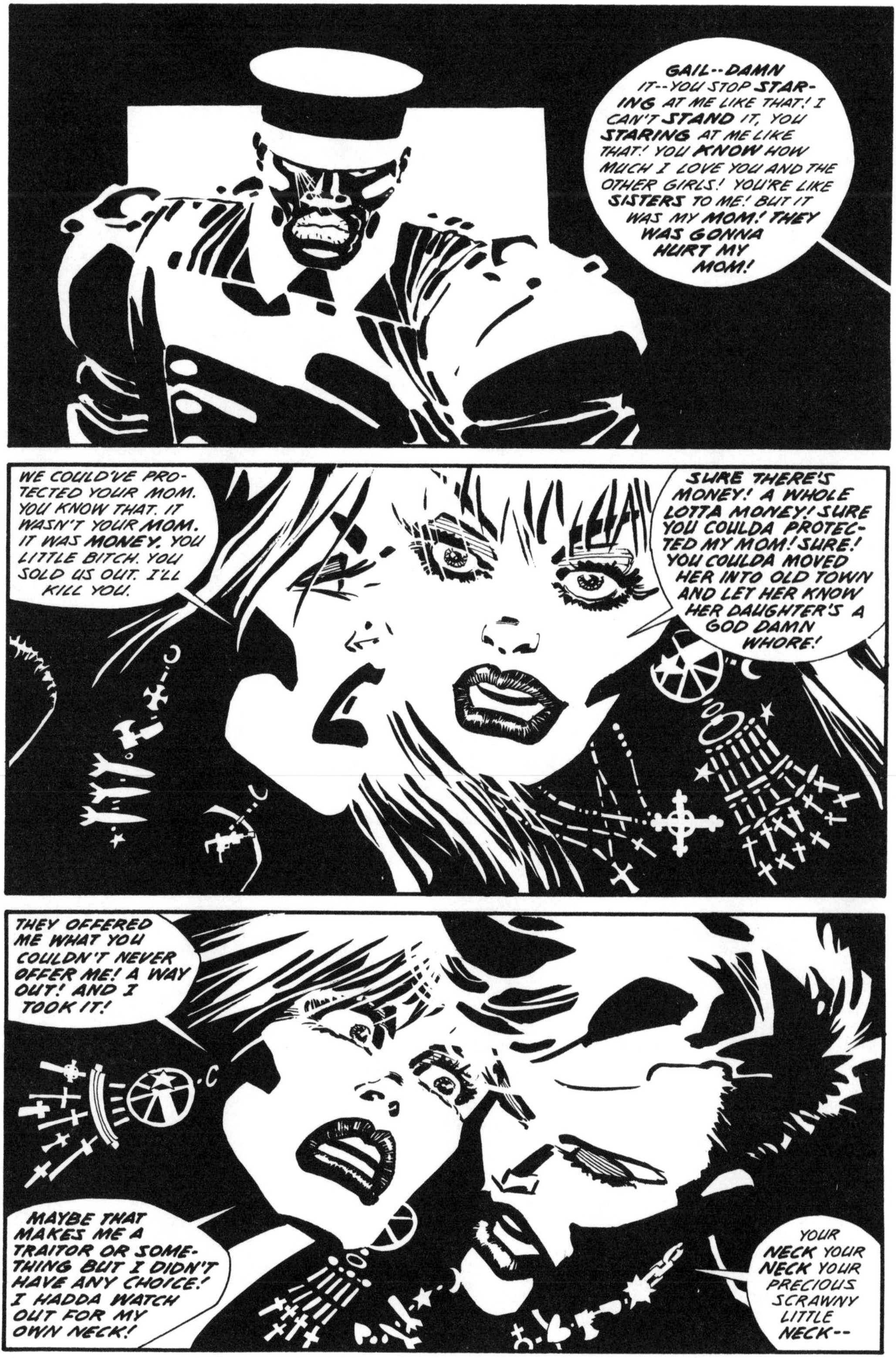
GAIL--DAMN IT--YOU STOP STARING AT ME LIKE THAT! I CAN'T STAND IT, YOU STARING AT ME LIKE THAT! YOU KNOW HOW MUCH I LOVE YOU AND THE OTHER GIRLS! YOU'RE LIKE SISTERS TO ME! BUT IT WAS MY MOM! THEY WAS GONNA HURT MY MOM!
WE COULD'VE PROTECTED YOUR MOM. YOU KNOW THAT. IT WASN'T YOUR MOM. IT WAS MONEY. YOU LITTLE BITCH. YOU SOLD US OUT. I'LL KILL YOU.
SURE THERE'S MONEY! A WHOLE LOTTA MONEY! SURE YOU COULDA PROTECTED MY MOM! SURE! YOU COULDA MOVED HER INTO OLD TOWN AND LET HER KNOW HER DAUGHTER'S A GOD DAMN WHORE!
THEY OFFERED ME WHAT YOU COULDN'T NEVER OFFER ME! A WAY OUT! AND I TOOK IT!
MAYBE THAT MAKES ME A TRAITOR OR SOMETHING BUT I DIDN'T HAVE ANY CHOICE! I HADDA WATCH OUT FOR MY OWN NECK!
YOUR NECK YOUR NECK YOUR PRECIOUS SCRAWNY LITTLE NECK--

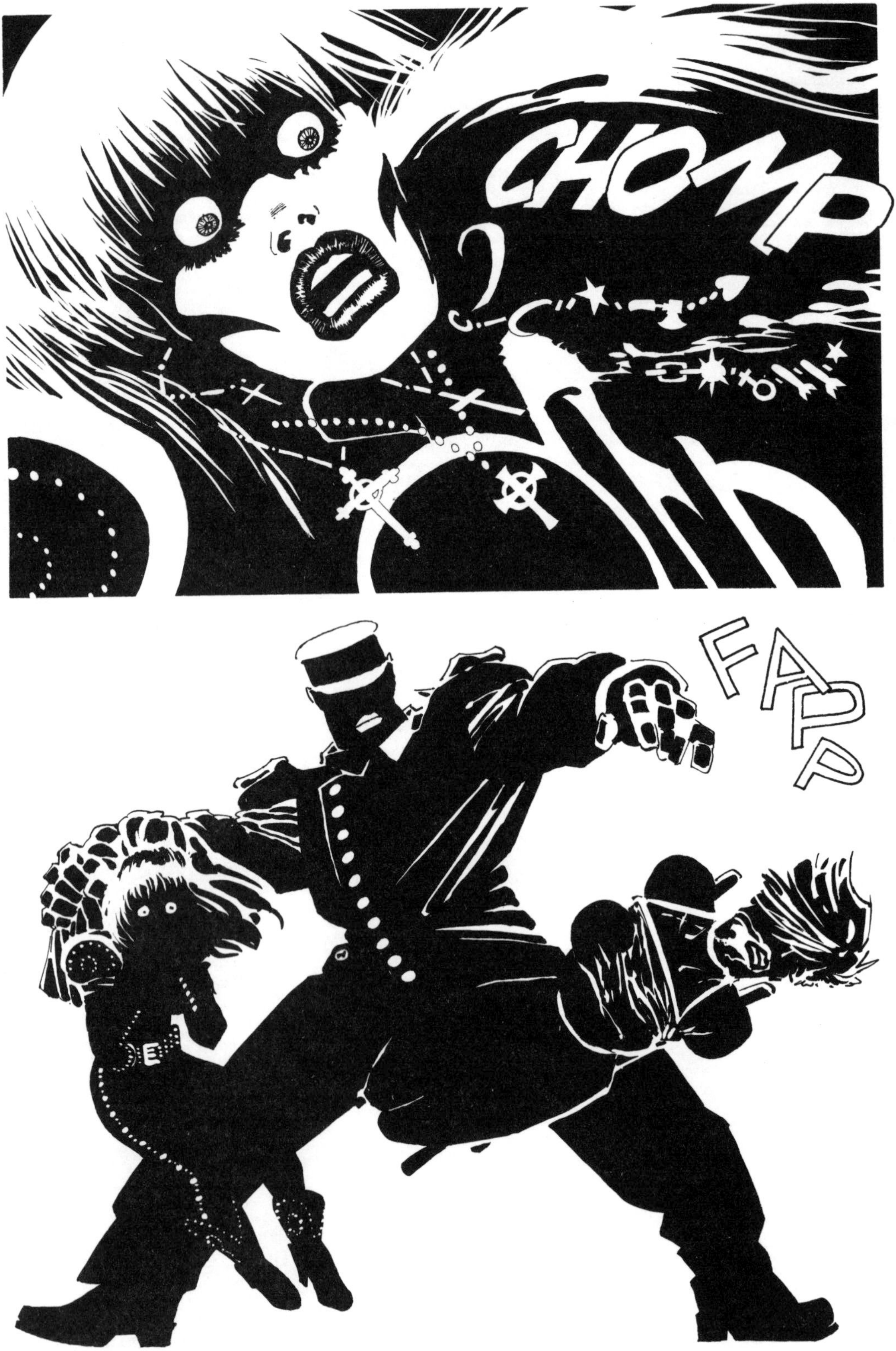
CHOMP
FAPP

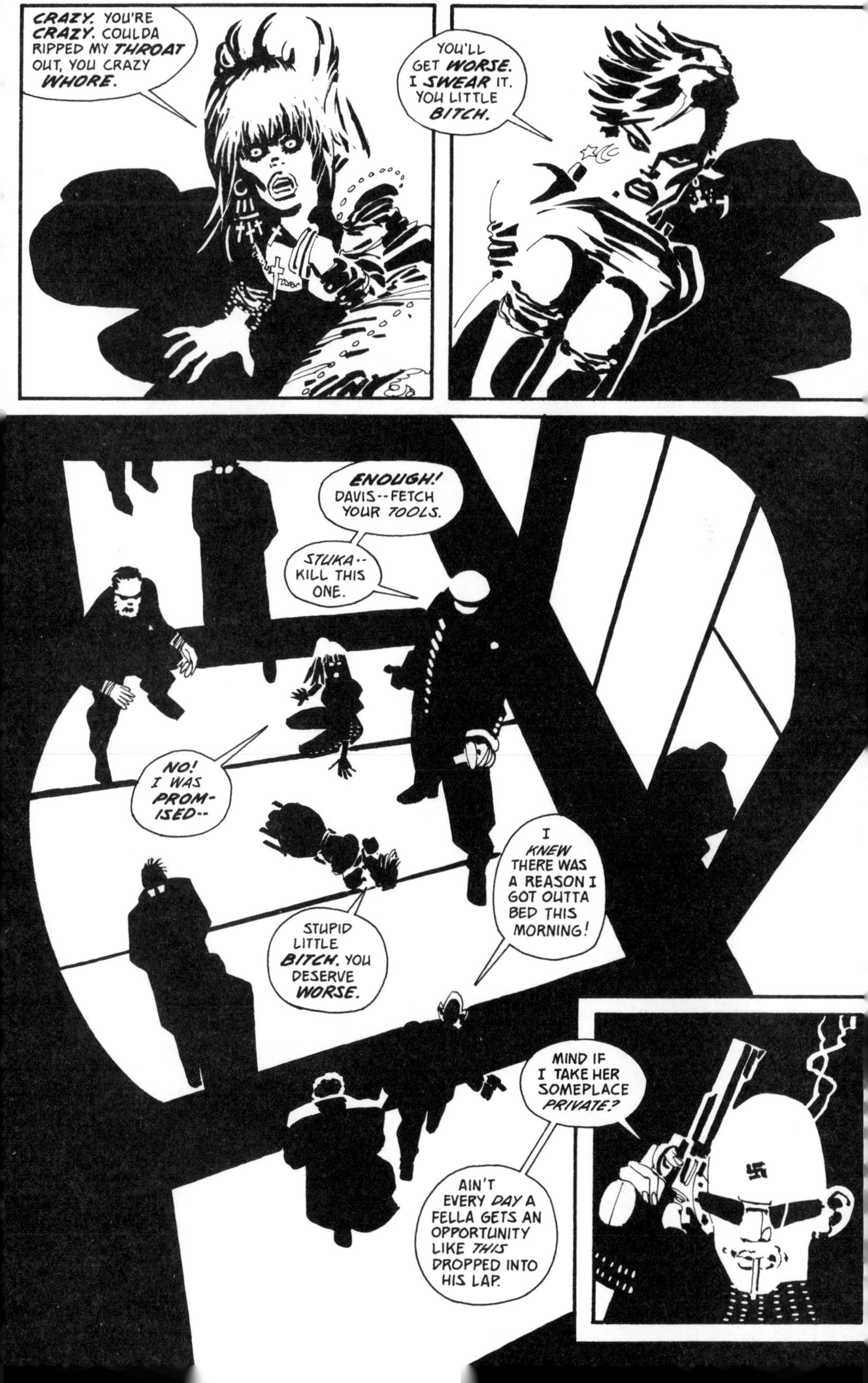
CRAZY. YOU'RE CRAZY. COULDA RIPPED MY THROAT OUT, YOU CRAZY WHORE.
YOU'LL GET WORSE. I SWEAR IT. YOU LITTLE BITCH.
ENOUGH! DAVIS--FETCH YOUR TOOLS.
STUKA-- KILL THIS ONE.
NO! I WAS PROMISED--
I KNEW THERE WAS A REASON I GOT OUTTA BED THIS MORNING!
STUPID LITTLE BITCH. YOU DESERVE WORSE.
MIND IF I TAKE HER SOMEPLACE PRIVATE?
AIN'T EVERY DAY A FELLA GETS AN OPPORTUNITY LIKE THIS DROPPED INTO HIS LAP.

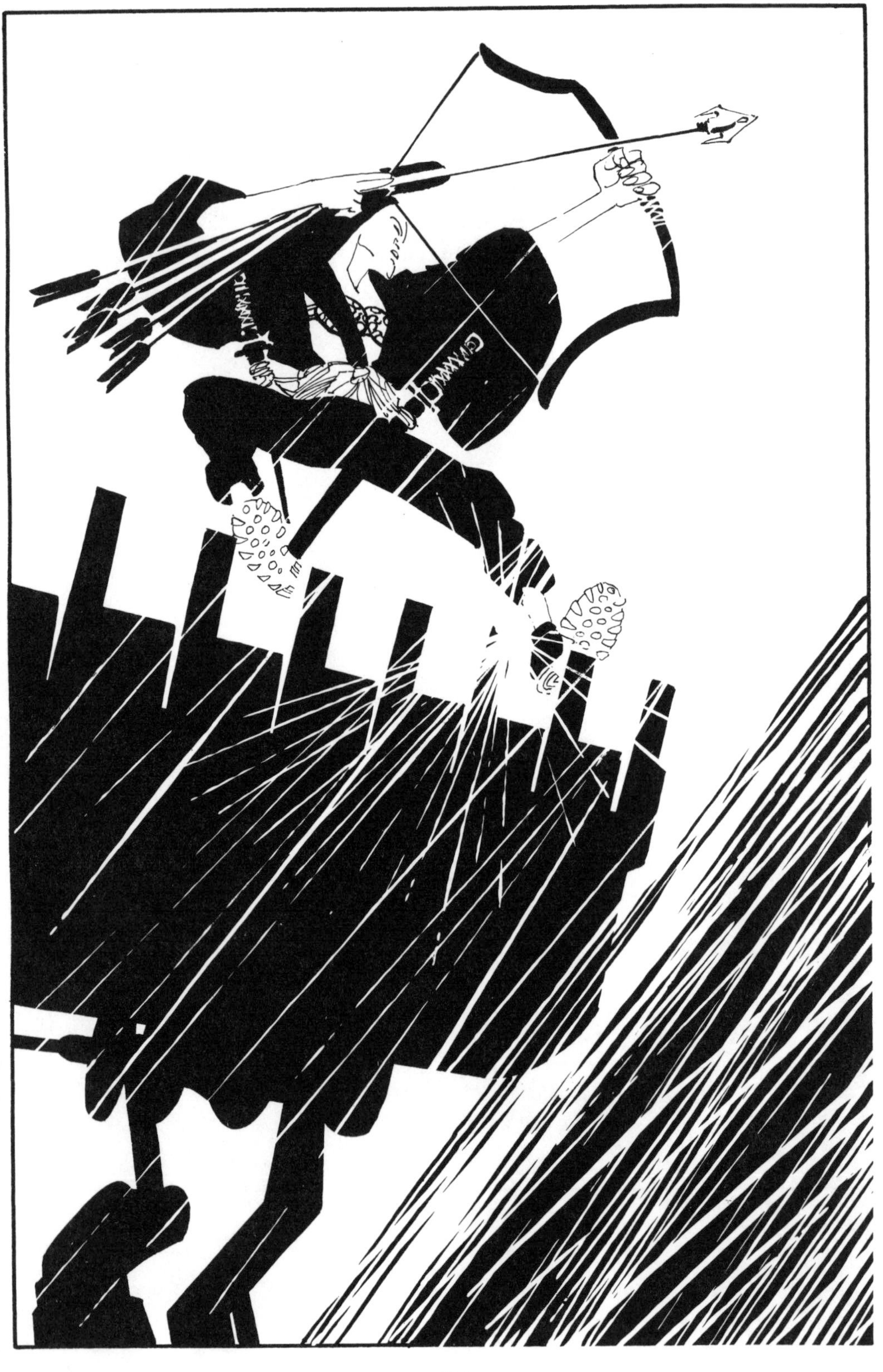

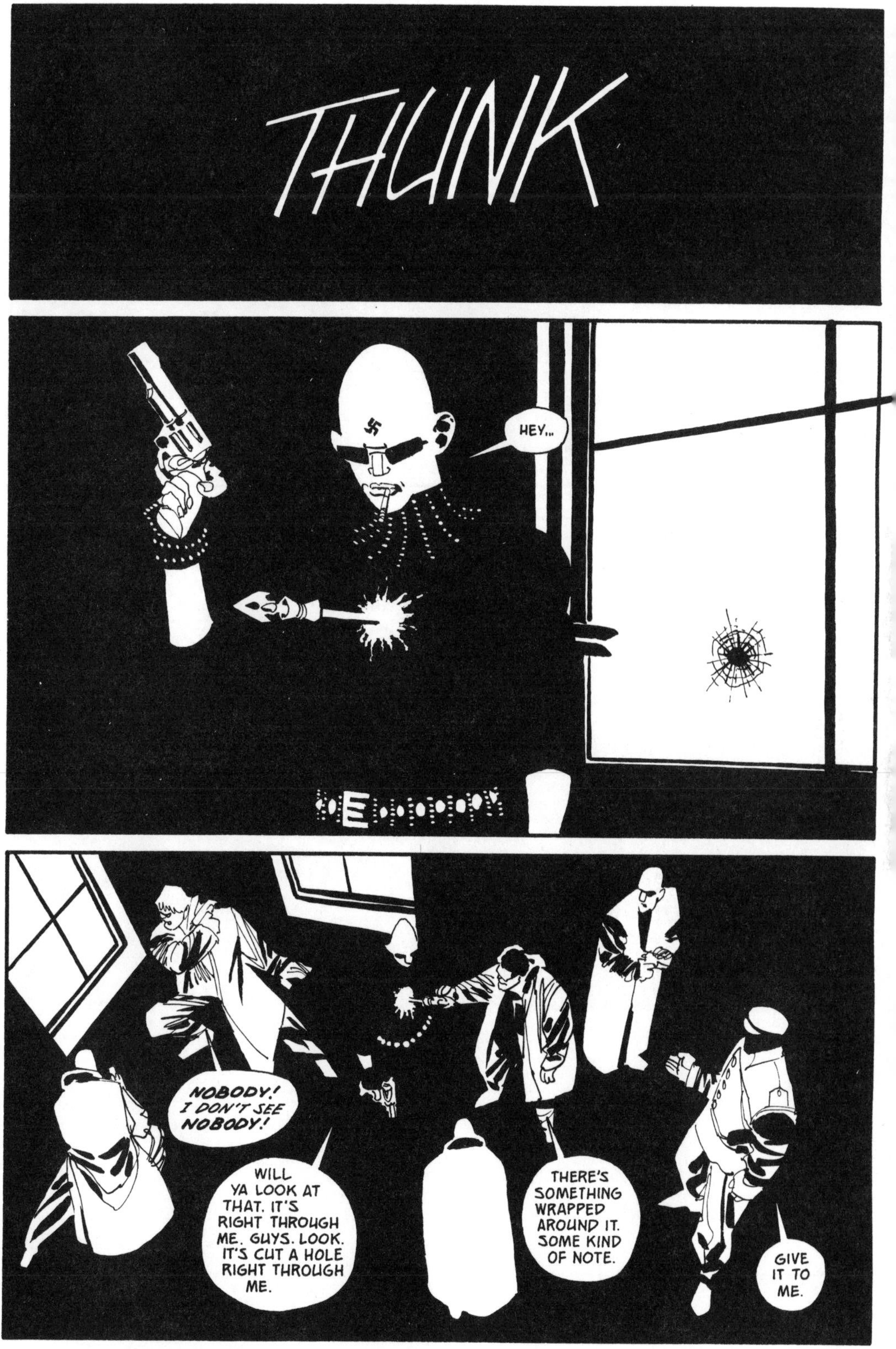
THUNK
HEY...
NOBODY! I DON'T SEE NOBODY!
WILL YA LOOK AT THAT. IT'S RIGHT THROUGH ME. GUYS. LOOK. IT'S CUT A HOLE RIGHT THROUGH ME.
THERE'S SOMETHING WRAPPED AROUND IT. SOME KIND OF NOTE.
GIVE IT TO ME.

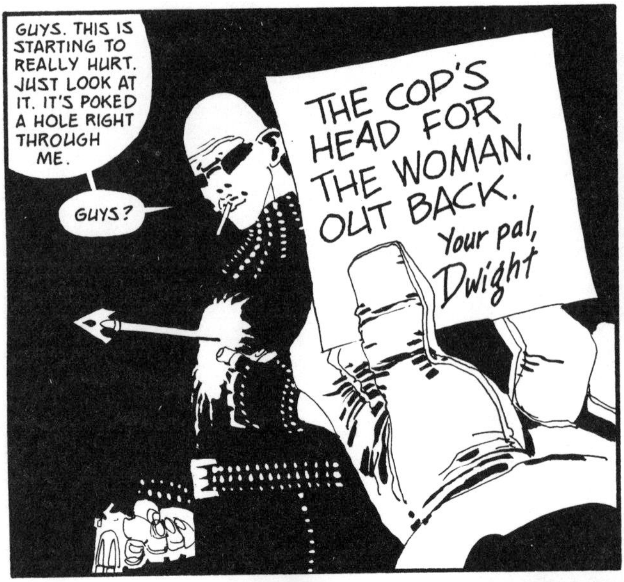
GUYS. THIS IS STARTING TO REALLY HURT. JUST LOOK AT IT. IT'S POKED A HOLE RIGHT THROUGH ME.
GUYS?
THE COP'S HEAD FOR THE WOMAN. OUT BACK.
Your pal, Dwight

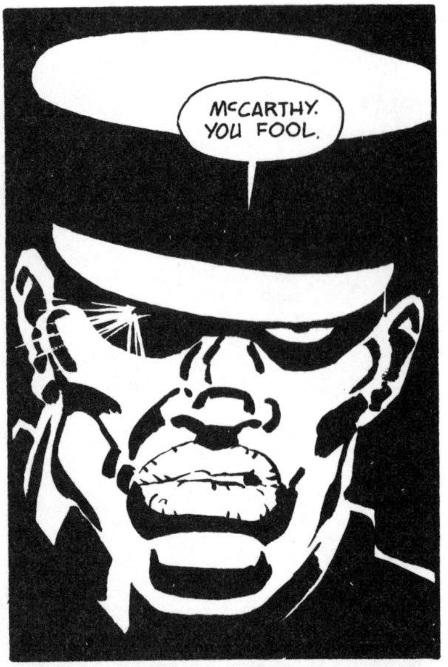
McCARTHY. YOU FOOL.

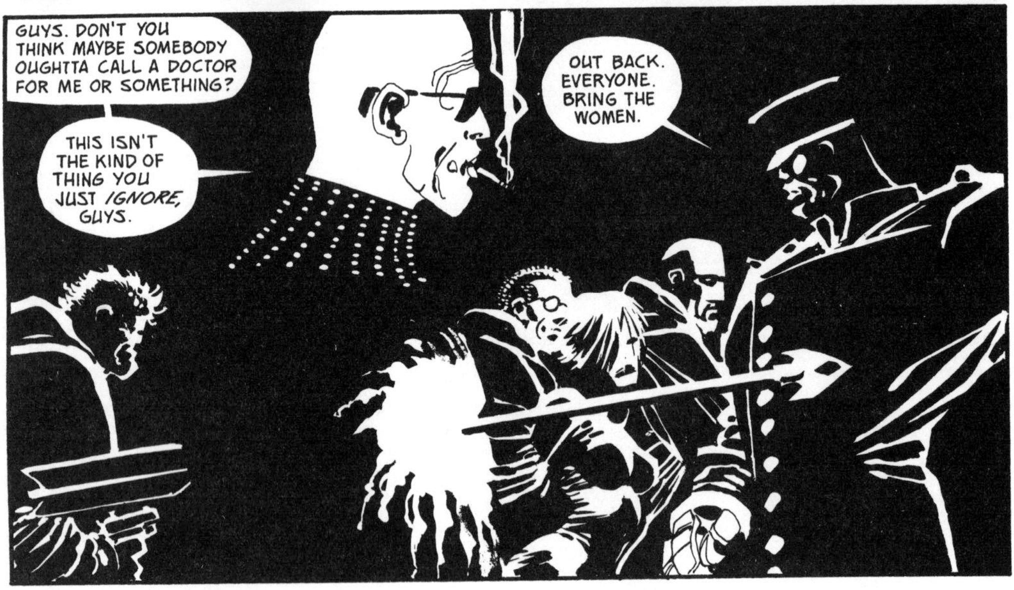
GUYS. DON'T YOU THINK MAYBE SOMEBODY OUGHTTA CALL A DOCTOR FOR ME OR SOMETHING?
THIS ISN'T THE KIND OF THING YOU JUST *IGNORE,* GUYS.
OUT BACK. EVERYONE. BRING THE WOMEN.

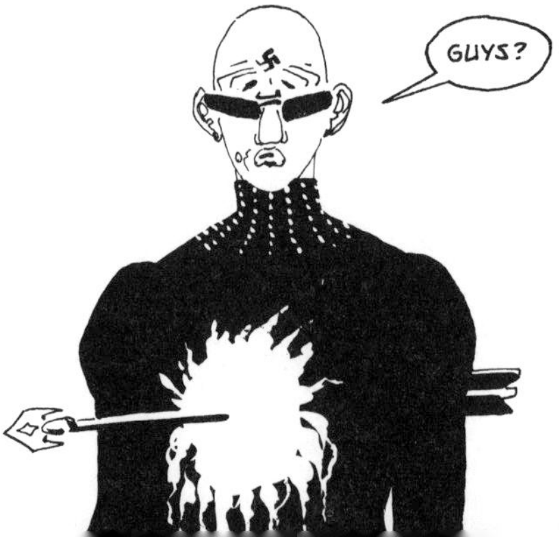
GUYS?

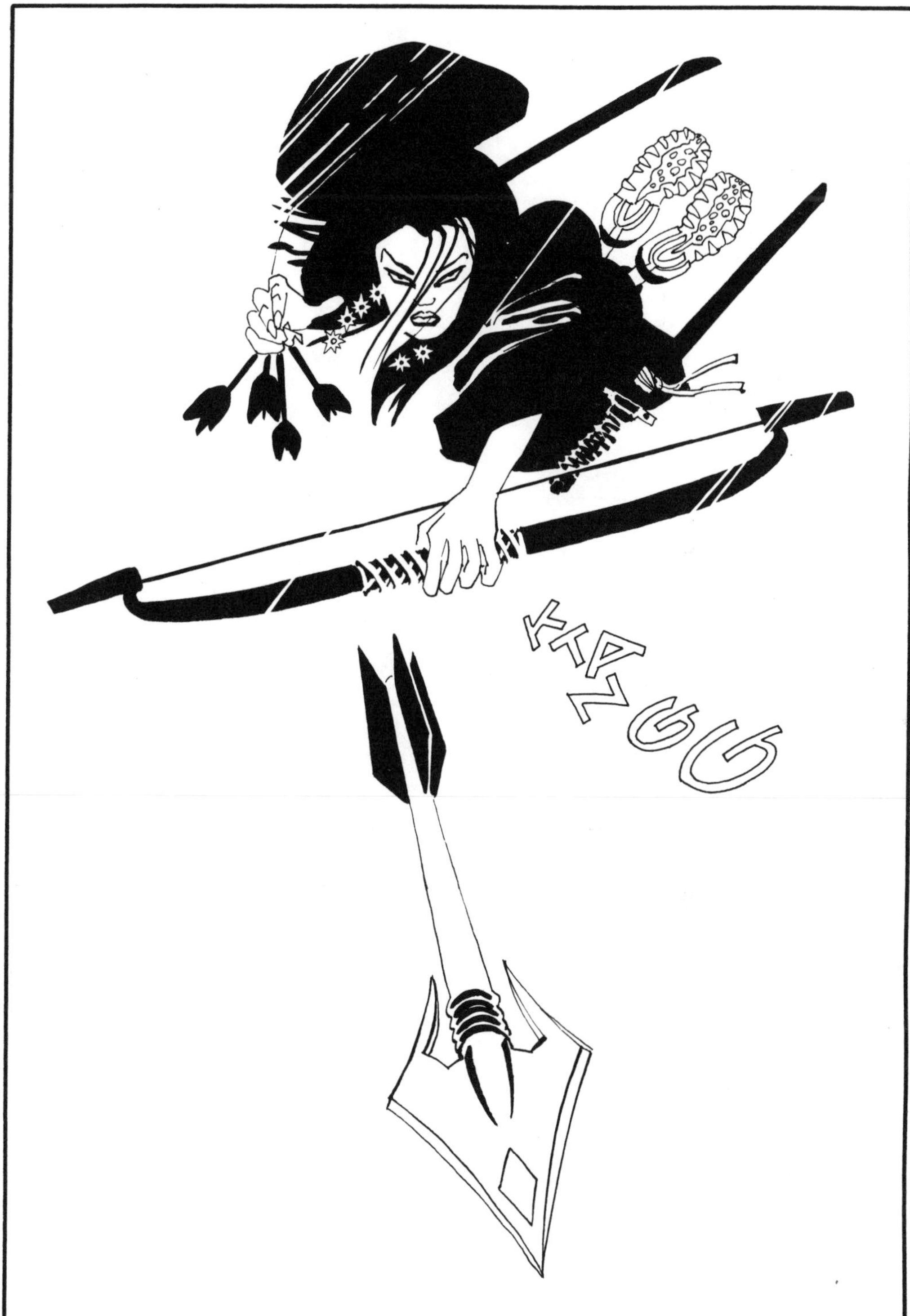
KTANGG

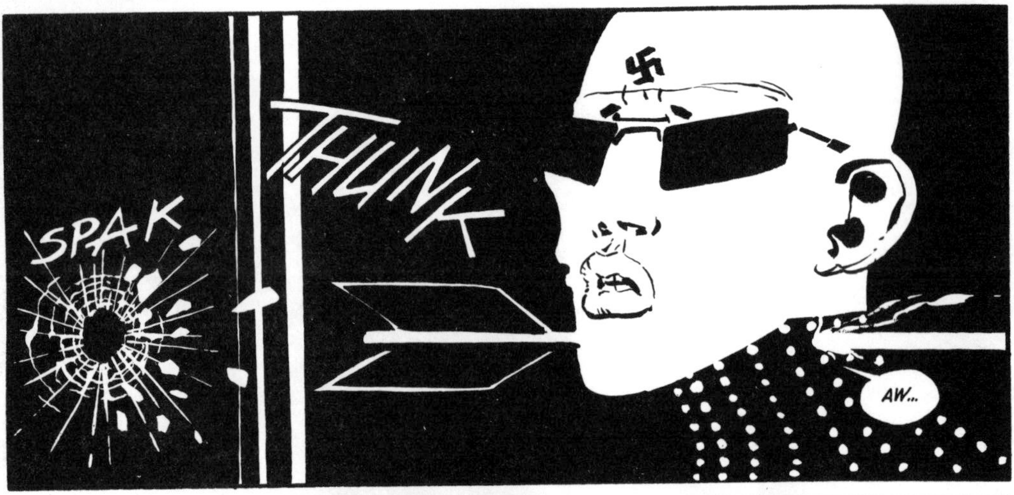
SPAK
THUNK
AW...

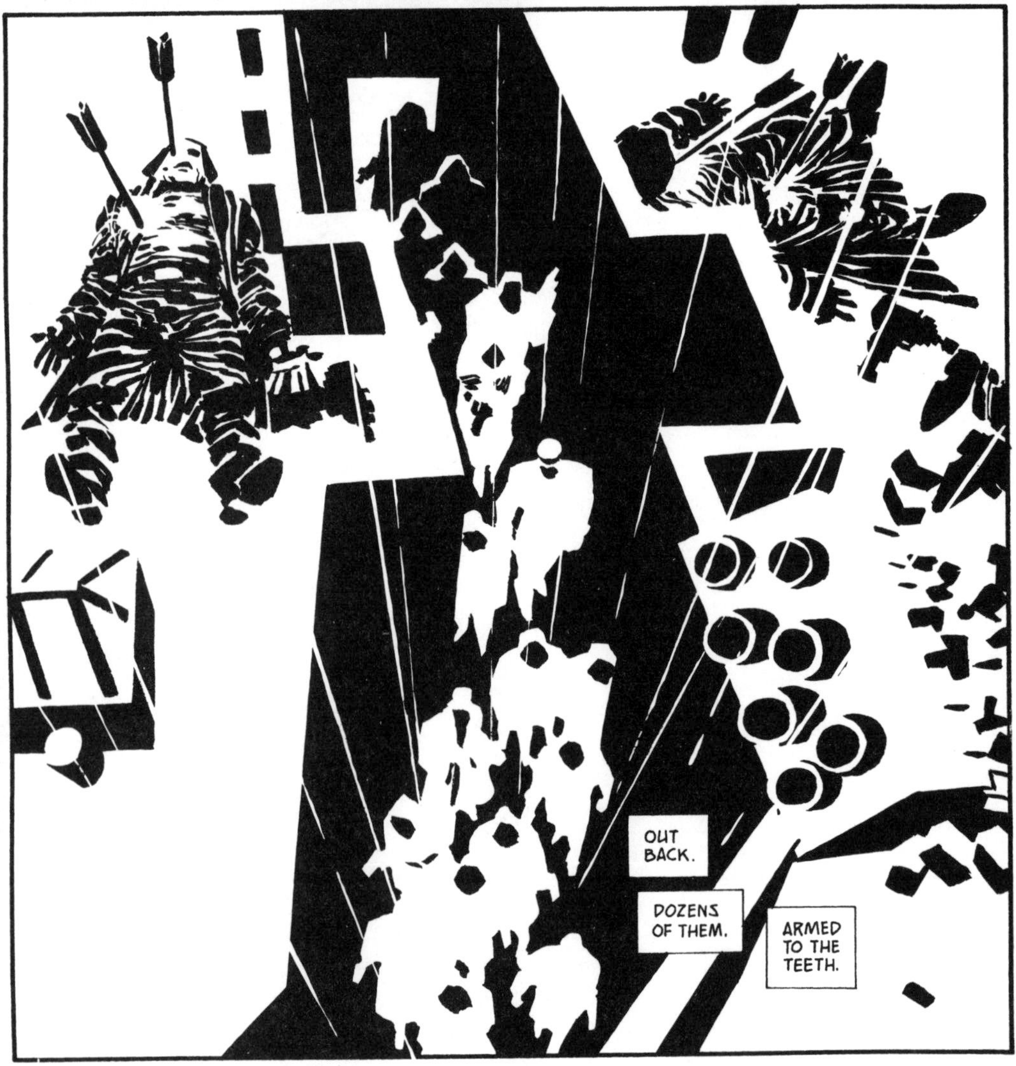
OUT BACK.
DOZENS OF THEM.
ARMED TO THE TEETH.

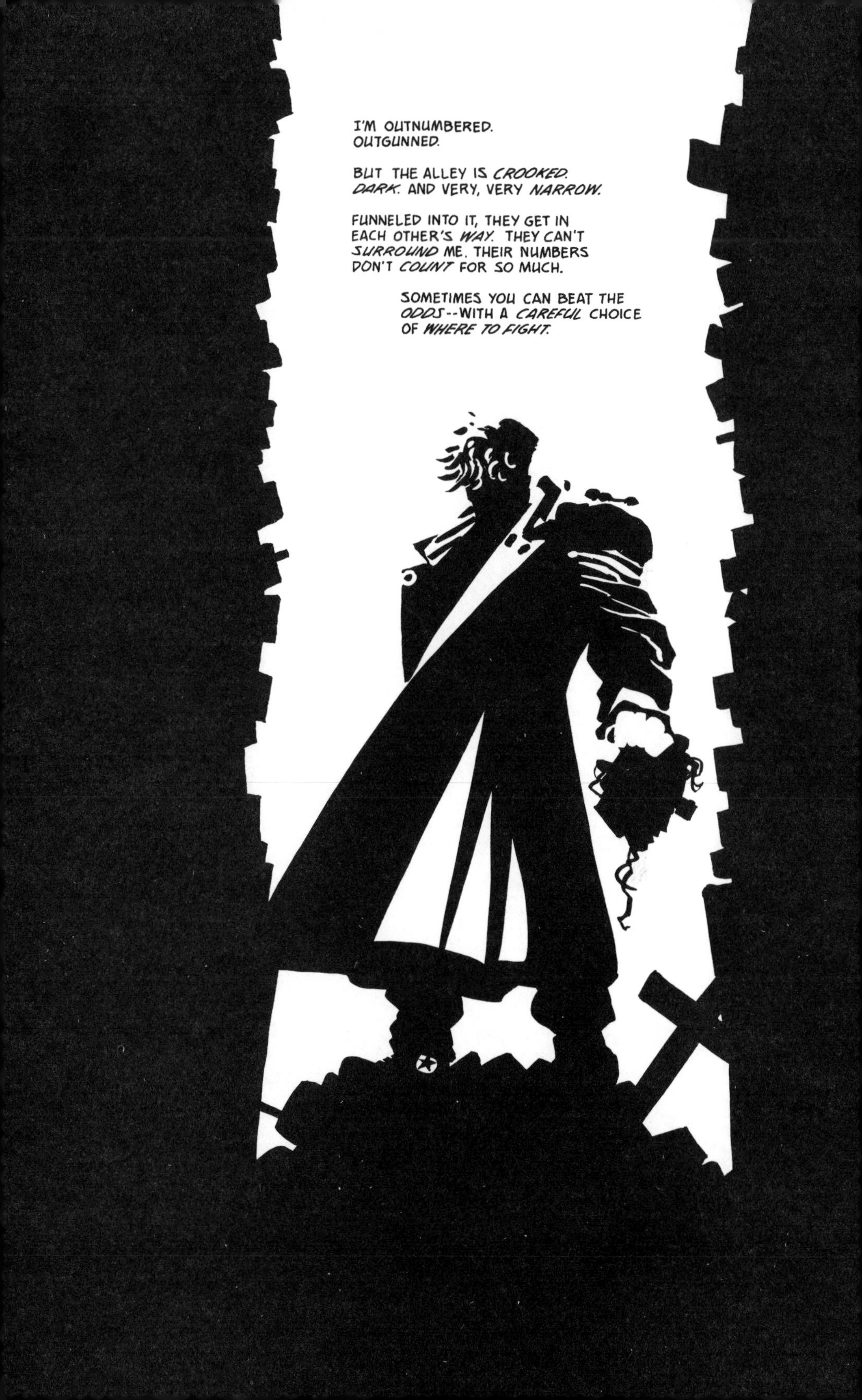
I'M OUTNUMBERED. OUTGUNNED.
BUT THE ALLEY IS *CROOKED.* *DARK.* AND VERY, VERY *NARROW.*
FUNNELED INTO IT, THEY GET IN EACH OTHER'S *WAY.* THEY CAN'T *SURROUND* ME. THEIR NUMBERS DON'T *COUNT* FOR SO MUCH.
SOMETIMES YOU CAN BEAT THE *ODDS*--WITH A *CAREFUL* CHOICE OF *WHERE TO FIGHT.*

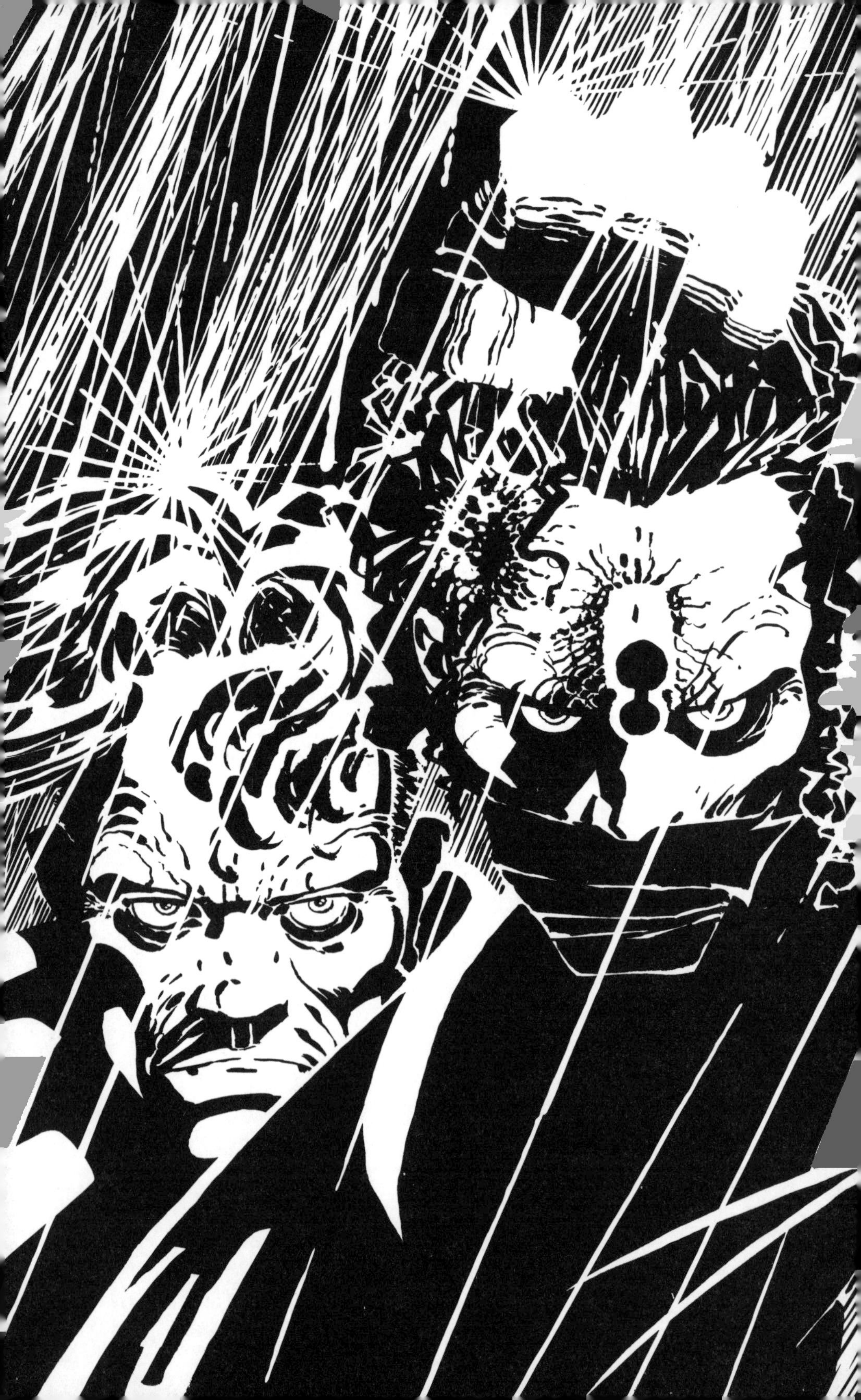

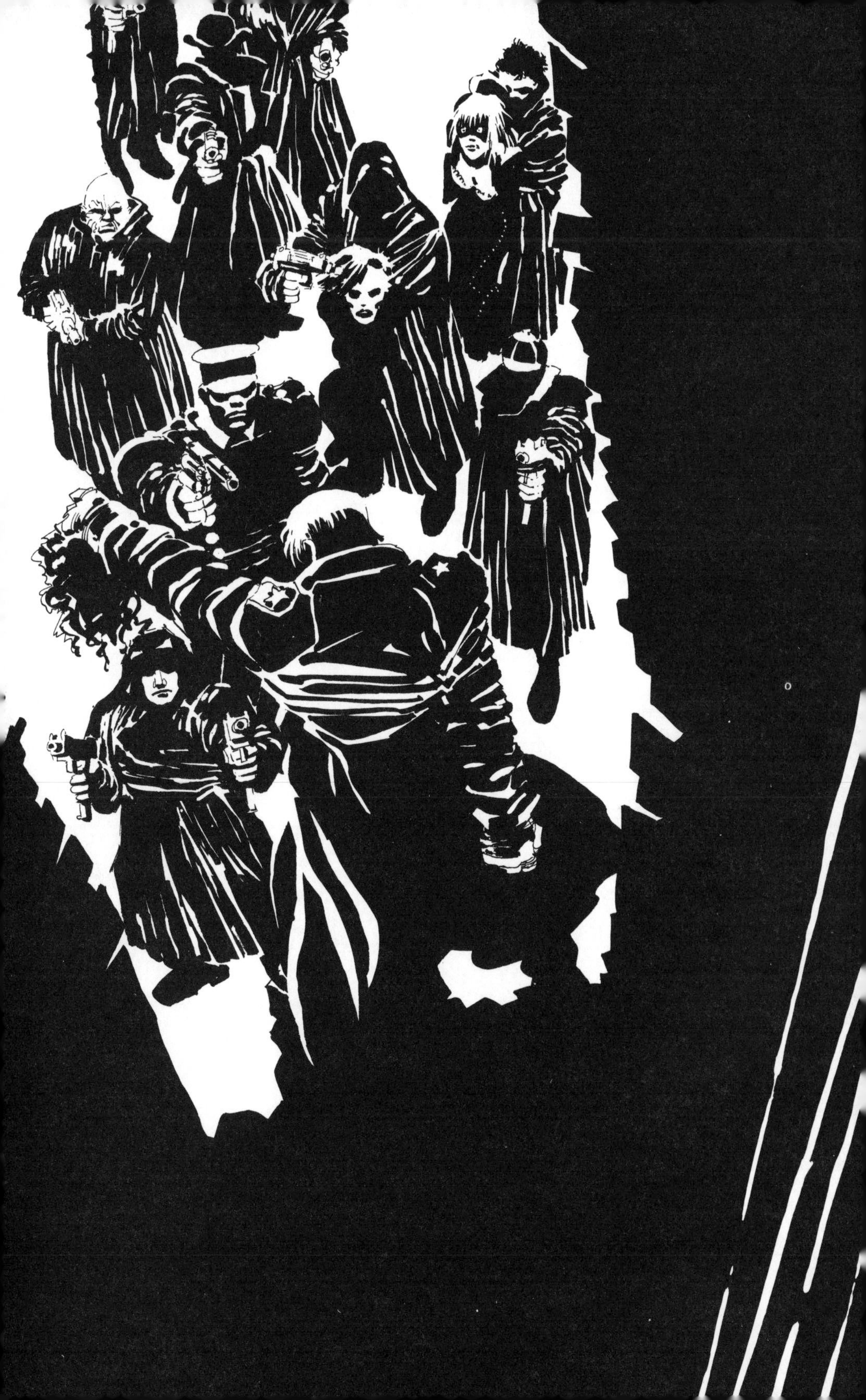

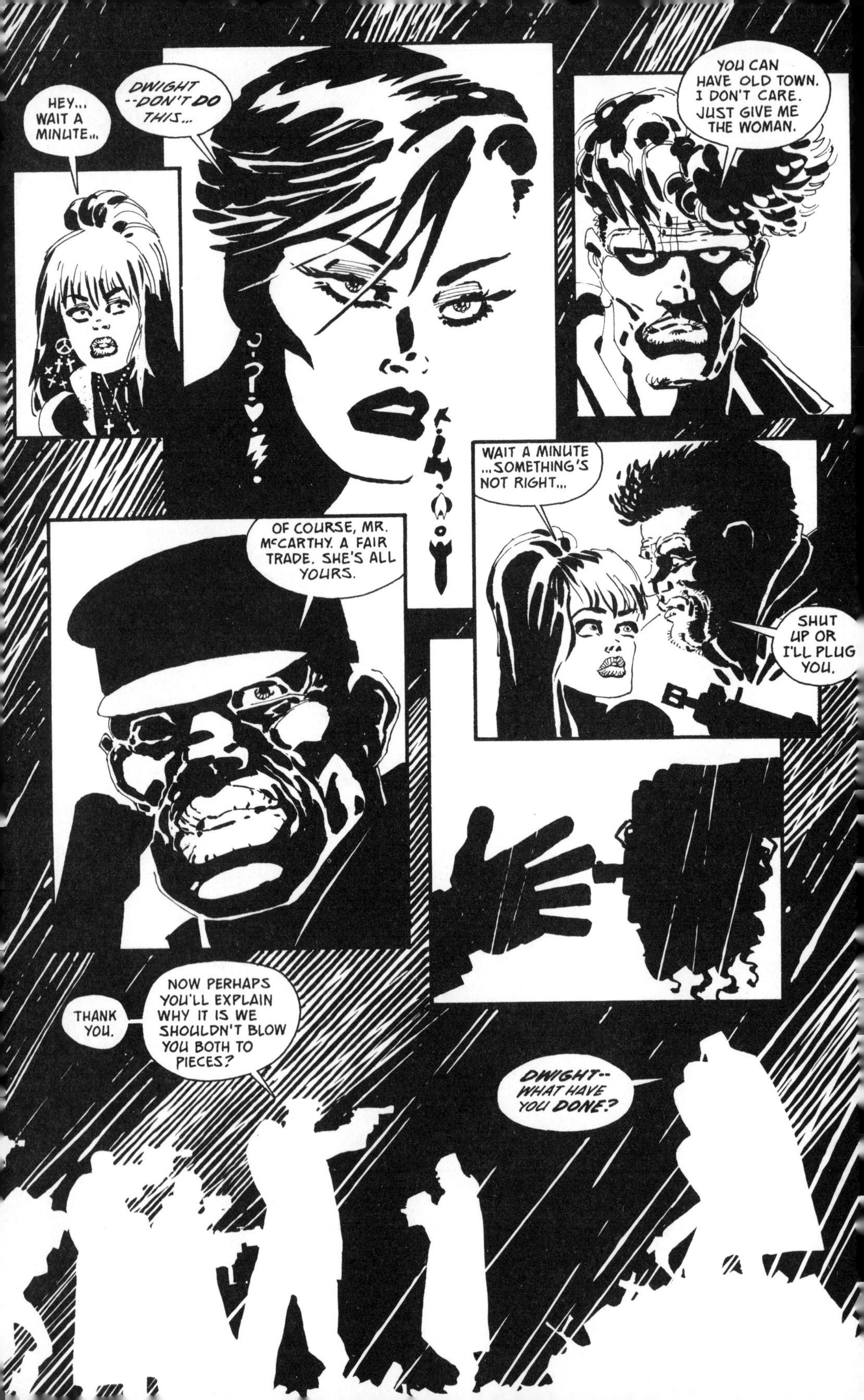
HEY... WAIT A MINUTE...
DWIGHT --DON'T DO THIS...
YOU CAN HAVE OLD TOWN. I DON'T CARE. JUST GIVE ME THE WOMAN.
OF COURSE, MR. McCARTHY. A FAIR TRADE. SHE'S ALL YOURS.
WAIT A MINUTE ...SOMETHING'S NOT RIGHT...
SHUT UP OR I'LL PLUG YOU.
THANK YOU.
NOW PERHAPS YOU'LL EXPLAIN WHY IT IS WE SHOULDN'T BLOW YOU BOTH TO PIECES?
DWIGHT-- WHAT HAVE YOU DONE?

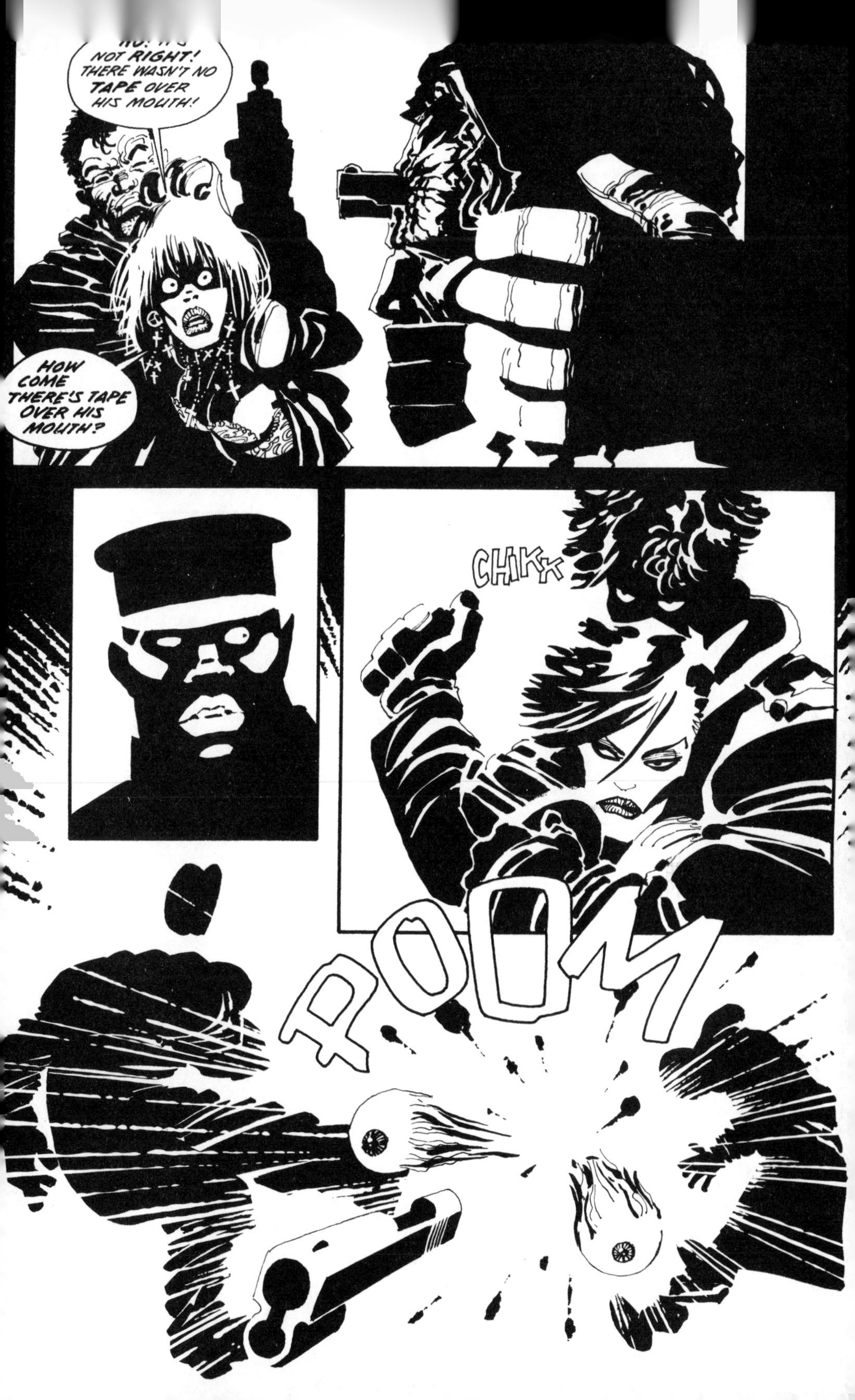
NOT RIGHT! THERE WASN'T NO TAPE OVER HIS MOUTH!
HOW COME THERE'S TAPE OVER HIS MOUTH?
CHIKK
BOOM

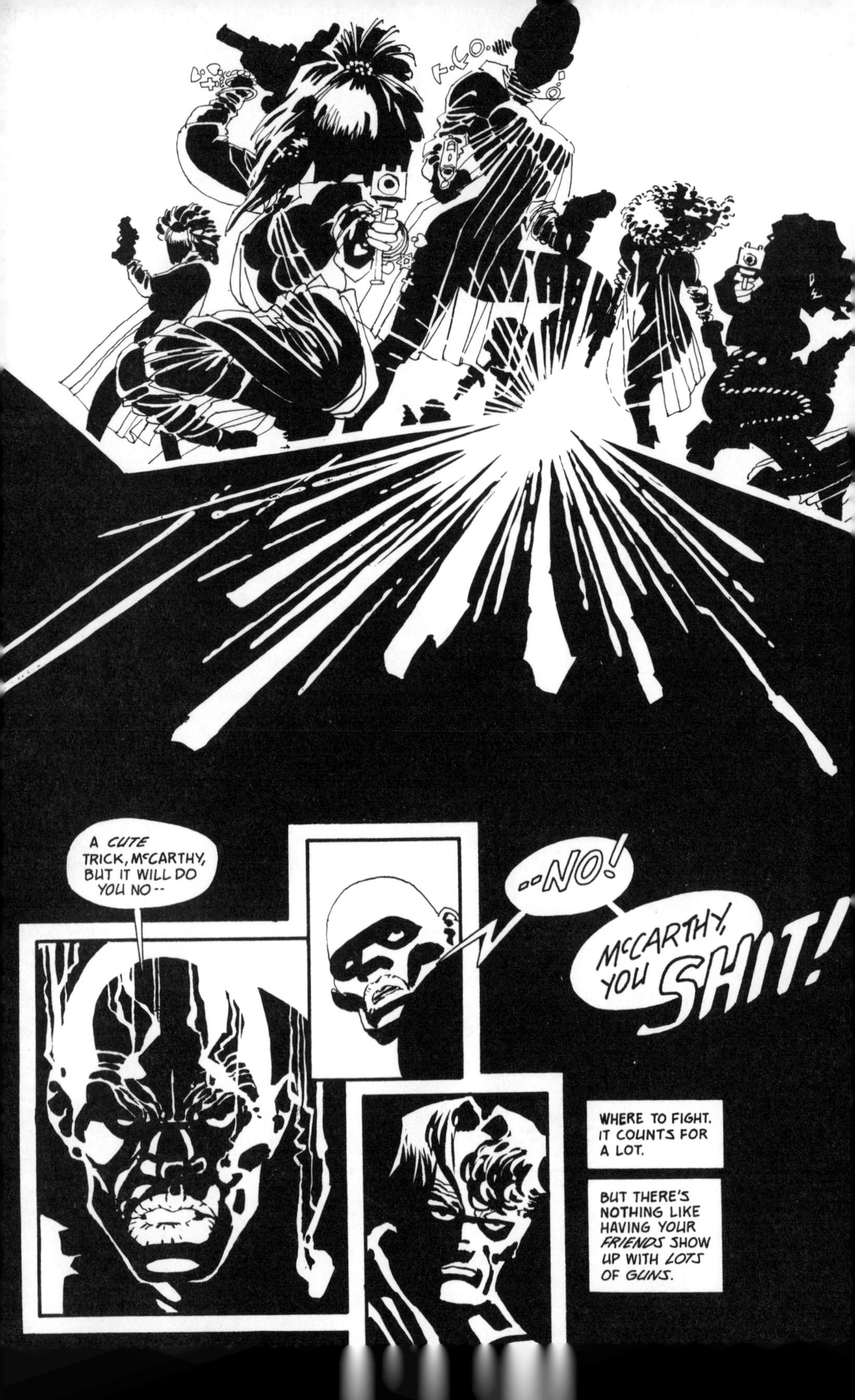
A *CUTE* TRICK, McCARTHY, BUT IT WILL DO YOU NO--
--NO!
McCARTHY, YOU SHIT!
WHERE TO FIGHT. IT COUNTS FOR A LOT.
BUT THERE'S NOTHING LIKE HAVING YOUR *FRIENDS* SHOW UP WITH *LOTS* OF *GUNS*.

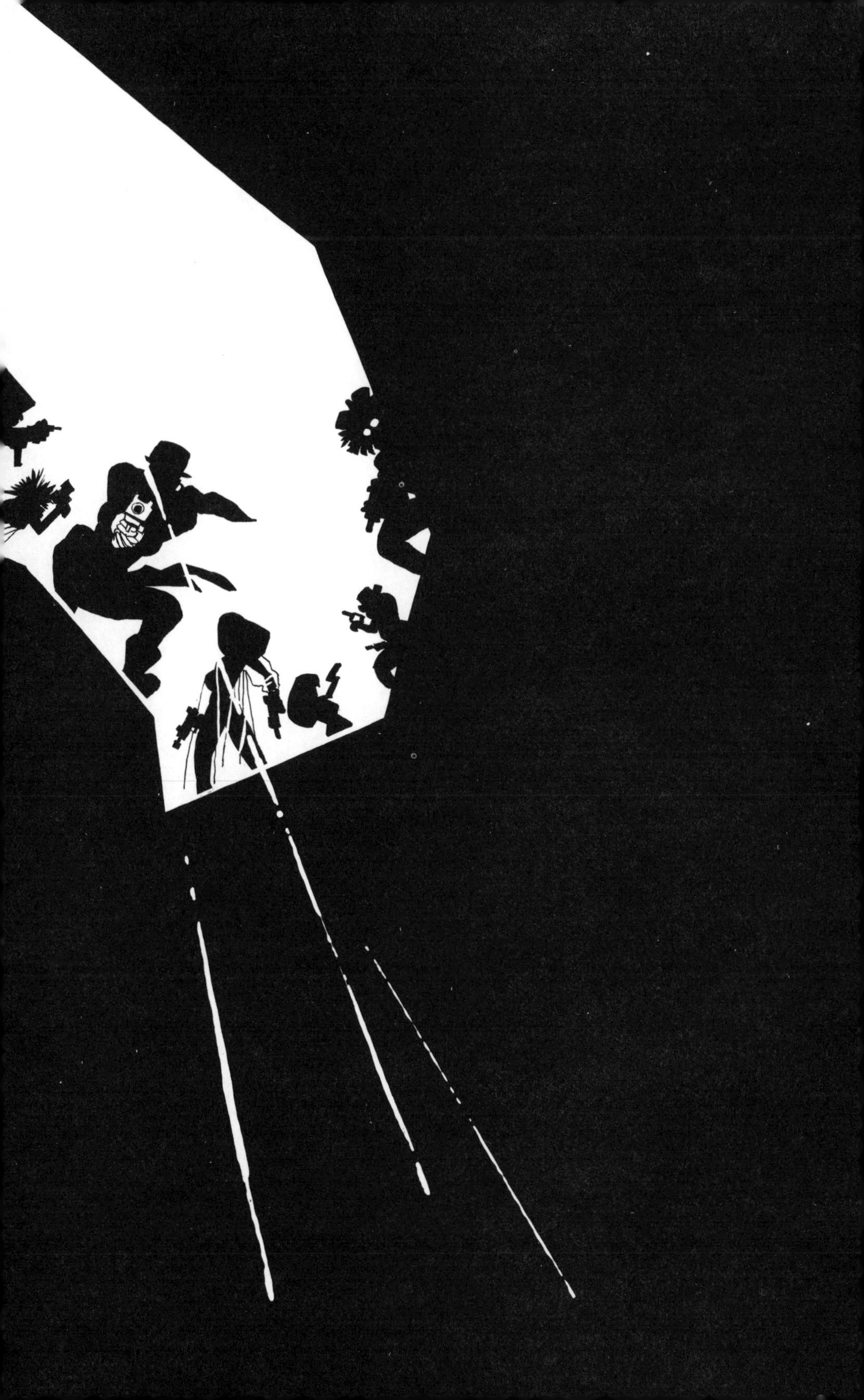

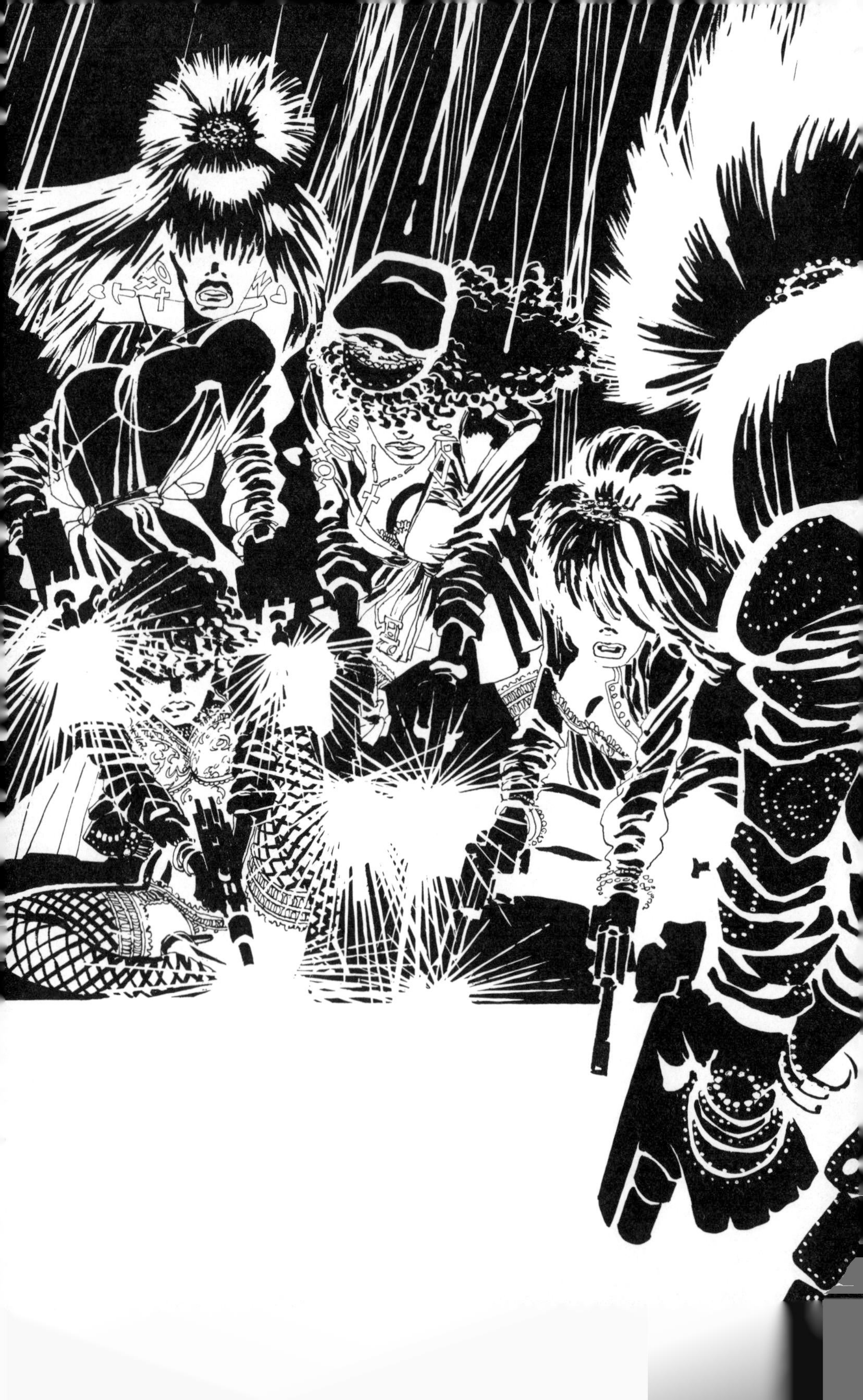

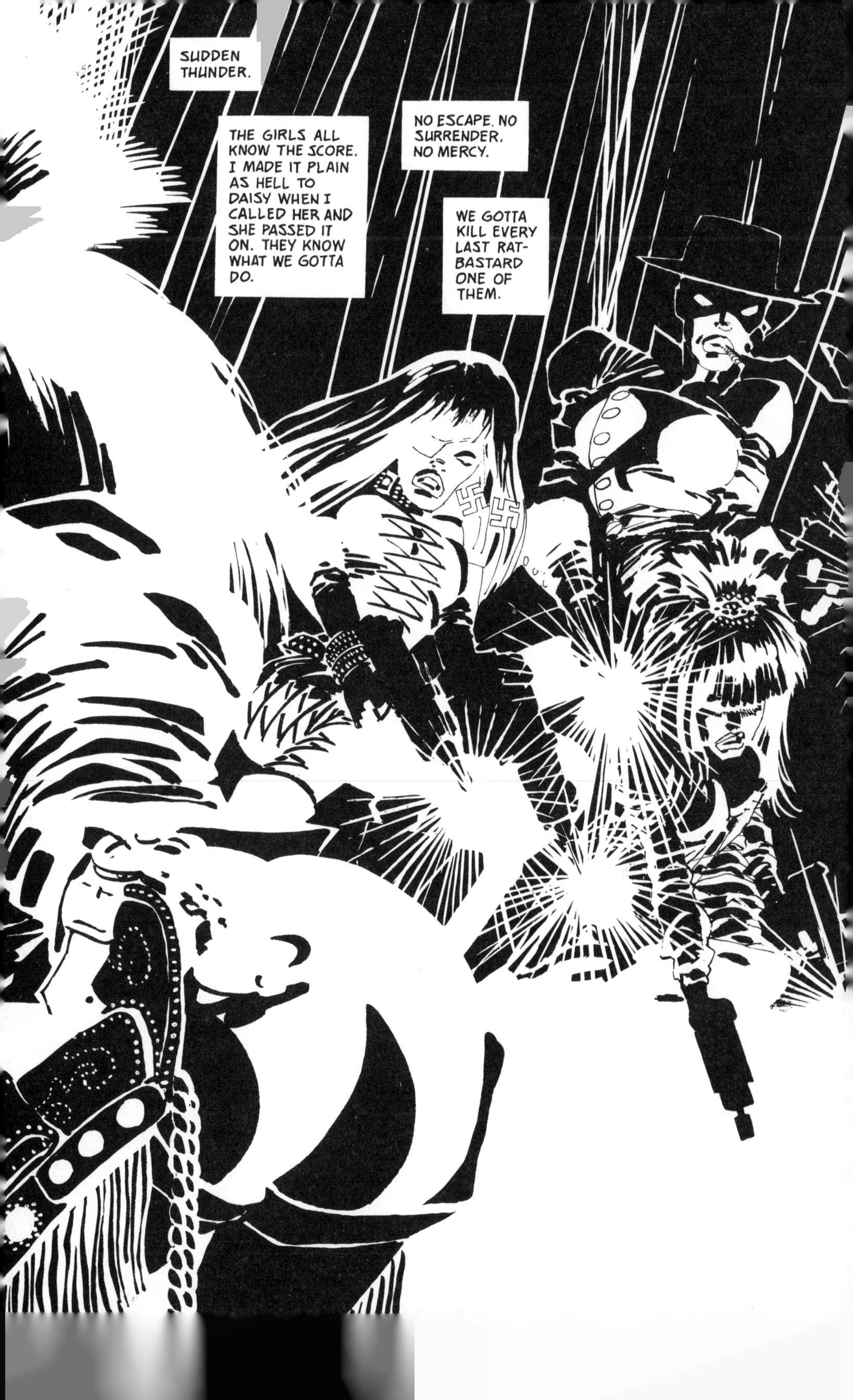
SUDDEN THUNDER.
THE GIRLS ALL KNOW THE SCORE. I MADE IT PLAIN AS HELL TO DAISY WHEN I CALLED HER AND SHE PASSED IT ON. THEY KNOW WHAT WE GOTTA DO.
NO ESCAPE. NO SURRENDER. NO MERCY.
WE GOTTA KILL EVERY LAST RAT-BASTARD ONE OF THEM.

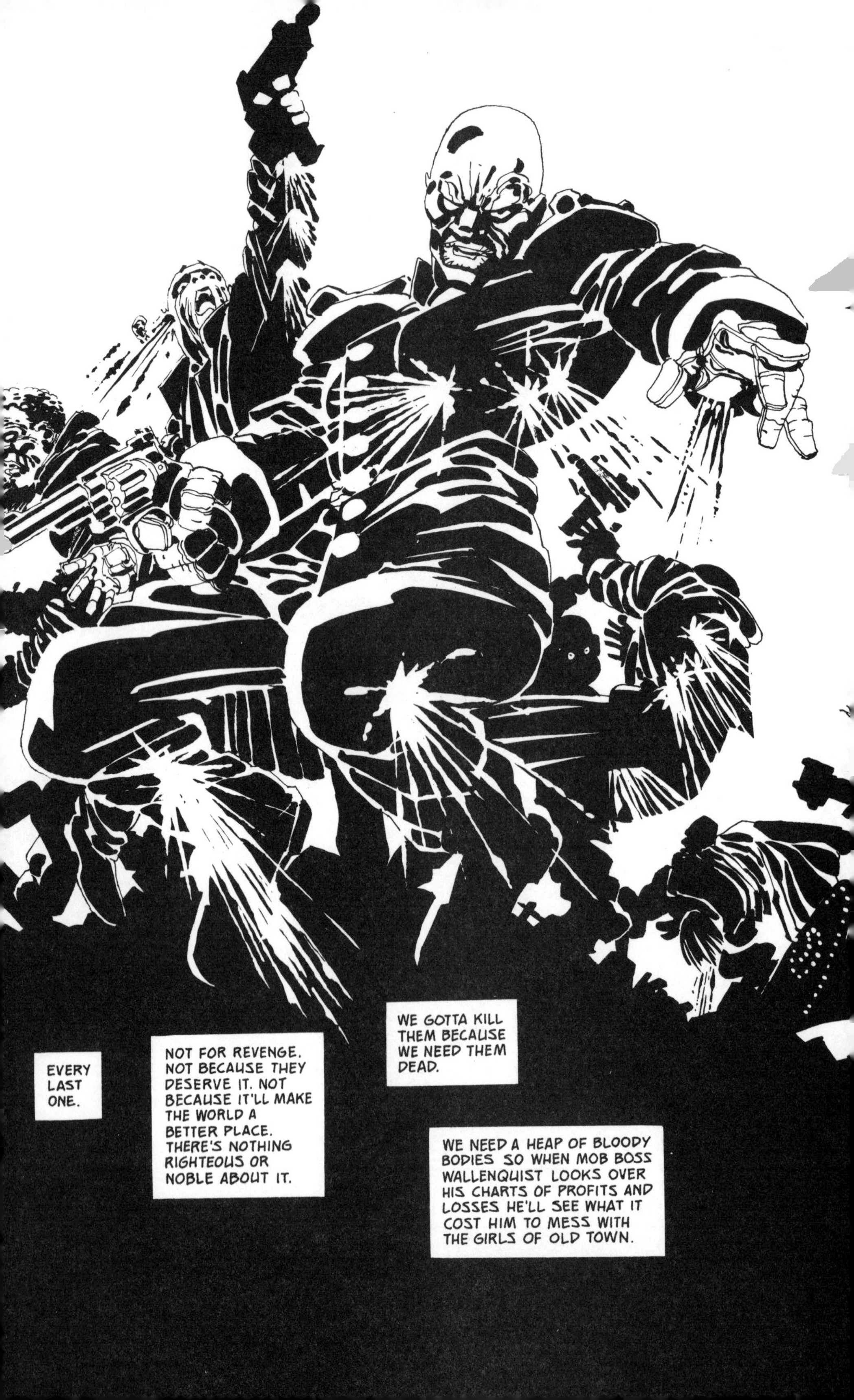

EVERY LAST ONE.
NOT FOR REVENGE. NOT BECAUSE THEY DESERVE IT. NOT BECAUSE IT'LL MAKE THE WORLD A BETTER PLACE. THERE'S NOTHING RIGHTEOUS OR NOBLE ABOUT IT.
WE GOTTA KILL THEM BECAUSE WE NEED THEM DEAD.
WE NEED A HEAP OF BLOODY BODIES SO WHEN MOB BOSS WALLENQUIST LOOKS OVER HIS CHARTS OF PROFITS AND LOSSES HE'LL SEE WHAT IT COST HIM TO MESS WITH THE GIRLS OF OLD TOWN.

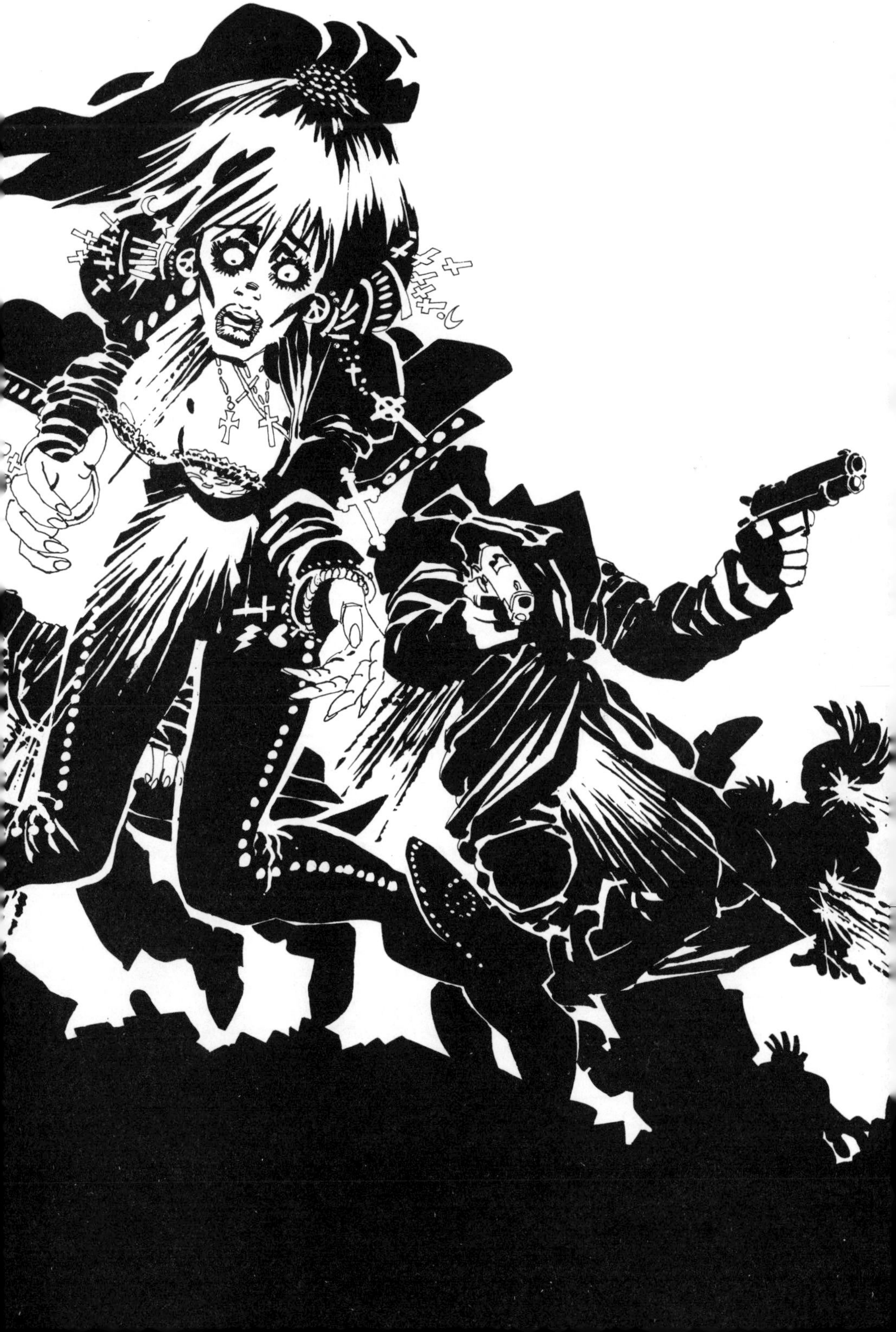

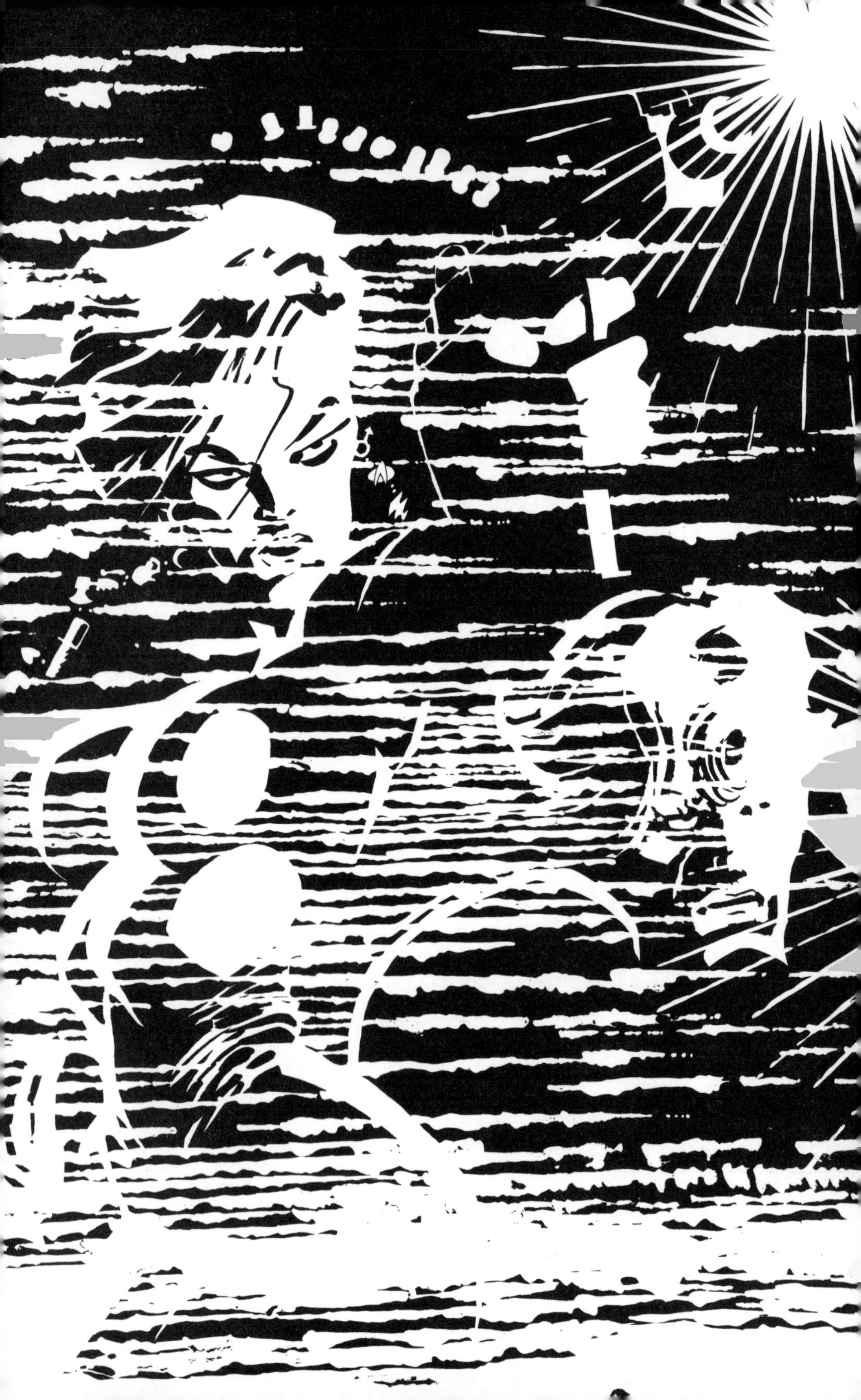

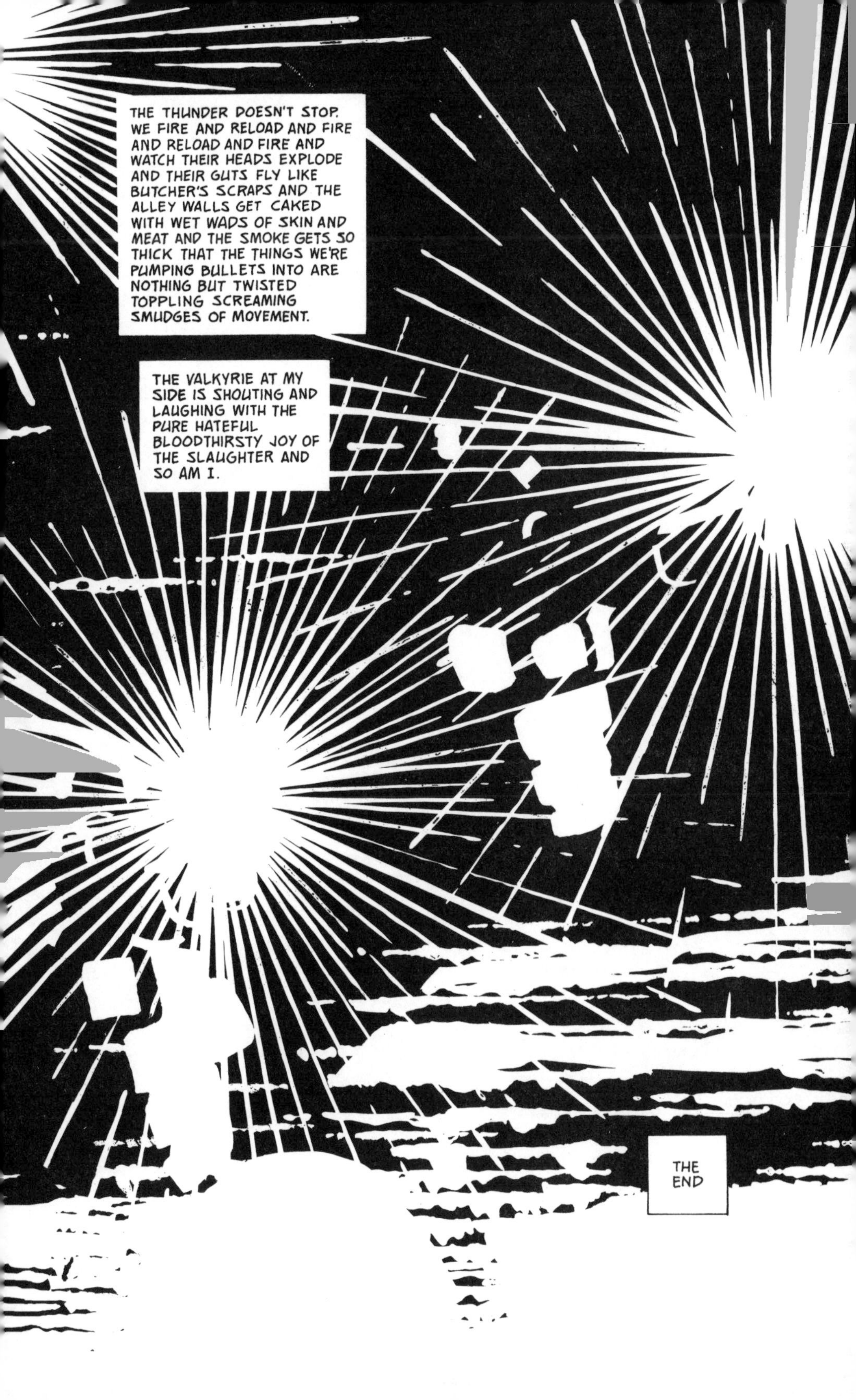
THE THUNDER DOESN'T STOP. WE FIRE AND RELOAD AND FIRE AND RELOAD AND FIRE AND WATCH THEIR HEADS EXPLODE AND THEIR GUTS FLY LIKE BUTCHER'S SCRAPS AND THE ALLEY WALLS GET CAKED WITH WET WADS OF SKIN AND MEAT AND THE SMOKE GETS SO THICK THAT THE THINGS WE'RE PUMPING BULLETS INTO ARE NOTHING BUT TWISTED TOPPLING SCREAMING SMUDGES OF MOVEMENT.
THE VALKYRIE AT MY SIDE IS SHOUTING AND LAUGHING WITH THE PURE HATEFUL BLOODTHIRSTY JOY OF THE SLAUGHTER AND SO AM I.
THE END

Dedicated to
JOHNNY **CRAIG**

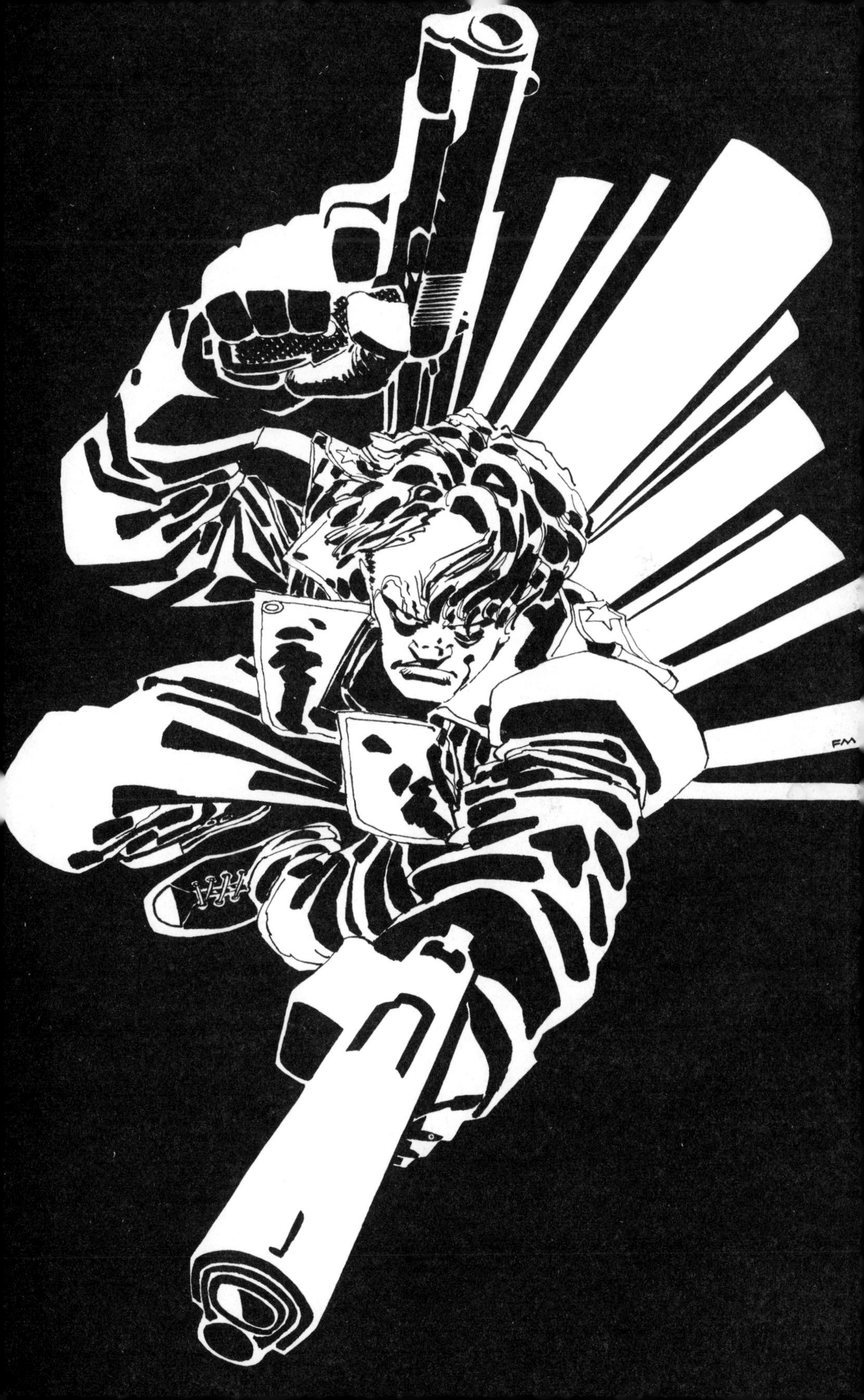
FM

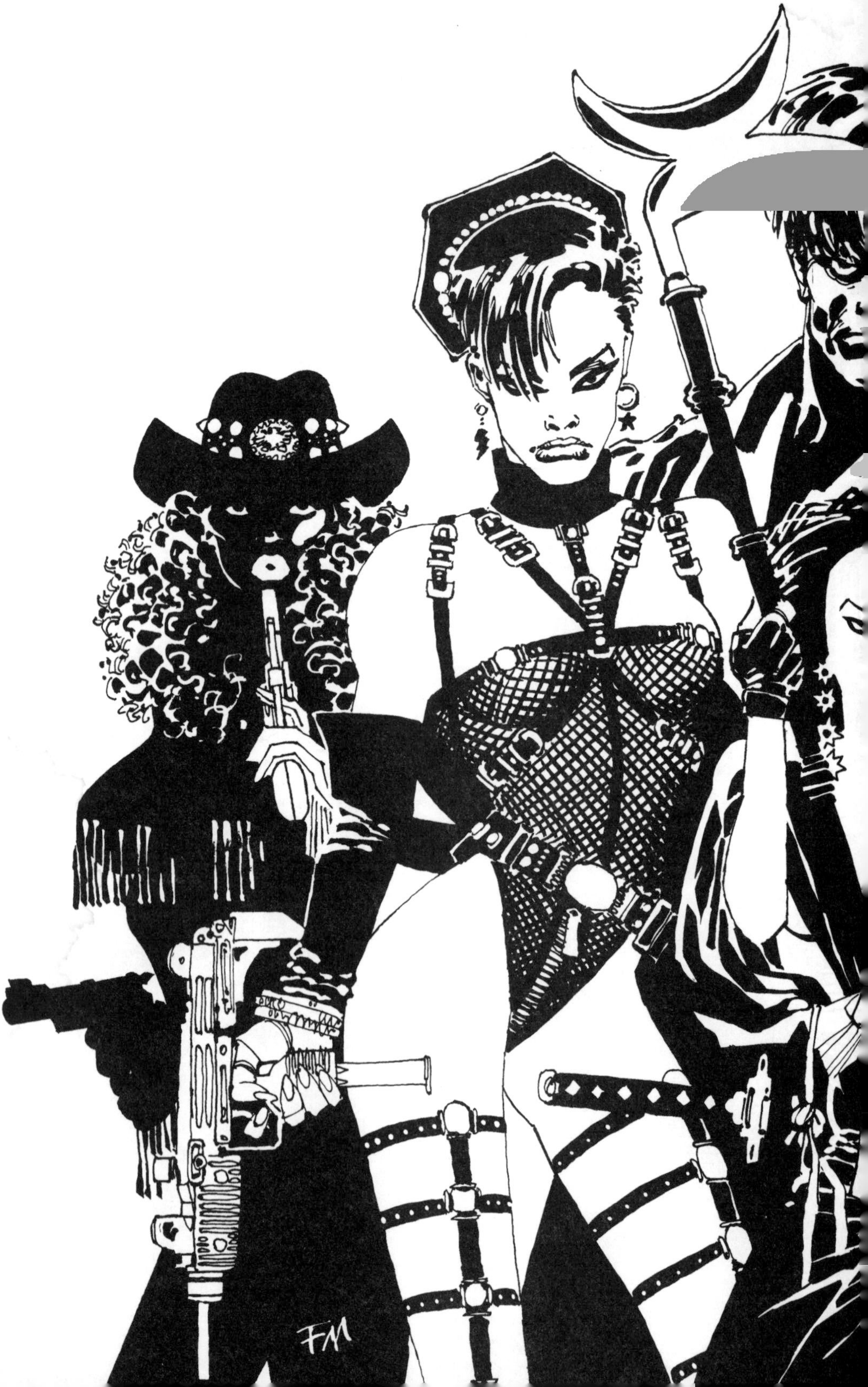
FM

GALLERY

ARTHUR **ADAMS**

MIKE **ALLRED**

SERGIO **ARAGONÉS**

PAUL **CHADWICK**

JOE **KUBERT**

MIKE **MIGNOLA**

JOHN **ROMITA**

JIM **SILKE**

WALTER **SIMONSON**

SERGIO **TOPPI**

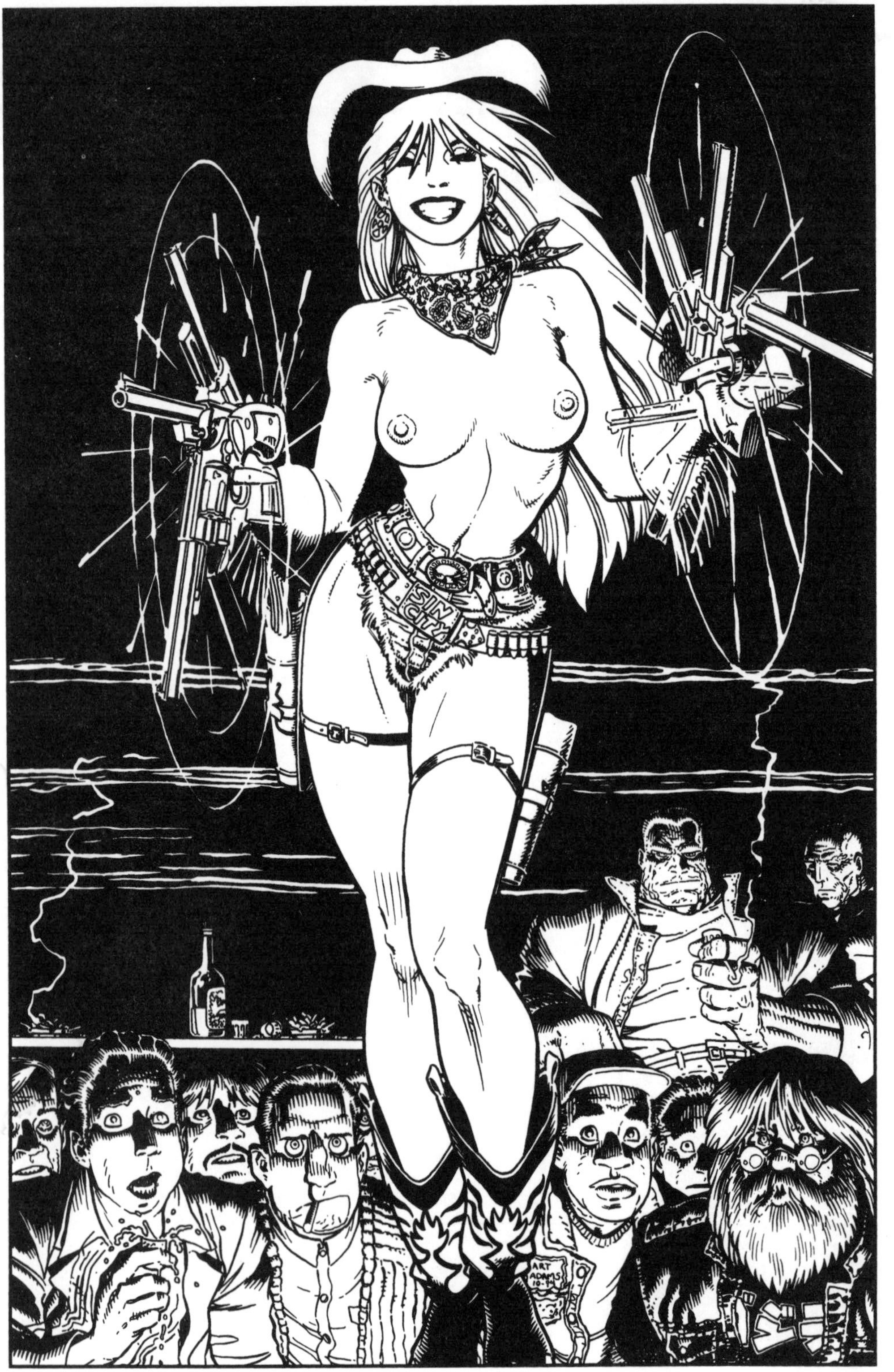
SIN CITY
ART ADAMS 10-94

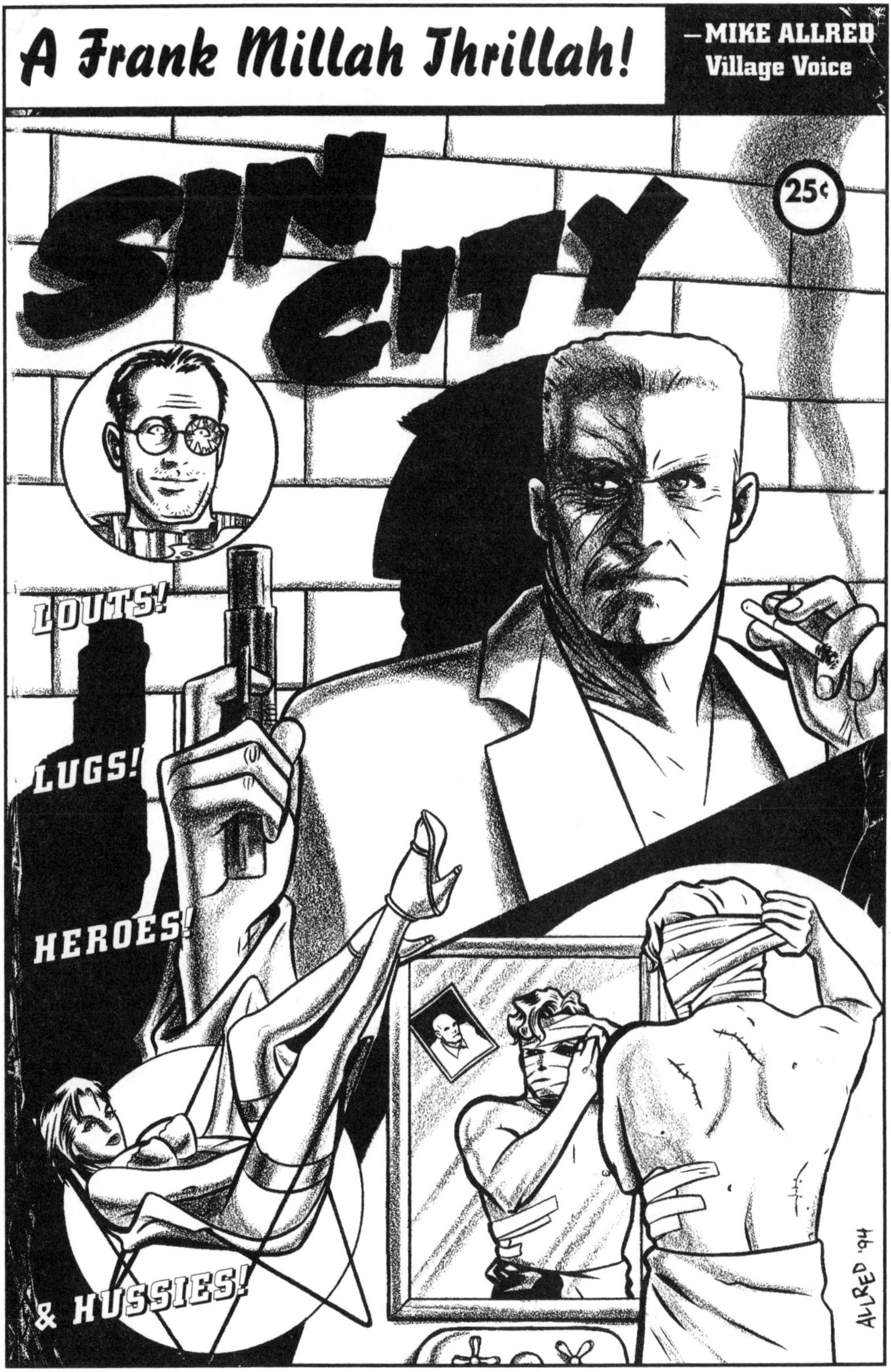
A Frank Millah Thrillah!
—MIKE ALLRED
Village Voice
SIN CITY
25¢
LOUTS!
LUGS!
HEROES!
& HUSSIES!
ALLRED '94

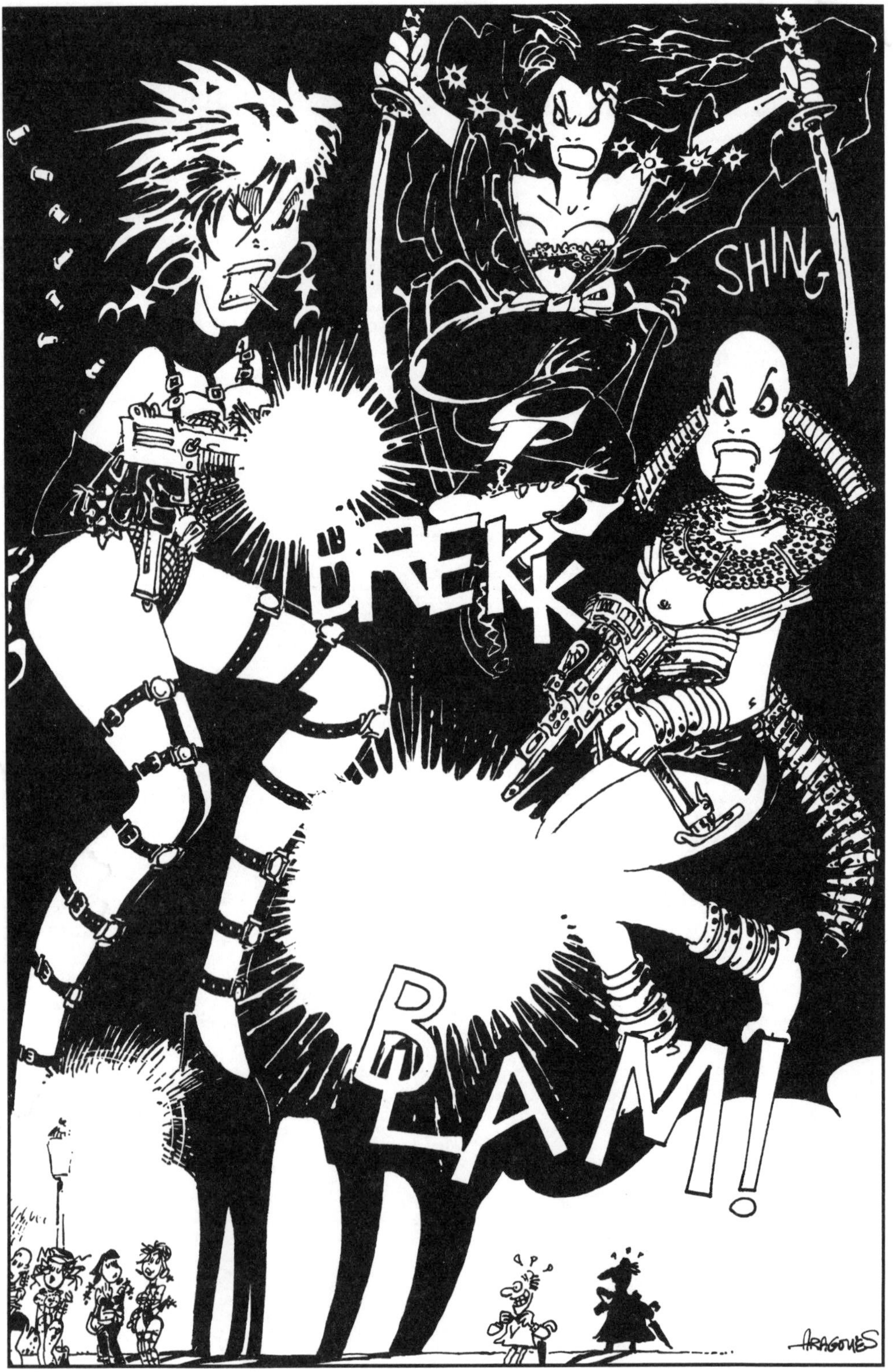
SHING
BREKK
BLAM!
ARAGONES

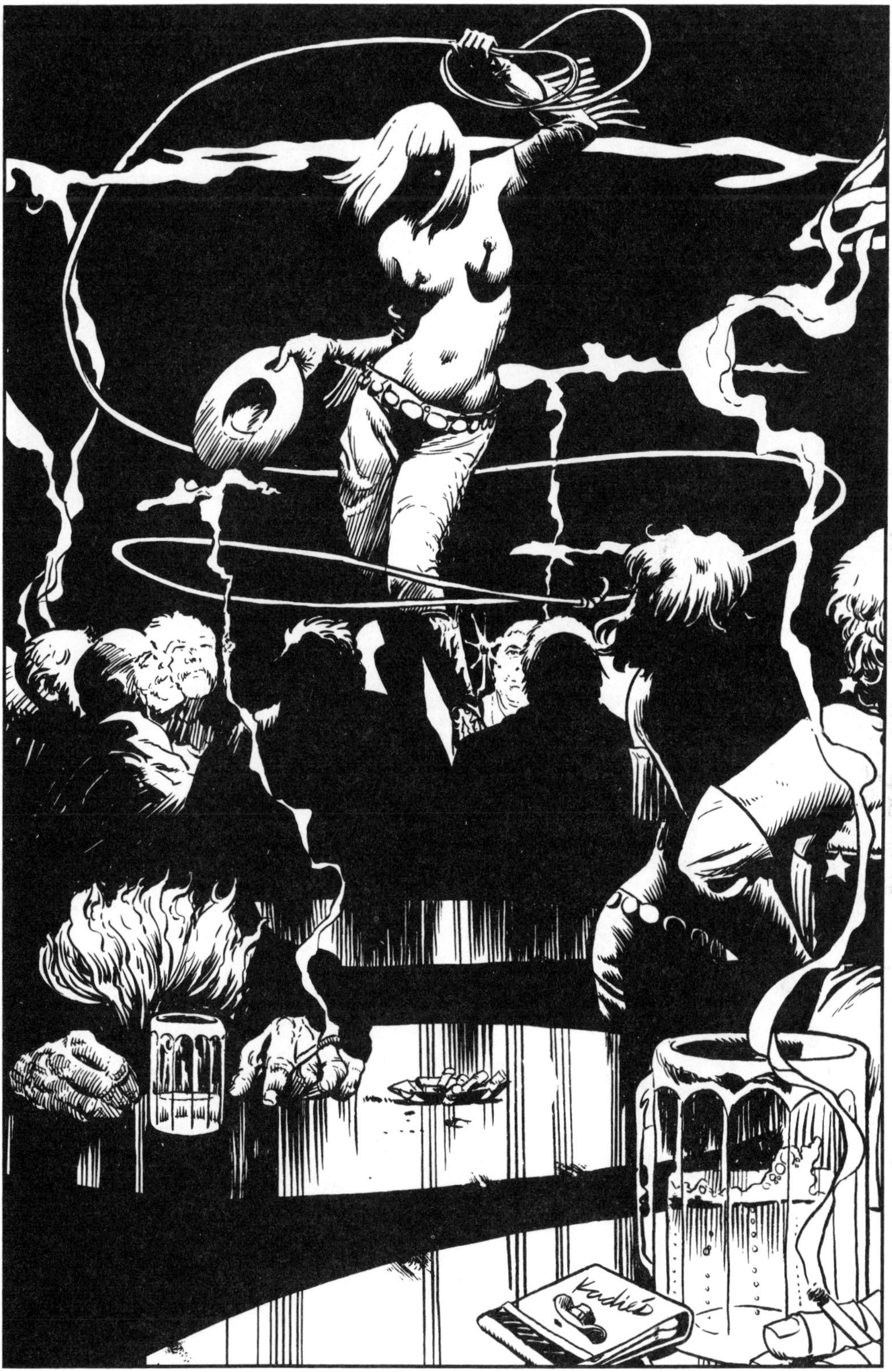
Kadie's

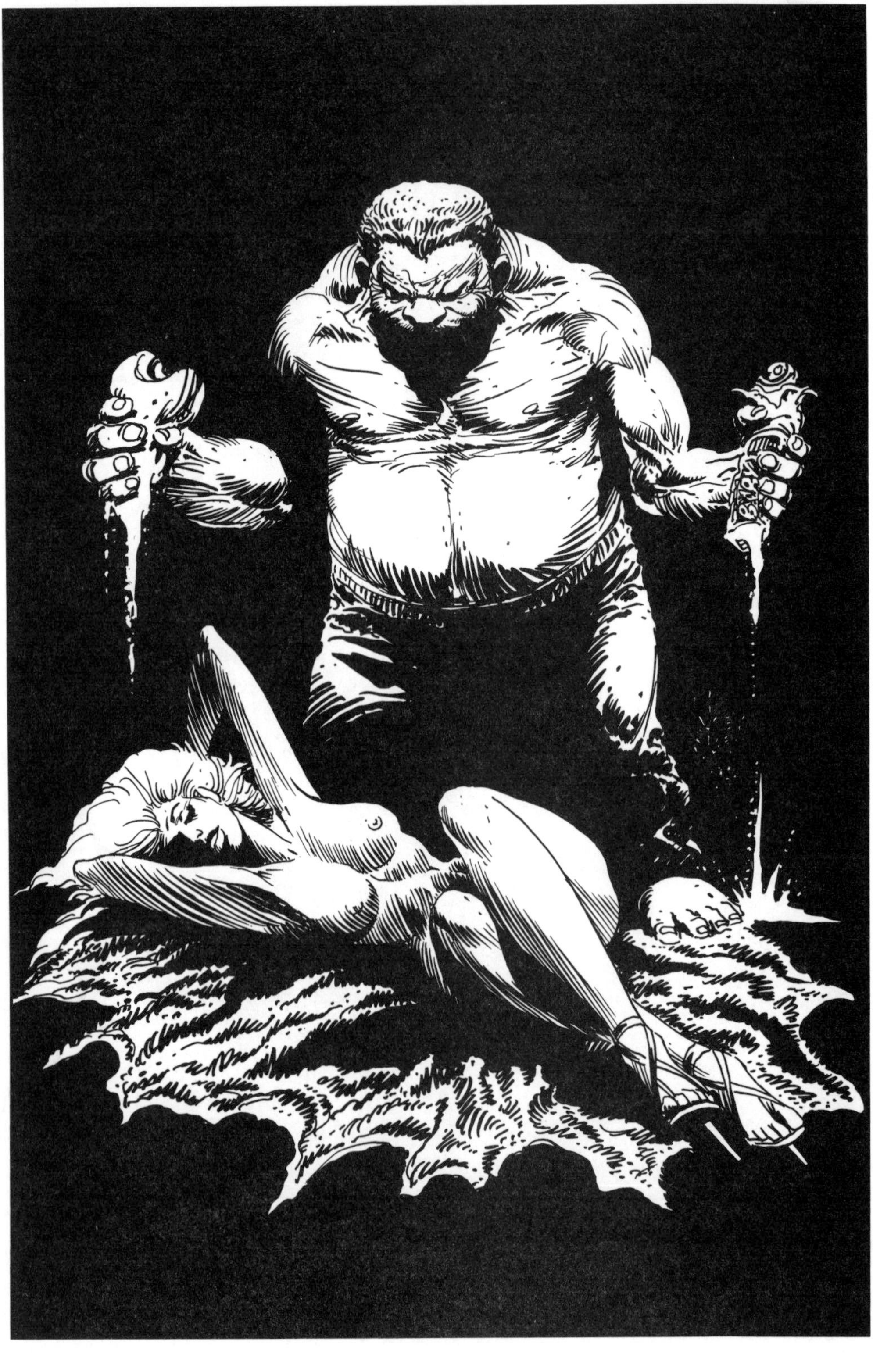

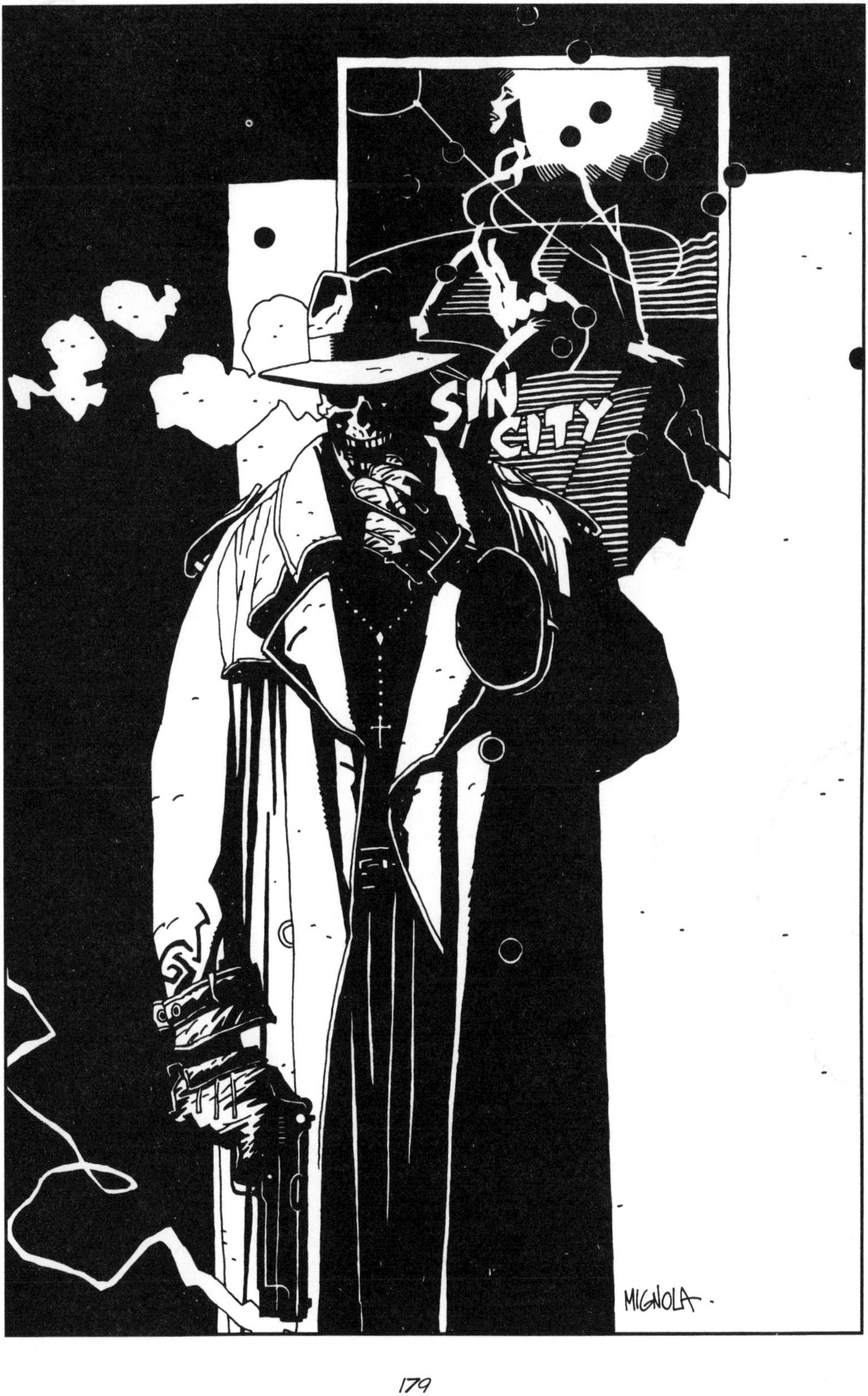
SIN CITY
MIGNOLA

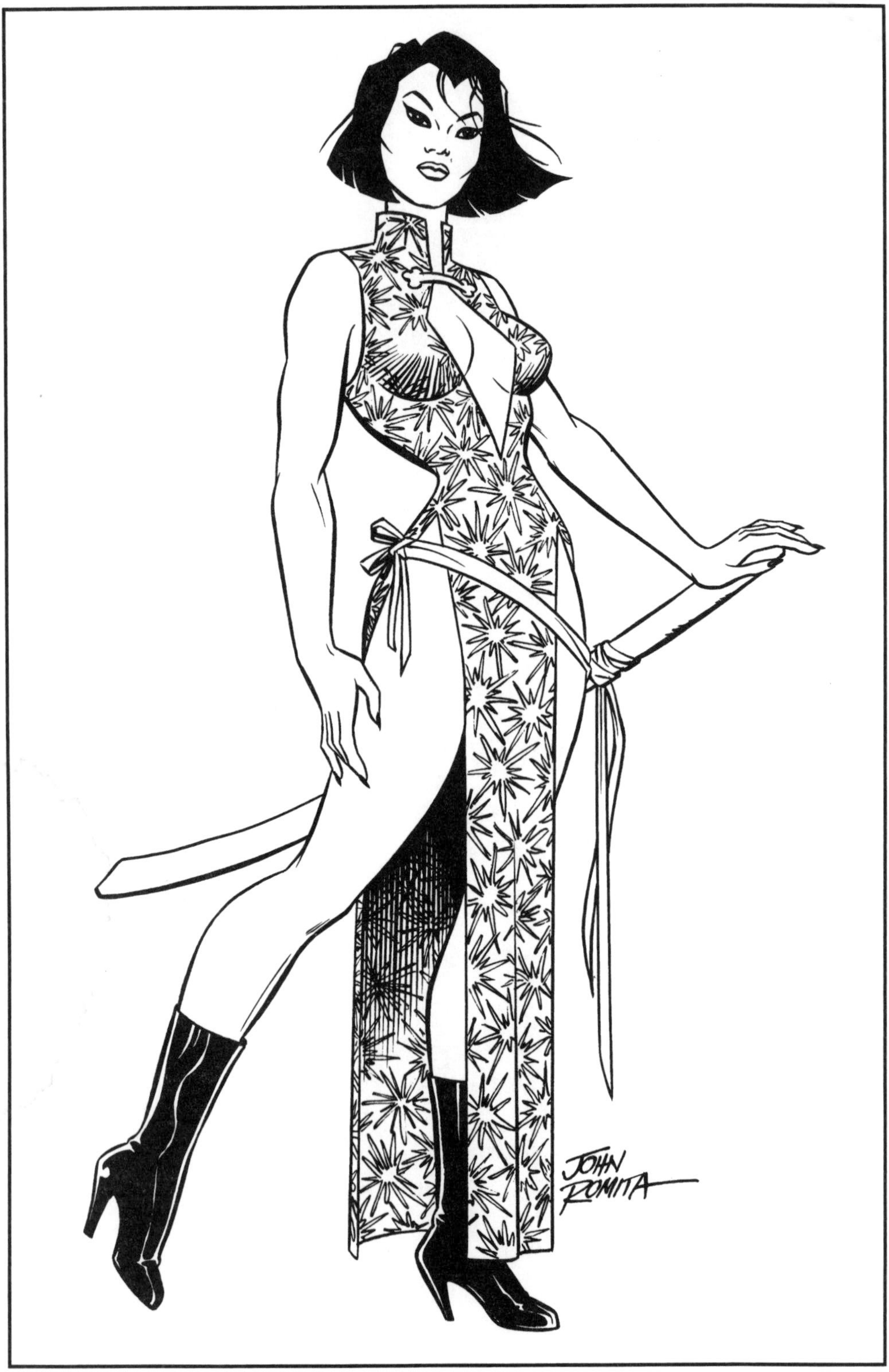
JOHN
ROMITA

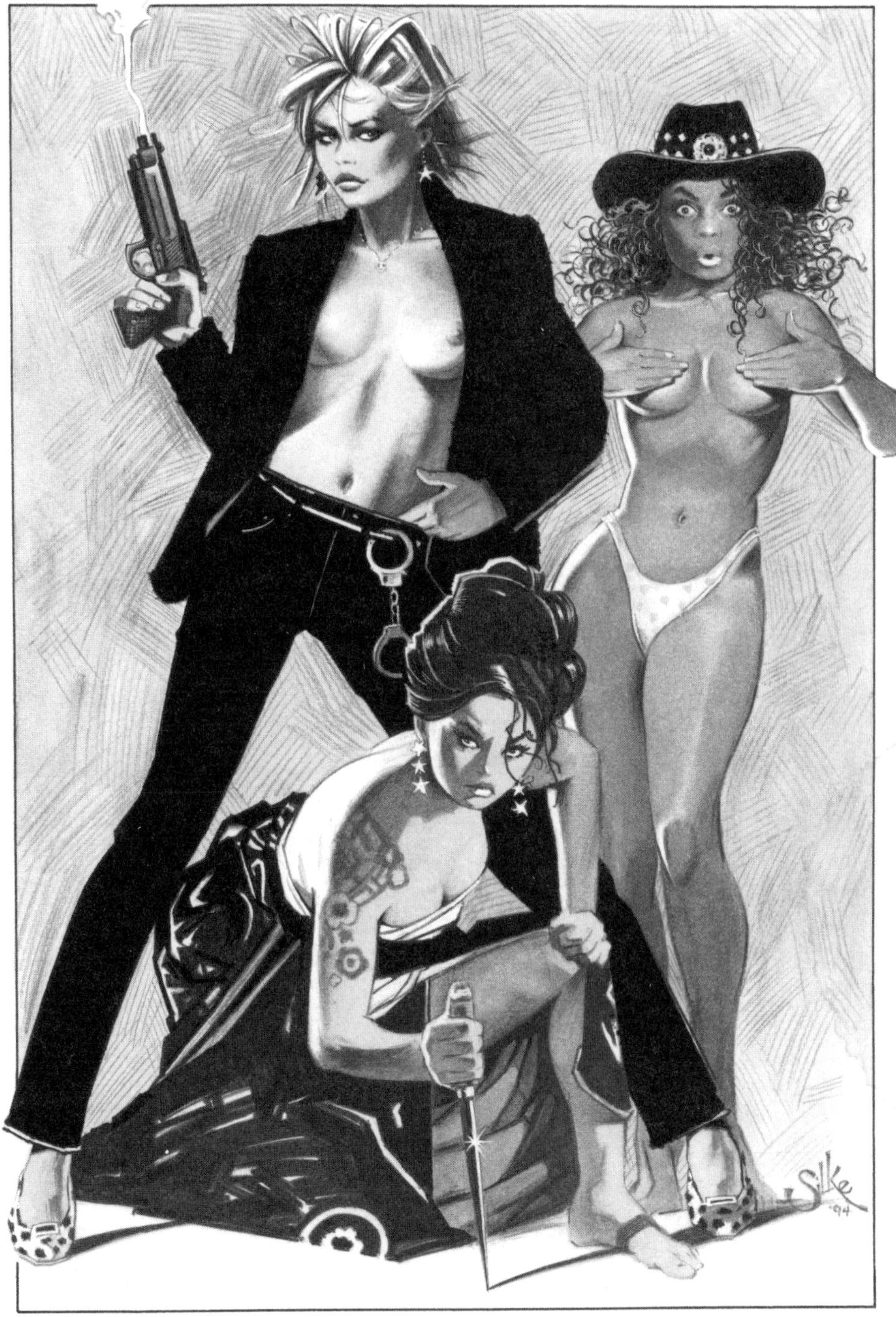
Silke
'94

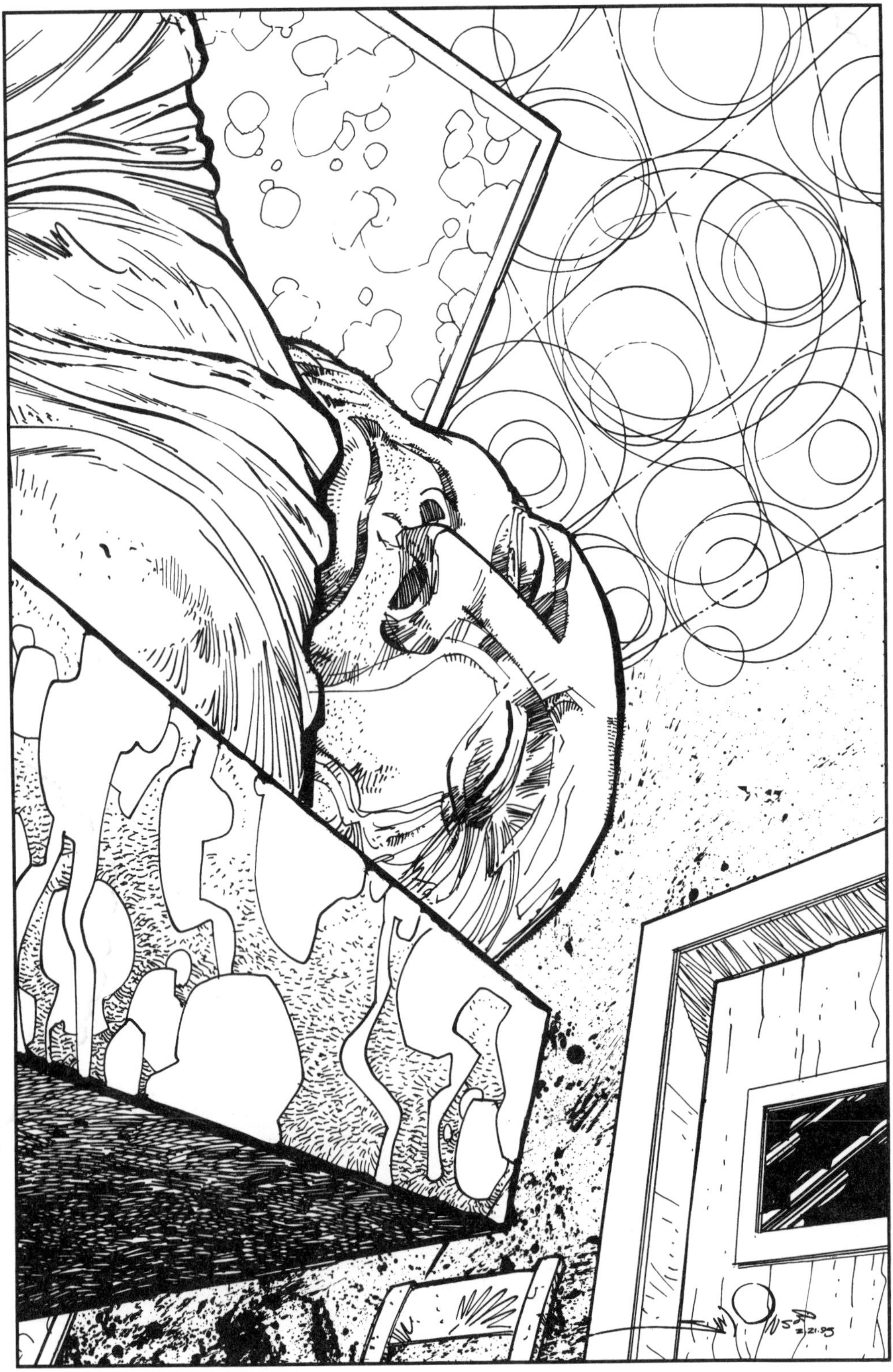

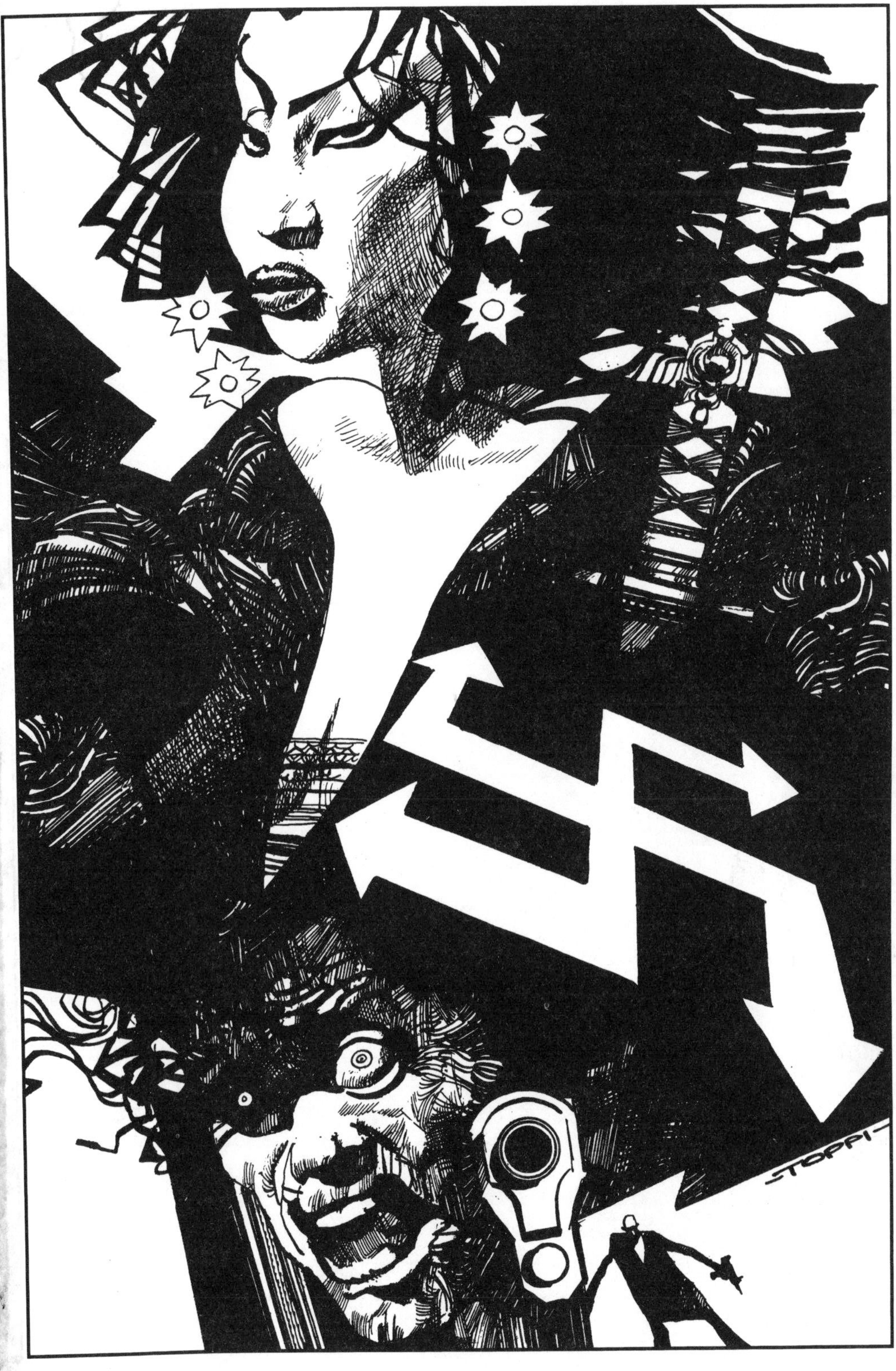
TOPPI

publisher
MIKE RICHARDSON

editor
BOB SCHRECK

cover gallery color
LYNN VARLEY

sin city classic logo design
STEVE MILLER

cover design
CHIP KIDD

book design
MARK COX
CHIP KIDD
LIA RIBACCHI

FRANK MILLER'S SIN CITY® VOLUME 3: THE BIG FAT KILL

This volume collects issues one through five of the Dark Horse comic book series *Sin City®: The Big Fat Kill*.

Published by
Dark Horse Books
A division of Dark Horse Comics, Inc.
10956 SE Main Street
Milwaukie, Oregon 97222

darkhorse.com

Second Edition: February 2005
ISBN 1-59307-295-3

1 0 9 8 7 6 5

PRINTED IN CANADA